T0281014

Lecture Notes in Computer Science　　14351

Founding Editors

Gerhard Goos
Juris Hartmanis

The series Lecture Notes in Computer Science (LNCS), including its subseries Lecture Notes in Artificial Intelligence (LNAI) and Lecture Notes in Bioinformatics (LNBI), has established itself as a medium for the publication of new developments in computer science and information technology research, teaching, and education.

LNCS enjoys close cooperation with the computer science R & D community, the series counts many renowned academics among its volume editors and paper authors, and collaborates with prestigious societies. Its mission is to serve this international community by providing an invaluable service, mainly focused on the publication of conference and workshop proceedings and postproceedings. LNCS commenced publication in 1973.

Demetris Zeinalipour · Dora Blanco Heras ·
George Pallis · Herodotos Herodotou ·
Demetris Trihinas · Daniel Balouek ·
Patrick Diehl · Terry Cojean · Karl Fürlinger ·
Maja Hanne Kirkeby · Matteo Nardelli ·
Pierangelo Di Sanzo
Editors

Euro-Par 2023: Parallel Processing Workshops

Euro-Par 2023 International Workshops
Limassol, Cyprus, August 28 – September 1, 2023
Revised Selected Papers, Part I

 Springer

Editors
Demetris Zeinalipour (iD)
University of Cyprus
Nicosia, Cyprus

George Pallis (iD)
University of Cyprus
Nicosia, Cyprus

Demetris Trihinas (iD)
University of Nicosia
Nicosia, Cyprus

Patrick Diehl (iD)
Louisiana State University
Baton Rouge, LA, USA

Karl Fürlinger (iD)
Ludwig-Maximilians-Universität
Munich, Germany

Matteo Nardelli (iD)
Bank of Italy
Rome, Italy

Dora Blanco Heras (iD)
University of Santiago de Compostela
Santiago de Compostela, Spain

Herodotos Herodotou (iD)
Cyprus University of Technology
Limassol, Cyprus

Daniel Balouek (iD)
Inria
Nantes, France

Terry Cojean (iD)
Karlsruhe Institute of Technology
Karlsruhe, Germany

Maja Hanne Kirkeby (iD)
Roskilde University
Roskilde, Denmark

Pierangelo Di Sanzo (iD)
Roma Tre University
Rome, Italy

ISSN 0302-9743 ISSN 1611-3349 (electronic)
Lecture Notes in Computer Science
ISBN 978-3-031-50683-3 ISBN 978-3-031-50684-0 (eBook)
https://doi.org/10.1007/978-3-031-50684-0

Preface

Euro-Par is the prime European conference covering all aspects of parallel and distributed processing, ranging from theory to practice, from small to the largest parallel and distributed systems and infrastructures, from fundamental computational problems to applications, from architecture, compiler, language and interface design and implementation, to tools, support infrastructures, and application performance aspects.

To provide a meeting point for researchers to discuss and exchange new ideas on more specialized themes, cross-cutting issues, and upcoming trends and paradigms, Euro-Par 2023 co-located Workshops, a Demos/Posters track, a PhD Symposium track and, for the first time, a minisymposia track (i.e., scientific sessions that bring together experts to discuss specific topics in a particular field but without publications in the proceedings.) These events complementary to the main conference were held in Limassol, Cyprus between August 28 and September 1, 2023, following the well-established format of their predecessors. The conference was organized by the University of Cyprus at the St. Raphael Resort, Limassol, Cyprus with local arrangements by Easyconferences Ltd.

LNCS volumes 14351 and 14352 contain the papers and extended abstracts presented at the Euro-Par 2023 Workshops, divided into 9 track sections (one per Workshop, one for the Demos/Posters track and one for the PhD Symposium track). Overall, the following seven Workshop proposals were submitted and all of them met the criteria set out in the guidelines and were accepted:

1. The 1st International Workshop on Scalable Compute Continuum (WSCC 2023)
2. The 1st International Workshop on Tools for Data Locality, Power and Performance (TDLPP 2023)
3. The 1st International Workshop on Urgent Analytics for Distributed Computing (QuickPar 2023)
4. The 21st International Workshop on Algorithms, Models and Tools for Parallel Computing on Heterogeneous Platforms (HeteroPar 2023)
5. The 2nd International Workshop on Resource AWareness of Systems and Society (RAW 2023)
6. The 3rd International Workshop on Asynchronous Many-Task systems for Exascale (AMTE 2023)
7. The 3rd International Workshop on Performance and Energy-efficiency in Concurrent and Distributed Systems (PECS 2023)

The following two minisymposia proposals were submitted and both of them met the criteria set out in the guidelines and were accepted:

1. The 1st Minisymposium on Applications and Benefits of UPMEM commercial Massively Parallel Processing-In-Memory Platform (ABUMPIMP 2023)
2. The 1st Minsymposium on Adaptive High Performance Input/Output Systems (ADAPIO 2023)

Each Euro-Par Workshop had an independent program committee, which was in charge of selecting the papers. The Euro-Par Workshops received 55 submitted Workshop papers, with each submission being single-blind reviewed by at least three technical program committee members of the respective Euro-Par Workshops program committee. After the thorough peer-reviewing process, 42 submissions were accepted for presentation at the Euro-Par 2023 Workshops, resulting in an acceptance rate of 76%. LNCS volumes 14351 and 14352 contain the following number of contributions from co-located Workshops, with each paper being 12 pages: 7 papers from WSCC 2023, 5 papers from TDLPP 2023, 3 papers from QuickPar 2023, 12 papers from HeteroPar 2023, 7 papers from RAW 2023, 4 papers from AMTE 2023 and 4 papers from PECS 2023.

The Euro-Par Demos/Posters track received 16 submissions, with each submission being reviewed by at least two technical program committee members. After a thorough single-blind peer-reviewing process, 14 submissions were accepted and included as 4-page papers in these proceedings. The Euro-Par PhD Symposium track received 12 submissions, with each submission being single-blind reviewed by at least three technical program committee members. After a thorough peer-reviewing process, 10 submissions were accepted and included as 6-page papers in these proceedings.

The success of the Euro-Par Workshops/Minisymposia, Demos/Posters track and PhD Symposium track depended on the work of many individuals and organizations. We therefore thank all the organizers and reviewers for the time and effort that they invested. We would also like to express our gratitude to the members of the Euro-Par 2023 Organizing Committee, the General Chair George A. Papadopoulos (University of Cyprus, Cyprus), the Program Co-Chairs Marios D. Dikaiakos (University of Cyprus, Cyprus) and Rizos Sakellariou (University of Manchester, UK), as well as the local staff of Easyconferences Ltd. (Petros Stratis, Nicolas Stratis and Boyana Slavova). Lastly, we thank all participants, panelists, and keynote speakers of the Euro-Par Workshops for their contribution to bring forward a number of productive events that have enriched the diversity and scope of the main conference in significant ways. It was a pleasure to organize and host the Euro-Par 2023 Workshops/Minisymposia, Demos/Posters track and PhD Symposium track in Limassol, Cyprus.

August 2023

Demetris Zeinalipour
Dora Blanco Heras
George Pallis
Herodotos Herodotou
Demetris Trihinas

Organization

Steering Committee

Fernando Silva (Steering Committee Chair)	University of Porto, Portugal
Dora Blanco Heras (Workshops Chair)	University of Santiago de Compostela, Spain
Maciej Malawski (Virtualization Chair)	AGH Univ. of Science and Technology, Poland
Henk Sips (Finance Chair)	Delft Univ. of Technology, The Netherlands
Massimo Torquati (Artifacts Chair)	University of Pisa, Italy
Marco Aldinucci	University of Turin, Italy
Luc Bougé	ENS Rennes, France
Jesus Carretero	Carlos III University of Madrid, Spain
Christos Kaklamanis	Computer Technology Institute and University of Patras, Greece
Paul Kelly	Imperial College London, UK
Thomas Ludwig	University of Hamburg, Germany
Tomś Margalef	Autonomous University of Barcelona, Spain
Wolfgang Nagel	Dresden University of Technology, Germany
George Papadopoulos	University of Cyprus, Cyprus
Francisco Fernández Rivera	University of Santiago de Compostela, Spain
Krzysztof Rządca	University of Warsaw, Poland
Rizos Sakellariou	University of Manchester, UK
Leonel Sousa	University of Lisbon, Portugal
Phil Trinder	University of Glasgow, UK
Felix Wolf	Technical University of Darmstadt, Germany
Ramin Yahyapour	GWDG and University of Göttingen, Germany

Honorary Members

Christian Lengauer	University of Passau, Germany
Ron Perrott	Oxford e-Research Centre, UK
Karl Dieter Reinartz	University of Erlangen-Nürnberg, Germany

General Chair

George A. Papadopoulos   University of Cyprus, Cyprus

Program Chairs

Marios D. Dikaiakos   University of Cyprus, Cyprus
Rizos Sakellariou   University of Manchester, UK

Workshop Chairs

Dora Blanco Heras   University of Santiago de Compostela, Spain
Demetris Zeinalipour   University of Cyprus, Cyprus

Publication Chairs

José Cano   University of Glasgow, UK
Miquel Pericàs   Chalmers University of Technology, Sweden

Local Chairs

Chryssis Georgiou   University of Cyprus, Cyprus
George Pallis   University of Cyprus, Cyprus

Contents – Part I

**The 1st International Workshop on Urgent Analytics for Distributed
Computing (QUICKPAR 2023)**

**The 21st International Workshop on Algorithms, Models and Tools
for Parallel Computing on Heterogeneous Platforms (HETEROPAR
2023)**

Contents – Part II

The 3rd International Workshop on Performance and Energy-efficiency in Concurrent and Distributed Systems (PECS 2023)

Minisymposia

Demos and Posters

The 1st International Workshop on Scalable Compute Continuum (WSCC 2023)

International Workshop on Scalable Compute Continuum (WSCC)

Workshop Description

Compute Continuum promises to manage the heterogeneity and dynamism of widespread computing resources, aiming to simplify the execution of distributed applications improving data locality, performance, availability, adaptability, energy management as well as other non-functional features. This is made possible by overcoming resource fragmentation and segregation in tiers, enabling applications to be seamlessly executed and relocated along a continuum of resources spanning from the edge to the cloud. Besides consolidated vertical and horizontal scaling patterns, this paradigm also offers more detailed adaptation actions that strictly depend on the specific infrastructure components (e.g., to reduce energy consumption, or to exploit specific hardware such as GPUs and FPGAs). This enables the enhancement of latency-sensitive applications, the reduction of network bandwidth consumption, the improvement of privacy protection, and the development of novel services aimed at improving living, health, safety, and mobility. All of this should be achievable by application developers without having to worry about how and where the developed components will be executed. Therefore, to unleash the true potential offered by the Compute Continuum, proactive, autonomous, and infrastructure-aware management is desirable, if not mandatory, calling for novel interdisciplinary approaches that exploit optimization theory, control theory, machine learning, and artificial intelligence methods.

The workshop attracted the attention of the distributed systems research community aiming to investigate novel platforms, systems, applications, policies, and autonomic features capable of dealing with the peculiarities of compute continuum, such as variable workloads and environmental events, while taking the best of heterogeneous and distributed infrastructures.

The International Workshop on Scalable Compute Continuum (WSCC 2023) was held in Limassol, Cyprus. WSCC 2023 was organized in conjunction with the Euro-Par annual international conference. The format of the workshop included an invited presentation by Alessandro Margara (Politecnico di Milano, Italy) titled "Compute continuum: the missing abstraction in data-intensive systems", followed by technical presentations of accepted papers.

The workshop was attended by around 20 people on average. We received 9 submissions for review from 10 countries. Each paper received from three to four single-blind from members of the Program Committee (PC). The PC comprised 14 members with expertise in various aspects of distributed systems, edge computing, and high-performance computing. After an accurate and thorough peer-review process, we selected 7 submissions to be presented at the workshop. The review process focused on the quality of the papers, their scientific novelty, and their relation to compute continuum problems and frameworks. The acceptance of the papers was the result of the PC discussion and agreement.

The accepted articles covered a diverse range of topics, techniques, and applications, including placement strategies, design of communication libraries, adaptive memory compression policies, evaluation of micro-batching techniques for GPU, and an electrical energy forecasting use case.

Finally, we would like to thank the WSCC 2023 Program Committee, whose members made the workshop possible with their rigorous and timely review process, and all the authors and participants for their valuable contributions to and their interest in the workshop. We would also like to thank Euro-Par 2023 for hosting the workshop, and the Euro-Par 2023 workshop chairs for their valuable help and support.

Organization

Program Chairs

Valeria Cardellini	University of Rome Tor Vergata, Italy
Patrizio Dazzi	University of Pisa, Italy
Gabriele Mencagli	University of Pisa, Italy
Matteo Nardelli	Bank of Italy, Italy
Massimo Torquati	University of Pisa, Italy

Program Committee

Atakan Aral	Umeå University, Sweden
Luiz Fernando Bittencourt	University of Campinas, Brazil
Antonio Brogi	University of Pisa, Italy
Daniele De Sensi	Sapienza University of Rome, Italy
Schahram Dustdar	TU Wien, Austria
Maria Fazio	University of Messina, Italy
Dalvan Griebler	PUCRS, Brazil
Vincenzo Gulisano	Chalmers University of Technology, Sweden
Stefan Nastic	TU Wien, Austria
Guillaume Pierre	Rennes 1 University, France
Fabiana Rossi	Bank of Italy, Italy
Gabriele Russo Russo	University of Rome Tor Vergata, Italy
Stefan Schulte	Hamburg University of Technology, Germany
Shuhao Zhang	Singapore University of Technology and Design, Singapore

Compute Continuum: What Lies Ahead?

Matteo Nardelli[1]([✉]) [iD], Gabriele Russo Russo[2] [iD], and Valeria Cardellini[2] [iD]

[1] Bank of Italy, Rome, Italy
matteo.nardelli@bancaditalia.it
[2] University of Rome Tor Vergata, Rome, Italy
russo.russo@ing.uniroma2.it, cardellini@ing.uniroma2.it

Abstract. Modern computing environments are evolving towards the compute continuum paradigm, which promises to manage the heterogeneity and dynamism of geographically spread computing resources, supporting the execution of distributed and pervasive applications. As a complete understanding of all the implications and challenges posed by this new paradigm is still far, we give an overview of the key features and concepts of the compute continuum and discuss the most relevant research opportunities we envision in the field.

Keywords: Compute continuum · IoT-edge-cloud · distributed systems

1 Introduction

Recently, the compute continuum emerged as a new distributed computing paradigm that combines centralized cloud data centers with heterogeneous and decentralized fog/edge computing resources (e.g., [27,36]). The idea behind compute continuum is all but new and builds on the convergence between end devices, edge, fog, and cloud computing; so, it proposes an infrastructure full of a wide range of heterogeneous resources. Based on the resulting decentralized infrastructure, the compute continuum promises to host distributed applications with benefits on their performance, availability, and energy footprint. This requires an efficient representation of the computing infrastructure, as well as the design of novel, efficient, and scalable management policies for computing, storage, and networking resources. To do so, a thorough understanding of the novel computing paradigm is necessary, especially to identify its key features.

Related Work: So far, only a limited number of papers investigated the compute continuum aiming to identify its key features and the most relevant open issues (e.g., [5,9,27]). Beckman et al. [5] envision the adoption of compute continuum for designing future applications that can exploit the heterogeneity and distribution of computing resources. Other papers focus on different problems, mostly related to resource management. For example, Dustdar et al. [12] suggest a holistic view to trade-off resource, quality, and cost of applications running on

D. Zeinalipour et al. (Eds.): Euro-Par 2023 Workshops, LNCS 14351, pp. 5–17, 2024.
https://doi.org/10.1007/978-3-031-50684-0_1

continuum resources. Preliminary mechanisms and (offloading) policies have also started to be proposed (e.g., [33,45]); nonetheless, they mostly focus on specific infrastructure features only. Kumar et al. [29] are among the first to explicitly model the heterogeneity of compute continuum, aiming to allocate tasks with minimum predicted completion time. Kimovski et al. [27] analyze energy and performance in offloading applications across the computing continuum.

Contribution: Differently from previous works, we aim to systematize knowledge on the emerging computing paradigm, by summarizing its key features and identifying the most relevant open challenges, whose investigation can help to better exploit the promising but complex computing continuum. In this paper, we first briefly analyze the latest computing paradigms that move computation from the cloud to the edge (Sect. 2). Then, we present the fundamental features of compute continuum (Sect. 3) and detail relevant research challenges (Sect. 4).

2   From Cloud to Edge Computing

Fog Computing. Since its first presentation in 2012 [7], different definitions have been proposed for *fog computing* (e.g., [22,37,40,52]). According to NIST, fog computing is "a horizontal, physical or virtual resource paradigm that resides between smart end-devices and traditional cloud or data centers. This paradigm supports vertically-isolated, latency-sensitive applications by providing ubiquitous, scalable, layered, federated, and distributed computing, storage, and network connectivity" [22]. The OpenFog Consortium also puts emphasis on distributing computing, storage, control, and networking functions "along a cloud-to-thing continuum" [37]. Fog computing is aimed to extend (and not completely replace) resources provided from logically centralized and powerful data centers with resources towards the network edge, including Internet-of-Things (IoT) devices. The combination of fog and cloud computing resources is indeed especially useful to timely deal with load bursts, large volumes of data, and decentralized processing. An ancestor of fog computing has been proposed in 2009 by Satyanarayanan et al. [48], who introduced the concept of *cloudlet*. Cloudlets are micro-data centers placed in the proximity of mobile users, with the aim of boosting the interactive performance of mobile applications [49].

Edge Computing. A similar paradigm also stems from the networking community in 2015: *edge computing* [50]. With edge computing, computation is performed at the edge of the network, thus moving it closer to data sources and final information consumers [17,26]. Preliminary definitions did not explicitly consider cloud computing, as edge computing also tends to be limited to a small number of peripheral devices [22]. Although not popular as previous paradigms, *mist computing* [39] proposes to process data only among IoT devices, without recurring to nearby gateways or edge computing devices. The difference between edge and fog computing is quite subtle, and several researchers nowadays consider these terms interchangeably (e.g., [44,49]). Ren et al. [41] present a detailed analysis of these paradigms, highlighting the key features.

Mobile Cloud and Edge Computing. In the last decade, the pervasive Internet connectivity enabled the interaction of mobile users with cloud and fog applications. Therefore, different research efforts also proposed novel paradigms, such as Mobile Cloud Computing [25], Mobile Edge Computing [30] or Multi-access Edge Computing [46], that explicitly consider cloud or edge environments with a special focus on mobility. Elazhary [13] presents a survey aimed at disambiguating all the different paradigms introduced in this section.

All these paradigms consider a layered architecture, where each layer is conceptually well-separated from its upper and lower layers (e.g., [4,11,19]).

3 Compute Continuum

3.1 Definition and Key Features

To the best of our knowledge, the idea behind compute continuum started to be developed with the introduction of fog computing. In 2018, several contributions already presented the idea of a continuity of resources, referred to as *cloud-to-things*, e.g., [40], *IoT-fog-cloud*, e.g., [6], or *IoT-edge-cloud*, e.g., [38], continuum. Similarly, the so-called *osmotic computing* [54] uses the analogy of physical pressure to distribute computation across a continuum of resources spanning from the IoT to the cloud. The compute continuum is a system-level architecture that distributes computing, storage, control, and networking functions along a cloud-to-things continuum. Differently from fog computing, compute continuum places emphasis on overcoming the segregation of resources into tiers (e.g., IoT, edge, cloud), emphasizing the need for a simple-to-use infrastructure as well as latency and energy-awareness (e.g., [23]). The compute continuum infrastructure includes heterogeneous computing, storage, and networking resources, which are usually geographically distributed: in addition to not being always available, the connection links between resources are also characterized by non-negligible delays. However, this complexity should not be translated into complexity of application design and management. Therefore, the management of heterogeneous resources should be decoupled as much as possible from the specific processing to perform. This complexity should be managed by specifically designed frameworks that expose simple management APIs while transparently optimizing resource utilization to meet Quality-of-Service (QoS) requirements of applications (e.g., [3]).

To the best of our knowledge, and building on previous works [5,11,12,23], we summarize the essential features of the compute continuum.

- Heterogeneity: the continuum includes a wide range of heterogeneous resources in terms of computing, storage, networking, and energy capacity;

- Geographic distribution: resources can be physically located into different data centers, hence exposing non-negligible inter-communication delays;
  however, resource distribution can exploited by services and application to
  improve performance and privacy-awareness;
- Multi-tenancy and multi-proprietary: multiple users can use the same infrastructure, which can include resources from different providers; interoperabil-
  ity enables applications/services to operate on resource *federations* spanning
  multiple providers and/or administrative domains;
- Dynamicity and mobility: the infrastructure can encompass also mobile nodes
  exposing computing, sensing, and actuating capacity (e.g., IoT, wearable,
  smartphones); together with intermittent connectivity, this can lead to a
  highly dynamic infrastructure that calls for automation mechanisms.

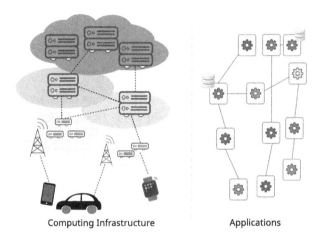

Computing Infrastructure   Applications

Fig. 1. Overview of compute continuum infrastructure, with (different types of) applications deployed on decentralized computing resources.

The compute continuum offers the possibility to deploy latency-sensitive
or privacy-aware applications by exploiting resources that are closer to data
sources or information consumers; hence, applications can more easily involve
real-time interaction. On the other hand, the continuum calls for novel and scalable approaches that simplify the management of the complex emerging infrastructure, thus handling varying workloads while avoiding resource wastage.

The following sections delve into the features of the infrastructure, platform,
and application layers in the compute continuum.

3.2 Infrastructure

Heterogeneous resources can include micro-controllers (interconnected using
Bluetooth, LTE, or WiFi), Array of Things, small servers, fog micro-data centers, medium-size clusters, and powerful data centers (usually interconnected

with high-speed wired network links) [5]. Resource heterogeneity also refers to the presence of specific hardware, such as sensors, actuators, FPGAs, GPUs, RISC-V and non-von Neumann architectures which can be exploited to run tailored applications (e.g., [1, 28]) or to efficiently perform computation—as it usually happens in the context of machine learning (e.g., [31]). Network links are heterogeneous as well, exposing different properties in terms of bandwidth, delay, and reliability. The *number* of devices also changes drastically when moving from the cloud to the edge, with edge resources usually more in number than large data centers. This is also due to differences in prices, which can be of several orders of magnitude lower for things and edge devices. *Energy capacity* cannot be neglected: edge devices usually rely on small batteries that limit their availability (e.g., [4, 19, 53]). All of these features require considering that computing, storage, and networking resources may not be always available, e.g., due to their mobility, reliability, limited energy, and limited connectivity. This is even more true as we get closer to the edge of the network.

Resources are usually organized into *geographically distributed* (micro, small, or large) data centers. This leads to non-negligible inter-data center network delays, which can, in turn, negatively affect application performance. As discussed in [7, 50], edge nodes often rely on nearby computing nodes instead of cloud resources to reduce application response times. Such ubiquitous resources can also belong to different *proprietaries*, who can expose them following different policies (in terms of both functional and non-functional requirements) [9].

Figure 1 gives a high-level overview of this compute continuum landscape from the perspective of the computing infrastructure and the hosted applications. Applications running in this environment are composed of several components, e.g., stream processing applications, microservices, or serverless functions, enabling their deployment at different locations of the continuum.

3.3   Platforms: Frameworks and Resource Management

The peculiar features of the compute continuum infrastructure requires the adoption of novel computing platforms that (i) rule the complexity of managing resources; (ii) optimize resource utilization; and (iii) simplify the design, deployment, and execution of distributed applications. We envision a scenario where multiple providers can offer computing or storage resources as a service, and expose such functionalities by means of high-level primitives or APIs (e.g., [3]). We imagine that the emerging landscape will be populated by multiple (both open and proprietary) frameworks. To successfully implement and exploit the idea of compute continuum, such frameworks should be highly *inter-operable* and ready to be *federated* in favor of ease the development of user-centric applications.

Locality Principle. Previous works showed the importance of exploiting data locality for data-intensive applications to improve performance (e.g. [11, 40]). The notion of locality is a pillar in the compute continuum, where different application components could be scattered across multiple and distant resources. Therefore, the infrastructure cannot be completely abstracted away. Frameworks for compute continuum should be able to explicitly and correctly take into account its key features while determining the application deployment.

Service Level Agreement. A representation of resources and applications enables the optimization of resource usage and application deployment. To conveniently express application requirements, novel Service Level Objectives (SLOs) are needed, possibly relying on high-level primitives, annotations, or alternative specification primitives [5]. SLOs are included in a *Service Level Agreement* (SLA) that the resource consumer stipulates with the resource provider; it also include penalties for the provider to pay if the agreement is disregarded.

Resource Management. Determining *where*, *when*, and *how* to run an application involves solving different tasks (see, e.g., [11,19,34]), mainly: resource discovery, admission control, scheduling, resource allocation, and deployment adaptation. *Resource discovery* deals with finding nodes that can provide computational, storage, or networking resources. Nodes may belong to different providers, where each one could adopt different mechanisms to collect information on ready-to-use nodes. Nodes can actively send availability information to a logically centralized repository. Alternatively, dedicated services can periodically pull this information (i.e., passive strategy). Cross-proprietary services could be envisioned as well to find nodes across different domains—almost as already happens in the Internet (e.g., [18,55]). *Admission control* helps providers to manage and account for the amount of resources rented to each consumer. Similar mechanisms are needed in the compute continuum (e.g., [20,47]). Besides business-oriented purposes, admission control helps to establish a rough control on the infrastructure load (and, in turn, to fulfil SLAs). When multiple applications arrive and go continuously, *scheduling* mechanisms enable the platform to collect application execution requests in a time frame before evaluating them in batches. Scheduling helps to partially deal with the uncertainty in predicting future resource demands and optimize for more convenient allocations (e.g., in terms of resource utilization or energy consumption). *Resource allocation* oversees the assignment of the available resources to the application execution requests. Different allocation policies have been explored in cloud and fog computing (e.g., [4,19]). However, the compute continuum calls for heterogeneity and energy-awareness and, secondly, mobility as well. Lightweight yet efficient heuristics are needed. When devices with limited capacity receive requests to execute large workloads, they can also recur to *offloading*, which moves computation away to another resource (e.g. [15]). Working conditions for (long-running) applications and services can likely change at run-time, e.g., due to load or resource availability variations. Therefore, it may be necessary to adjust resource allocation at run-time to meet SLAs and optimize resource utilization. Different *adaptation actions* can be performed, including *offloading*, *scaling*, and *migration* (e.g., [11,34]). While offloading refers to computation that is moved before being started, migration allows to move partially executed computation to another resource. These mechanisms should be carefully used in the compute continuum, as the communication latency between nodes is usually non-negligible and overheads are involved (e.g. [45]). Scaling applications on multiple edge-cloud resources also leads to higher variance in experienced latency. Run-time adaptation can be performed in a reactive or in a proactive manner. Also, the compute continuum can present both temporary and long-term performance degradation. Temporary performance degradation can be experienced more frequently towards the edge of the network, e.g., due to limited connectivity of endpoints and edge devices (e.g., [7,49]). Several approaches also exist for statically or dynamically updating the processing and topology of applications; we do not investigate them. The interested reader can find an overview of such approaches in the context of distributed data stream processing in [8].

Existing Frameworks. To the best of our knowledge, so far only few frameworks focus on running applications that exploit resources in the edge-cloud continuum (e.g., [33,45]). Both works consider the execution of serverless functions, and investigate the benefits of performing both vertical (i.e., from the edge to the cloud) and horizontal (i.e., within an edge zone) offloading. Frameworks that address also the other challenges of compute continuum (e.g., heterogeneous resources, mobility) are needed. In the context of fog computing, the literature offers a large number of frameworks that integrate IoT, fog, and cloud resources, which nonetheless reside in separate tiers. A review of existing fog computing frameworks can be found in, e.g., [11,19]. We also mention approaches aimed at running and orchestrating software containers on edge and IoT resources, such as K3s[1] and MicroK8s[2]. Although effort has been spent on running containers with reduced overhead, these frameworks only target a single segment of the continuum (the last mile). The ability to run containers with limited overhead has been boosted by the rapid diffusion of the serverless paradigm, which enables the execution of very small code units, defined as (mostly stateless) functions, on computing resources exploiting lightweight virtualization (e.g., OpenWhisk[3], [2,21,29,33,45]). To the best of our knowledge, no framework exists for long-running applications (e.g., data stream processing [8]).

3.4   Applications

In the last 15 years, the way applications are defined has deeply changed. With the advent of cloud computing, we assisted to the design of so-called *cloud-native applications* (e.g., [16]). These applications are usually organized as a bunch of loosely coupled components (microservices or functions) that strongly rely on

---

[1] https://k3s.io/.
[2] https://microk8s.io/.
[3] https://openwhisk.apache.org/.

lightweight virtualization for deployment (e.g., [33,45]). Besides exposing functionalities through standardized (REST or gRPC) APIs, the architecture aims to provide a clean separation between stateless and stateful services to fully exploit the features of an elastic computing environment. Microservices and serverless functions are usually adopted to define general-purpose applications that are deployed also on fog resources (e.g., [19,41]). Stream processing frameworks (e.g., Apache Flink), or other application-specific frameworks, usually expose high-level abstractions for specification and integration of user-defined code. We motivate the need for inter-operable solutions that could run seamlessly across hardware devices and software environments, while achieving good performance and a high level of security–a critical requirement for code and data processed off-premises. A promising technology is WebAssembly, a platform-independent portable binary code that can be executed client-side in browsers or in standalone environments. Using virtualization, protected within trusted execution environments, and equipped with a set of core services and libraries, WebAssembly allows us to meet both performance and high levels of security [35]. Some WebAssembly runtime (e.g., WasmEdge[4]) already supports edge computing.

4 Challenges and Opportunities

This section outlines some of the most relevant challenges of the compute continuum from a system perspective. We acknowledge that the list is not exhaustive.

4.1 Resource Management

Making efficient use of resources remains an open issue for computing systems, especially for those deployed at the edge of the network. These challenges are made even trickier by the intrinsic features of the compute continuum. We envision a few key research topics that might be highly relevant in the near future.

Lightweight virtualization. Virtualization techniques have played a key role in the cloud ecosystem. With modern infrastructures, there is increasing interest for lightweight virtualization techniques, due to resource-constrained devices within the continuum. Also, the dynamic nature of the compute continuum requires the ability of quickly allocating, migrating, or terminating (virtualized) application instances. Although technologies for lightweight virtualization (e.g., microVMs [2]) have recently appeared, their usage is still not widespread.

Computation Offloading. The availability of resource-rich yet distant cloud data centers alongside resource-constrained devices at the edge has motivated a lot of research on computation offloading [15], which trades off computational power with additional communication overhead. A multitude of different devices

---

[4] https://wasmedge.org.

and locations will be available to offloading fine-grained portions of applications. As offloading has significant implications in terms of performance, data transfers, and energy consumption, refined or novel offloading policies will be necessary to master the emerging complexity and take advantage of the continuum.

Energy-Aware Scheduling and Execution. Computing devices in the continuum are heterogeneous also in terms of energy supplies they rely on. On the one hand, it will be difficult (or even impossible) to execute some energy-demanding applications in certain parts of the continuum. On the other hand, some users may impose requirements related to the use of renewable energy for their tasks. We expect energy-aware strategies to emerge and integrate with existing solutions for application scheduling, offloading, and execution.

Multi-proprietary. The multi-proprietary infrastructure introduces further challenges for computing continuum. This requires investigating how existing approaches for federated cloud (e.g., [14,32,42]) can be adopted in this context.

4.2   Application Requirements

To successfully ensure performance while autonomously managing resources, we need a proper description of the application SLOs. Different approaches exists, e.g., including annotation or configuration files (e.g., [5,34]). If an application consists of multiple components (services or functions), specifying requirements for each component is not trivial. To overcome this issue, Dustdar et al. [12] propose to define high-level SLOs, which then relate to a set of hierarchically connected SLOs, down to SLOs for single resources. Within a single high-level SLO, there are SLOs at different levels of abstraction, which describe the system performance from different perspectives. Note that, since different applications for the compute continuum can have very different SLOs, different adaptation policies might be needed as well. This topic calls for further investigation.

4.3   Monitoring

The heterogeneity of the compute continuum infrastructure (also in terms of availability) requires monitoring, so to efficiently use computing, storage, and networking resources. Monitoring is also important to verify how applications are performing and whether their SLOs are attended. Local monitoring functions and external watchdogs can together provide information about the node's resource status. This information can be then used to plan resource allocation and offloading. Tracing historical performance metrics is also important to discover utilization patterns and improve resource management in a proactive manner.

4.4   Security and Privacy

Besides performance improvements, decentralized and multi-proprietary resources can result in applications being executed in untrusted environments. When data travels across different locations, it can be exposed to leakage, forgery, or stealing. The presence of multiple tenants also introduces further concerns. Costa et al. [11] show that only a limited number of works so far consider security in application deployment. Casamayor Pujol et al. [9] suggest to recur to Zero Trust [51], which is a set of cybersecurity paradigms that assumes no implicit trust granted to assets or users based on their network location. On the other hand, we are witnessing interesting developments in the field of cryptography, e.g., with homomorphic encryption techniques that can perform computation on opaque data with acceptable processing time (e.g., [10]). Research is also needed to investigate security and confidentiality of compute continuum applications.

4.5   Benchmarks

To support future research, there is an urgent need for tools that ease experimentation and comparison among novel proposals. Researchers need updated tools that capture the unique features and challenges of the continuum. Researchers would need reference application suites to use for benchmarking, reference workloads, network topologies, system simulators. While some initial effort has been spent on this aim (e.g., [24,43]), we expect more developments in this direction.

5   Conclusion

We have presented an overview of the key features and concepts of the emerging compute continuum paradigm. Then, we have identified relevant open issues representing opportunities for future research, especially as regards application specification, resource management, monitoring, privacy and security, and benchmarking tools.

References

1. Aazam, M., Zeadally, S., Harras, K.A.: Deploying fog computing in industrial internet of things and industry 4.0. IEEE Trans. Industr. Inform. **14**(10), 4674–4682 (2018)
2. Agache, A., Brooker, M., Florescu, A., Iordache, A., et al.: Firecracker: lightweight virtualization for serverless applications. In: Proceedings of NSDI 2020 (2020)
3. Aldinucci, M., Birke, R., Brogi, A., Carlini, E., et al.: A Proposal for a continuum-aware programming model: from workflows to services autonomously interacting in the compute continuum. In: Proceedings of IEEE COMPSAC 2023, pp. 1852–1857 (2023)
4. Bachiega, J.J., Costa, B., Carvalho, L.R., Rosa, M.J.F., Araujo, A.: Computational resource allocation in fog computing: a comprehensive survey. ACM Comput. Surv. **55**, 1–31 (2023)

5. Beckman, P., Dongarra, J., Ferrier, N., Fox, G., et al.: Harnessing the computing continuum for programming our world. In: Fog Computing, chap. 7, pp. 215–230. Wiley (2020)
6. Bittencourt, L., Immich, R., Sakellariou, R., Fonseca, N., et al.: The internet of things, fog and cloud continuum: integration and challenges. Internet Things **3**, 134–155 (2018)
7. Bonomi, F., Milito, R., Zhu, J., Addepalli, S.: Fog computing and its role in the internet of things. In: Proceedings of MCC 2012, pp. 13–16. ACM (2012)
8. Cardellini, V., Lo Presti, F., Nardelli, M., Russo Russo, G.: Runtime adaptation of data stream processing systems: the state of the art. ACM Comput. Surv. **54**(11s), 1–36 (2022)
9. Casamayor Pujol, V., Morichetta, A., Murturi, I., Kumar Donta, P., Dustdar, S.: Fundamental research challenges for distributed computing continuum systems. Information **14**(3), 198 (2023)
10. Chillotti, I., Gama, N., Georgieva, M., Izabachène, M.: TFHE: fast fully homomorphic encryption over the torus. J. Cryptol. **33**(1), 34–91 (2020)
11. Costa, B., Bachiega, J., de Carvalho, L.R., Araujo, A.P.F.: Orchestration in fog computing: a comprehensive survey. ACM Comput. Surv. **55**(2), 1–34 (2022)
12. Dustdar, S., Pujol, V.C., Donta, P.K.: On distributed computing continuum systems. IEEE Trans. Knowl. Data Eng. **35**(4), 4092–4105 (2023)
13. Elazhary, H.: Internet of things (IoT), mobile cloud, cloudlet, mobile IoT, IoT cloud, fog, mobile edge, and edge emerging computing paradigms: disambiguation and research directions. J. Netw. Comput. Appl. **128**, 105–140 (2019)
14. Elmroth, E., Marquez, F.G., Henriksson, D., Ferrera, D.P.: Accounting and billing for federated cloud infrastructures. In: Proceedings of GCC 2009, pp. 268–275 (2009)
15. Feng, C., Han, P., Zhang, X., Yang, B., et al.: Computation offloading in mobile edge computing networks: a survey. J. Netw. Comput. Appl. **202**, 103366 (2022)
16. Gannon, D., Barga, R., Sundaresan, N.: Cloud-native applications. IEEE Cloud Comput. **4**(5), 16–21 (2017)
17. Garcia Lopez, P., Montresor, A., Epema, D., Datta, A., et al.: Edge-centric computing: vision and challenges. SIGCOMM Comput. Commun. Rev. **45**(5), 37–42 (2015)
18. Gedeon, J., Zengerle, S., Alles, S., Brandherm, F., Mühlhäuser, M.: Sunstone: navigating the way through the fog. In: Proceedings of IEEE ICFEC 2020 (2020)
19. Goudarzi, M., Palaniswami, M., Buyya, R.: Scheduling IoT applications in edge and fog computing environments: a taxonomy and future directions. ACM Comput. Surv. **55**(7), 1–41 (2022)
20. Halén, J., Hellkvist, S., Baucke, S., Wuhib, F., Yazir, Y.O.: Wind: management and orchestration in the distributed heterogeneous cloud. In: Proceedings of IEEE SERVICES 2015, pp. 39–46 (2015)
21. Hendrickson, S., Sturdevant, S., Harter, T., Venkataramani, V., Arpaci-Dusseau, A.C., Arpaci-Dusseau, R.H.: Serverless computation with OpenLambda. In: Proceedings of HotCloud 2016. USENIX (2016)
22. Iorga, M., Feldman, L., Barton, R., Martin, M., Goren, N., Mahmoudi, C.: The NIST definition of fog computing. Tech. Rep. SP 800–191, NIST (2017)
23. Jansen, M., Al-Duilamy, A., Papadopoulos, A.V., Trivedi, A., Iosup, A.: The SPEC-RG reference architecture for the compute continuum. In: Proceedings of IEEE/ACM CCGRID 2023 (2023)

24. Jansen, M., Wagner, L., Trivedi, A., Iosup, A.: Continuum: automate infrastructure deployment and benchmarking in the compute continuum. In: Proceedings of ICPE 2023 Companion (2023)
25. Khan, A.u.R., Othman, M., Madani, S.A., Khan, S.U.: A survey of mobile cloud computing application models. IEEE Commun. Surv. Tutor. **16**(1), 393–413 (2014)
26. Khan, W.Z., Ahmed, E., Hakak, S., Yaqoob, I., Ahmed, A.: Edge computing: a survey. Future Gener. Comput. Syst. **97**, 219–235 (2019)
27. Kimovski, D., Mathá, R., Hammer, J., Mehran, N., et al.: Cloud, fog, or edge: where to compute? IEEE Internet Comput. **25**(4), 30–36 (2021)
28. Kimovski, D., Saurabh, N., Jansen, M., Aral, A., et al.: Beyond von Neumann in the computing continuum: architectures, applications, and future directions. IEEE Internet Comput. 1–11 (2023). https://doi.org/10.1109/MIC.2023.3301010
29. Kumar, R., Baughman, M., Chard, R., Li, Z., et al.: Coding the computing continuum: fluid function execution in heterogeneous computing environments. In: Proceedings of IEEE IPDPSW 2021, pp. 66–75 (2021)
30. Li, H., Shou, G., Hu, Y., Guo, Z.: Mobile edge computing: progress and challenges. In: Proceedings of IEEE MobileCloud 2016, pp. 83–84 (2016)
31. Li, P., Luo, Y., Zhang, N., Cao, Y.: HeteroSpark: a heterogeneous CPU/GPU spark platform for machine learning algorithms. In: Proceedings of IEEE NAS 2015 (2015)
32. Liaqat, M., Chang, V., Gani, A., Hamid, S.H.A., et al.: Federated cloud resource management: review and discussion. J. Netw. Comput. Appl. **77**, 87–105 (2017)
33. Lordan, F., Lezzi, D., Badia, R.M.: Colony: parallel functions as a service on the cloud-edge continuum. In: Proceedings of Euro-Par 2021, pp. 269–284 (2021)
34. Mahmud, R., Ramamohanarao, K., Buyya, R.: Application management in fog computing environments: a taxonomy, review and future directions. ACM Comput. Surv. **53**(4), 1–43 (2020)
35. Ménétrey, J., Pasin, M., Felber, P., Schiavoni, V.: WebAssembly as a common layer for the cloud-edge continuum. In: Proceedings of FRAME 2022, pp. 3–8. ACM (2022)
36. Moreschini, S., Pecorelli, F., Li, X., Naz, S., et al.: Cloud continuum: the definition. IEEE Access **10**, 131876–131886 (2022)
37. OpenFog consortium architecture working group: OpenFog reference architecture for fog computing. Tech. Rep. OPFRA001.020817, OpenFog Consortium (2017)
38. Pahl, C., Ioini, N.E., Helmer, S., Lee, B.: An architecture pattern for trusted orchestration in IoT edge clouds. In: Proceedings of FMEC 2018, pp. 63–70 (2018)
39. Preden, J.S., Tammemäe, K., Jantsch, A., Leier, M., et al.: The benefits of self-awareness and attention in fog and mist computing. IEEE Comput. **48**(7), 37–45 (2015)
40. Puliafito, C., Mingozzi, E., Longo, F., Puliafito, A., Rana, O.: Fog computing for the internet of things: a survey. ACM Trans. Internet Technol. **19**(2), 1–41 (2019)
41. Ren, J., Zhang, D., He, S., Zhang, Y., Li, T.: A survey on end-edge-cloud orchestrated network computing paradigms: transparent computing, mobile edge computing, fog computing, and cloudlet. ACM Comput. Surv. **52**(6), 1–36 (2019)
42. Rochwerger, B., Breitgand, D., Levy, E., Galis, A., et al.: The reservoir model and architecture for open federated cloud computing. IBM J. Res. Dev. **53**(4), 1–11 (2009)
43. Rosendo, D., Silva, P., Simonin, M., Costan, A., Antoniu, G.: E2Clab: exploring the computing continuum through repeatable, replicable and reproducible edge-to-cloud experiments. In: Proceedings of IEEE CLUSTER 2020, pp. 176–186 (2020)

44. Ruay-Shiung-Chang, Gao, J., Gruhn, V., He, J., et al.: Mobile cloud computing research - issues, challenges and needs. In: Proceedings of IEEE SOSE 2013, pp. 442–453 (2013)
45. Russo Russo, G., Mannucci, T., Cardellini, V., Lo Presti, F.: Serverledge: decentralized function-as-a-service for the edge-cloud continuum. In: Proceedings of IEEE PerCom 2023, pp. 131–140 (2023)
46. Saeik, F., Avgeris, M., Spatharakis, D., Santi, N., Dechouniotis, D., et al.: Task offloading in edge and cloud computing: a survey on mathematical, artificial intelligence and control theory solutions. Comput. Netw. **195**, 108177 (2021)
47. Santoro, D., Zozin, D., Pizzolli, D., De Pellegrini, F., Cretti, S.: Foggy: a platform for workload orchestration in a fog computing environment. In: Proceedings of IEEE CloudCom 2017, pp. 231–234 (2017)
48. Satyanarayanan, M., Bahl, P., Caceres, R., Davies, N.: The case for VM-based cloudlets in mobile computing. IEEE Pervasive Comput. **8**(4), 14–23 (2009)
49. Satyanarayanan, M., Chen, Z., Ha, K., Hu, W., et al.: Cloudlets: at the leading edge of mobile-cloud convergence. In: Proceedings of MobiCASE 2014, pp. 1–9 (2014)
50. Satyanarayanan, M., et al.: Edge analytics in the internet of things. IEEE Pervasive Comput. **14**(2), 24–31 (2015)
51. Stafford, V.: Zero trust architecture. NIST Spec. Publ. **800**, 207 (2020)
52. Vaquero, L.M., Rodero-Merino, L.: Finding your way in the fog: towards a comprehensive definition of fog computing. SIGCOMM Comput. Commun. Rev. **44**(5), 27–32 (2014)
53. Vatanparvar, K., Al Faruque, M.A.: Energy management as a service over fog computing platform. In: Proceedings of ACM/IEEE ICCPS 2015, pp. 248–249. ACM (2015)
54. Villari, M., Fazio, M., Dustdar, S., Rana, O., Ranjan, R.: Osmotic computing: a new paradigm for edge/cloud integration. IEEE Cloud Comput. **3**(6), 76–83 (2016)
55. Zavodovski, A., Mohan, N., Bayhan, S., Wong, W., Kangasharju, J.: ExEC: elastic extensible edge cloud. In: Proceedings of EdgeSys 2019, pp. 24–29. ACM (2019)

An Algorithm for Tunable Memory Compression of Time-Based Windows for Stream Aggregates

Vincenzo Gulisano[(✉)] [iD]

Chalmers University of Technology, Gothenburg, Sweden
vincenzo.gulisano@chalmers.se

Abstract. Cloud-to-edge device continuums transform raw data into insights through data-intensive processing paradigms such as stream processing and frameworks known as Stream Processing Engines (SPEs). The control of resources in streaming applications within and across such continuums has been a prominent topic in the literature. While several techniques have been proposed to control resources like CPU, limited control exists for other resources such as memory.

Based on this observation, this work proposes an algorithm for streaming aggregation that allows for control of memory usage through lossless compression. The algorithm provides a "knob" to control the amount of state that should be compressed, prioritizing the compression of old over fresh data when performing streaming aggregation. Together with a detailed algorithmic description, this work presents preliminary results from a fully implemented prototype on top of the Liebre SPE, showing the effectiveness of the proposed approach.

Keywords: Stream Processing · Stream Aggregate · Compression

1 Introduction

Cloud-to-edge device continuums support pipelines transforming edge data into cloud-based insights/decisions. These pipelines often rely on data-intensive processing paradigms like stream processing where applications are defined as Directed Acyclic Graphs (DAGs) of operators and run by Stream Processing Engines (SPEs). SPEs allow control of how pipelines are deployed through the distribution and parallelization of the operators of a DAG.

Despite the increasing computational power of the cloud-edge continuum, resources are typically dedicated to critical tasks, with limited room for custom analysis, especially at the edge (e.g., as in modern vehicles, where powerful devices are primarily utilized for critical driving applications [18]).

The ability to control resource utilization of stream processing applications has been a prominent topic in the literature, e.g., with adaptive distribution and elasticity [8,9], shedding [20], and thread scheduling [22,23]. However, current

© The Author(s), under exclusive license to Springer Nature Switzerland AG 2024
D. Zeinalipour et al. (Eds.): Euro-Par 2023 Workshops, LNCS 14351, pp. 18–29, 2024.
https://doi.org/10.1007/978-3-031-50684-0_2

solutions offer limited control over memory usage, which is crucial for streaming applications with operators maintaining state over analyzed data to manage their memory footprint. In this context, this work introduces an algorithm for streaming aggregation that allows for control of memory usage through compression. By defining a single additional parameter to existing streaming aggregation parameters, the algorithm provides a "knob" to control the amount of state that should be compressed, prioritizing the compression of old over fresh data.

This work provides a detailed algorithmic description of the proposed solution, along with a fully implemented prototype on top of the Liebre SPE [21]. The results demonstrate the effectiveness of the approach in managing memory usage while maintaining the desired level of aggregation accuracy.

2   Preliminaries

2.1   Stream Processing Basics and Streaming Aggregation

According to DataFlow [2], a *stream* S is an unbounded sequence of *tuples*, each defined by its *type* $\langle \tau, v_1, \ldots, v_n \rangle$, where τ is the timestamp attribute, always included in the type of a tuple, and $v_1, \ldots, v_n$ are application-specific attributes. Streams are homogeneous: every tuple t of the same stream S has the same type.

Stream processing queries (or simply queries) are composed of *ingresses*, *operators*, and *egresses*. Ingresses forward tuples (e.g., events reported by sensors or other applications) to operators, the basic units manipulating tuples. Operators connected in a Directed Acyclic Graph (DAG) process and forward/produce tuples; eventually, tuples are fed to egresses, which deliver results to end-users or other applications. Multiple copies of the same operator can be deployed within the same DAG, each analyzing a portion of a given stream (e.g., tuples sharing the same key in *key-by* parallelism, as explained in the remainder).

As an ingress tuple t corresponds to an event, $t.\tau$ is the *event time* set by the ingress when the event took place. Event time is expressed in time units from a given epoch and progresses in SPE-specific δ increments (e.g., milliseconds [11]).

Operators are distinguished into *stateless* and *stateful*. FlatMap, Filter, and Map are stateless operators that do not maintain a state that evolves according to the tuples they process. Stateful operators produce results from a state, dependent on one or more tuples. This work targets stateful operators defined over delimited groups of tuples called *time-based windows* (or simply windows) which are commonly provided by SPEs [11,21,25]: *Aggregates* over windows.

An Aggregate $A(WA, WS, S_I, f_K, f_A, f_O, f_S)$ is defined by parameters:

Window Advance (WA), Size (WS): the epochs $[\ell WA, \ell WA + WS)$, with $\ell \in \mathbb{N}$, covered by A. Each epoch is referred to as a window *instance* γ. If $WA < WS$, consecutive *sliding* γs overlap and a tuple can fall into several γs. If $WA = WS$, each tuple falls in exactly one *tumbling* γ.

Stream S_I: the input stream fed to A.

Function f_K: which specifies the subset (possibly empty) of S_I tuples' attributes used to maintain dedicated γs for tuples that share the same *key*. Note that f_K affects the way in which A is parallelized, as discussed next.

Function $f_A(\gamma, t)$ to add to γ the contribution of t.
Function $f_O(\gamma)$ to compute the values of an output t_o from γ.
Function $f_S(\gamma, l)$ to advance γ to its new left boundary l, increasing l by WA.

A γ's left boundary (inclusive) is referred to as $\gamma.l$ (omitting γ if clear from the context). The right (exclusive) boundary is $\gamma.l + WS$. When an output tuple t_o is created from γ, $t_o.\tau$ is set by A to $\gamma.l + WS - \delta$ [6,11,25].

As aforementioned, SPEs parallelize the execution of an operator by deploying multiple copies of such an operator. To achieve this, SPEs let users define operators as *logical*, and later convert them into *physical instances*. Since stateless operators do not maintain a state that evolves based on the tuples they process, the data fed to multiple instances of the same logical operator can be shuffled or fed in a round-robin fashion. For logical stateful operators like A, SPEs rely on key-by routing/partitioning, splitting the data sent to such instances so that tuples sharing the same f_K value are correctly processed by the same instance.

2.2 Correctness Conditions

Users expect SPEs' executions to enforce A's semantics correctly:

Definition 1. *A's execution is correct if any subset of tuples from S_I sharing the same key and falling in the same γ is jointly processed by f_O exactly once and the resulting output tuple is forwarded to A downstream peers.*

For A, Definition 1 implies that all the tuples falling into γ should be added to γ by f_A and jointly processed by f_O exactly once. Correct execution can be achieved by consistently maintaining A's *watermarks* [17]:

Definition 2. *A's watermark W_A^ω at wall-clock time ω is the earliest event time a tuple t_i fed to A can have from ω on (i.e., $t_i.\tau \geq W_A^\omega, \forall t_i$ fed to A from ω on).*

Watermarks are commonly maintained assuming ingresses periodically output special watermark tuples with monotonically increasing timestamps [11,17]. They serve as notifications of how event-time advances from the perspective of ingresses, and operators use them to (1) make progress even in the absence of regular tuples and/or (2) reorder tuples from out-of-timestamp-order streams.

Upon receiving a watermark, A can store the watermark's time and update W_A^ω to the smallest value among those in the set comprised of the latest watermark from each input stream. Upon reception of a watermark that increases W_A^ω, A can output the results of all γs whose right boundary is not greater than W_A^ω (i.e., invoke f_O on any $\gamma|\gamma.l + WS \leq W_A^\omega$) since no more tuples will fall in such γs, and then forward W_A^ω to its downstream peers.

3 Problem Definition

This study aims at defining an Aggregate operator that lets users customize its behavior through its common parameters (see Sect. 2.1) allowing to control which portion of its γs should be compressed, ranging from none to all, prioritizing the compression of γs updated least recently over those updated more recently.

Since the additional compression and decompression of γs can ease memory consumption but also incurs a computational cost besides the data handling and data analysis ones already defined by an Aggregate, this work assesses the memory/performance trade-offs based on the following metrics:

- Throughput: the number of tuples processed per unit of time,
- Latency: the delay in the production of an output tuple once the tuple triggering the production of such an output is fed to A,
- Number of compressions/decompressions (cumulative) over time,
- Memory usage: the total memory used by A's state, and
- Percentage of compressed/uncompressed γs (over the total number of γs).

This work assumes that each one of the input streams fed to an instance of A is sorted on its timestamp attributes or, alternatively, that it can be sorted by relying on watermarks before being fed to A [15]. If multiple streams are fed to A, then they are first merge-sorted based on their timestamp, for instance, like in [16]. Notice that, with such an assumption in place, the timestamp of each tuple fed to A is in fact an update of the A's watermark, since any later tuple fed to A will have an equal or greater timestamp, according to Definition 2. For A's downstream operators/sinks to also count with sorted streams, the algorithm should also produce A's output tuples in timestamp order [16].

When presenting the proposed algorithm, for ease of exposition, the SPE running the A is assumed to define two main methods: `process(t)`, invoked by the SPE to signal A that a new input tuple t can be processed by the latter, and `forward(t)`, invoked by A when a new output tuple t can be forwarded to downstream operators/sinks, after $t.\tau$ is set by the SPE according to the A's WA and WS parameters (see Sect. 2.1).

4   Proposed Algorithm and Aggregate Operator

This section overviews the algorithm proposed for an operator A_C that can compress part of the γs that have updated least recently, later decompressing/compressing them based on updates or results production.

Besides the parameters covered in Sect. 2.1, A_C defines an additional parameter D, to express the maximum time distance in event time that can elapse from the update of a γ to its compression. Note such a parameter allows tuning the fraction of γs that are compressed by A_C in a range that goes from $D = 0$, where all γs will be immediately compressed after their update, to $D = \infty$, where no γ will be compressed. Also, note that for $D \neq \infty$, any compressed γ must be decompressed before invoking f_A, f_O, or f_S on it.

Algorithm 1 shows A_C's variables and methods. A_C's variables include WA and WS (L 1), parameter D (L 2), two `Map` objects $uncomp_\gamma$ and $comp_\gamma$ maintaining uncompressed and compressed γs, respectively (L 3), the earliest left boundary e_l of any γ maintained by A_C (L 4), a `TreeMap` linking a given event

---

Algorithm 1: Aggregate A_C supporting compression, run by the SPE.

Local variables:

1 WA, WS // window advance and size

2 D // max event-time diff. from last insertion to trig compression

3 Map<k,γ> $uncomp_\gamma$, $comp_\gamma$ // uncompressed/compressed γs

4 e_l // earliest left boundary of any γ kept by A

5 TreeMap<τ,Set<k>> $\tau_\mathbb{K}$ // keys for each latest contrib. timestamp

6 Map<k,τ> k_τ // latest contribution for key k

Auxiliary Methods:

7 getEarliestLeftBound(τ) // get γ's earliest left bound for τ

8 getOrCreate(k,τ) // get (decompress if needed) or create γ

9 compress(γ),decompress(γ) // compress/decompress γ

10 Method process(t) // process tuple t

11 $\quad$ while $e_l + WS < t.\tau$ do // Output and advance γs

12 $\quad\quad$ for $k \in uncomp_\gamma$ do // Output and advance uncompressed γs

13 $\quad\quad\quad$ forward($f_O(uncomp_\gamma[k])$)

14 $\quad\quad\quad$ $uncomp_\gamma[k] \leftarrow f_S(uncomp_\gamma[k], e_l + WA)$

15 $\quad\quad\quad$ if $|uncomp_\gamma[k]| == 0$ then // remove if γ is empty

16 $\quad\quad\quad\quad$ $uncomp_\gamma$.remove(k)

17 $\quad\quad$ for $k \in comp_\gamma$ do // Output and advance compressed γs

18 $\quad\quad\quad$ $\gamma \leftarrow$decompress($comp_\gamma[k]$) // decompress γ

19 $\quad\quad\quad$ forward($f_O(\gamma)$)

20 $\quad\quad\quad$ $\gamma \leftarrow f_S(\gamma, e_l + WA)$

21 $\quad\quad\quad$ if $|\gamma| == 0$ then // remove if γ is empty

22 $\quad\quad\quad\quad$ $comp_\gamma$.remove(k))

23 $\quad\quad\quad$ else // compress γ again

24 $\quad\quad\quad\quad$ $comp_\gamma[k] \leftarrow$ compress(γ)

25 $\quad\quad$ $e_l \leftarrow e_l + WA$ // advance earliest left boundary of γs kept by A

26 $\quad$ $k \leftarrow f_K(t)$ // get t's key

27 $\quad$ $l \leftarrow$ getEarliestLeftBound($t.\tau$) // get γ's earliest left bound for t

28 $\quad$ $\gamma \leftarrow$ getOrCreate(k,l) // get (decompress if needed) or create γ

29 $\quad$ $\gamma \leftarrow f_A(\gamma, t)$ // add the tuple

30 $\quad$ if $k \in k_\tau$ then // update k_τ and $\tau_\mathbb{K}$ based on t

31 $\quad\quad$ $\tau_\mathbb{K}[k_\tau[k]]$.remove($k$)

32 $\quad$ $k_\tau[k] \leftarrow t.\tau$

33 $\quad$ $\tau_\mathbb{K}[t.\tau]$.add(k)

34 $\quad$ for $\tau \in \tau_\mathbb{K}$ do // compress γs not updated in the last D time units

35 $\quad\quad$ if $t.\tau - \tau \geq D$ then

36 $\quad\quad\quad$ for $k' \in \tau_\mathbb{K}[\tau]$ do

37 $\quad\quad\quad\quad$ $comp_\gamma[k'] \leftarrow$ compress($uncomp_\gamma[k']$)

38 $\quad\quad\quad\quad$ $uncomp_\gamma$.remove(k')

39 $\quad\quad\quad\quad$ k_τ.remove(k')

40 $\quad\quad\quad$ $\tau_\mathbb{K}$.remove(τ)

41 $\quad\quad$ else

42 $\quad\quad\quad$ break

---

time τ with all keys for which τ represents the last event time at which the corresponding γ has been updated (L 5), and a Map storing, for each key, the latest event time at which the corresponding γ has been updated (L 6).

Notation: $M[k]$ refers to the entry k of Map or TreeMap M, M.remove(k) indicates key k is being removed from M, S.add(k) indicates the k is being added to set S, "if $(k \in M)$ {}" checks if k is a key maintained by M, $|\gamma|$ refers to the number of tuples in γ. The keys of a TreeMap M are traversed in increasing order when running "for $(k \in M)$ {}".

In Algorithm 1, the auxiliary method getEarliestLeftBound(τ) computes the left bound of the earliest γ to which a tuple with timestamp τ contributes to (L 7). Method getOrCreate(k, τ) retrieves the γ for key k and timestamp τ. If γ exists but is compressed, the method decompresses γ before returning it, while if γ does not exist, the method creates it (L 8). Methods compress(γ)/ decompress(γ) compress/decompress γ, respectively (L 9).

Upon reception of a new input tuple (method process(t), L 10), A_C produces all the output tuples that can be produced based on $t.\tau$. As discussed in Sect. 3, $t.\tau$ represents in this case A_C's latest watermark (see Sect. 2.2). A_C keeps producing, in timestamp order, the results of the γs it maintains as long as their left boundary indicates such γs are expired (i.e., as long as $e_l + WS < t.\tau$, L 11), increasing e_l by WA at each iteration (L 25), and thus meeting the requirement of producing output tuples in timestamp order (see Sect. 3). Within each iteration, A_C begins by producing the results for uncompressed γs. For each γ, the result is retrieved and forwarded by A_C. Subsequently, γ is advanced and either maintained or discarded depending on whether it is empty or not once advanced (L 12-16). Results for compressed γs are produced similarly, with additional calls to methods decompress, before producing the result of a γ and advancing it, and compress, before storing back in $comp_\gamma$ a non-empty γ (L 17-24).

Once the output tuples (if any) that could be produced based on the incoming t are forwarded, A_C retrieves $k = f_K(t)$ (L 26), the left boundary of the earliest γ to which t contributes (L 27), the corresponding γ, decompressing or creating it if necessary (L 28), and proceeds adding t to γ (L 29). Then, it proceeds to update the information about the latest event time at which k has been updated. If k was previously updated it removes K from the set of keys for the corresponding event time update. Then, it proceeds to update $k_\tau[k]$ and $\tau_\mathbb{K}$ (L 30-33). Finally, A_C traverses all the keys of the uncompressed γs it maintains based on the latest event time at which each key updated its corresponding γ. The γs that refer to keys whose last update is far away from $t.\tau$ more than D time units are compressed and moved from $uncomp_\gamma$ to $comp_\gamma$, updating $k_\tau[k]$ and $\tau_\mathbb{K}$ accordingly. Note the traversal stops as soon as the distance between $t.\tau$ and the latest update of a given set of is less than D (L 34-42).

5   Evaluation

The evaluation begins by discussing hardware/software, data, and how experiments are conducted for A_C. Then, it discusses how the performance metrics introduced in Sect. 3 behave for various setups of the experiments' parameters.

Hardware/Software. Experiments run on an Intel Xeon E5-2637 v4 @ 3.50 GHz (4 cores, 8 threads) server with 64 GB of RAM with Ubuntu 18.04. The server is representative of a device that could be deployed at the edge end of the cloud-edge continuum in connection to the use-case presented next. Algorithm 1 has been implemented using the Liebre SPE [21] and the Snappy [1] compressor.

Data. For S_I (see Sect. 2.1), the data comes from the Linear Road benchmark [5], a popular benchmark in stream processing that simulates a real-time traffic monitoring system. Its data models individual vehicles with a given number of highways, generating a stream of reports of vehicles' position and speed, with new reports being generated every second. Consecutive reports from the same vehicle are 30 s apart (in event time). Each vehicle starts/ends producing reports within a given event time interval, lasting a few to tens of minutes. The simulated traffic covers 3 h (in event time) and results in ∼ 44 million tuples.

Experimental Setup. A_C's f_O (see Sect. 2.1) counts the number of stops each vehicle performs during its journey, where a stop is a sequence of at least one position report with zero speed in-between reports with non-zero speed (or happening at the very beginning/end of the journey), over a window with WA and WS set to 1 min and 3 h, respectively. A_C's f_A and f_S store and remove tuples in a γ's internal state, respectively. The experiments study A_C's performance for varying injection rates – $5*10^3$, $10*10^3$, $20*10^3$, $25*10^3$, and $40*10^3$ t/s – up to the rate sustainable for an A_C that does not compress its γs, and D values (see Sect. 4) – ∞, 20 m, 10 m, 1 m, 15 s and 0 s. Note that, for a fair comparison, the original Liebre Aggregate is used when $D = \infty$ (i.e., when no γ is to be compressed). Each experiment lasts 10 min. The data collected during the first (warm-up) and last (cool-down) minutes is excluded from the results. For each experiment, given the performance metrics introduced in Sect. 3, throughput and latency metrics refer to the average value observed during the experiment, while ratio, compression, decompression, and memory metrics refer to the value at the end of the experiment. All results are averaged over 10 repetitions. Shaded areas in the plots represent the 99% confidence interval. Since accurate runtime memory estimation in Java is costly, runtime measurements are based on precomputed measurements, obtained using the Jamm library[1], of tuples' sizes and per-tuple overheads (e.g., for maintaining a tuple in a `LinkedList`), later used as a multiplicative factor of the total number of tuples maintained by A_C.

Results. Figure 1(a) presents the legend for the different injection rates used in all the subsequent plots, while Figs. 1(b) and 1(c) present the throughput and latency metrics, respectively, for the various injection rates and D values. As shown, the throughput degrades for decreasing D values, and, the higher the injection rate, the more severe the degradation. Similar trends are observed for

---

[1] https://github.com/jbellis/jamm.

the latency, with an increasing overhead as D increases and higher overheads observed for higher injection rates.

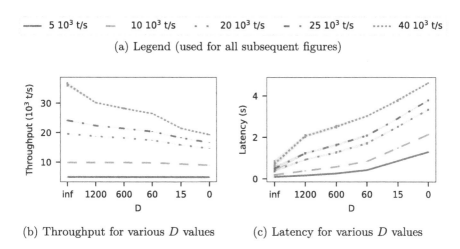

(a) Legend (used for all subsequent figures)

(b) Throughput for various D values   (c) Latency for various D values

Fig. 1. Legend for all figures(a), and throughput(b)/latency(c) performance figures.

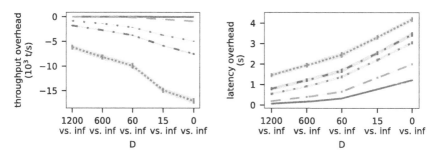

(a) Throughput overhead for various D values, compared with $D = \infty$ (b) Latency overhead for various D values, compared with $D = \infty$

Fig. 2. Throughput (b) and latency (c) overheads.

The actual overheads (in t/s for throughput and s for latency) observed when comparing the performance of an A_C that does not rely on compression (i.e., when $D = \infty$) and one that does (i.e., when $D \neq \infty$) are shown in Fig. 2(a) and Fig. 2(b), respectively. As shown, the degradation can grow to e.g., -40% throughput and $+9\times$ latency for a low D value (15 s) and high injection rate $(40{*}10^3$ t/s). To contextualize the overheads with respect to the gains in memory, though, one can observe from Fig. 3(a) and Fig. 3(b) that the values 15 s and 0 s for D are the values at which the total number of compressions/decompressions spikes. If this is expected when $D = 0$ s, since each γ is immediately compressed once a tuple is added to it, it is also expected for $D = 15$ based on the data being processed: since 15 s is less than the time interleaving two reports from the same tuple, such a value implies each γ, once a tuple is added to it, is compressed before any subsequent tuple from the same vehicle is again added to it.

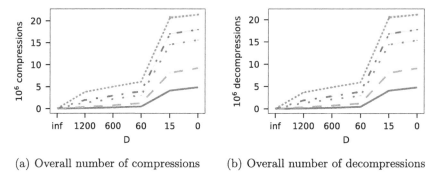

(a) Overall number of compressions   (b) Overall number of decompressions

Fig. 3. Overall number of compression (a) and decompression (b) actions

For a larger D value such as 60s, one can nonetheless observe that the benefits from the memory perspective are visible even for a less aggressive compression threshold, as shown in Fig. 4(a) and Fig. 4(b). For a medium injection rate, one can observe a reduction of approximately 2/3 in the overall memory (from 3 to 1 GB), with approximately 40% of the overall γs being compressed, with a throughput degradation of about 15%.

In general, the preliminary results indicate several configurations of the D parameter, for several of the studied rates, have overheads that lead to performance figures in the same order of magnitude as those without compression, while they allow reducing memory usage by at least one-third.

6   Related Work

Managing access to computational resources in streaming applications is a widely researched topic, as evidenced by the literature [3,7,9,19,22,23]. While several proposed techniques/tools focus on CPU resource control [9,23] memory management (in general) and compression (in connection to this work) have received less attention, unlike in databases where they have been discussed in major depth [26]. Examples in stream processing are e.g., discussed in [23], including the provisioning and scheduling of threads to queries and their operators.

Focusing on the existing solutions for streaming applications, memory control has been discussed in [12–14] but with a focus on specific hardware like FPGAs. The compression technique proposed in [14] is also for stream aggregation but for

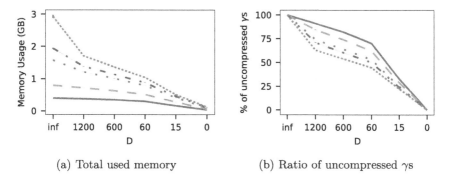

(a) Total used memory   (b) Ratio of uncompressed γs

Fig. 4. Overall memory usage (a) and ratio of uncompressed/compressed γs (b)

tuple-based windows, which differ from the windows considered in this work. The tuple-based windows are chosen for FPGAs because they allow the exact size of each window instance to be known in advance, enabling allocation and control of the required memory for that window instance. Expanding the discussion to generic hardware, other complementary approaches have been proposed in [10, 18]. However, these techniques differ from this work in that they apply lossy (with a controllable error bound) instead of lossless compression and apply compression to streams across operators rather than within an Aggregate operator. Similarly, [24] proposes a compression scheme for tuples maintained outside individual operators' states. While [24] evaluates compression for stream aggregation, the proposed solution only supports tumbling windows with $WA=WS$, unlike this work. Additional work that relates to stream aggregation is discussed in [4]. However, this contribution focuses on a data structure (the Compressed Buffered Tree) that can be leveraged by any operator rather than on the internal state of stream Aggregates. Additionally, the data structure supports continuous stream aggregation on a per-key basis but does not discuss window semantics.

7   Conclusions and Future Work

This work introduced a novel algorithm for tunable memory compression in stream aggregation. By defining a single additional parameter besides the common parameters defined for streaming aggregation over time-based windows, the algorithm allows controlling the amount of compressed window instances, prioritizing the compression of those not recently updated.

Initial results show the proposed algorithm can be beneficial and compress memory by at least one-third, with overheads in throughput/latency performance figures in the same order of magnitude as those without compression. This initial study can be expanded in several research directions: extended empirical studies, with more use-cases, setups (e.g., parallel/distributed executions) and heterogenous hardware, comparison with state-of-the-art baselines, and amounts of available memory, studying also the behavior of an Aggregate when memory is exhausted or in high contention with e.g., a garbage collector; generalization of the proposed technique to accommodate different compression techniques, possibly extending to lossy compression too, and study of different compression levels for a given technique, and joint use of the proposed technique with AI-based agents adjusting parameter D based on e.g., Quality-of-Service requirements.

Acknowledgements. This work is supported by the Marie Skłodowska-Curie Doctoral Network project RELAX-DN, funded by the European Union under Horizon Europe 2021–2027 Framework Programme Grant Agreement number 101072456, by Chalmers Un. AoA frameworks Energy and Production, proj. INDEED, and WP "Scalability, Big Data and AI", respectively, and by the Swedish Government Agency for Innovation Systems VINNOVA, proj. "Automotive Stream Processing and Distributed Analytics (AutoSPADA)" (DNR 2019-05884) in the funding program FFI: Strategic Vehicle Research and Innovation.

References

1. Snappy, a fast compressor/decompressor. https://github.com/google/snappy
2. Akidau, T., et al.: The dataflow model: a practical approach to balancing correctness, latency, and cost in massive-scale, unbounded, out-of-order data processing. Proc. Endowment **8**(12), 1792–1803 (2015)
3. Aldinucci, M., Danelutto, M., Kilpatrick, P., Torquati, M.: Fastflow: high-level and efficient streaming on multicore, chap. 13, pp. 261–280. Wiley (2017)
4. Amur, H., et al.: Memory-efficient groupby-aggregate using compressed buffer trees. In: Proceedings of the 4th Annual Symposium on Cloud Computing, pp. 1–16 (2013)
5. Arasu, A., et al.: Linear road: a stream data management benchmark. In: Proceedings of the Thirtieth International Conference on Very large data bases-Volume 30, pp. 480–491. VLDB Endowment (2004)
6. Apache beam. https://beam.apache.org/. Accessed 12 Nov 2020
7. Cardellini, V., Grassi, V., Presti, F.L., Nardelli, M.: On QoS-aware scheduling of data stream applications over fog computing infrastructures. In: 2015 IEEE Symposium on Computers and Communication (ISCC), pp. 271–276. IEEE (2015)
8. Cardellini, V., Nardelli, M., Luzi, D.: Elastic stateful stream processing in storm. In: 2016 International Conference on High Performance Computing Simulation (HPCS), pp. 583–590. IEEE (2016)
9. De Matteis, T., Mencagli, G.: Keep calm and react with foresight: strategies for low-latency and energy-efficient elastic data stream processing. ACM SIGPLAN Notices **51**(8), 1–12 (2016)
10. Duvignau, R., Gulisano, V., Papatriantafilou, M., Savic, V.: Streaming piecewise linear approximation for efficient data management in edge computing. In: Proceedings of the 34th ACM/SIGAPP Symposium on Applied Computing (2019)
11. Apache flink. https://flink.apache.org. Accessed 27 Jan 2023
12. Geethakumari, P.R., Gulisano, V., Svensson, B.J., Trancoso, P., Sourdis, I.: Single window stream aggregation using reconfigurable hardware. In: 2017 International Conference on Field Programmable Technology (ICFPT). IEEE (2017)
13. Geethakumari, P.R., Gulisano, V., Trancoso, P., Sourdis, I.: Time-SWAD: a dataflow engine for time-based single window stream aggregation. In: 2019 International Conference on Field-Programmable Technology (ICFPT), pp. 72–80. IEEE (2019)

14. Geethakumari, P.R., Sourdis, I.: Stream aggregation with compressed sliding-windows. ACM Trans. Reconfigurable Technol. Syst. **16**, 1–28 (2023)
15. Gulisano, V., Nikolakopoulos, Y., Cederman, D., Papatriantafilou, M., Tsigas, P.: Efficient data streaming multiway aggregation through concurrent algorithmic designs and new abstract data types. ACM Trans. Parallel Comput. **4**(2), 11:1–11:28 (2017). https://doi.org/10.1145/3131272
16. Gulisano, V., Nikolakopoulos, Y., Papatriantafilou, M., Tsigas, P.: ScaleJoin: a deterministic, disjoint-parallel and skew-resilient stream join. IEEE Trans. Big Data **7**(2), 299–312 (2021). https://doi.org/10.1109/TBDATA.2016.2624274
17. Gulisano, V., Palyvos-Giannas, D., Havers, B., Papatriantafilou, M.: The role of event-time order in data streaming analysis. In: Proceedings of the 14th ACM International Conference on Distributed and Event-based Systems (2020)
18. Havers, B., Duvignau, R., Najdataei, H., Gulisano, V., Koppisetty, A.C., Papatriantafilou, M.: Driven: a framework for efficient data retrieval and clustering in vehicular networks. In: 2019 IEEE 35 th International Conference on Data Engineering (ICDE), pp. 1850–1861. IEEE (2019)
19. Hirzel, M., Soulé, R., Schneider, S., Gedik, B., Grimm, R.: A catalog of stream processing optimizations. ACM Comput. Surv. (CSUR) **46**(4), 1–34 (2014)
20. Kalyvianaki, E., Fiscato, M., Salonidis, T., Pietzuch, P.: Themis: fairness in federated stream processing under overload. In: Proceedings of the 2016 International Conference on Management of Data, pp. 541–553 (2016)
21. Liebre SPE. https://github.com/vincenzo-gulisano/liebre. Accessed 27 June 2022
22. Palyvos-Giannas, D., Gulisano, V., Papatriantafilou, M.: Haren: a framework for ad-hoc thread scheduling policies for data streaming applications. In: Proceedings of the 13th ACM International Conference on Distributed and Event-based Systems, pp. 19–30 (2019)
23. Palyvos-Giannas, D., Mencagli, G., Papatriantafilou, M., Gulisano, V.: Lachesis: a middleware for customizing OS scheduling of stream processing queries. In: Proceedings of the 22nd International Middleware Conference, pp. 365–378 (2021)
24. Pekhimenko, G., Guo, C., Jeon, M., Huang, P., Zhou, L.: TerseCades: efficient data compression in stream processing. In: 2018 USENIX Annual Technical Conference (USENIX ATC 18), pp. 307–320 (2018)
25. Apache storm. https://storm.apache.org. Accessed 1 Mar 2019
26. Zhang, H., Chen, G., Ooi, B.C., Tan, K.L., Zhang, M.: In-memory big data management and processing: a survey. IEEE Trans. Knowl. Data Eng. **27**(7), 1920–1948 (2015)

Latency-Aware Placement of Stream Processing Operators

Raphael Ecker[1], Vasileios Karagiannis[2(✉)], Michael Sober[3], Elmira Ebrahimi[3], and Stefan Schulte[3]

[1] TU Wien, Vienna, Austria
[2] Center for Digital Safety & Security, Austrian Institute of Technology, Vienna, Austria
vasileios.karagiannis@ait.ac.at
[3] Christian Doppler Laboratory for Blockchain Technologies for the Internet of Things, TU Hamburg, Hamburg, Germany
{michael.sober,elmira.ebrahimi,stefan.schulte}@tuhh.de

Abstract. The rise of the Internet of Things and Fog computing has increased substantially the number of interconnected devices at the edge of the network. As a result, a large amount of computations is now performed in the fog generating vast amounts of data. To process this data in near real time, stream processing is typically employed due to its efficiency in handling continuous streams of information in a scalable manner. However, most stream processing approaches do not consider the underlying network devices as candidate resources for processing data. Moreover, many existing works do not take into account the incurred network latency of performing computations on multiple devices in a distributed way. Consequently, the fog computing resources may not be fully exploited by existing stream processing approaches. To avoid this, we formulate an optimization problem for utilizing the existing fog resources, and we design heuristics for solving this problem efficiently. Furthermore, we integrate our heuristics into Apache Storm, and we perform experiments that show latency-related benefits compared to alternatives.

Keywords: Stream Processing · Fog Computing · Edge Computing · Internet of Things · Apache Storm

1 Introduction

Data stream processing is widely used for processing data in near real time, e.g., in factory automation or banking scenarios [4]. While a stream processing application could in theory be executed on a single computational resource, the scale and scope of many applications require distributing the stream processing operators on different computational resources. Distributing the operators also allows to parallelize tasks, which aids significantly in scaling the operations. Originally, most approaches to enable distributed data stream processing relied on cloud-based resources [3]. However, more recently, the utilization of fog resources in addition to the cloud has gained a lot of attention [11].

D. Zeinalipour et al. (Eds.): Euro-Par 2023 Workshops, LNCS 14351, pp. 30–41, 2024.
https://doi.org/10.1007/978-3-031-50684-0_3

The fog can be seen as a continuum stretching from the edge of the network to the cloud, allowing to make use of computational resources anywhere in between [12]. These resources can be, e.g., single-board computers, sensor nodes, cloudlets at the edge of the network, routers and switches, or virtual machines in the cloud [25]. Notably, the fog does not replace the cloud; instead, cloud-based resources can be included in the fog [13]. If compared to the centralized data centers of the cloud, fog computing provides geographically distributed resources closer to the data sources [12]. This is especially helpful in scenarios where the data sources are also geographically distributed, e.g., in the Internet of Things (IoT), since it allows to decrease the communication overhead both regarding network latency and the amount of data to be transferred to the cloud.

When applying fog computing principles in data stream processing, the overall processing response time depends on how the operators are arranged based on the location of the data sources. With the geographical distribution of computational resources in the fog, the distances and therefore also the network latency between the resources become larger. This leads to the question of how operators should be distributed on available resources in order to meet the near real-time requirements of many stream processing applications. This is also known as the stream operator placement problem [24].

While many approaches to optimize the placement of stream processing operators have been introduced, most of them do not consider the network latency between the operators. Consequently, existing approaches may not be taking full advantage of fog environments which can include a variety of distributed computational resources. To address this concern, this work aims at designing a latency-aware stream operator placement approach for the fog. To this end, we formulate the placement of the operators on fog resources as an optimization problem. Since similar problems are typically NP-hard [16], we focus on designing heuristics that approximate the optimal solution efficiently. Furthermore, we build a prototype based on Apache Strom, and we perform experiments that show great potential due to reducing the stream processing latency, compared to alternatives.

The remainder of this paper is structured as follows: In Sect. 2, we provide an overview of related work. Afterward, Sect. 3 offers information regarding the utilized system model, and Sect. 4 presents the design of our latency-aware placement heuristics. Then, we experiment with the performance of the heuristics in Sect. 5, and we conclude this paper in Sect. 6.

2   Related Work

So far, optimizing the placement of stream processing operators has been mostly investigated with a focus on cloud-based resources. Nevertheless, fog-based approaches also exist [11]. Since placing operators on computational resources is usually considered an NP-hard problem (as mentioned in Sect. 1), aiming for an optimal solution may be too computationally intensive. To avoid this, efficient heuristics can be used. Some existing works apply a greedy heuristic that finds a fitting resource allocation [24]. However, greedy solutions may suffer from finding local optimums which may differ significantly from the global optimum. Another approach is to decompose the problem into multiple partitions, which can be solved more efficiently. In the case of fog computing, the usage of location for the partitioning has been discussed, while networking aspects have been mostly neglected [20]. For instance, Eskandari et al. [8] present *P-Scheduler* which allows the partitioning of nodes and edges in a hierarchical way. Instead of geographical separation, other approaches organize the fog in a logical hierarchy. For example, Nardelli et al. [16] present a solution whereby fog-based resources are arranged into a hierarchical tree based on network capabilities. Notably, the aforementioned approaches do not focus on the latency of the underlying network links which is within the scope of our work.

Approaches that consider the underlying network also exist. For example, Pietzuch et al. [18] apply spring relaxation to estimate latencies in a three-dimensional Euclidean space. However, this paper presents early work without details regarding integration into cloud and fog computing environments. Interestingly, subsequent work by Cardellini et al. [5,6] integrates similar concepts into Apache Storm for finding fog resources with low utilization and high availability. Prosperi et al. [19] present *Planner* which identifies subgraphs of a topology to be deployed in the cloud or at the edge. Thus, several approaches have been proposed for taking into account some networking aspects of placing operators in the fog. However, most of them do not focus on the latency of the underlying network links that connect the operators. In this work, we formulate an optimization problem that considers these links to reduce the latency of the processing.

3   System Model

Previous approaches define a strict separation of resources into a multi- or often three-layer fog model including edge, fog and cloud. In the work at hand, the system is viewed as a computing continuum in which the type of resource is not considered relevant in the context of the operator placement decisions. Instead, a resource is characterized by the computational capabilities it can provide. This way, all available resources are taken into account whether they are network devices, single-board computers at the edge, or powerful servers. In addition, all the network links between the resources of the system are taken into account, which is essential to achieve an efficient distribution of operators, e.g., with reduced latency and increased throughput [19].

Resource-constrained IoT devices such as wireless sensor nodes are not considered full-fledged resources in our system. The reason for this decision is that such resources may be highly unreliable due to lossy wireless transmissions or limited battery lifespans. Nevertheless, since such devices are omnipresent in IoT

Algorithm 1: Process to update a supervisor's position in the latency cost space.

Input: estimatedPosition=current coordinate, minEpsilon=minimum required
            movement to continue iterating
Output: updated estimated position
1 peers=peerSelection()
2 getUpdatedPeerPositions(peers)
3 measurePeerLatencies(peers)
4 maxMovement=MAXFLOAT
5 iteration=0
6 **while** *maxMovement>minEpsilon* **and** *iteration<100* **do**
7 | movement=Vector(0,0,0)
8 | **foreach** *peer in peers* **do**
9 | | d=calculateForce(peer,estimatedPosition)
10 | | movement=movement+d
11 | **end**
12 | estimatedPosition+=movement
13 | maxMovement=movement.length
14 | iteration++
15 **end**
16 **return** *estimatedPosition*;

---

and fog environments, we take them into account through their connection to a supervisor. A *supervisor* is a component that is integrated into a resource to be responsible for task allocation locally. If resource-constrained devices that can offer computational capabilities are connected to a resource, the supervisor is responsible for assigning tasks to them. We also model the way whereby the performance of network links between supervisors is measured. For the estimation of link latencies, an approach using spring relaxation is used due to its decentralized design that does not require coordination [18]. Each supervisor independently estimates its coordinates in a three-dimensional cost space. In this space, the distance between two coordinates correlates to the estimated latency between the supervisors. Initially, each supervisor's coordinates are randomized and are then adjusted based on periodic latency measurements [18].

Algorithm 1 shows the process of executing a periodic latency measurement. When a supervisor can communicate with other supervisors, these are referred to as peers. Few peers are assumed to be known in the beginning to bootstrap the algorithm. First, a supervisor adjusts its position by assuming the coordinates of other peers as fixed (Lines 1–3). Spring relaxation is then applied between the supervisor and its peers to pull the supervisor into a position closer to the measured latencies (Lines 8–12). This is repeated iteratively until the total movement across all peers becomes insignificant or a maximum number of iterations is reached (Line 6) [18]. The new position is then returned (Line 16). After this process, the supervisor saves the new position in a key-value store and waits until the periodic latency estimation starts again to refine the coor-

---

Algorithm 2: Process to calculate the force based on spring relaxation.

   Input: peer, estimated Position
   Output: d=movement update vector
1 d=peer.position-estimatedPosition
2 force=multiplierConstant*log(d.length/peer.latency)
3 d=d/d.length
4 d=d*force
5 **return** d;

---

dinates based on new measurements or updated positions of peers. The interval of the periodic estimation is slightly randomized to prevent peers from potentially being synchronized which can lead to cyclic updating based on outdated measurements.

To calculate the spring force in Line 9 of Algorithm 1, we present Algorithm 2. First, a unit vector of the distance between the supervisors is calculated (Lines 1, 3). The force is defined as $c_1 * log(d/c_2)$, with c_1 being a constant, c_2 the distance (e.g., using network ping), and d the distance in the latency space (Line 2). This force is then applied in the correct direction by multiplying it with the unit vector (Line 4). The logarithmic scale is used for preventing the forces between very distant positions from becoming too large in comparison to the smaller forces [14].   After the position of a supervisor in the latency cost space is updated, only a few other supervisors are considered as peers [22]. These are selected based on latency so that the peers of a supervisor can be used for operator placement with low communication latency. This way, a heuristic for operator placement can use these peers for achieving low-latency stream processing.

4   Optimization Problem

In this section, we present the proposed approach. First, Sect. 4.1 formulates an optimization problem tailored to the system model discussed in Sect. 3. Then, Sect. 4.2 presents heuristics for solving this problem efficiently.

4.1   Formulation

The placement problem is formulated as a cost-minimization problem. The cost function is shown in Eq. 1. This equation consists of four weighted parameters with weights w_1 to w_4 which regulate the amount of influence of each parameter.

$$s(x) = w_1 * s_{lat}(x) + w_2 * s_{sup}(x) + w_3 * s_{co}(x) + w_4 * s_{event}(x) \qquad (1)$$

$s_{lat}(x)$ is the highest estimated network latency that is accumulated during the processing of an event in the topology T. For any operator, $s \in T_{source}$ we define that $s_{lat}(s) = 0$. For the other operators in the topology, applies that

$\forall o \in T : s_{lat}(o) = max(s_{lat}(p) + l_{p,o} : p \in o_{predeccesors})$ with $l_{a,b}$ being the estimated network link latency from the operator a to b. The latency score of the topology is the maximum among all sinks: $s_{lat}(T) = max(s_{lat}(s) : s \in T_{sinks})$. $s_{sup}(x)$ is used to condense the placement of operators, and is defined as $s_{sup}(x) = \frac{|supervisors \in x|}{|supervisors|}$. This parameter aims at reducing the total number of employed supervisors allowing to temporarily shut down redundant supervisors. This reduces unused resources. $s_{co}(x)$ is a measure of the co-location of operators. If $p(o)$ is the placement of an operator o then $s_{co}(x) = \frac{|e_{o_1,o_2} \in T : p(o_1) \neq p(o_2)|}{|e_{o_1,o_2} \in T|}$. Finally, $s_{event}(x)$ counts the events emitted over not co-located edges. With $t(e)$ being the events emitted on an edge e, $s_{event}(x)$ can be defined as $s_{event}(x) = \frac{\sum_{e_{o_1,o_2} \in T : p(o_1) \neq p(o_2)} t(e_{o_1,o_2})}{\sum_{e_{o_1,o_2} \in T} t(e_{o_1,o_2})}$. In practice, $t(e)$ might not be measured exactly because most stream processing frameworks only have a metric about the emitted events for each operator. Nevertheless, $t(e)$ can be approximated by dividing the operator-based statistic by the count of outgoing edges. Thus, $s_{co}(x)$ relates to the general performance while $s_{event}(x)$ focuses on important operators being co-located. All parameters have a range of $[0, 1]$ except for the latency $s_{lat}(x)$ that has a range of $[0, \infty]$. To account for this range, w_1 is set to $\frac{1}{1000000}$ so that it becomes insignificant and acts mostly as a deciding factor between similarly scored solutions. All the other weights w_2 to w_4 are set to 1.

Regarding constraints, every operator is assigned to one supervisor, while each supervisor can have operators of one topology. Furthermore, the memory and CPU usage of the supervisors cannot exceed the integrated capacities. Overall, the cost function favors co-located placements, while the constraints ensure the efficient use of the available computational resources.

4.2   Heuristics

To solve the aforementioned optimization problem, we design three heuristics: hill-climbing, ant-system, and hybrid. All heuristics aim at using computational resources sparingly so that they can be executed iteratively for online scheduling. Thus, instead of striving to find an optimal solution (that may be too computationally intensive), our heuristics aim at approximating the optimal solution, which is preferred for real-time stream processing. To further reduce the computational overhead of the heuristics, a topology is rescheduled periodically, e.g., every 30 s, and only if there have been system updates.

Hill-Climbing: This heuristic tries to find a modification of a placement that reduces the cost while also reducing the number of constraint violations, or maintaining it the same [23]. This means that a suboptimal placement will never be selected. Consequently, this heuristic might lead to getting stuck in local optimums. Hill-climbing uses the following three operations to modify a placement:

1. Moving one operator to a different supervisor.
2. Swapping the placement of two operators which are not co-located.
3. Moving all operators of a supervisor to a different supervisor.

Algorithm 3: Process of finding a placement based on the ant system.

Input: currentPlacement
Output: new optimised placement
1 bestAnt=currentPlacement
2 pheromone=initialisePheromone(bestAnt)
3 **while** *no exit condition fulfilled* **do**
4 | ants=generatePopulationOfAntsWithPaths()
5 | bestAnt=selectBestAnt(ants,bestAnt)
6 | pheromone=placeAndDecayPheromone(pheromone,ants)
7 | updateExitConditions()
8 **end**
9 **return** *bestAnt*;

Ant System: This heuristic is based on the real-world collaborative pathfinding of ants [7]. A placement is represented by a path (in a graph) that starts at an operator, ends at a supervisor, and alternates between supervisors and operators until all operators are included in the path exactly once. Edges from the operators to the supervisors represent individual operator assignments. When the same edges are frequently chosen, they are given priority in future assignments based on a calculated pheromone. Notably, the order of the operators can affect the placement since the first operators are preferred. This can lead to local optimums. To avoid local optimums, the operator order is randomized for every placement.

Algorithm 3 shows the process of the ant system. First, the pheromone of each edge (i, j) is initialized with a configurable parameter p_i. A previous placement can also affect the initial pheromones by executing the pheromone placement p_c times for a path that is equivalent to the current placement (Lines 1–2). Then, m ants are generated each one having a random path (Line 4). The best ant is updated (Line 5) and the pheromones on the graph edges are modified accordingly (Line 6). The iteration count and the number of iterations since the last score are used as exit conditions (Lines 3,7). When the algorithm ends, the best placement is returned (Line 9). The mathematic formulations to execute the path generation (Line 4), scoring (Line 5), and pheromone update (Line 6) are explained below.

The probability of an ant k at time t to move from a node i in the graph to j is shown in Eq. 2. It consists of an a priori heuristic, for which a custom one is defined in Eq. 3, and an a posteriori heuristic, i.e., the pheromone. α and β are used as parameters to weigh the importance of both elements [7].

$$p_{ij}^k = \begin{cases} \dfrac{|\mathcal{T}_{ij}(t)^\alpha| \cdot |\eta_{ij}(t)^\beta|}{\sum_{k \in \text{allowed movements}} |\mathcal{T}_{ik}(t)^\alpha| \cdot |\eta_{ik}(t)^\beta|} & j \in \text{allowed movements} \\ 0 & \text{otherwise} \end{cases} \quad (2)$$

The a priori heuristic in Eq. 3 is used for finding solutions with more co-locations. The output value of this heuristic is multiplied by 2 if another operator of the topology is placed on the supervisor, or if a predecessor or successor operator is placed on the supervisor (to achieve co-location). If the placement overloads the resources, the value is divided by 2. This way, the pheromone encourages or discourages certain decisions, thereby guiding the exploration.

$$\eta_{ij} = 1 \cdot 2^{\text{pre or suc on } j} \cdot 2^{j \text{ already used}} \cdot \frac{1}{2^{\text{overloads } j\text{'s CPU}}} \cdot \frac{1}{2^{\text{overloads } j\text{'s mem}}} \quad (3)$$

Equation 4 shows the decay of the pheromone which is based on the parameter ρ and the newly placed pheromone of all ants for an edge (i, j) [7]. In this ant system variant, a minimum pheromone amount p_m on each edge is enforced to ensure that the random exploration of alternate paths never stops [21].

$$\mathcal{T}_{ij}(t) = \max(\rho \cdot \mathcal{T}_{ij}(t-1) + \sum_{k=1}^{m} \Delta \mathcal{T}_{ij}^{k}, p_m) \quad (4)$$

The pheromone placed on an edge (i, j) by the ant k is defined in Eq. 5. This equation uses a constant Q to scale the placed pheromone and S_k as the score of the ant k's solution. This ensures that a lower score results in more pheromones placed, thereby attracting more ants to better solutions [7].

$$\Delta \mathcal{T}_{ij}^{k} = \begin{cases} \frac{Q}{S_k} & k\text{th ant uses edge (i,j) in path} \\ 0 & \text{otherwise} \end{cases} \quad (5)$$

To ensure that constraint violations are reduced, S_k is defined using a combined score, i.e., $S_k = score(k) + 10000 * constraintViolations(k)$.

Hybrid: This heuristic combines the benefits of hill-climbing and the ant system [23]. The placement selection of the ant system is very effective at exploring the solution space by avoiding local optimums. At the same time, hill-climbing is more effective in performing smaller adjustments (with the risk to get stuck in local optimums). The hybrid approach first runs the ant system for effective exploration and then executes hill-climbing for making small adjustments.

5   Evaluation

To evaluate our approach, we build a system for stream operator placement, and we run preliminary experiments to compare our heuristics with existing alternatives. To make this evaluation more comprehensible, Sect. 5.1 describes the evaluation environment, and Sect. 5.2 presents the produced results.

5.1   Environment

In this evaluation, we experiment using a custom implementation of our heuristics, which we integrate into Apache Storm. In addition, we run experiments using two other approaches: the default scheduler of Apache Storm, and the

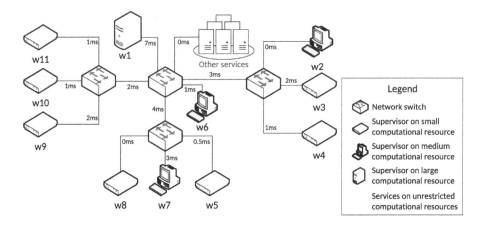

Fig. 1. Emulated network topology for the evaluation.

Resource-Aware Scheduler [1, 2, 17]. The former assigns operators in a round-robin way, while the latter aims at high resource utilization with reduced latency.

Figure 1 shows the emulated network topology we use. This topology includes $w1$ to $w11$ which are the Apache Storm supervisors running in Docker containers. The symbol *other services* in Fig. 1 represents ancillary services required for running the experiments (such as Nimbus, Zookeeper and Redis). The resource capacities that are available for each supervisor are: $w1$ has 1.5 logical cores of CPU and 2048 Megabytes (MB) of memory, $w2, w6$ and $w7$ have 1 logical core of CPU and 1024 MB of memory, and $w3$ to $w5$, as well as $w8$ to $w11$, have 0.3 logical cores of CPU and 768 MB of memory. Notably, the resource capacities of the supervisors vary to represent different devices used in fog computing. The link latencies also vary (as shown in Fig. 1) to represent the distance of distributed computational resources found in fog computing environments [9, 10, 15]. The network emulation is executed on an Intel i7-4770k with 3.5 GHz, four CPU cores and eight threads using memory of 16 GB DDR3 with 1600 MHz. Ubuntu 20.04.4 LTS was used as the operating system with version 2.4.0 of Apache Storm. Finally, Containernet is used for running the containers as hosts in the topology, while the Quagga routing suite handles the routing.

5.2   Results

To produce preliminary results which show how each examined approach performs, we run experiments using a randomly generated topology. Specifically, to generate this topology, we start from a single source and add either one (with 60% probability) or two (with 40% probability) operations. The resulting topology has 12 operations and 22 operators. The CPU and memory requirements of the operations are also randomized. As input data for the topology, we implement a data generator that always sends the current timestamp. This timestamp is propagated to the sink, which helps us measure the latency of the processing.

Figure 2 shows a representative case of the minimum latency measured during the experiments for each examined approach. The Y axis represents the latency value in milliseconds (ms), while the X axis represents the utilized vCPU capacity. A vCPU capacity of 100 corresponds to the consumption of an entire core. Each point in Fig. 2 represents a deployment, i.e., an execution of a stream operator placement heuristic that deploys the operators. For example, the default scheduler is executed to perform a deployment, which results in (around) 110 ms of latency for the stream processing while utilizing a vCPU capacity of (around) 90.

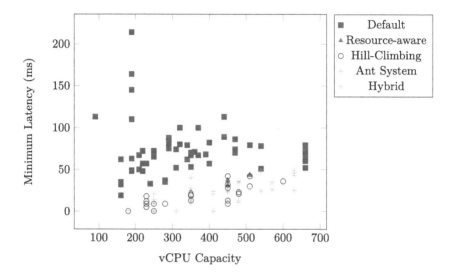

Fig. 2. Minimum latency of the placements for all the examined heuristics.

The results of Fig. 2 show clearly that the default scheduler, which does not aim for co-location of operators, incurs the highest latency. The resource-aware scheduler, which aims for lowering latency, produces results with much lower values which are, however, relatively high compared to the other heuristics. Hill-climbing performs similarly or better than the resource-aware scheduler due to performing frequent adjustments. The ant system exhibits a wide variance of results with latency that is close to the minimum and the maximum, compared to the other heuristics (apart from the default scheduler). Finally, the hybrid heuristic performs similarly or slightly better than hill-climbing without much variance in the results.

Overall, we note that our preliminary results show that the three heuristics we design for solving the stream operator placement problem, i.e., hill-climbing, ant system, and hybrid, tend to outperform the baselines when it comes to processing latency. This can be attributed, to a large degree, to the formulation of the optimization problem presented in Sect. 4.1. Specifically, the presented formulation in combination with the hybrid heuristic exhibit a lot of potential due to combining the powerful exploration phase of the ant system with the smaller adjustments of hill-climbing.

6 Conclusion

In this paper, we formulate an optimization problem for the placement of stream operators that is designed for processing IoT data in fog computing environments. This optimization problem takes into account the potentially distributed computational resources of the fog and favors the co-location of operators, which can lead to lower processing latency. Furthermore, we design heuristics for solving this optimization problem efficiently. Since the presented preliminary results show great potential, we plan to refine our Apache Storm-based prototype to record various metrics, e.g., regarding throughput, and resource utilization, so that we can take additional measurements. In addition, we plan to perform an exhaustive evaluation considering various diverse topologies in order to acquire a comprehensive view of the heuristics' performance.

Acknowledgements. The financial support by the Austrian Federal Ministry for Digital and Economic Affairs, the National Foundation for Research, Technology and Development as well as the Christian Doppler Research Association is gratefully acknowledged.

References

1. Apache software foundation: apache storm documentation: resource aware scheduler. https://storm.apache.org/releases/2.4.0/Resource_Aware_Scheduler_overview.html#Enhancements-on-original-DefaultResourceAwareStrategy (2022). Accessed 31 Mar 2022
2. Apache software foundation: apache storm documentation: scheduler. https://storm.apache.org/releases/2.4.0/Storm-Scheduler.html (2022). Accessed 31 Mar 2022
3. de Assunção, M.D., Veith, A.D.S., Buyya, R.: Distributed data stream processing and edge computing: a survey on resource elasticity and future directions. Netw. Comput. Appl. **103**, 1–17 (2018)
4. Axenie, C., Tudoran, R., Bortoli, S., Hassan, M.A.H., Sánchez, C.S., Brasche, G.: Dimensionality reduction for low-latency high-throughput fraud detection on datastreams. In: 18th IEEE International Conference On Machine Learning And Applications, pp. 1170–1177. IEEE (2019)
5. Cardellini, V., Grassi, V., Presti, F.L., Nardelli, M.: Distributed QoS-aware scheduling in storm. In: 9th ACM International Conference on Distributed Event-Based Systems, pp. 344–347. ACM (2015)
6. Cardellini, V., Grassi, V., Presti, F.L., Nardelli, M.: On QoS-aware scheduling of data stream applications over fog computing infrastructures. In: 2015 IEEE Symposium on Computers and Communication, pp. 271–276. IEEE (2015)
7. Dorigo, M., Maniezzo, V., Colorni, A.: Ant system: optimization by a colony of cooperating agents. IEEE Trans. Syst. Man Cybern. Part B **26**(1), 29–41 (1996)

8. Eskandari, L., Huang, Z., Eyers, D.M.: P-Scheduler: adaptive hierarchical scheduling in apache storm. In: Australasian Computer Science Week Multiconference, p. 26. ACM (2016)
9. Hasenburg, J., Grambow, M., Bermbach, D.: Mockfog 2.0: automated execution of fog application experiments in the cloud. IEEE Trans. Cloud Comput. **11**(01), 58–70 (2021)
10. d Hasenburg, J., Grambow, M., Grünewald, E., Huk, S., Bermbach, D.: MockFog: emulating fog computing infrastructure in the cloud. In: IEEE International Conference on Fog Computing, pp. 144–152. IEEE (2019)
11. Hiessl, T., Karagiannis, V., Hochreiner, C., Schulte, S., Nardelli, M.: Optimal placement of stream processing operators in the fog. In: 3rd IEEE International Conference on Fog and Edge Computing, pp. 1–10. IEEE (2019)
12. IEEE: IEEE Standard 1934–2018 for adoption of OpenFog reference architecture for fog computing (2018)
13. Karagiannis, V., Frangoudis, P.A., Dustdar, S., Schulte, S.: Context-aware routing in fog computing systems. IEEE Trans. Cloud Comput. **11**(01), 532–549 (2021)
14. Kobourov, S.G.: Spring embedders and force directed graph drawing algorithms. CoRR abs/1201.3011 (2012)
15. Mayer, R., Graser, L., Gupta, H., Saurez, E., Ramachandran, U.: EmuFog: extensible and scalable emulation of large-scale fog computing infrastructures. In: IEEE Fog World Congress, pp. 1–6. IEEE (2017)
16. Nardelli, M., Cardellini, V., Grassi, V., Presti, F.L.: Efficient operator placement for distributed data stream processing applications. IEEE Trans. Parallel Distrib. Syst. **30**(8), 1753–1767 (2019)
17. Peng, B., Hosseini, M., Hong, Z., Farivar, R., Campbell, R.H.: R-Storm: resource-aware scheduling in storm. In: 16th Annual Middleware Conference, pp. 149–161. ACM (2015)
18. Pietzuch, P.R., Ledlie, J., Shneidman, J., Roussopoulos, M., Welsh, M., Seltzer, M.I.: Network-aware operator placement for stream-processing systems. In: 22nd International Conference on Data Engineering, p. 49. IEEE (2006)
19. Prosperi, L., Costan, A., Silva, P., Antoniu, G.: Planner: Cost-efficient execution plans placement for uniform stream analytics on edge and cloud. In: 2nd IEEE/ACM Workflows in Support of Large-Scale Science, pp. 42–51. IEEE (2018)
20. Skarlat, O., Nardelli, M., Schulte, S., Dustdar, S.: Towards QoS-aware fog service placement. In: IEEE International Conference on Fog and Edge Computing, pp. 89–96. IEEE (2017)
21. Stützle, T., Hoos, H.H.: MAX-MIN ant system. Futur. Gener. Comput. Syst. **16**(8), 889–914 (2000)
22. Szymaniak, M., Presotto, D.L., Pierre, G., van Steen, M.: Practical large-scale latency estimation. Comput. Netw. **52**(7), 1343–1364 (2008)
23. Tsai, C., Rodrigues, J.J.P.C.: Metaheuristic scheduling for cloud: a survey. IEEE Syst. J. **8**(1), 279–291 (2014)
24. Varshney, P., Simmhan, Y.: Characterizing application scheduling on edge, fog and cloud computing resources. Softw. Pract. Experience **50**(5), 558–595 (2020)
25. Yousefpour, A., et al.: All one needs to know about fog computing and related edge computing paradigms: a complete survey. J. Syst. Architect. **98**, 289–330 (2019)

Scalable and Efficient Architecture for Random Forest on FPGA-Based Edge Computing

Cuong Pham-Quoc[1,2(✉)] ⓘD

[1] Ho Chi Minh City University of Technology (HCMUT), Ho Chi Minh City,
Vietnam
cuongpham@hcmut.edu.vn
[2] Vietnam National University - Ho Chi Minh City (VNU-HCM), Ho Chi Minh City,
Vietnam

Abstract. This paper proposes a scalable and efficient architecture to accelerate random forest computation on FPGA devices targeting edge computing platforms. The proposed architecture with efficient decision tree units (DTUs) executes samples in a pipeline model for improving performance. Moreover, a size-effective memory organization is also introduced with the architecture to save the on-chip block ram used for reducing the latency and improving working frequency of the implementation system on FPGA devices. We target edge computing platforms that suffer from the limitations of resources and power consumption. Therefore, the proposed architecture can reconfigure the number of DTUs according to the target platform's available resources. We build a system with a PYNQ Z2 FPGA board for testing, validating, and estimating the proposed architecture. In this system, we exploit different numbers of DTUs, from 1 to 15, to test our scalability. Experimental results with certified datasets show that we achieve speed-ups by up to $170.39\times$ and $90.27\times$ compared to Intel core i7 desktop version and core i9 high-performance computing version processors, respectively.

Keywords: FPGA · Hardware accelerator · Decision tree · Random forest · Edge Computing · Scalability

1 Introduction

Random Forest (RF) is a powerful and versatile machine learning algorithm that offers several key advantages for a wide range of applications. This ensemble learning method, which combines multiple decision trees, has gained popularity due to its ability to address various challenges in predictive modeling and classification tasks. Compared to other machine learning models, RF offers better results when datasets include many features with fewer samples [20]. Besides, RF outperforms various algorithms for classification with mixed data types in both categorical and continuous [16]. However, along with many advantages, RF also

D. Zeinalipour et al. (Eds.): Euro-Par 2023 Workshops, LNCS 14351, pp. 42–54, 2024.
https://doi.org/10.1007/978-3-031-50684-0_4

suffers from drawbacks, including highly intensive computation and resources, especially storage required for large datasets with many features. These requirements prevent implementing RF on edge computing platforms where computing performance, storage, and energy capacity are limited compared to traditional and cloud computing platforms [19].

Field-Programmable Gate Arrays (FPGAs) are revolutionizing the landscape of edge computing by offering a dynamic and highly customizable hardware platform [3]. Unlike traditional CPUs and GPUs, FPGAs allow developers to define and implement their own hardware functions and accelerators, tailored specifically to the unique requirements of edge devices. Moreover, low-cost FPGAs are good platforms for machine learning inference phases in IoT/edge computing applications [5]. Therefore, this research paper suggests an architecture tailored for edge computing platforms that leverages Field-Programmable Gate Arrays (FPGAs) to create a scalable and efficient solution for accelerating Random Forest. This adaptable architecture can be configured to prioritize different objectives, such as maximizing performance, conserving hardware resources, or minimizing energy consumption. Within our design, multiple Decision Tree Units (DTUs) operate concurrently to compute decision trees, with each DTU employing a 5-stage pipeline architecture to enhance throughput. To manage the computational load efficiently, we partition decision trees into subsets for pipeline processing. Additionally, we address the storage demands associated with numerous trees by introducing an optimized memory structure for the DTUs, which utilizes a memory footprint of just 4 bytes per node.

We have constructed a testing framework following the hardware accelerator approach [15], employing the Xilinx PYNQ-Z2 edge computing platform equipped with a Xilinx MPSoC Zynq FPGA device [6]. Within this setup, our proposed architecture is realized within the FPGA fabric, while the ARM-hardwired processor is responsible for preprocessing data and making final decisions based on the results of the random forest computation. To demonstrate the system's scalability, we conduct evaluations concerning hardware resource utilization and power consumption across a range of DTU quantities, spanning from 1 to 15. Furthermore, to show the effectiveness of our architecture and design, we employ two validated datasets and subject the random forest system to regression and classification tasks using varying DTU configurations, including 1, 5, 10, and 15 DTUs. The experimental results with the above platform show that with 15 DTUs, our system uses about 47% of LUTs (29K/53K) and 34% of Flip-Flops (35K/106K). Furthermore, the FPGA-based accelerator system with 15 DTUs outperforms Intel core i7 and Intel core i9 processors by up to $170.39\times$ and $90.27\times$, respectively. Moreover, our system also requires less energy than the processors by up to $464.11\times$ and $1,112.5\times$.

The main contributions of the paper can be summarized into three folds.

1. We propose an efficient and scalable FPGA-based architecture for accelerating random forest, targeting edge computing platforms;
2. We design and build decision tree units (DTUs) with a 5-stage pipeline model for processing decision trees for effective and high-throughput;

3. We evaluate the proposed architecture and system with certified datasets for future research reference.

The rest of the paper is organized as follows. Section 2 introduce the background of random forest and related hardware acceleration proposals in the literature. We present our proposed scalable and efficient architecture in Sect. 3. our prototype system based on an FPGA edge computing platform is depicted in Sect. 4. We analyze synthesis, performance, and energy results extracted from our experiments with different datasets for regression and classification models in Sect. 5. Finally, Sect. 6 concludes our paper.

2   Background and Related Work

In this section, we first present the fundamentals of random forests based on the design of the proposed architecture. We then summarize related work of FPGA-based random forest acceleration in the literature.

2.1   Random Forest

Random forest is an ensemble learning algorithm for solving classification and regression problems. It was first introduced by Ho in [9] and involved multiple decision trees contributing to the final prediction result. A decision tree is a binary tree consisting of internal and leaf nodes. An internal node has two child nodes and performs a test on an attribute of a sample to decide which branch to take next. The test involves comparing a feature with a threshold value, also known as a decision rule. The training process of a decision tree yields the appropriate thresholds for each internal node.

On the other hand, a leaf node does not have any child node and instead contains a prediction value, which can either be a class label for classification or a numeric value for regression. To make a prediction using a decision tree, we fetch a sample into the root node, and the sample traverses down the tree until a leaf node is reached. Decision trees are trained using the bootstrap aggregating (bagging) algorithm [4]. Finally, the prediction result of a random forest is obtained by taking the mean or average (for regression) or majority (for classification) of the results derived from individual trees.

2.2   Related Work

To execute random forest, like other machine learning approaches, both training and inference phases must be conducted, in which the training phase can be done offline. Therefore, much research focuses on accelerating the inference phase to achieve higher processing performance. Three architectures, memory-centric, comparator-centric, and synthesis-centric, were introduced in [13]. Study in [21] eliminated the floating-point execution by pre-computing and storing floating-point values in local memory. Researchers in [7] used a new partial reconfiguration technique for updating the large random forest models. Authors in [10,11] optimized the comparisons for accelerating random forest on FPGA. A 2-dimensional pipeline architecture was proposed in [18] for decision trees. A RISC-like architecture was introduced in [1] to achieve higher performance for random forests. Finally, research in [14] focused on improving random forests for computer vision.

These proposals target only modern and high-end FPGA platforms with massive hardware resources and nearly unlimited energy. Meanwhile, this work focuses on edge computing platforms with limited resources and energy. Therefore, we design a scalable architecture where the number of DTUs can be quickly scaled up or down according to available resources.

3   Proposed Architecture

This section introduces our proposed architecture for accelerating random forest targeting edge computing platforms. We then present our DTU architecture for processing decision trees with the pipeline technique applied for further improving performance. Finally, we depict the memory structure for storing decision trees.

3.1   Overview System Architecture

Figure 1 presents our proposed FPGA-based hardware accelerator architecture for random forest, which aims to deliver scalability and efficiency for edge computing applications. In this proposed architecture, a host processor, tailored to the specific FPGA device (either an embedded hardwired processor for MPSoC FPGA or a soft-processor for standard FPGA), is responsible for executing the software aspects of the random forest-based application. This entails tasks such as data pre/post-processing, I/O management, and network communication. Furthermore, the architecture incorporates a primary external memory dedicated to storing application data, alongside a DMA block responsible for facilitating data transfers between the main memory and the local memory within the programmable logic. These components are interconnected with both the host processor and the FPGA fabrics through a communication infrastructure, typically employing a bus-based interconnect.

The main contribution of this work is the architecture in the programmable logic (FPGA fabrics), where we build a bunch of DTU modules for processing decision trees. Details of DTU are presented in the next section. For the processing of DTUs, a set of exchange registers (ExRegs) is used for passing arguments and handling (start and done) DTUs. In addition, we build an efficient structure Local memory for storing datasets (samples) processed by DTUs for making decisions. The Accumulator module computes the outputs of DTUs for classification and regression techniques. The number of DTUs can be reconfigured before synthesizing so that the system can be suitable for various FPGA-based edge computing platforms with limited resources and energy.

3.2   The Efficient Local Memory Structure

To process the decision trees, we store the structures and parameters of the trees in the Local memory module that should be compact enough for keeping large amount of data. Therefore, this section presents our proposed structure of Local memory (as depicted in Fig. 2) upon which the DTU collects and processes the trees.

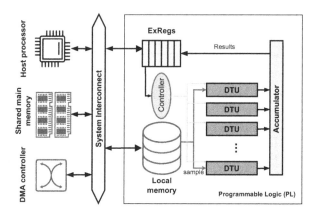

Fig. 1. The generic architecture of the proposed system

Since we design our DTU module in a 5-stage pipeline architecture that takes 5 cycles for processing a tree node, trees in a forest are divided into 5 subsets so that 5 trees (each from a subset) can be performed concurrently by a DTU. Therefore, starting addresses of each subset are stored in the 5 first memory words of the Local memory structure, the subset addresses part. The last bit in each subset address denotes whether this is the last subset or not. This allows the DTU architecture can be improved with more pipeline stages. As the figure shows, each subset stores trees continuously instead of allocating fixed space for each tree to save the memory. Since the trees' sizes (the number of nodes in a tree) vary, relative address of the next tree is stored in leaf nodes (the next tree field). Each tree contains two types of node, internal or leaf nodes, that requires a 32-bit word per node, as depicted in the figure.

Let's consider an internal/root node (the least significant bit, called isLeaf, is 0). The 10 most significant bits keep the right node's relative address (distance for the node to its right) while its left node is the consecutive word. The next 5 bits (f field) depict feature types which is computing by the node. Hence, our decision trees can manage up to 32 features. The threshold value of the feature in the node is stored in the next 16 bits. To cope with different applications, we use floating points for threshold values. Based on the processing results, the next executed node can be the left or the right. If the right node is asserted, 10-bit distance is accumulated to the current address while the consecutive memory word is used if the next is left.

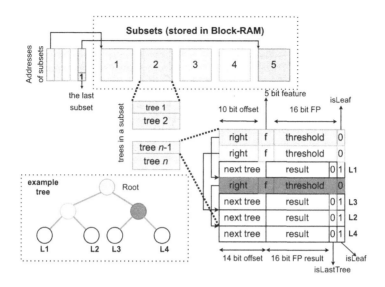

Fig. 2. The Block RAM-based memory structure of the proposed DTU

Let's consider a leaf node (`isLeaf = 1`), if this is not the last tree in the subset (second least significant bit is 0, `isLastTree` field), the 14 most significant bits store the distance to current position to the next tree in the subset. The result from this tree for the current sample is extracted from the `result` field of the node before jumping to the next tree. In case `isLastTree` is 1, the DTU finishes processing for the subset.

3.3 Decision Tree Unit (DTU)

Figure 3 represents our proposed FPGA-based pipeline DTU (decision tree unit) architecture for processing a decision tree. As depicted in the figure, our DTU requires five cycles for calculating (two cycles for reading Block-RAM, the Local memory, and three for comparisons). Hence, the pipeline processing is divided into 5 stages.

Two cycle pipeline `Block-RAMs` (storage) are used to store parameters and the decision tree's structure. The first ports of Block-RAMs are connected with the `system interconnect`, as shown in Fig. 1, for receiving data from and sending results to the `Shared main memory` through DMA (Direct Memory Access), while the DTU connect to the second port for processing samples. Although the Block-RAM requires two cycles for each read, it supports pipeline reading/writing so that the DTU can request and get data every cycle. Besides, to compare samples' values and nodes' parameters, we use three cycle pipeline `comparator` that accepts data inputs and produces results every cycle, like the storage. For processing each node, DTUs collect the node's threshold in the first two cycles and compare it to the sample's value. This comparison result determines the left or right node is executed next in case the current node is not a

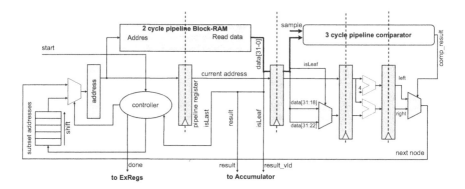

Fig. 3. The architecture of DTU

leaf. In contrast, node's result is forwarded to the `Accumulator` block for a leaf node.

To collect a node's information, the `Controller` modules determines the address of the node in the first pipeline stage by selecting from subset addresses or values computed according to results of previous nodes. Since, in this current version, we use a 5-stage pipeline model for DTUs, decision trees in a random forest are assigned to DTUs and partitioned into 5 subsets with n or $n + 1$ trees per subset. These subsets are stored in the Block-RAM memory following the efficient local memory structure in the previous section for the processing of a DTU. During the first five cycles, the Controller module selects values from subset addresses for collecting the first trees of each subset while next nodes will be obtained after that. When isLastTree values from all subsets are obtained, the DTU responsible for these subsets is done.

4   FPGA-Based Edge Computing Platform Implementation

In order to evaluate the proposed system and DTU cores, we deploy our proto-type using the Xilinx PYNQ-Z2 edge computing platform [17] hosting a Xilinx MPSoC FPGA Zynq 7000 xc7z020 device equipped with 53.2K Lookup tables (LUTs), 106.4K Flip-Flops (FFs), and 140 Block-RAMs (4.9 Mbit). Addition-ally, this device is embedded a hardwired dual-core ARM Cortex-A9 Application Unit Processor, which functions as our primary host processor.

We develop the proposed system and DTU architecture using parameterized SystemVerilog, enabling swift configuration of the number of DTUs as needed. To facilitate data transfer between the main memory and local memories of the DUTs, we exploit the Xilinx AXI-lite bus as the communication infrastructure. For the storage of decision tree parameters, we utilize Block-RAM IP cores, adhering to the structure outlined earlier.

Within this implementation, we construct an Accumulator capable of han-dling both regression and classification tasks. For the evaluation of regression performance, we employe the Scikit-learn California housing dataset [12], which comprises eight features. In this test, we create one hundred decision trees with a maximum depth of nine, distributing them across five subsets. To assess the classification capability, we apply the Glass classification dataset, consisting of one thousand decision trees and nine features. It's worth noting that both datasets contain floating-point numerical features.

For synthesizing and building the system on the designated platform, we employ Xilinx Vivado 2022 [2]. To assess the scalability of the proposed system, a variable numbers of DTUs is considered and analyzed, from 1 to 15 units. Finally, for evaluating the efficiency of the system, performance and energy consumption are measured with the above datasets using 1, 5, 10, and 15 DTUs.

5 Experiments

In this section, we present our experiments to validate and estimate the acceleration ability of the above system. At first, we present our synthesis results with various numbers of DTUs used ranging from 1 to 15. We then provide performance and energy consumption evaluations to validate the efficiency of our proposed system.

5.1 Synthesis Results

As described above, we synthesize the system with the number of DTUs ranging from 1 to 15. Table 1 presents the percentage of hardware resources usage, maximum frequency, and power consumption when different numbers of DTUs are exploited. The synthesis and implementation process with the above edge computing platform is conducted without any constraints or optimization directives.

Table 1. Synthesis results for the proposed system

HW	Number of Decision Tree Units (DTUs)										
	15	10	9	8	7	6	5	4	3	2	1
LUTs (%)	56.3	39.3	37.2	34.7	31.5	29.2	25.2	23.0	20.5	17.7	14.9
FFs (%)	33.5	23.8	22.7	20.8	19.5	18.0	16.2	14.7	13.2	11.7	10.1
BRAMs (%)	70.0	59.3	66.8	65.7	60.7	43.9	60.0	61.1	61.8	60.4	58.9
Freq. (MHz)	125		167	143	167			143			125
Power (W)	2.204	1.877	2.089	1.946	1.978	1.855	1.824	1.696	1.663	1.66	1.588

As shown in the table and compared with the total amount of available resources of the chip, when 15 DTUs are deployed, our system requires at most 70.0% Block-RAMs for storing decision trees' parameters and structure and 56.3% computing resources (LUTs and FFs). It is possible to scale up the system with more DTUs. However, the more DTUs are implemented, the higher power consumption is required. Regarding working frequency, the system achieves the best working frequency with a reasonable number of DTUs (9, 7, 6, or 5). The frequency is reduced when the number of DTUs is small or large because of the longer physical paths used for routing hardware resources. This issue can be eliminated with area constraints for the placement and routing process. However, it is out of the scope of the paper.

5.2   Performance and Energy Analysis

To validate the efficiency of the proposed system, we compare our system with Intel core i7-8565U 1.8 GHz (desktop version) and core i9-9820X 3.30 GHz (high-performance version) processors. When running on CPUs, all cores of the CPUs are used to process the datasets.

Regression Technique: As stated above, we use the Scikit-learn California housing regression data for evaluating the system with the regression technique. Our system processes one hundred decision trees with 1, 5, 10, and 15 DTUs. We also conduct the same testing with Intel CPUs to get the execution time of CPUs Intel core i7 and core i9 performing with all cores for comparisons. Table 2 shows the execution time of our system and the CPUs.

Table 2. Execution time of our system with different number of DTUs and Intel CPUs for the regression dataset

Systems	Number of DTUs			
	15	10	5	1
Our system	1.340 ms	1.706 ms	2.040 ms	8.842 ms
Intel core i7	26.750 ms			
Intel core i9	16.087 ms			

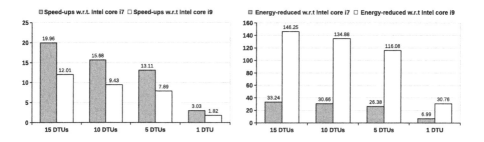

Fig. 4. Speed-ups and energy reduction w.r.t Intel processors with regression

As shown in the table, the execution time of our system does not scale linearly according to the number of DTUs used because the system is responsible for transferring data from the main memory to the local memories of DTUs. This moving time is not scalable. Figure 4 compares speed-ups and an energy reduction of our system with Intel core i7 (desktop version) and core i9 (high-performance version). The energy consumption is computed based on execution time and power consumption (power consumption of the Intel core i7 and core i9 when processing the dataset is 3.67 W and 26.849 W, respectively). As shown in the figure, we achieve speed-ups by up to 19.96× and 12.01× compared to the two Intel processors. Regarding energy consumption, thanks to the reconfigurable technology, our system can save up to 146.25× and 33.24× energy compared to Intel core i9 and core i7 processors, respectively. This result illustrates our system's efficiency, especially for edge computing platforms.

Classification: The Glass classification dataset [8] with one thousand decision trees and nine features is used for testing the performance and energy of our system with the classification technique. Like the regression above, we process the dataset with 1, 5, 10, and 15 DTUs and compare our execution time with the two Intel processors. Table 3 presents our system's processing time with different DTUs and the two Intel processors.

Table 3. Execution time of our system with different number of DTUs and Intel CPUs for the classification dataset

Systems	Number of DTUs			
	15	10	5	1
Our system	0.770 ms	0.869 ms	1.487 ms	3.612 ms
Intel core i7	131.2 ms			
Intel core i9	69.51 ms			

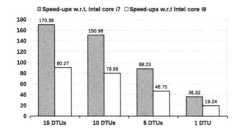 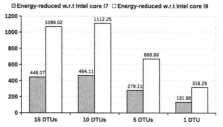

Fig. 5. Speed-ups and energy reduction w.r.t Intel processors with classification

Due to the high number of trees (1000), Intel processors suffer from high memory accesses while our system uses each local memory for each DTU. Hence, our system is better scalable according to the number of trees. Figure 5 depicts our system's speed-ups and energy reduction with the classification dataset compared to the two Intel processors. The power consumption of our system is fixed, while the Intel processors' power consumption is 5.77 W and 26.1 W for core i7 and core i9, respectively. As shown in the figure, compared to the Intel core i7 processor, our system achieves the most optimized speed-up of 170.39× with the dataset when 15 DTUs are deployed. However, regarding the energy consumption, the proposed system with 10 DTUs obtains the most reduction of 464.11× compared to the processor. Compared to Intel core i9 processor, our system outperforms the processor in terms of execution time 90.27× when we use 15 DTUs. The system with 10 DTUs offers the most optimized energy reduction by 1,112.25× compared to the Intel core i9 processor.

6   Conclusion

In this paper, we proposed a scalable and efficient architecture for accelerating random forest on FPGA-based edge computing platforms. We also present our architecture for the decision tree units (DTUs) where the pipeline technique is applied to improve performance. To store the decision tree's parameters sufficiently, we introduce our DTU's memory structure with five subsets for the pipeline processing of a DTU. We implement our proposed architecture with SystemVerilog to make the number of DTUs used for the system scalable. We build a prototype system with an edge computing platform using a Xilinx Zynq device. Experiments are conducted and compared with Intel core i7 desktop version and Intel core i9 high-performance computing version processors. Experimental results show that with the regression dataset, our system outperforms core i7 and core i9 19.96× and 12.01× in terms of execution time, respectively. We also save 146.25× and 33.23× energy consumption compared to the core i7 and core i9 processors. Furthermore, when the classification dataset is used, our system obtains speed-ups by up to 170.39× and 90.27× compared to the core i7 and core i9 processors, respectively. Regarding the energy, we saved 464.11× and 1,112.5× compared to the two processors.

Acknowledgement. We acknowledge Ho Chi Minh City University of Technology (HCMUT), VNU-HCM for supporting this study.

References

1. Alcolea, A., Resano, J.: FPGA accelerator for gradient boosting decision trees. Electronics **10**(3) (2021). https://doi.org/10.3390/electronics10030314
2. AMD Xilinx: Vivado overview (2023). https://www.xilinx.com/products/design-tools/vivado.html

3. Biookaghazadeh, S., Zhao, M., Ren, F.: Are FPGAs suitable for edge computing? In: USENIX Workshop on Hot Topics in Edge Computing (HotEdge 18). USENIX Association, Boston, MA, July 2018

4. Breiman, L.: Random forests. Mach. Learn. **45**(1), 5–32 (2001)

5. Chen, R., Wu, T., Zheng, Y., Ling, M.: MLoF: machine learning accelerators for the low-cost FPGA platforms. Appl. Sci. **12**(1) (2022). https://doi.org/10.3390/app12010089

6. Crockett, L., Northcote, D., Ramsay, C.: Exploring Zynq MPSoC: With PYNQ and Machine Learning Applications. Strathclyde Academic Media (2019)

7. Damiani, A., Sozzo, E.D., Santambrogio, M.D.: Large forests and where to "partially" fit them. In: 2022 27th Asia and South Pacific Design Automation Conference (ASP-DAC), pp. 550–555 (2022). https://doi.org/10.1109/ASP-DAC52403.2022.9712534

8. Dua, D., Graff, C.: UCI machine learning repository (2017). https://archive.ics.uci.edu/ml

9. Ho, T.K.: Random decision forests. In: Proceedings of 3rd International Conference on Document Analysis and Recognition, vol. 1, pp. 278–282 (1995). https://doi.org/10.1109/ICDAR.1995.598994

10. Ikeda, T., Sakurada, K., Nakamura, A., Motomura, M., Takamaeda-Yamazaki, S.: Hardware/algorithm co-optimization for fully-parallelized compact decision tree ensembles on FPGAs, pp. 345–357 (2020). https://doi.org/10.1007/978-3-030-44534-8_26

11. Jinguji, A., Sato, S., Nakahara, H.: An FPGA realization of a random forest with K-means clustering using a high-level synthesis design. IEICE Trans. Inf. Syst. **E101.D**, 354–362 (2018). https://doi.org/10.1587/transinf.2017RCP0006

12. scikit learn: scikit-learn California housing dataset. https://scikit-learn.org/stable/modules/generated/sklearn.datasets.fetch_california_housing.html. Visited 15 Feb 2023

13. Lin, X., Blanton, R.S., Thomas, D.E.: Random forest architectures on FPGA for multiple applications. In: Proceedings of the on Great Lakes Symposium on VLSI 2017, GLSVLSI 2017, pp. 415–418. Association for Computing Machinery, New York, NY, USA (2017). https://doi.org/10.1145/3060403.3060416

14. Oberg, J., Eguro, K., Bittner, R., Forin, A.: Random decision tree body part recognition using FPGAs. In: 22nd International Conference on Field Programmable Logic and Applications (FPL), pp. 330–337 (2012). https://doi.org/10.1109/FPL.2012.6339226

15. Pham-Quoc, C., Heisswolf, J., Werner, S., Al-Ars, Z., Becker, J., Bertels, K.: Hybrid interconnect design for heterogeneous hardware accelerators. In: 2013 Design, Automation & Test in Europe Conference & Exhibition (DATE), pp. 843–846 (2013). https://doi.org/10.7873/DATE.2013.178

16. Prasad, A.M., Iverson, L.R., Liaw, A.: Newer classification and regression tree techniques: bagging and random forests for ecological prediction. Ecosystems **9**(2), 181–199 (2006). https://doi.org/10.1007/s10021-005-0054-1

17. PYNQ: Pynq: Python productivity. https://www.pynq.io/. Visited 6 Nov 2022

18. Qu, Y.R., Prasanna, V.K.: Scalable and dynamically updatable lookup engine for decision-trees on FPGA. In: 2014 IEEE High Performance Extreme Computing Conference (HPEC), pp. 1–6 (2014). https://doi.org/10.1109/HPEC.2014.7040952

19. Roman, R., Lopez, J., Mambo, M.: Mobile edge computing, fog et al.: a survey and analysis of security threats and challenges. Future Gener. Comput. Syst. **78**, 680–698 (2018). https://doi.org/10.1016/j.future.2016.11.009

20. Yang, P., Hwa Yang, Y., Zhou, B.B., Zomaya, A.: A review of ensemble methods in bioinformatics. Current Bioinform. **5**(4), 296–308 (2010). https://doi.org/10.2174/157489310794072508
21. Zhao, S., Sun, Y., Chen, S.: A discretization method for floating-point number in FPGA-based decision tree accelerator. In: 2018 IEEE 4th International Conference on Computer and Communications (ICCC), pp. 2698–2703 (2018). https://doi.org/10.1109/CompComm.2018.8780932

MTCL: A Multi-transport Communication Library

Federico Finocchio⬤, Nicoló Tonci⬤, and Massimo Torquati⁽✉⁾⬤

Computer Science Department, University of Pisa, Pisa, Italy
`massimo.torquati@unipi.it`

Abstract. To pave the way toward adopting the Compute Continuum paradigm, there is the need to support highly distributed heterogeneous application workflows that require the simultaneous use of multiple communication protocols in different parts of the application. In this work, we present for the first time the MTCL C++ communication library. It aims to abstract multiple transport protocols (e.g., MQTT, MPI, TCP) and related implementations under a single connection-oriented API, offering point-to-point and collective communication patterns to the programmers. We discuss the main design choices and preliminary performance results measured using the OSU micro-benchmarks. Finally, through a simple Federated Learning application, we showcase the flexibility of the MTCL library.

Keywords: Multi-Transport · Communication Protocols · Collectives

1 Introduction

The increasing availability of Internet of Things (IoT) devices has caused the explosion of data production rates and the development of data-intensive application workflows, motivating the shift toward highly decentralized and heterogeneous computing environments [4,14]. Extracting information from data is a task at every stage of the path from Edge to Cloud, and the heterogeneity of devices participating in the data processing workflow makes developing efficient and scalable applications challenging. The path toward Exascale Computing requires leveraging the entire set of available resources, ranging from resource-constrained IoT devices to High-Performance Computing (HPC) infrastructures. Additionally, as the difference between Big Data (BD) and HPC shrinks, and the *Compute Continuum* is emerging as the new computing paradigm [3], new frameworks, programming models, and tools have surfaced to help the programmer deal with the complexity of designing parallel and distributed applications in such a complex and heterogeneous scenarios [15,16]. However, while in the HPC domain the MPI interface is the de facto standard for distributed communications, the abstractions provided to the user in the context of BD and IoT domains are many, with different APIs and characteristics. Given the high heterogeneity of the Compute Continuum infrastructure that spans from tiny

D. Zeinalipour et al. (Eds.): Euro-Par 2023 Workshops, LNCS 14351, pp. 55–67, 2024.
https://doi.org/10.1007/978-3-031-50684-0_5

IoT devices to high-end multi/many-core servers to HCP clusters, to meet the performance and computational requirements of each device category, multiple communication protocols must be handled simultaneously in different parts of the application workflow graph to enable fast and reliable message exchange [14]. The selection of which communication protocol to use also depends on where the application workflow components are deployed over time to meet the scalability and performance needs. Therefore, supporting multiple protocols simultaneously (e.g., MPI for intra-cluster and TCP/MQTT for inter-clusters communications) is paramount to guarantee the execution of new distributed applications. Some frameworks and libraries offer support to multiple transport protocols. For example, MPI [11], and UCX [18], allow programmers to specify transport protocol preferences via command line arguments. However, the control of the actual protocols to be used is left to the library, which follows a set of rules and performance metrics to decide which transport is best suited for each computing resource. While this behavior is desirable for the end-user, it often restricts the choices to the expert programmers in the presence of heterogeneous networks. Additionally, the simultaneous use of different transport protocols in different parts of the workflow is generally challenging for the programmer. The ZeroMQ [9] communication library requires customizing specific proxies between different protocols, making the programming of the workflow more complex. To our knowledge, current solutions offer limited flexibility to simultaneous multi-protocol support. Also, they are often limited in the variety and purposes of the different transport protocols offered to the programmers, mainly trusting TCP, the lingua franca of distributed communications.

The *Multi-Transport Communication Library* (MTCL) stems from the necessity of enabling simultaneous multi-protocol support in distributed applications. The rationale is to provide flexibility to the distributed application developers, allowing them to take full advantage of the available network resources and their optimized protocols while providing a unified interface. Additionally, MTCL aims to: a) be easy to use by providing a familiar *connection-oriented* communication model, and b) introduce a low overhead for each offered protocol with respect to a native implementation. The contribution of this work is the MTCL C++ header-only, open-source library[1] a software engineering effort aiming to fill the lack of flexible and low-overhead communication libraries for implementing distributed applications using multiple heterogeneous communication protocols simultaneously. MTCL currently supports *point-to-point* as well as some of the most used *collective* communications on top of MQTT [21], MPI [11], UCX [18], TCP, and POSIX Shared Memory (SHM).

The paper is organized as follows. Section 2 describes the most relevant related works. Section 3 introduces the MTCL library, and some simple usage examples. Section 4 presents some tests aiming to assess the current implementation of the library as well as its flexibility in implementing a multi-protocol application use case. Finally, Sect. 5 provides some preliminary outcomes and the next steps.

---

[1] MTCL repository: https://github.com/ParaGroup/MTCL.

2   Related Work

The Message Passing Interface (MPI) [11] is the most used library in parallel computing. It boasts a solid API and supports both point-to-point and collectives communications. The many implementations of the MPI standard enable applications to scale to hundreds of thousands of cores due to their collective communication algorithms and efficient use of network interfaces. MPI collective operations assume that data producers and consumers use the same communicator. However, such a tightly-coupled cooperation model can only be used in the HPC domain. Big Data and highly decentralized distributed applications typically use the data-flow model of computations [10]. The MTCL library aims to support both communication models and provides support for heterogeneous communication collectives. The Unified Communication X (UCX) [18] and Open-Fabrics Interface (OFI) [8] are libraries for high throughput computing, targeting modern interconnects with massive parallelism. They are designed to provide a set of interfaces for implementing high-performance and scalable network stacks. UCX unifies, under a unique framework, both APIs and protocols while maintaining portability across different systems. OFI has two main components: the user-space API *libfabric*, and the *provider* layer that gives access to fabric hardware and services. Mercury [19] is a framework implementing RPC functionalities in HPC systems as a building block for communication services. It offers an abstracted network API whose implementation is provided by a set of *plugins*. The plugins offer compatibility with many network fabrics and protocols (including UCX and OFI) and allow the upper layers to be completely agnostic of the underlying network specification. MPI, UCX, OFI, and Mercury have in common that they all target HPC infrastructures and are hard to install and use in heterogeneous and decentralized infrastructures.

The Adaptable Input Output System (ADIOS) [6] is a framework designed to offer a unified API for different data transport technologies. ADIOS components are extensible and reusable to allow compatibility with different I/O functionalities over multiple means of transport. Its high-level API allows the user to focus on the application design of I/O functionalities reducing the effort required to develop applications for a target system. While ADIOS can be used as a high-performance multi-protocol communication library, its primary purpose is to target in-situ workflow analysis offering different I/O media. MTCL aims to provide more fundamental mechanisms than ADIOS, thus being easier to use, and open to broad usage.

In the context of IoT and Cloud settings, ZeroMQ [9] and gRPC [1] are two popular communication libraries leveraging TCP and HTTP/2, respectively. Commlib [13], is a protocol-agnostic Python library providing a high-level API for managing communications over MQTT [21], AMQP [20] and Redis [5] brokers. Commlib mainly targets asynchronous IoT and Edge-to-Cloud scenarios. To the best of our knowledge ZeroMQ, gRPC and Commlib do not provide support for high-performance interfaces such as OFI or UCX.

REST (REpresentational State Transfer) API is extensively adopted for implementing distributed services in the Cloud. It relies on the popular HTTP(S)

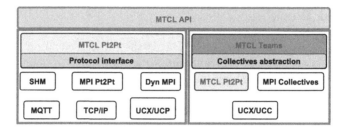

Fig. 1. The two main software layers of the MTCL library: Point-to-Point (MTCL Pt2Pt) and Collectives (MTCL Teams).

protocol enabling easy and safe communications for small-sized messages. Its simplicity made REST also used for interacting with key-value stores, non-relational databases, and message brokers [17].

3   The MTCL Library

Existing communication frameworks present some limitations on the flexibility offered to the application programmers, mainly when multiple transport protocols have to be used simultaneously. The MTCL library aims to address such limited flexibility. It has been designed taking in mind some important principles:

- **flexibility:** the library must ease the burden of programming, configuring, and executing a multi-protocol application in a distributed environment;
- **extensibility:** the provided network functionalities should be easy to extend to permit the integration of different transport protocols, not limited to a single programming model;
- **efficiency:** the performance of the implemented network functionalities should be comparable to the native interface. The abstraction layer must be thin enough to guarantee low overhead;
- **simplicity:** the library should remain easy to use and provide the user with a user-friendly programming environment.

The outlined properties are desirable in an ever-changing and heterogeneous scenario, where proprietary protocols and network fabrics have non-standardized APIs, and it is challenging to program efficient parallel and distributed applications harnessing the full potential of available network resources. For this reason, MTCL has a simple and generic interface that can be extended to support different protocols and programming models.

The MTCL library is layered in multiple components, designed to provide easy extensibility to integrate different transport protocols and communication libraries under a unique connection-oriented API. The component-based architecture of MTCL offers flexibility, portability, and extensibility down to the library's core. As sketched in Fig. 1, the MTCL library comprises two main software layers, one offering Point-to-Point (Pt2Pt) communications between peers (called *MTCL Pt2Pt*) and one offering Collective communications among multiple peers (called *MTCL Teams*). The *MTCL Teams* layer was partially built atop the *MTCL Pt2Pt* layer to implement a generic back-end, which does not leverage on optimized communication collectives and thus uses Point-to-Point connections among peers participating in the Team. Currently the protocols supported in the *MTCL Pt2Pt* layer are: *shared-memory* (SHM), *TCP/IP*, *MQTT*, *UCX*, and *MPI* with two distinct protocols: plain MPI (*MPI Pt2Pt*) and dynamic MPI (*dyn MPI*) [7].

The core components of the MTCL Pt2Pt layer are:

- **Manager:** Represents the library engine. It manages all the protocol-specific components in the application and provides functionalities to select the protocols to use. The Manager performs carefully controlled polling over the established connections to signal network events to the application.
- **Protocol Interface:** Provides the MTCL developers the interface to extend or add a new protocol. It defines protocol-specific functionalities to manage connection endpoints. The *Manager* orchestrates instances of the *Protocol Interface* to provide efficient and concurrent multi-protocol support.
- **Protocol Handle:** The interface for protocol-specific communication primitives, such as blocking *send*, blocking *receive*, and *probe*. Its instances are transparent to the user and accessed through a higher-level component.
- **User Handle:** The interface to perform network operations between different communicating peers. Its instances are created by the Manager as a result of an explicit connection or a network event.

MTCL network `Handles` are used to connect a pair of *peers*. The network primitives (`send` and `receive`) mimic the semantics of the POSIX socket interface. Network calls allow the detection of errors by means of return values and the system's `errno` value. In this way, an application can be programmed in the same way as one would program a POSIX socket-based application, even if the underlying communication transport belongs to a completely different model (e.g., MPI). Additionally, a connected `Handle` can be explicitly released to the `Manager` control loop to allow asynchronous signaling of network events on the `Handle`'s connection. The automated polling performed by the `Manager` enables an application to create as many connections as needed and only read data when available on the given communication channel.

In addition to peer-to-peer communications, the MTCL library allows structured communications between a pre-defined set of peers called *Teams*. *Communication topologies*, such as Fan-in/Fan-out, and *MPI-like* collectives, such as *Broadcast* and *Gather*, can be defined. The interface provided by the library is simple and allows the user to easily create groups of peers and perform communications among the identified participants with specific semantics in mind. A collective Team (or simply *Team*) is created by interacting with the `Manager`. The *Team* creation is a collective operation representing a synchronization point among the participants. It serves the purpose of informing each participant that the group is ready to receive and send messages according to the chosen communication pattern among those provided by the MTCL library. The chosen

Table 1. MTCL core API.

Function Name	Description
`Manager::init`	initialize the Manager
`Manager::finalize`	finalize the Manager
`Manager::listen`	start listening for incoming connections
`Manager::connect`	connect to a listening endpoint
`Manager::getNext`	return a handle ready for reading
`Manager::createTeam`	create a collective team with a fixed semantics
`Manager::registerType`	register a protocol type
`HandleUser::send`	send bytes to the connected handle
`HandleUser::receive`	receive bytes from the connected handle
`HandleUser::probe`	check for incoming data (blocking or non-blocking call)
`HandleUser::yield`	return the handle control back to the Manager
`HandleUser::close`	close the handle connection
`HandleUser::size`	return the size of the handle (≥ 1 for team handles)
`HandleUser::sendrecv`	send and receive data following collective semantics

Team pattern defines how messages are exchanged between participants. Moreover, the interface for communication patterns is the same as for point-to-point communications. The `Manager` is used to get communication `Handle`s, which can be used to perform network calls. Based on the participant's role in the *Team*, either `send` or `receive` calls might be inhibited to respect the team semantics. An additional `sendrecv` method has been defined to facilitate the user and to have a uniform interface between producers and consumers of the *Team*. When supplied by the protocol, the MTCL implementation integrates collective communications using proprietary optimizations. Instead, it emulates the collective whenever the underlying protocol has no native implementation. For example, for MPI and UCX protocols, MTCL relies on their collective support (for UCX, by using UCC). Moreover, the collectives interface design follows the same approach as peer-to-peer handles, hence it can be easily extended to introduce optimized algorithms for each available protocol.

3.1 MTCL API

In Table 1, we list the set of core API calls provided to the user. An MTCL-based application can be created by interacting with two library components, the `Manager` and the `HandleUser`. The former handles connections, network events, and protocols. The latter performs network operations, like sending and receiving data, checking for available data on existing connections, and closing connections. The `Init` method initializes the library components. The user may pass to the `Init` method a configuration filename (in JSON format) containing information about the protocols and the listening endpoints/addresses of each communicating pears. The configuration file is parsed, and all communication endpoints are set up during initialization. The JSON configuration file is mandatory only if Team components will be used. For Point-to-Point communications, the listening endpoints of a communicating peer can be initialized explicitly by using the `listen` method. The `getNext` method allows the programmer to wait until one handle has something available for reading, thus avoiding blocking the next `read` operation. Finally, the `sendreceive` method is used to participate in a collective communication defined on a Team. Several collective operations require peers to send and receive data simultaneously (e.g., Gather).

```
1  #include "mtcl.hpp"
2
3  int main(int argc, char** argv) {
4    Manager::init("ECHO-SERVER");
5    Manager::listen("TCP:0.0.0.0:42000
       ");
6    Manager::listen("UCX:0.0.0.0:42001
       ");
7
8    while(true) {
9      auto h=Manager::getNext(30ms);
10     if (!h.isValid()) continue;
11
12     size_t r, size;
13     h.probe(size, true);
14     char buff[size];
15     r=h.receive(buff, size);
16     h.send(buff, r);
17     // automatic h.yield() here
18   }
19   Manager::finalize();
20   return 0;
21 }
```

Listing 1.1. Echo-server example.

```
1  #include "mtcl.hpp"
2
3  int main(int argc, char** argv) {
4    Manager::init("ECHO-CLIENT");
5    auto h=Manager::connect("TCP:0.0.0.0:42000");
6
7    char* buff = "Hello";
8    // sending the string "hello" incrementally
9    for(int i=1;i<=5;++i) {
10     if(h.send(buff,i)<=0) break;
11
12     char rbuf[i+1];
13     if(h.receive(rbuf, i)<=0) break;
14
15     rbuf[i]='\0';
16     std::cout << "Read: \"" << rbuf << "\"\n";
17   }
18   h.close();
19   Manager::finalize();
20   return 0;
21 }
```

Listing 1.2. Echo-client example.

```
1  #include "mtcl.hpp"
2
3  int main(int argc, char** argv) {
4    const string s{"M:W1:W2"};
5    Manager::init("M", "config.json");
6    auto b = Manager::createTeam(s,"M"
       ,
7                      MTCL_BROADCAST);
8    auto g = Manager::createTeam(s,"M"
       ,
9                      MTCL_GATHER);
10   prepare(data,datasize);
11   b.sendrecv(data,datasize,nullptr
       ,0);
12   char* buf= new char[datasize*g.
       size()];
13   g.sendrecv(nullptr, 0, buf,
       datasize);
14   return 0;
15 }
```

Listing 1.3. Teams usage example.

```
1  {
2    "components":[
3    { "name": "M",
4      "host": "node1",
5      "protocols": ["MPI,TCP"],
6      "listen-endpoint": ["MPI:0:100",
7                          "TCP:10.0.10.1:13000"]
8    }, { "name": "W1",
9      "host": "node2",
10     "protocols": ["MPI,TCP"]
11   }, { "name": "W2",
12     "host": "node3",
13     "protocols": ["MPI,TCP"]
14   },
15   ]
16 }
```

Listing 1.4. JSON configuration file.

3.2   Usage Examples

In the Listing 1.1 (server) and Listing 1.2 (client) we show a usage example of the MTCL library to define a simple client-server application. Line 5 and 6 in the server code define the listening endpoints, each with a protocol and a listen address. To connect to a listening endpoint, the client connects with the selected protocol and the endpoint string (line 5 in Listing 1.2). At line 8, the server starts polling over the available protocols returning an invalid handle after 30 milliseconds if no communication events have been captured (lines 9 and 10). Valid handles can be used bidirectionally using `send`, `probe`, and `receive` calls. Moreover, handles can be moved to be managed by helping threads, for example, to implement a multi-threaded concurrent server.

In the Listing 1.3 we report a simple example of collectives definition and usage. An endpoint called "*M*" communicates with the endpoints "*W1*" and "*W2*" using two collectives: a *Broadcast* (whose Team is defined at lines 6 − 7) and a *Gather* (whose Team is defined at lines 8−9). The master peer of the groups is "*M*" for both collectives. The communication happens (synchronously) at line 11 and 13 for the two collectives, respectively. In the Listing 1.4 the JSON configuration file (which is automatically parsed by the `Manager::init` method) is used to define the peers, the protocols (MPI and UCX in this example), and the listening endpoint for the "M" peer (lines 6 and 7). If multiple protocols are set for Team members, the library automatically selects the one matching all of them.

4   Evaluation

In the first round of experiments, we measured the MTCL performances using a subset of the OSU micro-benchmark suite [2]. To accomplish this, we refactored the benchmark to use the MTCL API by replacing MPI calls with equivalent MTCL calls. The baseline for comparison was the default execution of the benchmark using MPI. We conducted these experiments on two different HPC clusters equipped with a 100 Gb/s Mellanox Infiniband network and running OpenMPI v4.1.3 and v4.1.1, respectively. The clusters were named *OpenHPC4*[2] and *GALILEO100*[3]. We reported the average result of 10 executions for each test presented in the plots.

The first test measures the *Point-to-Point* communication latencies using different transport protocols (i.e., MPI, UCX, and TCP). The results obtained running the `osu_latency` benchmark are presented in Fig. 2 (top plots). The additional software layers introduced by the MTCL library do not add significant overhead to the communications. Raw UCX performance is equivalent to or slightly worse than MPI over UCX. However, to achieve the reported performance figures, we had to set the UCX zero-copy threshold value to 8M, and many other parameters are available to fine-tune the UCX library for performance. For what concerns TCP, all the experiments use Ethernet over Infiniband with the MTU set to 2044 (the default value), and the `TCP_NODELAY` flag enabled by compiling the test with `-DMTCL_DISABLE_NAGLE`.

---

[2] Hosted by the Green Data Center of the University of Pisa.

[3] GALILEO100: https://www.hpc.cineca.it/hardware/galileo100 Tier-1 supercomputer hosted by the CINECA supercomputing center.

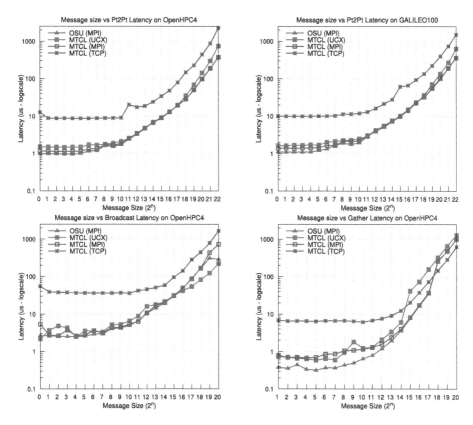

Fig. 2. OSU benchmark results. **Top**: *Point-to-Point* latency vs. message size on *OpenHPC4* (left) and *GALILEO100* (right). **Bottom**): Broadcast (left) and Gather (right) latency varying the message size and using 16 Team participants on *OpenHPC4*.

The second test measures the latency of *Broadcast* (osu_bcast) and *Gather* (osu_gatherv) collective communications using an MTCL Team of 16 peers. The results obtained on the *OpenHPC4* cluster using the Infiniband network are reported in Fig. 2 (bottom plots). Concerning the Broadcast tests, the performance gap between the raw MPI vs. MTCL MPI and MTCL UCX back-ends is fairly low. The MTCL TCP back-end running over Infiniband exhibits higher latency, as expected. As for the Gather test, surprisingly, latency for large messages is lower when using the TCP back-end. The TCP-based implementation uses Point-to-Point connections to emulate collective operations. For message sizes larger than 16K, the UCX back-end is the worst, and this behavior deserves further investigation. Lastly, the MPI MTCL back-end provides performance close to raw MPI.

A second experiment aims to validate the MTCL library to implement application workflows in which different parts of the workflow graph use different communication protocols simultaneously (e.g., MQTT and MPI). The use case

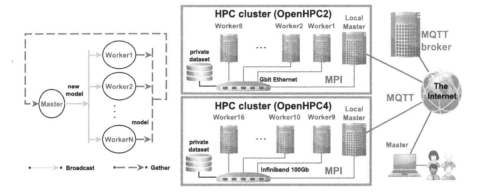

Fig. 3. Left: Communication patterns in the FL application. **Right**: Deployment of the FL application on 2 clusters. The application Master is on the user's laptop.

Table 2. Results of the FL tests using one and two clusters (5 iterations executed).

Cluster	Workers	Dataset	Time	Loss	Accuracy
OpenHPC2	8	20%	5.8 s	0.501	87.1%
OpenHPC4	8	80%	6.3 s	0.214	92.4%
Both clusters	8+8	80+20%	10.9 s	0.345	90.2%

is a simple cross-silo Federated Learning (FL) application deployed on distinct federations as described in [12]. Multiple parties (clients) collaborate in solving a learning task using their private data. Each client's data is not exchanged or transferred to any participant for privacy reasons. Instead, clients collaborate by exchanging locally trained models via a central server (the Master or Aggregator). The Master, which can be deployed on a different federation, collects and aggregates models to produce a new global model. The global model is then sent back to the clients, who use it to update their local models. Then, by using their private data, they further update/improve the local model and this process is repeated until the global model converges to a satisfactory solution or another termination condition is met (e.g., a maximum number of rounds). The application workflow defines a Master-Worker communication pattern sketched in Fig. 3 (left-hand side), in which the Master executes a *Broadcast* of the new aggregated model and a *Gather* of the models computed by each Worker independently on their local partition of the dataset. In our test, Workers are partitioned into 2 federations (i.e., 2 HPC clusters in our use case), each having a Local Master process to communicate with the application Master. The application Master is deployed on a third separate federation (a laptop in our tests). Communications between the Master and the Local Masters use the MQTT protocol relying on a publicly available MQTT broker. Instead, communications between the Local Master and the 8 Workers occur via MPI (see Fig. 3 right-hand side). The FL algorithm exploits a Multilayer Perceptron (MLP) of three fully connected layers trained to recognize digits from the MNIST dataset as described in [12]. The Master performs a simple *FedAvg* aggregation algorithm. To simulate a realistic scenario, the MNIST training dataset was split into two disjoint partitions using an IID distribution, one containing about 20% of the training data assigned to the *OpenHPC2* federation, and the second one containing about 80% of the data to the *OpenHPC4* federation.

We reported the results obtained in Table 2. The first two lines represent the FL algorithm applied separately on the two dataset partitions using only local Workers (i.e., 1 Local Master and 8 Workers) and MTCL MPI. The third line shows the results of combining the two clusters using MPI and MQTT protocol simultaneously. The time increases because of distributed inter-cluster communications via MQTT. From the algorithm standpoint, employing the FedAvg algorithm in the Master leads to slightly worst accuracy and data loss results when aggregating all 16 locally computed models. However, the federation owning the smallest dataset obtains a better-trained final model. This simple tests demonstrate the flexibility and simplicity of using multiple protocols in MTCL.

5   Conclusions and Future Work

We described MTCL, a multi-transport C++ header-only communication library, which abstracts multiple communication transport protocols and related implementations under a single connection-oriented API offering point-to-point and collective communication patterns. Unlike other multi-protocol libraries, MTCL can handle different protocols simultaneously. The library implementation is in its early stage. However, preliminary experimental results using some standard benchmarks are promising. The current implementation does not introduce significant performance overheads for small to medium message sizes, even though there is room for improvement compared to the "raw" protocol usage (particularly MPI) for large message sizes.

We are working to enlarge the number of collective communications supported by MTCL, fine-tuning the performance of already supported protocols, and extending the number of transport back-end. Additionally, we plan to enrich MTCL with a new component called `Proxy`, capable of abstracting MTCL communications and acting as a message broker between transport protocols and connected peers.

Acknowledgements. This work was partially funded by Spoke 1 "FutureHPC & Big-Data" of the Italian Research Center on High-Performance Computing, Big Data and Quantum Computing (ICSC) funded by MUR Missione 4 Componente 2 Investimento 1.4: Potenziamento strutture di ricerca e creazione di "campioni nazionali di R&S (M4C2-19)" - Next Generation EU (NGEU), and by the European Union's Horizon 2020 under the ADMIRE project, grant Agreement number 956748. We acknowledge the CINECA award under the ISCRA initiative, for the availability of high-performance computing resources and support.

References

1. gRPC. https://grpc.io/
2. OSU Microbenchmarks. https://mvapich.cse.ohio-state.edu/benchmarks/
3. Beckman, P., et al.: Harnessing the computing continuum for programming our world, pp. 215–230 (2020). https://doi.org/10.1002/9781119551713.ch7
4. Belcastro, L., Marozzo, F., Orsino, A., et al.: Edge-cloud continuum solutions for urban mobility prediction and planning. IEEE Access **11**, 38864–38874 (2023). https://doi.org/10.1109/ACCESS.2023.3267471
5. Carlson, J.L.: Redis in Action. Manning Publications Co. (2013)
6. Godoy, W.F., Podhorszki, N., Wang, R., et al.: ADIOS 2: the adaptable input output system. A framework for high-performance data management. SoftwareX **12**, 100561 (2020). https://doi.org/10.1016/j.softx.2020.100561
7. Gropp, W., Lusk, E.: Dynamic process management in an MPI setting. In: Proceedings, Seventh IEEE Symposium on Parallel and Distributed Processing, pp. 530–533 (1995). https://doi.org/10.1109/SPDP.1995.530729
8. Grun, P., Hefty, S., Sur, S., et al.: A brief introduction to the OpenFabrics interfaces - a new network API for maximizing high performance application efficiency. In: 2015 IEEE 23rd Annual Symposium on High-Performance Interconnects, pp. 34–39 (2015). https://doi.org/10.1109/HOTI.2015.19
9. Hintjens, P.: ZeroMQ: Messaging for Many Applications. O'Reilly Media (2013)
10. Kamburugamuve, S., Wickramasinghe, P., Govindarajan, K., et al.: Twister: net-communication library for big data processing in HPC and cloud environments. In: 2018 IEEE 11th International Conference on Cloud Computing (CLOUD), pp. 383–391. IEEE (2018). https://doi.org/10.1109/CLOUD.2018.00055
11. Message Passing Interface Forum: MPI: A Message-Passing Interface Standard Version 4.0, June 2021. https://www.mpi-forum.org/docs/mpi-4.0/mpi40-report.pdf
12. Mittone, G., Tonci, N., Birke, R., et al.: Experimenting with emerging arm and RISC-V systems for decentralised machine learning. arXiv preprint arXiv:2302.07946 (2023). https://doi.org/10.48550/arXiv.2302.07946
13. Panayiotou, K., Tsardoulias, E., Symeonidis, A.: Commlib: an easy-to-use communication library for cyber-physical systems. SoftwareX **19**, 101180 (2022). https://doi.org/10.1016/j.softx.2022.101180
14. Perera, C., Qin, Y., Estrella, J.C., et al.: Fog computing for sustainable smart cities: a survey. ACM Comput. Surv. **50**(3) (2017). https://doi.org/10.1145/3057266
15. Ramon-Cortes, C., Alvarez, P., Lordan, F., et al.: A survey on the distributed computing stack. Comput. Sci. Rev. **42**, 100422 (2021). https://doi.org/10.1016/j.cosrev.2021.100422
16. Reed, D.A., Dongarra, J.: Exascale computing and big data. Commun. ACM **58**(7), 56–68 (2015). https://doi.org/10.1145/2699414
17. Sellami, R., Bhiri, S., Defude, B.: ODBAPI: a unified rest API for relational and NoSQL data stores. In: 2014 IEEE International Congress on Big Data, pp. 653–660 (2014). https://doi.org/10.1109/BigData.Congress.2014.98
18. Shamis, P., Venkata, M.G., Lopez, M.G., et al.: UCX: an open source framework for HPC network APIs and beyond. In: 2015 IEEE 23rd Annual Symposium on High-Performance Interconnects, pp. 40–43 (2015). https://doi.org/10.1109/HOTI.2015.13

19. Soumagne, J., Kimpe, D., Zounmevo, J., et al.: Mercury: enabling remote procedure call for high-performance computing. In: 2013 IEEE International Conference on Cluster Computing (CLUSTER), pp. 1–8 (2013). https://doi.org/10.1109/CLUSTER.2013.6702617
20. Vinoski, S.: Advanced message queuing protocol. IEEE Internet Comput. **10**(6), 87–89 (2006). https://doi.org/10.1109/MIC.2006.116
21. Yassein, M.B., Shatnawi, M.Q., Aljwarneh, S., Al-Hatmi, R.: Internet of things: survey and open issues of MQTT protocol. In: 2017 International Conference on Engineering & MIS (ICEMIS), pp. 1–6 (2017). https://doi.org/10.1109/ICEMIS.2017.8273112

Towards a Scalable Compute Continuum Platform Applied to Electrical Energy Forecasting

Mohamad Moussa[1,3]([envelope]) [iD], Nabil Abdennahder[1] [iD], Raphaël Couturier[2] [iD],
and Giovanna Di Marzo Serugendo[3] [iD]

[1] University of Applied Sciences and Arts, Geneva, Switzerland
{nabil.abdennadher,mohamad.moussa}@hesge.ch
[2] Université de Franche-Comté, CNRS, institut FEMTO-ST, 90000 Belfort, France
raphael.couturier@univ-fcomte.fr
[3] Computer Science Center, University of Geneva, Geneva, Switzerland
giovanna.dimarzo@unige.ch

Abstract. The electricity market is witnessing an increasingly digital transition and market liberalisation. To support this transition and promote market liberalisation, digital platforms employed in the power energy market must incorporate smart services and enable seamless deployment of these services in proximity to smart meters. The emergence of Compute Continuum and Edge-to-Cloud solutions provide a promising avenue in this regard. This paper discusses such a distributed computing continuum architecture and accompanying services for predicting/planning local household as well as a whole microgrid electric consumption/production.

We present two compute continuum strategies for load forecasting in electrical grids: (1) a centralised approach, which involves training a model on a centralised server, and (2) a decentralised approach using Federated Learning (FL). The former approach involves centralising data from multiple sources onto a single server, while the latter distributes the training process across edge devices and preserves data privacy and security. In both cases the inference model is deployed on edge devices close to the collected data. Results show that our suggested FL forecasting model offers privacy-preserving advantages compared to non-private centralised models, with a slight trade-off in prediction accuracy.

Keywords: Compute Continuum · Edge · Cloud · Federated learning

1 Introduction

Renewable energy sources, along with the energy market opportunities and entrepreneurial developments, may promote the establishment of new industries directly or indirectly involved in the renewable energy value chain, potentially leading to new paradigms. The diversification of energy sources, including solar,

D. Zeinalipour et al. (Eds.): Euro-Par 2023 Workshops, LNCS 14351, pp. 68–80, 2024.
https://doi.org/10.1007/978-3-031-50684-0_6

wind, and others, along with their widespread distribution, are significantly disrupting the management of the electric grid. On the other hand, this decentralisation of energy sources will involve a shift in the current business models and create an opportunity for the development of peer-to-peer networks (microgrids). To address this challenge, new "smart energy services" are needed. They will offer supply/usage prediction, flexibility and energy transaction negotiation while upholding grid stability.

One key aspect of this transformation is the requirement for advanced smart meters capable of supporting advanced "services". Traditional smart meters, despite being labelled as "smart", are essentially digital meters that primarily monitor overall electricity consumption at a measurement point. However, the next generation of smart meters will assume a broader role, providing features such as monitoring/controlling home appliances, forecasting local consumption/production and communicating/negotiating with other advanced smart meters. These innovative smart meters, which we call Grid Edge Devices (GED), need to adapt to the evolving landscape by enabling collaborative management. In addition to monitoring power cycles of individual home appliances, they must also gather data from other households to facilitate the prediction and planning of local consumption/production. The main idea is to develop GEDs able to communicate and collaborate to forecast energy production and consumption at the medium (microgrid) and low (household) voltage as shown in Fig. 1.

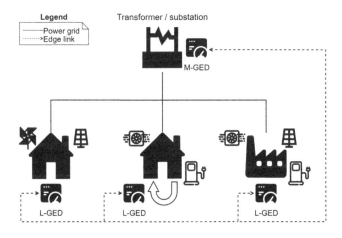

Fig. 1. Network L-GED and M-GED

Low-GED (L-GED) and Medium-GED (M-GED) are able respectively to act on behalf of households and microgrids. They learn and anticipate the consumption/production of electric power at low (household) and mid (microgrid) levels. In previous works we developed the concept of spatial services [1,2], a type of autonomous self-adaptive compute continuum (CC) service spanning geographic areas and exploiting IoT, edge and cloud. We also leveraged this work in the energy context, and developed a CC system specific for smart grids involving various services such as energy negotiation, peak shaving, and energy consumption and production prediction [3,4].

In this paper, we focus on the CC prediction services exploiting various ML algorithms in dedicated CC architectures. Two approaches are studied: (1) a centralised learning approach deployed through edge-to-cloud (E2C) architecture, and (2) a decentralised Federated Learning (FL) approach deployed through edge-to-edge (E2E) architecture. In the centralised E2C approach, ML models are continuously improved through feedback loops and updated prediction models. In the decentralised using an E2E setup, GEDs collaborate and leverage distributed data sources for collaborative model training.

The rest of the paper is structured as follows. Section 2 presents the state-of-the-art related to CC, E2C solutions and provides an overview of FL algorithms applied to smart microgrids. Section 3 describes our CC architectures applied to microgrids. Section 4 discusses our CC prediction services and results based on various ML techniques. Section 5 presents the ongoing deployment and the potential additional costs that may emerge, upon the chosen deployment approach. Finally, Sect. 6 concludes the paper.

2   Related Works

2.1   Compute Continuum and Edge-to-Cloud Solutions

The proliferation of sensing device technologies, and the growing demand for data-intensive IoT applications, are paving the way to the next wave of transformation in IoT systems architecture. The goal today is to design, implement and deploy a seamless interconnection of IoT, edge and cloud resources in one computing system, to form a CC, also referred to as edge-to-cloud or fog-to-cloud.

In this paper, CC refers to the deployment and execution of self-adaptive machine learning-based (ML) applications employing IoT sensors. Because of their distributed nature over constrained resources devices, these applications leverage the cloud infrastructure for learning tasks while exploiting edge devices for inference tasks on data coming from local IoT sensors.

Generally speaking, a self-adaptive ML based application deployed on an E2C solution is composed of a set of cloud modules (such as database, learning algorithms, etc.) and edge modules supporting ML Models (MLMs) and optimised for a limited resource edge devices. As detailed in our previous work [5], the scenario is the following: An artificial intelligence-based (AI) with an MLM trained in the cloud is deployed on the edge device to make predictions on input data. This setup allows for efficient task and resource management, even with dependencies between tasks.

Several research projects and industrial products are addressing CC needs as defined in this paper. AWS Amazon and Microsoft Azure offer proprietary solutions: GreenGrass [6] and IoT Edge Azure [7]. Google [8] proposes a solution based on a dedicated hardware edge device. Open-source solutions are also provided by Balena [9], SixSq [10] and EdgeXfoundry [11]. Research projects such as ACES [12] and ICOS [13] are proposing alternatives to build operating systems applied to CC.

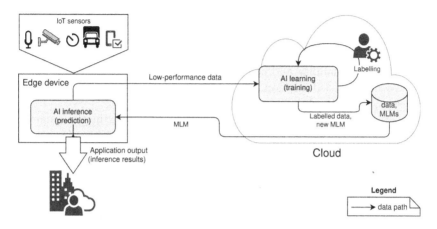

Fig. 2. A self-adaptive ML-based E2C application scenario (operation feedback loop) [5].

As shown in Fig. 2, the system enters a feedback loop enabling continuous intelligence adaptation. The edge device autonomously processes IoT sensors' data. Two cases may occur: The prediction is satisfying or not satisfying. The related sensing input which is failing inference is uploaded to the Cloud as "low-performance" data. This bad data is again labelled and fed for ML training to the AI learning module: a new MLM is generated which is then redeployed to the edge device.

As detailed in our previous work [5] and in Fig. 1, a CC ecosystem, as defined above is composed of six components: IoT Infrastructure Manager, Edge Framework, Container Facilities, Communication Hub, Storage Facilities and ML Facilities.

2.2 Federated Learning for Electric Load Forecasting

Electric load forecasting in the context of smart grids and renewable energies has been the subject of extensive research, employing a range of AI algorithms. One emerging and rapidly gaining paradigm in this field is FL [14]. FL is revolutionising traditional techniques by enabling collaborative ML models to be trained on local datasets that are distributed across multiple sources. The fundamental principle of FL is the decentralised nature of the learning process, which ensures the preservation of data privacy while still achieving highly accurate predictions. Instead of centralising data from various sources into a single location, FL allows the models to be trained directly on the devices where the data is generated.

Recent advances in FL as presented in [15], offer significant potential to further enhance accuracy and privacy within decentralised computing continuum systems. Moreover, as discussed in [16,17], the authors delve into the data analysis complexities found in distributed computing continuum systems and introduce a governance model inspired by self-healing mechanisms with implications for system monitoring, prediction and AI/ML integration.

To tackle the challenge of load forecasting, an online learning method was used for load forecasting, adapting to new patterns with incoming information [18]. To address scalability and computing power constraints, the authors proposed a recent FL-based solution [19], enabling distributed model training without accessing users' local data.

Another study investigated short-term load forecasting in the smart grid using edge-computing and FL [20]. The approach involved decentralized training of a MLM using energy consumption as the sole input feature. The dataset included 200 clients with one-hour resolution, where 180 were used for model training and 20 for evaluation. Similarly, Li et al. [21] proposed a secure FL-based approach, focusing on data privacy.

A FL-based framework using LSTM models was proposed for short-term energy consumption forecasting [22]. It employed customer grouping based on socioeconomic affinities and consumption patterns, along with additional features like weather and calendar data, to improve accuracy.

In this study, we'll evaluate ML algorithms effectiveness for electric load forecasting through comparative analysis in E2C and E2E settings.

3   Compute Continuum-Oriented Architectures for Smart Grid

In this section, we present an overview of the two approaches within the CC. The first approach, as discussed in Sect. 2, is E2C setup, where data from GEDs is processed and analysed at both the edge and cloud levels. This centralised approach enables efficient utilisation of resources across the continuum. Data from all GEDs are collected and stored in the cloud, where the training process occurs in a centralised fashion leveraging the collective insights and patterns present in the data coming from various GEDs.

Our main contribution lies in the second approach, which is a decentralized E2E setup depicted in Fig. 3. This approach fosters collaboration among GEDs, leveraging the power of FL. In this decentralised learning paradigm, GEDs work collectively to train models while preserving data privacy and minimising the need for data transmission to a central server. By focusing on the E2E setup and leveraging the power of FL, our work highlights the significant potential of decentralisation within the CC framework. Figure 3 shows a network of GEDs where each GED (or group of GEDs) trains its own MLM using only its local data while sharing model weights with its neighbours. The decentralised FL allows each GED to leverage its local data to train a personalised model. In this setup, the GEDs share model weights with their neighbouring devices, facilitating collaborative learning and knowledge exchange. An underlying coordination platform will provide communication, sharing and aggregation of data and learning models among the various GEDs. The coordination platform provides a collective adaptive approach to FL as it allows a flexible choice of: the data aggregation operator, and the spreading option (to which neighbouring GEDs and to which hopping distance).

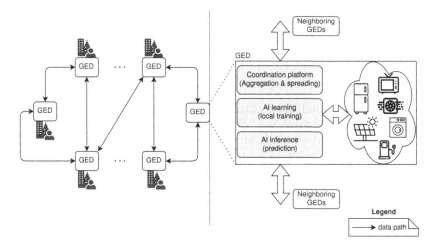

Fig. 3. Decentralised FL-based approach: GED-collaborative intelligence.

3.1 Limitations and Advantages

We examine the limitations and advantages between the centralised learning approach implemented via E2C architecture and the decentralised FL approach implemented through E2E architecture. Table 1 summarizes the key differences between the two approaches, based on the following criteria:

– Privacy: E2C raises privacy concerns as data is transferred and processed in a centralised data center, while E2E prioritises privacy by performing local training at the edge devices, ensuring data remains on the devices without being shared with a central entity.
– Latency: E2E enables local training at the edge devices, eliminating the need for data transfer to a central server, resulting in efficient network usage.
– Scalability: E2E approach supports large-scale training as it can be distributed across multiple edge devices via FL.
– Generic: In both approaches, the model is trained on multiple client devices, which ensures a diverse range of data sources. This diversity in data contributes to improving the generalisation of the model and enhances its ability to perform well on unseen data.

– Hardware (HW) constraints: E2C reduces dependency on resource-constrained edge devices by offloading heavy computational tasks to the cloud, while E2E performs local training at the edge devices themselves, necessitating addressing hardware limitations.

Table 1. E2C vs. decentralised FL

Learning/Architecture	Aspects				
	Privacy	Latency	Scalability	Generic	HW constraints
Centralised learning/E2C	×	×	×	✓	✓
Decentralised learning/E2E	✓	✓	✓	✓	×

By addressing the limitations of traditional centralised learning through E2C methods and respecting privacy concerns, we propose a novel decentralised FL-based E2E setup. This approach involves communication between GEDs and emerges as a promising solution for handling sensitive data at the edge.

4   Experimental Results and Analysis

In this section, we start by discussing a range of ML algorithms used. Next, we delve into the process of data acquisition, highlighting the methods employed for data preparation and modeling techniques. Lastly, we examine the evaluation methodologies employed to assess the performance of the forecasting models.

4.1   ML Algorithms

In order to address the challenges inherent in dealing with time-varying load data, which demands an approach that is carefully tailored to its unique characteristics, neural networks (NN) with a recurrent structure were employed due to their ability to retain knowledge from previous time steps. Among these NN architectures, both Long Short-Term Memory (LSTM), convolutional neural networks (CNN) and its variants were extensively investigated, primarily due to their successful track record as a deep learning model.

The LSTM [23], CNN-LSTM [24], and Attention-based [25] CNN-LSTM algorithms have been carefully selected for our decentralized FL strategy because their NN architectures are well suited for FL. These algorithms demonstrate exceptional proficiency in handling complex and nonlinear data models commonly encountered in decentralised scenarios. Their ability to identify intricate correlations and patterns within distributed datasets makes them ideal for efficient collaboration and accurate learning across distributed GEDs.

4.2   Data Acquisition and Preparation

The data are provided by a Swiss electric utility company. It consists of energy usage and production data in kilowatts (kW) from $1,153$ households. Spanning a 2-year period with a 15-min sampling interval from January 2021 to December 2022, a total of $69,601$ readings per household were recorded. The dataset contains comprehensive information on energy usage patterns, including voltage, current, and power measurements for all three phases of the metering device, along with corresponding timestamps. However, we focus solely on active power measurements, disregarding other measurements. The training set spans 21 months from January 2021 to September 2022, is used to train the model, while the test set covers the remaining 3 months from October 2022 to December 2022 to evaluate model accuracy. Additionally, temporal features such as month, day, hour, minute, and weekday have been incorporated into the dataset to enhance the model's training.

4.3   Evaluation

In this study and all subsequent experiments, the decentralised FL-based approach is implemented with an all-to-all communication pattern among GEDs. Our analysis investigates the architectural configurations of the three selected algorithms:

1. LSTM. It consists of a stack of two LSTM layers, where each layer has 128 units. The multiple layers allow for the propagation of information over longer sequences, enabling the model to learn and represent dependencies across different time steps more effectively.
2. CNN-LSTM. It consists of two CNN layers followed by max pooling, which extract spatial features from the input data. Then, the data is fed into an LSTM layer to capture temporal dependencies. Finally, a fully connected layer maps the LSTM output to the desired output size. This hybrid architecture allows the model to effectively learn complex patterns by leveraging both spatial and temporal information in the data.
3. Attn-CNN-LSTM. It extends the capabilities of the CNN-LSTM model by integrating attention mechanisms. Initially, the architecture mirrors that of CNN-LSTM that allows the model to effectively learn spatial, temporal, and attention-based representations for enhanced prediction accuracy.

All three models were trained for 100 epochs using the Adam optimizer [26] with a learning rate of 0.001. We compare the performance of these models using the normalized Root Mean Square Error (NRMSE) metric under two different approaches, namely centralised E2C and decentralised E2E. The RMSE is a commonly used metric to evaluate the accuracy of regression models. It measures the difference between the predicted values and the actualvalues by calculating the square root of the average of the squared differences. The RMSE formula is given by:

$$RMSE = \sqrt{\frac{1}{n}\sum_{i=1}^{n}(y_{actual}^{(i)} - y_{predicted}^{(i)})^2}$$ (1)

Here, n represents the total number of samples, y_{actual} denotes the actual values, and $y_{predicted}$ represents the predicted values. The NRMSE formula is:

$$NRMSE = \frac{RMSE}{\max(y_{actual}) - \min(y_{actual})}$$ (2)

where $\max(y_{actual})$ and $\min(y_{actual})$ denotes, respectively, the maximum and minimum of the actual observations. NRMSE measures the normalized RMSE between predicted and actual electric load values, facilitating fair model comparisons. Its adoption is based on its ability to standardise comparisons across models with different scales, which is crucial in electric load forecasting. With diverse smart meter datasets and varying electric load patterns across contexts and time periods, employing a metric that accommodates variability and enables fair comparisons across scenarios is paramount.

Table 2 presents the average NRMSE score of the three models implemented in both centralised and decentralised FL. The models were evaluated on a dataset of 50 consumers and their average test error was computed for both one-hour (1 h) and one-day (1D) ahead forecasts.

Table 2. NRMSE for Decentralised FL and centralised approaches on a set of 50 Consumers: 1-h (1 h) ahead and 1-day (1D) ahead prediction.

Algorithm	NRMSE Centralised		NRMSE FL	
	1 h ahead	1D ahead	1 h ahead	1D ahead
LSTM	0.040	0.027	0.065	0.109
CNN-LSTM	0.043	0.060	0.108	0.110
Attn-CNN-LSTM	0.043	0.011	0.078	0.039

Table 3 presents the results for 1H ahead forecasting using different sets of GEDs, including 100, 200, and 300. Across all three cases, the centralised approach outperforms the decentralised FL approach in terms of prediction accuracy. As the number of GEDs increase, FL errors also rise compared to the centralised E2C method. This observation may be attributed to several factors, including the possibility that training concluded prematurely, leading to the observed effects.

Table 3. NRMSE for Decentralised FL and centralised approaches on a set of 100, 200 and 300 Consumers: 1-h (1 h) ahead prediction.

Algorithm	NRMSE Centralised			NRMSE FL		
Number of GEDs	100	200	300	100	200	300
LSTM	0.045	0.056	0.047	0.075	0.131	0.327
CNN-LSTM	0.047	0.093	0.053	0.077	0.164	0.242
Attn-CNN-LSTM	0.049	0.055	0.046	0.072	0.147	0.240

Additionally, inherent complexities and potential noise introduced by the FL design could also impact the overall prediction accuracy. Despite the observed accuracy difference between the decentralised FL approach and the centralised one, the focus on data privacy, the distributed nature of learning, and the trade-off between privacy and accuracy are crucial considerations.

5   Deployment

We conducted a field study in "Meyrin", a commune in the canton of Geneva (Switzerland), deploying GEDs in operational microgrid infrastructures, specifically at a school. We selected the CLEMAP device [27] as GED; and NuvlaEdge [10] a cutting-edge edge computing software solution provided by SixSq, to configure the GED. This integration of GEDs and NuvlaEdge software establishes a resilient CC infrastructure, where GEDs collect and transmit data while NuvlaEdge orchestrates the necessary computing power and intelligent analytics for data processing and analysis at the edge. With this seamless integration and our ongoing data collection efforts, we are strategically positioned to fully leverage the potential of CC technologies.

The Living Lab of "Les Vergers" [28] in Meyrin consists of four school buildings: Gymnastic room, After-school building, Primary school and an Underground space. Currently, our deployment is reliant on an E2C infrastructure, but we are pursuing the development of an E2E alternative. Seven Clemap (GEDs) are installed in those 4 different buildings. They measure the power flows of different electrical appliances. Since May 2022, we have been collecting measurement data from this living laboratory. Each GED collects power, voltage and amperage measurements every 10 s. The GEDs regularly send the collected measurements to a cloud server Exoscale [29].

However, the E2C approach, as discussed in our previous study [5], introduces additional costs associated with infrastructure provisioning, data storage, and computational resources, depending on the scale of the deployment, data volume, and retraining frequency. Retraining, driven by unsatisfactory predictions, can lead to increased cloud resource utilisation and subsequently higher expenses. Cloud computing resources commonly follow a pay-as-you-go model, where the cost scales with the amount of computational power and storage required. Hence, large-scale applications with extensive training datasets may face significant expenses due to frequent retraining. These considerations align with the pillars characterising ML-based applications in an E2C setup:

- Event rate and MLM triggering rate
- Raw data footprint representing the size of each input item for the MLM.
- ML error rate indicating the percentage of events the MLM fails to predict.
- ML training times denoting the duration required for training the MLM.
- ML training rate representing the frequency of training rounds for Cloud-based MLM.

In this study, we evaluated prediction services using two deployment strategies in a CC-oriented architecture, considering accuracy, data privacy, and costs.

6 Conclusion

This paper presents two compute continuum-oriented architectures we used to deploy ML-based prediction services over smart grids. The E2C architecture provides a centralised approach where the learning process is centrally managed in the cloud. The E2E approach provides a decentralised FL approach, where GEDs share their local learning results with their neighbours. We experimented the architecture with actual deployed GEDs in our living lab in Meyrin, Geneva; and with three different ML techniques. Results show that the centralised approach consistently outperforms the decentralised FL approach in terms of prediction accuracy, both for 1 h and 1 day predictions. A possible explanation is the possibility of premature training completion. However, the trade-off between privacy and accuracy make the decentralised FL-based approach a relevant and reasonable choice for applications where data privacy is a critical concern. Future work involves exploiting the coordination platform for providing decentralised solutions with higher accuracy results. This involves investigating the effects of training FL models for longer durations to enhance accuracy and reduce the performance gap with the centralized approach. In parallel, we will also develop and deploy further services exploiting the prediction service discussed in this paper such as transactive energy, peak shaving or higher-level self-adaptive user applications. In all cases the services follow a compute continuum approach.

References

1. Di Marzo Serugendo, G., Abdennadher, N., Ben Mahfoudh, H., De Angelis, F.L., Tomaylla, R.: Spatial edge services. In: 2017 Global Internet of Things Summit (GIoTS), pp. 1–6 (2017)
2. Ben Mahfoudh, H., Di Marzo Serugendo, G., Naja, N., Abdennadher, N.: Learning-based coordination model for spontaneous self-composition of reliable services in a distributed system. Int. J. Softw. Tools Technol. Transfer **22**, 417–436 (2020)
3. Ben Mahfoudh, H., Di Marzo Serugendo, G., Abdennadher, N., Rumsch, A., Upegui, A.: Spatial services for decentralised smart green energy management. In: 2018 IEEE International Energy Conference (ENERGYCON), pp. 1–6 (2018)

4. Glass, P., Di Marzo Serugendo, G.: Plateforme de coordination et collaboration pour échanger l'énergie, réguler et prédire la production/consommation dans le cadre d'un réseau électrique intelligent. University Claude-Bernard Lyon 1, University of Geneva, Technical report (2021). https://archive-ouverte.unige.ch/unige: 155369
5. Poleggi, M.E., Abdennadher, N., Dupuis, R., Mendonça, F.: Edge-to-cloud solutions for self-adaptive machine learning-based IoT applications: a cost comparison. In: Economics of Grids, Clouds, Systems, and Services: 19th International Conference, GECON: Proceedings, pp. 89–102. Springer, Cham (2022). https://doi.org/ 10.1007/978-3-031-29315-3_8
6. Amazon Web Services: IoT Greengrass. https://aws.amazon.com/greengrass/
7. Microsoft: Azure IoT Edge. https://azure.microsoft.com/en-us/products/iot-edge/
8. Google: Google Cloud IoT Core. https://cloud.google.com/iot-core
9. Balena: Balena. https://www.balena.io/
10. SiqSq SA: Nuvla. https://sixsq.com/products
11. EdgeXfoundry: EdgeX. https://www.edgexfoundry.org/software/platform/
12. Autopoietic Cognitive Edge-cloud Services, ACES. https://www.aces-edge.eu/ partners/
13. Towards a functional continuum operating system, ICOS. https://www.icos-project.eu
14. Konečný, J., McMahan, H.B., Yu, F.X., Richtárik, P., Suresh, A.T., Bacon, D.: Federated learning: strategies for improving communication efficiency. arXiv preprint arXiv:1610.05492 (2016)
15. Li, Y., et al.: Federated domain generalization: a survey (2023)
16. Donta, P.K., Dustdar, S.: The promising role of representation learning for distributed computing continuum systems. In: IEEE International Conference on Service-Oriented System Engineering (SOSE) 2022, pp. 126–132 (2022)
17. Donta, P.K., Sedlak, B., Casamayor Pujol, V., Dustdar, S.: Governance and sustainability of distributed continuum systems: a big data approach. J. Big Data 10(1), 1–31 (2023)
18. Fekri, M.N., Patel, H., Grolinger, K., Sharma, V.: Deep learning for load forecasting with smart meter data: online adaptive recurrent neural network. Appl. Energy 282, 116177 (2021)
19. Fekri, M.N., Grolinger, K., Mir, S.: Distributed load forecasting using smart meter data: federated learning with recurrent neural networks. Int. J. Electric. Power Energy Syst. 137, 107669 (2022)
20. Taïk, A., Cherkaoui, S.: Electrical load forecasting using edge computing and federated learning. In: ICC 2020–2020 IEEE International Conference on Communications (ICC), pp. 1–6. IEEE (2020)
21. Li, J., Ren, Y., Fang, S., Li, K., Sun, M.: Federated learning-based ultra-short term load forecasting in power internet of things. In: 2020 IEEE International Conference on Energy Internet (ICEI). IEEE, pp. 63–68 (2020)
22. Savi, M., Olivadese, F.: Short-term energy consumption forecasting at the edge: a federated learning approach. IEEE Access 9, 95 949–95 969 (2021)
23. Hochreiter, S., Schmidhuber, J.: Long short-term memory. Neural Comput. 9(8), 1735–1780 (1997)
24. O'Shea, K., Nash, R.: An introduction to convolutional neural networks. arXiv preprint arXiv:1511.08458 (2015)
25. Vaswani, A.: Attention is all you need. In: Advances in Neural Information Processing Systems, vol. 30 (2017)

26. Kingma, D.P., Ba, J.: Adam: a method for stochastic optimization. CoRR, abs/1412.6980 (2014)
27. With CLEMAP into the energy future. https://en.clemap.ch
28. Les Vergers | Ecoquartier Meyrin Les Vergers. https://www.lesvergers-meyrin.ch/ecoquartier/les-vergers
29. A solid European cloud hosting alternative. https://www.exoscale.com/

Evaluation of Adaptive Micro-batching Techniques for GPU-Accelerated Stream Processing

Ricardo Leonarczyk[1]($\boxtimes$) (ID), Dalvan Griebler[1] (ID), Gabriele Mencagli[2] (ID),
and Marco Danelutto[2] (ID)

[1] School of Technology, Pontifical Catholic University of Rio Grande do Sul, Porto
Alegre, Brazil
`ricardo.leonarczyk@edu.pucrs.br`
[2] Computer Science Department, University of Pisa, Pisa, Italy

Abstract. Stream processing plays a vital role in applications that
require continuous, low-latency data processing. Thanks to their extensive parallel processing capabilities and relatively low cost, GPUs are
well-suited to scenarios where such applications require substantial computational resources. However, micro-batching becomes essential for efficient GPU computation within stream processing systems. However,
finding appropriate batch sizes to maintain an adequate level of service is often challenging, particularly in cases where applications experience fluctuations in input rate and workload. Addressing this challenge
requires adjusting the optimal batch size at runtime. This study proposes a methodology for evaluating different self-adaptive micro-batching
strategies in a real-world complex streaming application used as a benchmark.

Keywords: Parallel programming · Self-adaptive · Stream
parallelism · Shared-memory architecture

1 Introduction

Stream processing systems (SPSs) such as Apache Flink[1] and Apache Spark
Streaming[2] have traditionally been deployed in commodity clusters, aiming
at horizontal scalability [5]. In these scenarios, the emphasis is typically on
input/output (I/O), accompanied by relatively low computing requirements that
involve logic for data filtering and transformations. However, high-capacity computing infrastructures become critical when there is the need to maintain acceptable *service level objectives* (SLO) (e.g., bounds in terms of latency) for stream

---

This research has been supported by the Italian Resilience and Recovery Plan (PNRR)
through the National Center for HPC, Big Data and Quantum Computing.

[1] https://flink.apache.org.
[2] https://spark.apache.org/streaming.

D. Zeinalipour et al. (Eds.): Euro-Par 2023 Workshops, LNCS 14351, pp. 81–92, 2024.
https://doi.org/10.1007/978-3-031-50684-0_7

processing applications (SPAs) with high computational demands, such as those in computer vision and robotics.

Accelerators such as graphics processing units (GPUs) offer significant advantages in such cases due to their capacity for massive data parallelism. However, the integration of a GPU into an SPS can exhibit several challenges. In streaming analytics, data streams convey small items in the form of records of attributes (which we call *tuples*). Such tuples are often small (e.g., a few hundred bytes), so individually processing them on GPU leads to the under-utilization of its computing capacity.

A potential solution to the challenge of GPU integration into SPSs is the processing of stream tuples in micro-batches. Micro-batching is a technique used in SPSs to process small batches of data simultaneously rather than processing tuples individually. The SPS collects a defined number of incoming tuples, groups them into a batch, and processes them as a unit of computation. This is the default processing model for SPSs such as Spark Streaming. In contrast, for tuple-at-a-time SPSs like Flink, the user usually performs micro-batching manually when co-processors are present in the system.

Once micro-batching is adopted, a subsequent challenge arises in determining the optimal batch size. Increasing the batch size in GPU-accelerated SPAs leads to a rise in both buffering requirements and the time it takes for the GPU to start processing. This results in a trade-off between latency and throughput, which can be managed by finding a batch size that can satisfy the particular application SLO [7]. If the workload and input rate are stable, finding a suitable batch size can be a one-time task, which the user may manually find or use auto-tuning approaches. However, SPAs are often subjected to workload and input rate fluctuations, making the suitable batch size an evolving target.

Self-adaptation techniques can be used to determine a suitable batch size at different stages of the SPA's execution, as demonstrated in Sect. 2. Broadly defined, self-adaptation is the capability of a system to autonomously change itself to better respond to its dynamic environment [11]. In practice, a self-adaptive system will collect metrics data about the SPA, and based on them, it will perform adaptation actions (e.g., variating the batch size or the parallelism degree) at runtime to achieve defined SLOs.

A recent paper [9] presented four adaptation algorithms for adapting the batch size to keep the SPA's latency within a threshold around a target latency. Our goal in the current study is to provide a methodology (Sect. 3) consisting of a set of metrics that complement the metric used to compare the algorithms and workloads in this original study, offering a novel way to analyze experiments with SLO-constrained SPAs which use micro-batching techniques. Additionally, (in Sect. 4), we evaluate the adaptive strategies and algorithms with a new complex and real-world application. We believe that an understanding of how the algorithms in [9] behave with an entirely different use case will shed more light on their generalizability and usefulness beyond the basic scenarios they were originally evaluated. The application we selected is the *Military Server Benchmark* [2] (MSB), a SPA designed to exploit data parallelism and highly configurable to reflect workload variations and changes in the input rate. We also consider in the evaluation how latency sampling affects the adaptation. The original study did not address this aspect, which affects the average of a set of latencies corresponding to the process variable in control theory.

2   Related Work

Stein et al. [9] present a control-loop strategy driven by four algorithms for adapting the batch size to keep a user-defined latency SLO in streaming compression applications targeting GPUs. The proposed algorithms expect a target latency provided by the user. Internally, they also consider a threshold indicating an acceptable percentage of variation in latency, as well as a step size for changing the batch size. The metric used to compare the algorithms and workloads is named *SLO hit*, which is the percentage of batches that meet the SLO in relation to the overall batch count.

De Matteis et al. [5] propose Gasser, an SPS that offloads sliding-window operators on GPUs. Gasser adapts the batch size and parallelism to balance latency and throughput. It calibrates a predictive model at the beginning of execution based on the throughput achieved by different configurations on CPU and GPU. However, Gasser's predictive model does not react effectively to irregular workloads. The Chebyshev distance is used in the study to measure the effectiveness of Gasser's auto-tuning approach.

Das et al. [4] introduce the fixed-point iteration method to find the intersection between batch processing time and batch interval, providing adaptability without specifying a step size. However, this algorithm assumes the existence of a batch interval where the processing rate can keep up with the input rate and may suffer from control-loop delays in cases of sudden workload variations.

Zhang et al. [12] propose the DyBBS algorithm, which uses online historical statistics to adapt batch interval through isotonic regression and block interval through a heuristic approach. DyBBS prioritizes accuracy over convergence time but also assumes the presence of a stable batch interval.

In some studies, the batch size is associated with the efficiency of task schedulers. Venkataraman et al. [10] propose Drizzle, which organizes batches into groups and dynamically adapts the group size using a technique based on the additive-increase/multiplicative-decrease (AIMD) feedback control algorithm. Cheng et al. [3] propose adapting the batch interval through the expert fuzzy control (EFC) technique integrated with A-scheduler, a new Spark Streaming scheduler. They also use a reinforcement learning algorithm to adapt job parallelism based on historic workload variations.

From the studies presented, only [9] and [5] adapt the batch size for GPU-accelerated SPAs, demonstrating that this specific scenario is not currently receiving significant attention from the literature. The remaining studies focus on batch size adaptation for SPAs built upon the Spark DSPS. Besides the traditional latency and throughput metrics, [9] uses the SLO hit, while [5] use the notion of distance from a optimal configuration. Our work extends the SLO-related metrics from [9], and introduces distance-related metrics.

3   Evaluation Methodology

Our methodology consists of a new set of metrics: the *SLO hit* and the *SLO distance* metric. They are used to compare the adaptation algorithms among themselves in terms of quality and effectiveness from different perspectives. Each metric has both a less and a more sensitive version. For the SLO hit, we propose a *batched* and an *itemized* definition. The batched SLO hit is described in Definition 1.

Definition 1 (B-SLH).   *Let t be the target SLO, h be a threshold percentage such that $0 < h < 1$, B be the set of batches processed during the whole or part of the application execution, and $\omega : B \rightarrow \mathbb{R}$ be a mapping of a batch $b_i \in B$ to its measured performance metric value (e.g., in terms of latency or throughput). The set $B' \subseteq B$ containing the batches which fell within threshold bounds is defined as $B' = \{b \in B \mid t * (1 - h) \leq \omega(b) \leq t * (1 + h)\}$. The batched SLO hit is defined as the percentage of batches that fall within threshold bounds, formally as:*

$$B\text{-}SLH = |B'|/|B| \tag{1}$$

What we refer to as the batched SLO hit was the metric chosen by Stein et al. [9] to evaluate the adaptation algorithms they proposed. This metric is useful to understand the effectiveness of the adaptation algorithms for achieving a defined SLO. However, it presents a notable limitation resulting from the focus on the batch level. Specifically, batches containing large quantities of items will have the same weight as batches containing only a few items. This can produce situations where the adaptation algorithm fails to achieve the SLO for the majority of the items processed by the application, but the resultant SLO hit still remains greater than 50%. The problem described with the batched SLO hit becomes more pronounced as the range of batch sizes is increased. To solve this problem, we propose the itemized SLO hit, formalized in Definition 2. It is fundamentally the same as the batched SLO hit, with the additional consideration of the batch sizes.

Definition 2 (I-SLH).   *Let the definition of the sets B and $B' \subseteq B$ be the same as in Definition 1, and let $\sigma : B \rightarrow \mathbb{N}$ be the mapping of a batch $b_i \in B$ to its size. The itemized SLO hit is defined as follows:*

$$I\text{-}SLH = \frac{\sum_{b' \in B'} \sigma(b')}{\sum_{b \in B} \sigma(b)} \tag{2}$$

The two SLO hit metrics are binary in the sense that a given batch is either inside or outside threshold bounds. Such metrics can work perfectly for users whose only concern is to know whether the application is meeting the SLO. However, they fail to provide information for the researcher/practitioner who wants to know how much the SLO is being met or not. In the latter case, proper SLO distance metrics can be defined to supplement the SLO hit metrics by providing a measure of how far the batches were from the target SLO.

We propose two distance metrics: the MAD-based SLO distance and the SD-based SLO distance. They are calculated in the same fashion as the population's mean absolute deviation (MAD) and the population's standard deviation (SD). The only difference from the standard statistical forms of MAD and SD is that the target SLO value is used instead of the mean. As the second and final step, we divide the value obtained in the first step by the target SLO value. We found that expressing the values in percentage helps with the interpretability because it is expected that the distance values will not surpass more than one time the target SLO. Furthermore, the percentage format fits naturally with the way the thresholds are specified (as a percentage of the target SLO).

We define below the MAD-based SLO distance in Definition 3 and the SD-based SLO distance in Definition 4.

Definition 3 (MAD-D). *Let t be the target SLO, and let the set B and the function ω be as defined in Definition 1. The MAD-based SLO distance is defined as:*

$$MAD\text{-}D = \frac{\sum_{b \in B}(|t - \omega(b)|)}{|B| \cdot t}. \tag{3}$$

Definition 4 (SD-D). *Let t be the target SLO, and let the set B and the function ω be as defined in Definition 1. The SD-based SLO distance is defined as:*

$$SD\text{-}D = \frac{\sqrt{\sum_{b \in B}(|t - \omega(b)|^2)}}{|B| \cdot t} \tag{4}$$

The MAD-based SLO distance arguably provides the most intuitive results when compared to the SD-based SLO distance. When applied over a single batch, it provides a value that can be directly compared with the threshold. In fact, the batched SLO hit metric can be derived from the MAD-based SLO distance by checking if every batch's distance value is less or equal to the threshold. The MAD-based SLO distance also exhibits the property of not being affected by a few large batch distance values (outliers). In contrast, the SD-based SLO distance is more sensitive to such values, given that it is based on squaring distances from the target.

4   Evaluation

4.1   Military Server Benchmark

The Military Server Benchmark (MSB) is an application developed by Araujo et al. [2] designed to leverage accelerated computing in stream processing. The benchmark is composed of heavy computations and allows for the exploitation of data parallelism within each input item (i.e., inputs are records of attributes also called tuples) or in batches (depending on the size of the tuples used). The problem domain involves allocating military units on a map while considering the location requirements specific to each unit type. Drones fly over designated coordinates of the map and collect data that will be used to allocate their assigned units. The system performs the required computations to allocate the military units efficiently using the data continuously received from the drones.

The application is structured as a pipeline of five computational stages. The first and the last are devoted to generating data and gathering results (I/O-bound source and sink stages). The three internal stages are each one parallel. The first executes a compute-intensive *map* pattern running on GPU, which extracts information for each coordinate explored by the drone. The second still runs on GPU and is based on the *map-reduce* pattern to find the most suitable coordinate for each military unit. The last stage is lightweight and still done by GPU. It performs final data validation.

The MSB implementation used in this work has been parallelized with Fast-Flow [1] and GSParLib [8]. FastFlow assembles and coordinates the pipeline stages, while GSParLib is responsible for the GPU offloading inside the stages. In the MSB pipeline, each tuple carries data from a specific drone. Batches are allocated in the GPU memory at the source stage and deallocated at the sink stage. As a result, batch sizes are defined for the entire pipeline rather than individually stage by stage.

Runtime performance variability in a SPA can be attributed to variables such as tuple inter-arrival time and tuple processing time. The time series generated by the moving average of these variables often demonstrates non-stationarities in real-world scenarios, such as increasing or decreasing trends and cyclic behaviors such as seasonal patterns. The overall software architecture of MSB is capable of reproducing workload variations called *computation patterns* applied to the computation time per tuple by the system (while the input rate is kept fixed for each execution). This is a realistic scenario for MSB, since drones generate data and transmit them at fixed rate. The algorithms to generate the computation patterns were based on [6]. Since they were originally designed for generating different frequency patterns of data arrivals, we adapted them to reproduce time-varying patterns affecting the tuple computation time.

We adopted a feedback control strategy [9] that turns the MSB pipeline into a closed loop in which the sink measures the end-to-end latencies of computed batches and transmits the measurements to the source stage. The source is responsible for receiving the measured latencies and applying the adaptation algorithm to decide the size for the next batches. The feedback loop should not result in additional delays for the source stage to process the incoming tuples. Hence, if the updated latencies did not arrive in time to decide the size of the next batch, the batch is delivered with the last computed size without blocking the data flow through the pipeline. We also perform sampling of the batch latencies, where the average of the samples is provided as input to the adaptation algorithm. Sampling is controlled by a parameter named *sample size*. This parameter can be used to try reducing interferences from specific batches containing latencies that significantly deviate from their neighbors.

Stein et al. [9] presented four adaptation algorithms for adapting the batch size, namely Fixed Adaptation Factor (FAF), Percentage-Based Adaptation Factor (PBAF), PBAF without threshold (PBAF-WT), and Multiplier-Based Adaptation Factor (MBAF). The algorithms accept as parameters a target latency (our SLO), a threshold region around the target latency, the current batch size, and step size (called adaptation factor by the authors). The goal is to regulate the batch size to keep the target latency inside the threshold region, which is expressed in percentage.

Regarding the main differences among the algorithms, the most straightforward is FAF. FAF increments or decrements the batch size by a fixed step when the actual latency exceeds the lower or upper bound respectively. PBAF behaves similarly but reduces the (user-specified) step size as it approaches the target latency, aiming for more precision and likely avoiding stepping out of threshold bounds. PBAF-WT focuses solely on the target, resulting in frequent batch size changes to improve precision but risking going out of bounds with larger step sizes. MBAF prioritizes reaching the threshold region quickly by scaling the step size based on the distance from the target, aiming at offering a faster response to workload variations.

4.2   Evaluation Results

In this section we present the results of our evaluation of the algorithms proposed by [9] applied in the Military Server Benchmark [2]. The experiments were executed in a computer equipped with an AMD Ryzen 5 processor (6 cores and 12 threads) and 32 GB of RAM. The GPU was an NVIDIA GeForce RTX 3090 (Ampere architecture) with 24 GB of VRAM and 10,496 CUDA cores. The operating system was Ubuntu 20.04 LTS. The software used was GCC 9.0.5, CUDA 11, FastFlow 3, and an optimized version of GSParLib provided by [2]. We used the GCC compiler-level optimization 3 (flag O3). There was no replicated stage in our stream processing pipeline, so each stage is run by a dedicated host thread offloading computation on GPU.

We execute MSB ten times for each parameter combination to obtain the means and standard deviations. The evaluation parameters are as follows:

– Target latency (SLO): 3 milliseconds
– Threshold value: 5%
– Step sizes (adaptation factors): 1, 5, 10, 15, and 20
– Latency sample sizes: 1, 5, 10 and 20
– Adaptation algorithms: FAF, PBAF, PBAF-WT, and MBAF

The execution time for processing our workload (containing 500k tuples) varied from 6.4 s to around 1 min and a half, depending on the parameters used. We consider the whole execution in the experiments, without warm-up or cool-down periods. We select the parameter values based on the characteristics of the MSB in the chosen hardware platform. The three-millisecond target latency has been chosen because empirically it is achievable at practically any point in the execution if the right batch size is applied by the system. It is (approximately) the highest tuple latency encountered when executing MSB without batching, such that it can be achieved with a batch size close to one in the most compute-intensive regions, while the lowest tuple latencies require batch sizes of around 300 tuples. The threshold values are kept the same as in [9].

Figure 1 presents the best results for the metrics discussed in Sect. 3. For each algorithm, the metrics values (in percentage) from the best batched and itemized SLO hits are shown, as well as the best MAD-based and SD-based distances. They are labelled using the abbreviations for the definitions in Sect. 3. Furthermore, in Tables 1 and 2 we present the metrics values, as well as the configuration (step size and latency sample size) used for achieving those metrics.

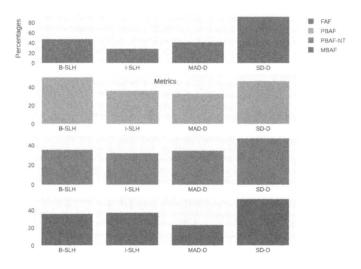

Fig. 1. Best SLO hit and distance metrics per algorithm.

Table 1 presents the best SLO hit metrics achieved by each algorithm, as well as the configuration used to achieve the metric value.

Table 1. Best SLO Hit metrics and configurations by algorithm.

Algo	Batched SLO Hit			Itemized SLO Hit		
	VALUE	STEP	SAMPLE	VALUE	STEP	SAMPLE
FAF	47.83	1	1	29.25	1	1
PBAF	51.02	5	1	36.35	10	1
PBAF-WT	35.72	5	5	32.28	5	1
MBAF	36.30	5	5	37.55	1	1

The algorithms were able to meet the latency SLO for 29% (FAF) to 37% (MBAF) of the 500K processed tuples. The SLO hit per batch ranged between

32% and 51%, with MBAF and PBAF-WT defining the lower end, and FAF and PBAF defining the higher end of the range. The best batched SLO hit results achieved in [9] for the 5% threshold range from 50.58% to 90.39%. The highest batched SLO hit we achieve in MSB with the same threshold is 53.452%, which is comparable with the lowest result from [9]. These results demonstrate that our workload is more challenging than the previous one from [9].

The algorithms achieve comparable results across all SLO hit metrics. However, the configuration they use to achieve their best results is not homogeneous. A step size of 5 or 10 yielded the best SLO hit results for PBAF and PBAF-WT, owing to their ability to use a fraction of the step size as they approach the threshold bounds. Conversely, the best SLO hit results for FAF and MBAF are achieved with a step size of 1 in most cases. This happens because larger step sizes for these algorithms, while allowing a faster reaction, also prevent them from fine-tuning the batch size when latencies are close to the target.

In Table 1 a consistent pattern can be discerned where the latency sample sizes are always 1 for the itemized SLO hit, while for the batched SLO hit they are set to 5 in half of the instances (rows). This behavior stems from a trade-off between two conflicting situations that favor one metric over the other. The first situation is that a latency sampling greater than 1 increases the SLO hit in regions with very frequent latency variations, such as in the workload segments belonging to the (gradually) increasing and decreasing computation patterns depicted in Fig. 2 across the green line. However, (as in the second situation) this increased sampling reduces reactivity since five latency samples must be collected before re-evaluating the strategy again. Consequently, the SLO hit will be lower in regions with abrupt latency changes necessitating high reactivity, e.g., spike and binary patterns. Furthermore, these patterns contain extensive regions with minimal computation, where large batch sizes (close to 300) are needed to keep the SLO. Specifically for the itemized SLO hit, batches missing the threshold bounds in these regions result in a greater cost than for the batched SLO hit. Consequently, the best results for the itemized SLO hit do not incorporate latency sample sizes greater than 1. Table 2 presents the best distance metrics achieved by each algorithm, as well as the configuration used to achieve the metric value.

Table 2. Best distance metrics and configurations by algorithm.

Algo	MAD-based Distance			SD-based Distance		
	VALUE	STEP	SAMPLE	VALUE	STEP	SAMPLE
FAF	41.78	5	1	92.64	20	1
PBAF	33.2	10	1	47.04	1	20
PBAF-WT	34.95	1	5	47.61	1	5
MBAF	23.73	5	5	53.3	1	20

Regarding the distance metrics, the best results for the MAD-based distance are similar for all algorithms except MBAF, predominantly staying within the range of the first five digits of 30. MBAF presented MAD-based distances around 25% smaller than the other algorithms. We attribute this behavior mainly to its high reactivity to spikes in latency.

The best configurations in terms of distance metrics do not necessarily match the best configurations in terms of SLO hit metrics. In Table 1, the maximum latency sample size used was 5. However, Table 2 includes configurations under the SD-based distance metric where the combination of the smallest step size (1) and the largest sample size (20) leads to significant delays in adaptation combined with minimal adjustments in batch size. This results in executions where the batch latencies converge towards the target from the lower threshold bound, albeit failing to cross into the threshold bounds most of the time. Figure 2 illustrates this behavior across the red lines. Keeping the latency closer to the lower threshold bound requires smaller batch sizes, which consequently contributes to avoiding extreme latency spikes caused by large-sized, computation-heavy batches. Another successful strategy for mitigating spikes is the use of large step sizes combined with small sample sizes to increase reactivity. Although the latency spikes are high with this strategy, they are reduced more quickly to a latency closer to the target. We do not observe the largest tested sample sizes being used in Table 2 for the MAD-based distance because this metric does not penalize latency spikes as much as the SD-based distance does. However, we observed that smaller values of the former are more indicative of greater SLO hits, an observation that does not always hold for the latter.

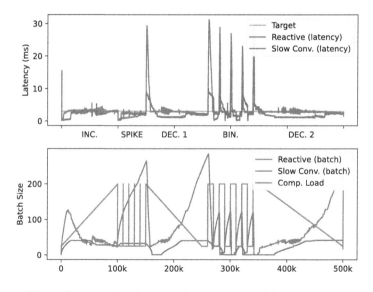

Fig. 2. Latency, batch size and computational load per item.

Figure 2 depicts the two most successful strategies concerning the SLO hit and distance metrics. We use strategy as a general term referring to the combinations of algorithms and configurations that generate a specific adaptation behavior. The strategies we chose to show are particularly remarkable due to their effectiveness in mitigating latency spikes through different means. The strategy we named *Reactive* comes from MBAF, which attained the best itemized and batched SLO hit, and the best MAD-based distance. The metrics and configuration for this strategy can be found in Table 1 in the row corresponding to MBAF. It is the same configuration found in Table 2 under the MAD-based distance. The second strategy, which we named *Slow Conv.*, comes from PBAF. It can be found in Table 2 under SD-based distance, having achieved the best result in this metric.

Figure 2 depicts the latency and the choice of batch sizes for two different algorithms and configurations along an execution time representation. In the x-axis, *time* is normalized across all executions, progressing based on a numerical identifier (id) associated with each tuple, according to the order that it was produced (which is fixed). Regarding the y-axis, the red lines represent the reactive configuration, labelled *Reactive*. The blue lines represent the slow convergence configuration, labelled *Slow Conv.*. The orange line represents the target latency.

The green line (named *Comp. Load*) is meant to represent the computational load of the item. It provides a (theoretical/conceptual) notion of the computation patterns (Sect. 4.1). For instance, if there is an increasing load, we will usually observe the batch size lines decreasing in an attempt to offset it. We name each pattern in Fig. 2. The abbreviated names are *Inc* for increasing, *Dec* for decreasing, and *Bin* for binary.

Summary. Our key findings can be summarized as follows. Firstly, the algorithms mostly achieve comparable results (although using different configurations) for the SLO hit metrics, while MBAF stands out mainly in the MAD-based distance. Secondly, the itemized SLO hits were consistently lower than the batched SLO hits, indicating that relying solely on the latter metric to assess SLO compliance can be misleading. Thirdly, the SLO hit, and distance metrics demonstrate that more reactive algorithms (such as MBAF) and configurations produce superior results. Lastly, the distance metrics indicate that less responsive configurations attaining low SLO hits can still be close to the threshold and mitigate large latency spikes.

5   Conclusion

In this paper we presented an evaluation of four self-adaptive algorithms for stream processing with GPUs from Stein et al. [9]. We implemented the self-adaptive strategy and algorithms with FastFlow [1] and GSParLib [8] in the Military Server Benchmark application [2].

One of the current limitations of the proposed algorithms is the exclusive focus on latency. Having only the latency as a target creates situations in which the batch size is increased with the sole purpose of artificially increasing latency, e.g., there is no gain in terms of throughput. This is not desirable, given that the reason for increasing latency is to achieve a greater throughput. In such cases, it would be preferable to disregard the lower threshold bound. Another notable limitation arises from the tradeoff presented by the current algorithms between reactivity (MBAF) and finer tuning near threshold bounds (PBAF and PBAF-WT). In future work, we plan to explore new approaches to overcome the aforementioned limitations of the evaluated algorithms, by targeting other SLOs besides latency, and by exploring adaptation algorithms that can adequately achieve both fine-tuning and reactivity.

References

1. Aldinucci, M., Danelutto, M., Kilpatrick, P., Torquati, M.: Fastflow: high-level and efficient streaming on multicore, chap. 13, pp. 261–280. John Wiley & Sons, Ltd. (2017)
2. Araujo, G.A.d, et al.: Data and stream parallelism optimizations on GPUs. Master's thesis, Pontifícia Universidade Católica do Rio Grande do Sul (2022)
3. Cheng, D., Zhou, X., Wang, Y., Jiang, C.: Adaptive scheduling parallel jobs with dynamic batching in spark streaming. IEEE Trans. Parallel Distrib. Syst. **29**(12), 2672–2685 (2018)
4. Das, T., Zhong, Y., Stoica, I., Shenker, S.: Adaptive stream processing using dynamic batch sizing. In: Proceedings of the ACM Symposium on Cloud Computing, SOCC 2014, pp. 1–13. Association for Computing Machinery, New York (2014)
5. De Matteis, T., Mencagli, G., De Sensi, D., Torquati, M., Danelutto, M.: Gasser: An auto-tunable system for general sliding-window streaming operators on gpus. IEEE Access **7**, 48753–48769 (2019)
6. Garcia, A.M., Griebler, D., Schepke, C., Fernandes, L.G.L.: Evaluating micro-batch and data frequency for stream processing applications on multi-cores. In: 2022 30th Euromicro International Conference on Parallel, Distributed and Network-based Processing (PDP), pp. 10–17. IEEE (2022)
7. Rockenbach, D.A., et al.: Stream processing on multi-cores with gpus: parallel programming models' challenges. In: 2019 IEEE International Parallel and Distributed Processing Symposium Workshops (IPDPSW), pp. 834–841 (2019)
8. Rockenbach, D.A.: High-level programming abstractions for stream parallelism on gpus. Master's thesis, Pontifícia Universidade Católica do Rio Grande do Sul (2020)
9. Stein, C.M., et al.: Latency-aware adaptive micro-batching techniques for streamed data compression on graphics processing units. **33**, 5786 (2021)
10. Venkataraman, S., et al: Drizzle: fast and adaptable stream processing at scale. In: Proceedings of the 26th Symposium on Operating Systems Principles, SOSP 2017, pp. 374–389. Association for Computing Machinery, New York (2017)
11. Vogel, A., Griebler, D., Danelutto, M., Fernandes, L.G.: Self-adaptation on parallel stream processing: a systematic review. Concur. Comput. Pract. Exper. **34**(6), e6759 (2022)
12. Zhang, Q., Song, Y., Routray, R.R., Shi, W.: Adaptive block and batch sizing for batched stream processing system. In: 2016 IEEE International Conference on Autonomic Computing (ICAC), pp. 35–44 (2016)

The 1st International Workshop on Tools for Data Locality, Power and Performance (TDLPP 2023)

Workshop on Tools for Data Locality, Power and Performance (TDLPP 2023)

Workshop Description

The goal of the TDLPP workshop was to provide a venue for developers and users of tools that address the important topic of memory access optimization. While hardware continues to evolve and high-bandwidth memory becomes available in accelerators and mainstream CPUs, the gap between compute capability (in terms of arithmetic operations per second) and the speed of memory (in terms of access latency or amount of bytes transferred) continues to widen. Tools are thus needed to help developers understand the behavior of their codes to support them with optimizing and modeling their applications. This is especially true in application areas that involve sparse matrices, tensors, or graphs.

In 2023 we organized the inaugural edition of the TDLPP workshop co-located with the Euro-Par 2023 conference in Limassol, Cyprus. We received seven submissions and an international workshop committee provided at least three single-blind reviews for each paper. Five papers were selected for presentation in person at the workshop covering topics describing general advances in performance tool technology as well as approaches specifically addressing sparse computing use cases. The latter was a special focus area of the workshop motivated by the Euro-HPC project SparCity (www.sparcity.eu), from which the idea for the TDLPP workshop developed.

In addition to the main session for presenting workshop papers, we continued the workshop with an interactive tool demo session to allow contributors more time showcasing their software to interested attendees. The tool demo session featured two contributions. The first contribution was provided by Fatih Taşyaran (Sabancı University), Osman Yasal (Koç University), and José António Carvalho Freire Morgado (INESC-ID) showcasing "SuperTwin: A Digital Twin for HPC Machines". The second contribution was provided by Olaf Krzikalla (Technische Universität Dresden) who provided an interactive demo of his tool for "Analyzing One-Sided Communication Using Memory Access Diagrams". The tool demo session was well received and should be considered again for future iterations of the workshop.

Organization

Organization Committee

Karl Fürlinger	LMU Munich, Germany
Didem Unat	Koç University, Turkey

Program Committee

Xing Cai	Simula Research Laboratory, Norway
Karl Fürlinger	LMU Munich, Germany
Aleksandar Ilic	INESC-ID, Portugal
Humayun Kabir	Microsoft, USA
Kamer Kaya	Sabancı University, Turkey
Johannes Langguth	Simula Research Laboratory, Norway
Leonel Sousa	INESC-ID, Portugal
Nathan Tallent	Pacific Northwest National Laboratory, USA
Miwako Tsuji	RIKEN, Japan
Didem Unat	Koç University, Turkey
Josef Weidendorfer	Leibniz Supercomputing Centre, Germany

Sparse-Aware CARM: Rooflining Locality of Sparse Computations

Afonso Coutinho, Diogo Marques, Leonel Sousa, and Aleksandar Ilic$^{(\boxtimes)}$

INESC-ID, Instituto Superior Técnico, Universidade de Lisboa, Lisboa, Portugal
{afonso.coutinho,diogo.marques,leonel.sousa,aleksandar.ilic}@inesc-id.pt

Abstract. Sparse computation is a centre focus of modern high performance computing research. However, the complexity associated with the variety of algorithms, storage formats and data diversity, makes improving the performance of sparse computations on general-purpose hardware a strenuous task. For this purpose, the Cache Aware Rooine Model (CARM) can be a useful tool, mainly due to its intuitive analysis of the application bottlenecks and the ability to pinpoint how close the examined application is to exploit the maximum attainable performance of a micro-architecture. However, the CARM's absolute architecture rooflines are not always sufficient to represent sparse computation scenarios, which are limited by indirect and irregular memory accesses, thus challenging the accuracy of characterization and insights obtained from the model. To improve the CARM insightfulness for sparse computations, this paper proposes a new modeling methodology that derives more representative processing upper-bounds for sparse computing scenarios, which can be applied to different formats and computation types. The proposed sparse-aware CARM is utilized to profile SpMV kernel providing more accurate cache locality insights regarding the memory accesses, for various multi-threaded execution scenarios. Additionally, possible optimization paths are explored, such as reordering for improving performance and core frequency scaling to boost energy efficiency.

Keywords: Sparse Computation · Roofline Modeling · Micro-benchmarking · Application Characterization · Performance and Energy Efficiency

1 Introduction

Sparse computation has been a topic of research for several years, due to its importance in fields such as graph analytics, artificial intelligence, data science and scientific computation [9]. Data in these applications is mostly comprised of zeros, thus it is represented with sparse matrices, where only non-zero elements are stored using diverse formats to reduce memory footprint. However, even for

This work was supported by FCT (Fundação para a Ciência e a Tecnologia, Portugal), through the UIDB/50021/2020 project and EuroHPC Joint Undertaking through grant agreement No 956213 (SparCity).

the most widely used sparse algorithms and formats, such as Sparse Matrix Vector Multiplication (SpMV) with Compressed Sparse Row (CSR), it is not trivial to identify the bottlenecks and improve their performance in current computing systems. This is mainly due to the diverse impact to performance, power consumption and energy efficiency when unpredictable and irregular memory access patterns dictated by the specific sparse matrix characteristics are coupled with increasing complexity of modern hardware.

For this purpose, performance models can be used to identify the main execution bottlenecks and give hints about optimization paths. One simple and insightful model that facilitates this process is CARM [6]. CARM offers intuitive analysis on the application bottlenecks through visual representation of the upper-bounds of the micro-architecture and application performance. However, when tackling sparse computation, this simplicity can lead to inaccurate characterization and optimization hints, due to the inability of the model to consider the realistic requirements of this type of computations, e.g., irregularity and indirect memory accesses.

In order to improve the applicability of CARM [6] to sparse computations, this paper proposes a novel micro-benchmarking methodology supported by a tool to achieve accurate and precise performance upper-bounds of current CPUs when performing sparse computations. The proposed methodology is used to build a sparse-aware CARM, which represent the limitations of the micro-architecture for the SpMV computation in a more accurate way. Rooflines are obtained based in micro-benchmarking with synthetic sparse matrices, specifically constructed to exercise the various component of the architecture. The proposed model retains the simplicity of the original model by relating the application performance with the hardware upper-bounds, while it significantly improves its insightfulness and applicability by providing additional hints for sparse-specific scenarios, such as possible reuse of involved data structures.

2   Background and Related Work

Most research on sparse computations are focused on SpMV, Sparse Matrix Multiplication (SpMM) and Sparse General Matrix Multiplication (SpGEMM), which are also components of more complex algorithms. One approach for improving performance and efficiency has been to develop specialized hardware accelerators [2,13]. These accelerators solve traditional computing systems' suboptimal efficiency when specialized for algorithms and storage formats. Other approach has been to investigate sparse algorithms for more conventional hardware structures, such as Central Processing Units (CPUs) or Graphics Processing Units (GPUs). There is a wide variety of new storage formats and corresponding computation kernels [3,5,12], matrix reordering algorithms [1,10,11] and computation libraries focused for optimized sparse computation [7,8,14].

However, there is a lack of research in what concerns the performance modeling and evaluation of algorithms to reach the maximum performance of the systems for sparse computation. Integrating insightful performance models, such as

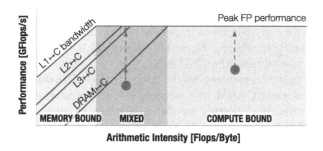

Fig. 1. Cache Aware Rooine Model (CARM) [6].

CARM, in the research work regarding sparse computation would add relevant information to the limitations of proposed algorithms, while also providing performance improvement hints. For example, Zhao et al [17] utilized Intel VTune Profiler, applying the Top-Down method [16], an advanced performance analysis approach based on hardware counters, to determine how a major hindrance to the performance of the analysed application was bad speculation. With this insight, research efforts could be funneled in solving the mentioned bottleneck to improve the overall performance, by relying on intuitive and simplified analysis, thus showing how useful these models can be.

The CARM [6] is based on the principle that computation and memory accesses are executed concurrently, due to the out-of-order engine contained in current systems. For this reason, in order to relate the application Arithmetic Intensity (AI) with system performance, it classifies applications as compute or memory bound and represent them in two corresponding modeling regions. While the compute bound region is associated with the peak Floating Point (FP) processor performance F_p, the memory system modeling is approached differently from other roofline approaches. Compared to the Original Rooine Model (ORM) [15], which considers memory bandwidth between consecutive memory levels, CARM considers bandwidth for each memory level from the core's viewpoint. This difference in approach also influences how each model views AI, specified as the ratio between compute operations performed and data traffic required. Given that CARM views memory traffic from the core perspective, accounting for all performed memory accesses, the AI used is consistent independently from the different memory level perceived, which ultimately allows the model to represent the entire memory hierarchy in a single plot.

As depicted in Fig. 1, the model is plotted using a logarithmic scale graph, in which y-axis represents the attainable performance in Flops/s, and x-axis represents the arithmetic intensity in Flops/Byte. The compute bound roofline is the peak FP performance, plotted in the graph as a straight line representing the hardware performance limit. The memory bound region is portrayed by CARM by presenting the slopes associated with the bandwidth of each memory level, measured from the core through careful micro-benchmarking. The intersection point between the bandwidth and peak performance lines is referred to as the *ridge point*, the minimum intensity that allows reaching F_p. This way, maximum performance P of an application in a specific platform, can be modelled, according to CARM, as $P_y = min\{F_p, B_y \times AI\}$, where B_y is the peak bandwidth of memory level y viewed from the CPU core.

Considering that the memory levels closer to the CPU core possess higher bandwidth, when using CARM in a memory bound application, the maximum attainable performance is limited by the L1 cache's bandwidth, and the lowest memory roof is limited by the Dynamic Random Access Memory (DRAM) bandwidth. When using this approach, modelling an application is then only dependent on its intensity. Optimizations can then be applied to the application, according to its bound region, such as: cache blocking, loop restructuring, improved hardware or software prefetching, for memory bound situations; improving Instruction-level Parallelism (ILP), and using Single Instruction Multiple Data (SIMD) for compute bound scenarios.

The insightfulness and simplicity of CARM, allow to easily relate application performance and the upper-bounds of a system. However, this simplicity can lead to inaccurate characterization and optimization hints in sparse computation scenarios, as the realistic requirements of this type of computations are not considered by the model, e.g., irregular and indirect memory accesses. The micro-benchmarking methodology proposed in this paper improves the applicability of the model to these scenarios. With this purpose, a tool is developed in the scope of this paper to achieve high micro-benchmarking precision and accuracy when performing sparse computation.

3   Micro-benchmarking SpMV Performance Upper-Bounds

The proposed methodology to experimentally assess the SpMV performance upper-bounds takes in account two key aspects: the SpMV algorithm implementation and the disposition of non-zero elements in the sparse matrix. For the former, we focus our analysis on the hand-tuned SpMV kernel, developed in x86 assembly and operating on the sparse matrices in the most commonly used CSR format. For the latter, we developed a set of synthetic sparse matrices to exercise different memory access and data reuse patterns with the aim of fully exploiting the memory hierarchy and compute resources of modern CPUs.

Figure 2-A presents the structural diagram of the developed SpMV kernel, performing $Ax=y$, where $A \in R^{N \times M}$ is a sparse matrix (with N rows and M columns), and $x \in R^M$ and $y \in R^N$ are dense vectors. The non-zero values of matrix A are represented in the CSR format, thus they are contained in a dedicated *vals* array (in a row-major order) with corresponding column indexes in the *cols* array. For each row i, the index of the respective first non-zero element in the *vals* vector is stored in $RowPtr[i]$ position. In order to maximize the kernel performance, we employ a sparse processing strategy with adaptive unrolling, which factor depends on the Number of Non-Zeros (NNZ) in a row, i.e., we strive

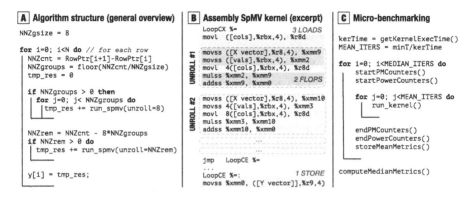

Fig. 2. SpMV algorithm: a) general structure (run_kernel function); b) x86 assembly kernel with adaptive unroll; and c) micro-benchmarking algorithm and procedure.

at minimizing the performance degradation caused by bad speculation due to unnecessary frequent branching when NNZ per row (NPR) is high.

For each row, the NNZ count is determined by assessing the difference between two successive *RowPtr* entries. Then, the processing is organized in groups of NNZs (in this case, 8 NNZs per group are considered), which is executed in an algorithm section with unroll factor of 8 (repeated $\lfloor (NNZperrow)/8 \rfloor$ times). Hence, each group of 8 non-zeros is multiplied with the corresponding 8 elements of the x vector and the result is locally accumulated. The remaining non-zeros of these rows and all rows with less than 8 non-zeros ($NNZrem$) are computed in distinct kernel sections that contain unrolling factor equal to $NNZrem$. Finally, the respective element of y vector is updated.

Figure 2-B depicts the generic version of the SpMV kernel unroll section in x86 assembly, where to reach the desired unroll factor, the instructions in the shaded regions should be replicated. As it can be observed, to avoid data dependencies and to maximize performance, the developed SpMV kernel favours the use of all available processor registers and it maximizes the distance between two subsequent re-uses of the same register. It is worth noting that this hand-tuned SpMV implementation attains performance close to the state-of-the-art Intel Math Kernel Library (MKL) kernel, which was not selected for analysis due to the aggressive auto-tuning that is generally employed in all device/vendor-specific sparse libraries. However, the proposed methodology is applicable to any SpMV kernel implementation, independently of the formats and processors.

By analysing the SpMV kernel in Fig. 2-B, it is possible to determine the total amount of memory and FP operations executed for any CSR-based input sparse matrix with N rows and NNZ non-zero elements. For each loaded non-zero in a row, its column index and the respective element of the x vector also need to be loaded (hence, 3 loads per non-zero), which are subsequently multiplied and accumulated in a temporary variable (2 FP per non-zero). After all non-zeros in a row are processed, the result is stored in the corresponding element of y vector

(1 store per row). As previously elaborated and presented in Fig. 2-A, to process a complete row, two elements of the *RowPtr* array also need to be fetched to determine the NNZ count per row (hence, 2 loads and 1 FP per row). As such, a total of $\mu = 3 \times NNZ + 3 \times N$ memory operations and $\phi = 2 \times NNZ + N$ FLOPs are performed within the SpMV kernel.

Given this analysis, it is possible to determine the range of Arithmetic Intensities (AIs) where any application is expected to be represented in CARM, which allows focusing the optimization task on a specific region of the model. Since the AI represents the ratio between the amount of performed FLOPs (ϕ) and transferred memory bytes ($4 \times \mu$, for single-precision FP and 32-bit integer data), it can be concluded that the AI is highly dependent on the characteristics of input sparse matrix, in particular NNZ per row (NPR), i.e., $AI = \frac{\phi}{4 \times \mu} = \frac{2}{4 \times (3 + 3NPR)} + \frac{1}{4 \times (3 + 3/NPR)}$. Hence, for single-precision FP and 32-bit integer CSR data structures, the minimumAI can be attained with the matrix containing 1 NNZ per row ($AI_{min} = 1/4 \times 2 = 1/8$), while the maximum AI is reached when NPR tends to infinity ($AI_{max} = 2/4 \times 3 = 1/6$).

To guarantee reproducible results, as shown in Fig. 2-C, the adopted micro-benchmarking method consists of three segments: *i) pre-run* – determines the number of kernel repetitions to reach the minimum execution time required for reliable measures ($minT \geq 200ms$, important for small matrices); *ii) mean loop* – repeated kernel execution with the mean value of collected metrics reported; and *iii) median loop* – repeated execution of *mean loop* (1024×), from which the median value of retrieved metrics is calculated. The most relevant metrics collected are: *a)* clock cycles – to measure kernel execution time; *b)* performance monitoring counters – total load, store and FP instructions performed (for bandwidth, performance and AI calculation), cache access, etc.; and *c)* RAPL counters – for package energy, used to evaluate the kernel's power consumption and efficiency.

This micro-benchmarking procedure is applied to experimentally validate the derived AI ranges and consequently assess the performance limits of SpMV processing on contemporary CPU platforms. However, for this evaluation, it is also needed to guarantee the maximum utilization of the available memory bandwidth for different levels of hierarchy. To achieve this goal, a special attention must be payed on the amount and disposition of non-zeros in the input matrix, since the accesses to the x vector are completely dependent on the distribution of non-zeros. As such, an irregular sparse matrix can negatively affect the reuse of the vector elements and not allow to fully exploit the bandwidth. For this purpose, the proposed methodology is based on computing upon a set of synthetic sparse matrices, which NNZ disposition resembles the fully dense matrices, but stored in a sparse format (CSR). By using these matrices, the memory accesses are guaranteed to be entirely coalesced and maximize the bandwidth. Increasing the matrix size enables the progressive utilization of diverse memory levels, while changing the amount of non-zeros per row enables the AI range analysis.

This methodology was experimentally verified in a computing platform with an octa-core Intel i7-7820X and Linux CentOS 7.5.1804, by varying the number

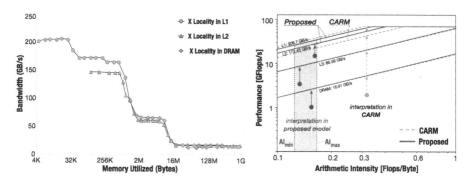

Fig. 3. Bandwidth variation (left) and sparse CARM (right) for multi-threaded SpMV.

of rows, non-zeros per row and ensuring the all data structures involved in SpMV fit in the L1 cache. It was observed that the lowest bandwidth was achieved for the matrix with 512 rows and 1 NPR (512×1), which increases towards 8 NPR, thus utilizing the SpMV algorithm segments with higher unrolling factor, reaching a maximum for the 128×16 matrix. To extend this evaluation to other memory levels, two approaches are adopted that allow preserving the locality of x vector in a specific level: $i)$ increase the number of rows while maintaining the number of columns (e.g., with 16 columns x is in L1 cache); and $ii)$ change the number of columns to provoke different data locality of x vector.

Figure 3 (left) shows the bandwidth variation for multi-threaded SpMV execution, as a function of the memory occupied by x and y vectors, and all CSR structures. For a given x vector locality, it can be seen that increasing the data size until exceeding the capacity of each memory level, causes a reduction in the maximum attainable bandwidth, since deeper memory levels are associated with higher access latency. The highest memory bandwidth is attained when the x vector fits in the L1 cache (for 16 columns, 206.7GB/s). When testing scenarios where x fits in other memory levels, e.g., in the L2 cache with 8702 columns, the resulting attainable L2 bandwidth suffers a bandwidth reduction. This difference in bandwidth is also noticeable for deeper memory levels (such as L3 and DRAM), where the increased access latency significantly reduces the impact of the locality of the x vector on overall bandwidth.

4 Sparse-Aware CARM: Fundamentals and Interpretation

The proposed micro-benchmarking strategy enables the accurate measurement of performance upper-bounds of the micro-architecture when performing sparse computations. Based on these findings, a novel sparse-aware CARM is proposed herein, which is capable of more accurately characterizing sparse computation kernels and their ability to exploit the micro-architecture compute and memory resources, when compared to the state-of-the-art CARM [6]. Based on the bandwidth evaluation conducted in Sect. 3, sparse-aware CARM is derived and presented in Fig. 3 (right), depicting the performance upper-bounds of the SpMV kernel, when the x vector locality is preserved in the L1 cache.

When compared to the original CARM roofs (see dashed roofs in Fig. 3), the proposed sparse-aware CARM (solid roofs) achieves lower maximum attainable performance for the L1 cache. This is mainly due to indirect accesses to the x vector and memory accesses to multiple arrays, which prevent the theoretical L1 bandwidth to be reached. However, proposed L2 roof is higher than the one in original CARM, since the locality of x vector is preserved in the L1 cache (original CARM L2 roof is obtained by maintaining locality only in L2 when streaming the data). Despite the x vector L1 data locality, the L3 and DRAM rooflines only slightly differ to the ones in original CARM, which indicates that indirect accesses with higher latency to the *cols* vector (stored in L3/DRAM) diminish the potential performance benefits from x vector L1 locality.

Given the different micro-benchmarking and model construction principles, the proposed model also has fundamentally different interpretation methodology when compared to the original CARM. As shown in Fig. 3 (see gray dot with dashed arrow), in the original CARM the execution bottlenecks and optimization hints are derived by observing all the roofs intersected at the application *AI*, always suggesting the potential to exploit the maximum architecture performance (either corresponding to the L1 bandwidth or FP performance). In other words, the optimization strategy is based on surpassing all roofs positioned above the application point. Although this method might be adequate for some general-purpose kernels with working set potentially fitting into L1 cache, it is certainly not sufficient to provide in-depth characterization of the considered sparse kernel.

In contrast, the rooflines in the proposed model are representative of both micro-architecture and sparse application features, since they are built via bandwidth micro-benchmarking where all data structures are stored in the respective memory level and accessed in a sequential and coalesced manner. Hence, for a warm-cache scenario, the maximum attainable performance with a sparse matrix whose data structures only fit in a specific cache level cannot exceed the performance of the corresponding memory roofline in the sparse-aware CARM (i.e., the roofline immediately above the application point, as shown in Fig. 3). As such, the optimization path is restricted to matrix reordering, where row and column permutations may yield improved accesses and better reuse of x vector data, thus providing higher performance.

The vertically dotted lines and shaded region in sparse-aware CARM, shown in Fig. 3, represent the theoretical AI range of the x86 SpMV kernel, as derived in Sect. 3. Figure 4 presents the experimental evaluation of this range by relying on a set of dense synthetic matrices with different dimensions. As elaborated before, the minimum AI is achieved with sparse matrices of 1 column (AI=0.125), then the AI shifts to the right as the NNZ per row increases, until reaching near-theoretical AI maximum with high column counts (AI≈0.16666).

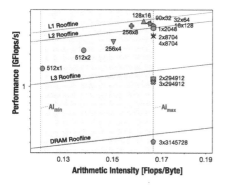

Fig. 4. AI variation with NNZ per row.

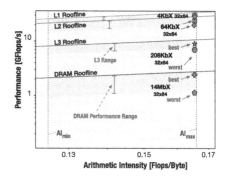

Fig. 5. Best-Worst cases in Sparse-CARM.

5 Sparse-Aware CARM: Experimental Usability Validation

Since reordering is the most important optimization approach to increase the SpMV performance (and potentially improve the x vector locality), we focus first on uncovering the realistically attainable ranges of performance improvements via reordering. For this, we create pairs of synthetic sparse matrices to mimic different execution scenarios: *i) worst case* matrix, which aims at minimizing the reuse of the x vector; and *ii) best case* matrix, which attempts to maximize the x locality. These matrices are obtained through a specific row and column permutation with dimensions and access patterns dictated by the cache specifics, and contain a set of diagonal dense blocks (each assigned to a specific core) [4]. Figure 5 presents the evaluation of several best and worst case matrices in the sparse-aware CARM. As it can be seen, performance improvements are achieved between the worst and the best cases for all memory levels, being the most notable for the groups of matrices that fit in DRAM ($14MbX$), L3 ($208KbX$) and L2 ($64KbX$), which may yield speedups of 2.13×, 1.3× and 1.23×, respectively.

Reordering real matrices: As presented in Fig. 6, we further extend the experimental evaluation to a set of 11 real sparse matrices from Suite Sparse, to which up to six different reordering algorithms are applied, i.e., RCM, AMD, ND, cut-net and connectivity from Patoh library and GrayRO [4]. This set of matrices are real, general and non-complex, with diverse number of rows, columns and non-zero elements, covering a wide range of execution scenarios. As it can be seen in Fig. 6, some reordering methods provide performance improvements for certain matrices (e.g., all for `poisson3Db`, all except GrayRO for `freescale`), but they might also provoke performance degradation (e.g., all for `torso1` or RCM for `wb-edu`). This effect is not surprising since some reordering methods are not developed with data locality in mind, e.g., RCM is a fill reducing method.

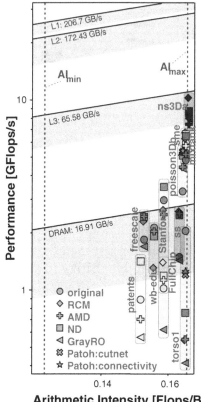

Fig. 6. Matrix reordering

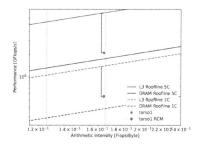

Fig. 7. Freescale in 6C/8C models.

Fig. 8. Torso1 in 5C/1C models.

Another noteworthy observation is that all considered matrices are placed within the modeled AI range, but not all of them are positioned within the best-worst case performance ranges (see grey regions below the rooflines). This is mainly due to the impact of reordering algorithms to the load balancing in multi-threaded execution. For example, AMD improves the average core utilization for `freescale1` from 6.19 (original) to 7.98, while RCM provokes its reduction for `torso1` from 5.32 to 1.46. This explains their characterization in the sparse-aware CARM, since `freescale1`-AMD obtains a speedup of 1.32×, while `torso1`-RCM incurs a slowdown of 0.26×. However, unbalanced execution may also impact the quality of insights derived from the sparse-aware CARM, since the application points are analyzed against the roofs that are not representative of that execution scenario. For example, in Fig. 6, `torso1`-RCM execution is no longer strictly associated with the x vector memory accesses across all 8 cores in parallel.

Adapted sparse-aware CARM: To counter-balance this issue by retaining the cache locality focus of the sparse-aware CARM, its analysis is extended to

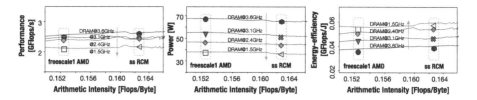

Fig. 9. SpMV performance, power and energy-efficiency variation with core frequency.

consider different core utilizations. These variants of the proposed model are obtained by applying the micro-benchmarking methodology from Sect. 3 to different number of cores (lower core counts should deliver lower memory bandwidth). This adapted sparse-aware CARM allows to improve the model insightfulness and isolate the cache locality analysis, thus providing the means to characterize the performance variations due to changes in x accesses and minimize the impact of load balancing.

For example, in Fig. 6, the initial 8-core sparse-aware CARM characterization suggests that `freescale1`-AMD achieves significantly better DRAM bandwidth utilization and data locality for x vector accesses. However, as presented in Fig. 7, the characterization in adapted sparse-aware CARM (based on the average core utilization), reveals that both original and AMD `freescale1` matrices are placed in the same relative position regarding the DRAM roof. This suggests that there are no changes in the main execution bottlenecks after reordering, which fully corroborates with the conducted VTune Top-Down analysis (see [4]). Similar discrepancy in analysis can be observed in Fig. 8, where the adapted sparse-aware CARM is applied for characterization of `torso1` RCM, which showcases the locality improvements due to reduced relative distance to its respective roof.

Overall, the adapted sparse-aware CARM offers additional insights on where the application optimization should focus. For example, if a specific matrix is represented on top of a memory roof that corresponds to its average core utilization, the next optimization step should focus on improving the load balancing (if the core utilization is lower than the maximum). If the application attains good average core utilization, but it is positioned significantly below the corresponding roof, then the techniques to improve the accesses to the x vector can be applied. Finally, in the case of a kernel that is represented below the roof in a model that does not correspond to its maximum core utilization, further optimization can be focused on both accesses to the x vector and load balancing.

Optimization for energy efficiency: We also investigate applicability of the proposed sparse-aware CARM methodology to explore the optimization space for improving the SpMV energy efficiency. For this purpose, the realistic upperbounds for performance, power consumption and energy-efficiency are obtained by running a set of synthetic matrices from Sect. 3 with increasing NNZ per row to iterate over the complete AI range and for a range of core frequencies. To validate model usability, the previously tested `freescale1`-AMD and `ss`-RCM are selected because they attain near perfect load balancing, with core utilization close to the maximum, thus allowing to showcase the benefits of the proposed strategy by limiting the impact of other execution factors.

Figure 9 presents the performance, power and energy efficiency analysis of these matrices for different core frequencies, by relying on the curves obtained for the memory levels which limit their performance (DRAM in this case). As it can be observed, the reordered matrices achieve close-to-modeled values in all three domain (see the difference between the point and the corresponding curve). Since the matrices are DRAM-bound, there is no significant variation in performance for different core frequencies (DRAM is clocked in a separate domain), while the minimum power consumption is obtained for the minimum frequency. As such, similar performance with reduced power results in the positive implications regarding energy efficiency, which is the highest for the minimum frequency.

6   Conclusions

The proposed methodology to extend the CARM insightfulness when characterizing sparse applications, when utilized to benchmark a SpMV kernel, allows the creation of a model with more representative rooflines for both single-threaded and multi-threaded execution. The profiling that results from this model offers insight that is related to relevant memory locality to the computation, being able to also deal with difficulties such as load balancing, and analyse the possible performance improvement to be obtained from applying reordering algorithms to the input matrices. Additionally, core frequency variation testing on real matrices also proves this optimization path to be an efficient approach to attaining better energy efficiency.

References

1. Amestoy, P.R., Davis, T.A., Duff, I.S.: An approximate minimum degree ordering algorithm. SIAM J. Matrix Anal. Apps **17**(4), 886–905 (1996)
2. Asgari, B., et al.: ALRESCHA: a lightweight reconfigurable sparse-computation accelerator. In: IEEE HPCA 2020, pp. 249–260. IEEE (2020)
3. Bian, H., et al.: A simple and efficient storage format for SIMD-accelerated SpMV. Cluster Comput. **24**(4), 3431–3448 (2021)
4. Coutinho, A.S.M.: CARM-based approach for sparse computation characterisation, Master's thesis, Instituto Superior Técnico, Universidade de Lisboa (2022)
5. Fukaya, T., et al.: Accelerating the SpMV kernel on standard CPUs by exploiting the partially diagonal structures. CoRR (2021)
6. Ilic, A., Pratas, F., Sousa, L.: Cache-aware roofline model: upgrading the loft. IEEE Comput. Archit. Lett. **13**(1), 21–24 (2013)
7. Intel: Intel® oneapi math kernel library. https://software.intel.com/en-us/mkl
8. Kjolstad, F., et al.: Taco: a tool to generate tensor algebra kernels. In: 2017 IEEE/ACM ASE, pp. 943–948. IEEE (2017)
9. Li, X., Wang, Y., Ruiz, R.: A survey on sparse learning models for feature selection. IEEE Trans. Cybern. **52**(3), 1642–1660 (2020)

10. Lipton, R.J., Rose, D.J., Tarjan, R.E.: Generalized nested dissection. SIAM J. Numer. Anal. **16**(2), 346–358 (1979)
11. Liu, W.H., Sherman, A.H.: Comparative analysis of the cuthill-mckee and the reverse cuthill-mckee ordering algorithms for sparse matrices. SIAM J. Numer. Anal. **13**(2), 198–213 (1976)
12. Liu, W., Vinter, B.: CSR5: an efficient storage format for cross-platform sparse matrix-vector multiplication. CoRR abs/1503.05032 (2015)
13. Pal, S., et al.: OuterSPACE: an outer product based sparse matrix multiplication accelerator. In: IEEE HPCA 2018, pp. 724–736. IEEE (2018)
14. Vuduc, R., et al.: OSKI: a library of automatically tuned sparse matrix kernels. In: Journal of Physics: Conference Series, vol. 16, p. 071. IOP Publishing (2005)
15. Williams, S., Waterman, A., Patterson, D.: Roofline: an insightful visual model for multicore architectures. ACM Commun. **52**(4), 65–76 (2009)
16. Yasin, A.: A top-down method for performance analysis and counters architecture. In: IEEE ISPASS 2014, pp. 35–44. IEEE (2014)
17. Zhao, H., et al.: Exploring better speculation and data locality in sparse matrix-vector multiplication on intel Xeon. In: IEEE ICCD 2020, pp. 601–609 (2020)

Enhancing Performance Monitoring in C/C++ Programs with EDPM: A Domain-Specific Language for Performance Monitoring

David Weisskopf Holmqvist and Suejb Memeti$^{(\boxtimes)}$ ⓘD

Department of Computer Science (DIDA), Blekinge Institute of Technology, 371 79
Karlskrona, Sweden
`daae19@student.bth.se` `suejb.memeti@bth.se`

Abstract. The utilization of performance monitoring probes is a valuable tool for programmers to gather performance data. However, the manual insertion of these probes can result in an increase in code size, code obfuscation, and an added burden of learning different APIs associated with performance monitoring tools. To mitigate these issues, EDPM, an embedded domain-specific language, was developed to provide a higher level of abstraction for annotating regions of code that require instrumentation in C and C++ programs. This paper presents the design and implementation of EDPM and compares it to the well-known tool PAPI, in terms of required lines of code, flexibility in configuring regions, and performance overhead. The results of this study demonstrate that EDPM is a low-resolution profiling tool that offers a reduction in required lines of code and enables programmers to express various configurations of regions. Furthermore, the design of EDPM is such that its pragmas are ignored by the standard compiler, allowing for seamless integration into existing software processes without disrupting build systems or increasing the size of the executable. Additionally, the design of the EDPM pre-compiler allows for the extension of available performance counters while maintaining a high level of abstraction for programmers. Therefore, EDPM offers a promising solution to simplify and optimize performance monitoring in C and C++ programs.

Keywords: performance monitoring · domain-specific languages · language abstractions · compilers

1 Introduction

Software optimization is a crucial process in the development of software systems, which aims to produce a more efficient and resource-friendly output. The effectiveness of optimization can only be ensured through empirical measurements of performance. Performance counters play a vital role in enabling users to extract essential information about the performance behavior of their programs, and to empirically verify the impact of code changes.

D. Zeinalipour et al. (Eds.): Euro-Par 2023 Workshops, LNCS 14351, pp. 110–122, 2024.
https://doi.org/10.1007/978-3-031-50684-0_9

However, the process of collecting such data has been challenging and prone to errors for application developers. The accessibility of hardware performance counters varies depending on the hardware manufacturer, and obtaining access is often not straightforward. Fortunately, several tools have been developed to unify access to such counters, mitigating this challenge for developers.

PAPI (Performance API) [2] is a widely used tool that facilitates the manual insertion of performance monitoring probes into the source code. Similarly, the Performance Counters Library (PCL) [1] offers similar functionality but with some limitations. While manual tools like PAPI and PCL provide programmers with the flexibility to collect performance counters selectively and precisely in different regions of the program, they also introduce foreign code that can obfuscate the application logic.

Alternatively, automated tools like gprof [6], valgrind [11], and TAU [12] do not require manual insertion of performance monitoring probes into the source code, freeing programmers from the burden of writing code related to collecting performance counters. However, automated tools often provide a uniform collection of counters throughout the whole program execution, making it challenging to identify discrete performance concerns in specific program regions.

This paper presents the design and implementation of an Embedded Domain-specific language for Performance Monitoring (EDPM) of C and C++ programs. The purpose of EDPM is to simplify the process of performance monitoring in software development by enabling programmers to annotate regions of code for monitoring using a high-level language, thereby reducing programming effort. Unlike existing alternatives, EDPM offers the added advantage of permitting nested code region hierarchies with varying performance counters.

EDPM is designed to allow for easy extension, such that additional performance counters can be collected by incorporating multiple back-ends. The prototype presented in this paper demonstrates that EDPM strikes a balance between flexibility and ease-of-use, thereby mitigating the typical increase in programming effort and line-of-code that is associated with manual profiling.

The main contributions of this paper include:

- The design and implementation of an Embedded Domain-specific Language for Performance Monitoring, incorporating pragma-based compiler directives and facilitating seamless integration with C/C++ programming languages.
- The creation of a pre-compiler capable of transforming the high-level compiler directives into low-level source code appropriate for the target system.
- A comparative analysis of the proposed solution with existing manual profiling tools, leveraging the current state of the art.

The following is the organizational structure of this paper: Sect. 2 provides a review of relevant background information and offers a comprehensive summary and comparative analysis of related works; Sect. 3 introduces the Embedded Domain-specific Language for Performance Monitoring (EDPM); Sect. 4 presents the evaluation of EDPM, providing empirical evidence of its effectiveness; and lastly, Sect. 5 concludes this paper and outlines potential directions for future research.

2   Background and Related Work

This section presents relevant background information about performance monitoring and domain-specific languages to provide a context for the later sections. Furthermore, it summarizes and comparatively analyses the related works.

2.1   Performance Monitoring

Performance monitoring is a crucial activity that involves generating performance measurements to describe the behavior of a software system. Various approaches are available to programmers, each with its own set of advantages and disadvantages. For instance, automated tools such as gprof [6] and valgrind [11] facilitate the collection of resource usage information and other relevant properties during program execution. However, such instrumentation tools generally consider the entire program and collect the same set of metrics throughout execution.

In contrast, tools like PAPI [2], PCL [1], and LIKWID [14] provide developers with more granular control over the code regions and specific metrics to be measured. However, this control comes at the cost of convenience, as application developers must include performance monitoring code within their application code. For example, Listing 1 provides an example of counting data and instruction cache misses at various call sites of **transpose** and **matmul** functions (highlighted lines), showcasing the many possibilities for configuring regions of interest and selecting counters.

Listing 1: Collecting data and instruction cache misses with PAPI

```
1   PAPI_library_init(PAPI_VER_CURRENT);
2   int EventSet1 = PAPI_NULL;
3   int Events1[3] = { PAPI_L1_DCM, PAPI_L2_DCM, PAPI_L3_DCM };
4   long long values1[3];
5   int EventSet2 = PAPI_NULL;
6   int Events2[3] = { PAPI_L1_ICM, PAPI_L2_ICM, PAPI_L3_ICM };
7   long long values2[3];
8   PAPI_create_eventset(&EventSet1);
9   PAPI_add_events(EventSet1, Events1, 3);
10  PAPI_create_eventset(&EventSet2);
11  PAPI_add_events(EventSet2, Events2, 3);
12  PAPI_start(EventSet1);
13  transpose(A, A_t);
14  transpose(B, B_t);
15  PAPI_stop(EventSet1, values1);
16  printf("L1_DCM:
17  values1[0], values1[1], values1[2]);
18  PAPI_start(EventSet2);
19  matmul(A_t, B_t, C);
20  PAPI_stop(EventSet2, values2);
21  printf("L1_ICM:
22  values2[0], values2[1], values2[2]);
23  PAPI_cleanup_eventset(EventSet1);
24  PAPI_destroy_eventset(&EventSet1);
25  PAPI_cleanup_eventset(EventSet2);
26  PAPI_destroy_eventset(&EventSet2);
27  PAPI_shutdown();
```

What is apparent from Listings 1 is the fact that incorporating performance monitoring code (lines 1–12, 15–18, and 20–27) can overwhelm the application logic (lines 13, 14, and 19). Utilizing tools that offer more granular control requires proficiency in their usage and API, which presents an additional hurdle.

The code above employs the low-level API, however, PAPI offers a more user-friendly high-level API [16], which aligns with the concept of defining regions of interest, as demonstrated in Listing 2. The list of counters of interest is specified through a `PAPI_EVENTS` environment variable. While this approach allows for modifying the counters without recompiling the application, it also poses the problem of collecting the same set of counters for all designated regions during program execution. The trade-off between convenience and control is evident in this example; with the increase of the abstraction level, programmers are relieved of the responsibility of initializing libraries and variables.

Listing 2: Collecting counters with PAPI's high-level API

```
1    PAPI_hl_region_begin("computation");
2    matmul(A_t, B_t, C);
3    PAPI_hl_region_end("computation");
```

The Performance Counter Library [1] is similar to PAPI, and also exposes a low-level interface for starting, stopping and reading from counters collected in regions. It supports nested regions with the limitation of any single nesting level being unable to accommodate for dynamic sets of counters.

Opari [10] is a performance monitoring tool, which utilizes the POMP monitoring library for measuring different performance related counters. Similarly to EDPM, Opari allows developers to annotate specific regions of OpenMP, for which to collect performance counters. In comparison to EDPM, the Opari API is not based on pragmas even though it targets OpenMP applications. The ompP [5] is built on top of Opari to abstract away some of the details and make the profiling process easier for developers. Similarly to EDPM, in ompP there is an *enter* and *exit* API function that wraps a region of interest.

2.2 Domain-Specific Languages

Abstraction is often deemed the most critical aspect of good software [7]. This notion is evidenced by the myriad of software design concepts that lack a corresponding hardware entity yet serve to reduce software engineering complexity. Examples of these concepts include classes, modules, and higher-order functions. Such concepts exist in general-purpose programming languages (GPLs), enabling programmers to create applications for diverse domains. However, a distinct class of languages, known as domain-specific programming languages (DSLs), employ domain-specific notations to succinctly express entities and their functions.

In the domain of performance analysis and optimization, examples of DSLs include the TigrisDSL [9], which allows programmers to specify events to be monitored by writing user definitions of so-called relevance criteria, which are used in its first phase to collect coarse-grained metrics. The collected data and the user-defined relevance specifications are then used in a second phase to identify relevant parts of the software system to be monitored for more fine-grained metrics. This two-phase approach decreases the performance monitoring overhead, which is crucial for runtime adaptation of a software system.

Another example is OpenMP [4] in the domain of parallelization of software. OpenMP is a set of compiler directives and runtime procedures that allow programmers to express shared-memory parallelism. OpenMP promised portability to allow application developers to adopt the shared-memory programming model; in the process, it is clear that a DSL was developed with constructs to express the different actions in the domain of data- and task-parallelism.

Performance monitoring is vital in High Performance Computing (HPC), where heterogeneous architectures pose significant challenges for developer.

ANTAREX [13] offers a novel approach to performance optimization by separating developers from the optimization process and entrusting support staff at HPC centers to handle it. The project has developed an aspect-oriented DSL that automates parallelization, offloading, and performance analysis and tuning. Domain-level experts can express functional properties like energy efficiency and performance using the ANTAREX DSL, enforced through runtime code generation using a "collect-analyze-decide-act" loop.

HSTREAM [8] introduces a compiler extension based on pragma directives that enables programmers to annotate parallel regions of code, in combination with a runtime system that, with the help of the code that is generated from the annotations, distributes the workload across the different processing units available on the architecture. In the paper, the authors show that HSTREAM, when compared to code that solely uses CPUs or GPUs, both provides greater performance and lower programming complexity.

EDPM provides a user-friendly interface for collecting performance counters without increasing programming complexity or disrupting application logic. Unlike other domain-specific languages such as ANTAREX, TigrisDSL, and HSTREAM, which aim to achieve different goals, EDPM employs linguistic abstraction to reduce programming complexity for performance monitoring. EDPM's use of pragma directives for generating code is similar to OpenMP and HSTREAM. Although currently relying solely on PAPI as its backend, EDPM has the potential to generate code for other backends, as discussed in Sect. 5. EDPM offers a valuable tool for programmers seeking to optimize program performance.

3   EDPM: C/C++ Language Extension for Ergonomic and Flexible Performance Monitoring

EDPM uses pragma directives to mark specific regions of code and specify which counters to collect for each region. This technique is similar to that used by

OpenMP and HSTREAM, and has the advantage of not interfering with regular program compilation. The user must still annotate points of initialization and termination, as demonstrated in Listing 3.

EDPM precompiles annotated source code and generates code for a specific performance monitoring backend (e.g., PAPI). EDPM offers a high degree of flexibility by allowing programmers to specify different counters for different regions in the same program. EDPM supports lexical nesting of regions (a feature inspired by the TAU [12] performance monitoring tool), enabling programmers to specify properly nested (where a region is fully contained within an outer region) or overlapping (where only one of the regions' boundaries lies within another region) regions. This flexibility makes it possible to handle diverse scenarios, such as an application that predominantly uses memory in one part and CPU in another. However, EDPM currently does not support dynamic nesting, which refers to nesting that becomes apparent during program execution.

Listing 3: EDPM-annotated region that collects counters related to memory

```
1    #pragma edpm init
2    #pragma edpm start region1 = { memory }
3    matmul(A_t, B_t, C);
4    #pragma edpm stop region1
5    #pragma edpm deinit
```

EDPM provides several directives for marking code regions and collecting counters. The directives are lines prefixed with #pragma edpm and include init/deinit (to initialize and deinitialize the counter collection mechanism), and start/stop (to start and stop a region to be monitored). The *start* directive takes a comma-separated list of region descriptions consisting of clauses specifying the counters to collect. The available counters are grouped by type, as shown in Table 1, and correspond to a selection of PAPI's API counters [2].

Listing 4: Excerpts of a matrix multiplication application that uses EDPM

```
44    void matmul(int* A, int* B, int* C){...}
45    int main() {
46      #pragma edpm init
47      int* A = malloc(N * N * sizeof(int));
48      ...
49      #pragma edpm start for-iterated = { branch }
50      for (int i = 0; i < ITERATIONS; i++) {
51        #pragma edpm start multiply-iterated = { memory, cache(l2-stores) }
52        matmul(A, B, C);
53        #pragma edpm stop multiply-iterated
54      }
55      #pragma edpm stop for-iterated
56      #pragma edpm deinit
57      return 0;
58    }
```

Table 1: List of counters available for collection, grouped by type

Type	Counters
cpu	cycles, instructions
memory	loads, stores
floating-point	instructions, operations, multiply, add, divide, sqrt, inverse
vector	single-precision, double-precision
branch	unconditional, conditional, taken, not-taken, mispredicted, correctly-predicted
cache	invalidation, l1-data, l2-data, l3-data, l1-instructions, l2-instructions, l3-instructions, l1-loads, l2-loads, l1-stores, l2-stores

A concrete example is described here to display how EDPM could be used to collect counters. We assume the presence of a file matmul.c as shown in Listing 4. In this file there are two regions, named in a describing manner to communicate the purpose of the regions: *for-iterated* that collects counters related to branching around the for loop, and *multiply-iterated* that collects counters related to memory and specifically L2 cache stores.

Listing 5 presents an example of the JSON output file produced by EDPM. It is noteworthy that the entries in the output file correspond to the names of the regions of interest, as exemplified by the name *multiply-iterated* in line 4, which corresponds to the region inside the loop body shown in lines 8–10 of Listing 4. Since regions may be executed multiple times, as in the case of the *multiply-iterated* region, which is executed inside a loop, a *temporal-id* field is included in the JSON file to distinguish between runs. For instance, the value *"temporal-id" : 0* in line 6 indicates that the collected counters correspond to the first iteration of the loop. Users can utilize their preferred JSON-aware tools to filter out specific regions and sum the counters to obtain the desired total.

Listing 5: Excerpt of the JSON file output when running EDPM with matmul.c

```
1   {
2       "file": "matmul.c",
3       "name": "multiply-iterated",
4       "start": 51,
5       "stop": 53,
6       "temporal-id": 0,
7       "memory": {
8           "loads": 18270944020,
9           "stores": 2151776592
10      },
11      "cache": {
12          "l2-stores": 9609
13      }
14  }
```

3.1   Design and Implementation

EDPM is a precompiler for C/C++ programs that follows the standard phases of a compiler. These phases include the reader, which combines the lexer and parser, semantic analysis, the intermediate representation, and code generation. The subsequent sections provide a brief overview of each of these phases.

Reader. The reader, consisting of the lexer and parser, receives a C/C++ source code file and produces a list of directive structures. These structures include the directive's type (init, deinit, start, or stop), name (applicable only for start and stop directives and refers to the region), a collection of clauses, and the line number from the source code file where it was obtained. A clause is also a structure type that comprises its type and counters, which align with Type and Counters columns in Table 1. EDPM only considers lines prefixed with `#pragma edpm` and currently is not aware of the syntax or semantics of C/C++ programs.

The EDPM formal grammar, is intentionally designed to be simple, which is a key advantage of the language. Enhancing EDPM with a static analysis step, could further simply the grammar by eliminating the *init* and *deinit* pragmas.

Semantic Analysis and Intermediate Representation. The semantic analysis generates a list of `ir-directive` structures, a list of `block` structures, and a region-table that maps region names to `region-info` structures. The list of directives undergoes several small passes to ensure semantic correctness. These passes check that only one init and deinit directive is provided, unique region names have been chosen for each region, and that unique types and counters have been specified for each start directive.

Following these passes, a small pass called "normalize" is executed to ensure that all types and counters provided by the user are recognized by EDPM, as per Table 1. This pass also expands any empty counter specifications, which results in a list of expanded directives that EDPM recognizes.

The list of expanded directives is then passed to a stack-based algorithm called "collect-blocks" that identifies all consecutive blocks by pushing counters onto the stack when encountering a start directive and popping them when encountering a stop directive. When the last set of counters is popped from the stack, a `block` structure type is created with the set union of all counters found. This enables users to collect the same set of counters in different regions within the same block. Information about the start and stop positions of the block, as well as reserved variable names for *eventsets* (an integer) and counters (a static array of *long long*), are also collected.

Next, the expanded directives are processed once more with "collect-regions," another stack-based algorithm that assigns indices into the values array variable. This algorithm uses the information collected in the previous pass and results in a region-table that maps region names to `region-info` structures, and a list of `ir-directive` structures.

The `region-info` structure contains the start and stop positions of the region, a `block-index` structure, another reserved variable name for counters (a static array of *long long*), and a reserved variable name for a temporal identifier that lets programmers differentiate between different executions of the same regions. The `block-index` structure contains a means of accessing the corresponding `block` structure and the assigned indices. While a block must allocate space for all the counters it needs to count, a region allocates space only for the counters it requires, consulting the block's values using the assigned indices.

The `ir-directive` is the intermediate representation for EDPM, containing information about the entity referenced by the directive, its type, an identifier reference, and a position representing the line number in the source code file where generated code will reside. When encountering a start directive during evaluation of `collect-regions` with an empty stack, a block is started (see Listing 6, lines 1–3). However, when the stack is not empty, the current counter values maintained by the block must be updated/accumulated, and the collection of counters is paused to prevent EDPM actions from influencing the counters and skewing performance monitoring results. The current counter values are then copied over into the region's array as a starting value, and finally, the block is resumed again (see Listing 6 lines 4–6).

Listing 6: Intermediate directives generated upon encountering a start directive when the maintained stack is empty (lines 1-3) and non-empty (lines 1-6)

```
1    (directive 'start 'region1 (list (clause 'cpu (list 'cycles 'instructions))) 12)
2    ;; =>
3    (list (ir-directive 'block 'accum 'block1 12)
4    (ir-directive 'block 'stop 'block1 12)
5    (ir-directive 'region 'copy 'region1 12)
6    (ir-directive 'block 'start 'block1 12))
```

Code Generation. EDPM uses information from the semantic analysis phase to generate object, header, and source code files. The bindings collected during semantic analysis, such as reserved variable names for event sets and counters, are used to create these files. Additionally, auxiliary bindings like global integers and file pointers are generated. EDPM's code generation phase generates code specific to the backend (in this case, PAPI) by utilizing the low-level API for PAPI. The library is initialized at the `"#pragma edpm init"` point, where event sets are created and counters are added to those event sets. At the `"#pragma edpm deinit"` point, the event sets are cleaned up and destroyed, and the library is shutdown. The resulting output is a file-spec structure for each file type, which is later passed to the runner for compilation and counter collection.

4   Empirical Evaluation

In this section, we evaluate EDPM in terms of code lines and performance overhead. We use a program with three functions, each containing four code blocks for performance analysis. We assess four configurations: E1 (which involve regions around function calls), E2 (regions around code blocks), E3 (properly nested regions around the code blocks), and E4 (alternating overlapping regions around the code blocks). The monitored code blocks involve naive matrix multiplication on 512×512 matrices. For each configuration, we compare EDPM and PAPI's low-level and high-level APIs in terms of programmability (lines of code and region configurations) and performance overhead.

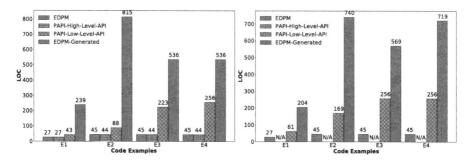

Fig. 1: Comparison of EDPM and PAPI for the static (left) and dynamic (right) code examples with respect to lines of code.

Figure 1 depicts the comparison of LOC required for the EDPM, PAPI high- and low-level API, and EDPM-generated code for the Static and Dynamic sample sets. Notably, EDPM demonstrates consistent behavior, requiring the same LOC for both sample sets. Conversely, PAPI high-level API fails to provide any data for the examples in the dynamic set, indicating its inadequacy for such scenarios, whereas for the static set it results with similar lines of code as EDPM. In contrast, the PAPI low-level API requires more effort and significantly more LOC compared to EDPM in both the Static and Dynamic sample sets.

Furthermore, on average, the EDPM-generated code contains approximately 12.69 and 13.15 times more LOC than the original EDPM code in the Static and Dynamic sample sets, respectively. The increase of LOC for the EDPM-generated code compared to the PAPI low-level APi is mainly because EDPM has to generalize and be flexible for future added features.

We may conclude that the LOC for EDPM and the high-level API provided by PAPI for the Static sample set are very similar. However, for the Dynamic sample set, since PAPI's high-level API does not permit having differing sets of counters for different regions in the same program execution, EDPM can be compared to the low-level API of PAPI, which allows this particular expression of configuration. The LOC required for the low-level API is approximately 3.3 to 4.3 times that of the equivalent using EDPM.

Figure 2 depicts the execution time of EDPM, PAPI high-level API, and PAPI low-level API compared to the original code that incurs no profiling. Each configuration was executed 10 times, and the results report the average values.

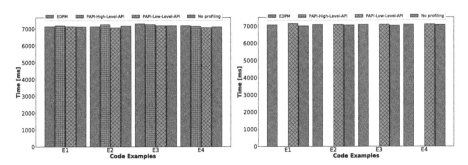

Fig. 2: Comparison of EDPM and PAPI for the static (left) and dynamic (right) code examples with respect to execution time.

One may observe from the figure that no significant performance overheads are added when profiling is enabled, which makes EDPM low-resolution profiling tool, a characteristic that is inherited by the PAPI library.

As described in Sect. 3, EDPM allows for the addition of new backends by creating a mapping from the intermediate representation to equivalent source code using the new backend, which enables potential source-code level performance monitoring tools to target programmers already familiar with EDPM by implementing necessary translations. If new backends require hooking into different phases of the precompiler, EDPM would have to evolve to provide the necessary flexibility. For programmers using EDPM, the level of abstraction remains constant regardless of changes to the backends or precompiler.

EDPM holds an advantage over PAPI in that when standard C/C++ compilers process source code annotated with EDPM-specific pragmas, these pragmas are ignored, leading to no increase in the executable file size. In contrast, when using PAPI the size of the target executable file increases. Integrating comparable features using PAPI or other manual profiling tools would require adapting the application logic, which would incur additional time and effort that is not reflected in the presented results related to LOC.

5   Conclusion and Future Work

The authors conclude that EDPM offers comparable user-friendliness to PAPI's high-level API for collecting a static set of counters, while also providing the ability to collect different sets of counters in various regions, which the high-level PAPI API cannot do. Compared to PAPI's low-level API, EDPM offers benefits such as reduced LOC and ease-of-use similar to PAPI's high-level API, while also providing the flexibility and possibilities of the low-level API.

Additionally, EDPM offers high-level abstractions for various configurations for performance monitoring regions. It can be integrated with existing source code without increasing the maintenance costs or disrupting the current build system. To collect and analyze performance data for a new software iteration, the source code can be passed to EDPM without modification.

Moreover, EDPM's design, which includes backends and an intermediate representation, allows for the implementation of new backends to enhance its feature set without reducing the level of abstraction for the end-user.

Future work can explore several areas. One possibility is to support dynamic nesting, as discussed in Sect. 3. Furthermore, EDPM could be enhanced with the functionality to monitor multi-threaded applications.

Currently, PAPI serves as EDPM's only backend. To broaden counter options and platform availability, new backends could be integrated. If these introduce unique requirements, such as specific precompiler phases, implementation mechanisms would be needed. EDPM could also be extended to include a generic backend-definition framework, acting as a plugin to facilitate the creation of new monitoring tools.

While energy efficiency in hardware has received considerable attention in recent years, less attention has been directed towards energy efficiency in software [3]. PAPI can collect system-wide energy usage [15], and EDPM could easily be extended to support this feature.

Finally, instead of focusing on program-local counters, we could examine system counters to assess the load that specific regions place on the system.

References

1. Berrendorf, R., Ziegler, H.: PCL - The Performance Counter Library: A Common Interface to Access Hardware Performance Counters on Microprocessors (1998). https://juser.fz-juelich.de/record/155195/files/FZJ-2014-04376.pdf
2. Browne, S., Dongarra, J., Garner, N., Ho, G., Mucci, P.: A portable programming interface for performance evaluation on modern processors. Int. J. High Perform. Comput. Appl. **14**(3), 189–204 (2000)
3. Capra, E., Francalanci, C., Slaughter, S.A.: Measuring application software energy efficiency. IT Prof. **14**(2), 54–61 (2012)
4. Dagum, L., Menon, R.: OpenMP: an industry standard API for shared-memory programming. IEEE Comput. Sci. Eng. **5**(1), 46–55 (1998)
5. Fürlinger, K., Gerndt, M.: ompP: a profiling tool for OpenMP. In: Mueller, M.S., Chapman, B.M., de Supinski, B.R., Malony, A.D., Voss, M. (eds.) IWOMP -2005. LNCS, vol. 4315, pp. 15–23. Springer, Heidelberg (2008). https://doi.org/10.1007/978-3-540-68555-5_2
6. Graham, S.L., Kessler, P.B., McKusick, M.K.: Gprof: a call graph execution profiler. SIGPLAN Not. **17**(6), 120–126 (1982)
7. Hudak, P.: Domain Specific Languages, vol. III, pp. 39–60. Macmillan Technical Publishers (1997)
8. Memeti, S., Pllana, S.: HSTREAM: a directive-based language extension for heterogeneous stream computing. In: 2018 IEEE International Conference on Computational Science and Engineering (CSE), pp. 138–145 (2018)
9. Mertz, J., Nunes, I.: Tigris: a DSL and framework for monitoring software systems at runtime. J. Syst. Softw. **177**(110963) (2021)
10. Mohr, B., Malony, A.D., Shende, S., Wolf, F., et al.: Towards a performance tool interface for OpenMP: an approach based on directive rewriting. In: Proceedings of the Third Workshop on OpenMP (EWOMP 2001) (2001)

11. Nethercote, N., Seward, J.: Valgrind: a program supervision framework. Electron. Notes Theor. Comput. Sci. **89**(2), 44–66 (2003)
12. Shende, S.S., Malony, A.D.: The TAU parallel performance system. Int. J. High Perform. Comput. Appl. **20**(2), 287–311 (2006)
13. Silvano, C., et al.: The ANTAREX domain specific language for high performance computing. Microprocess. Microsyst. **68**(0141–9331), 58–73 (2019)
14. Treibig, J., Hager, G., Wellein, G.: LIKWID: lightweight performance tools. In: Bischof, C., Hegering, H.G., Nagel, W.E., Wittum, G. (eds.) Competence in High Performance Computing 2010, pp. 165–175. Springer, Heidelberg (2012). https://doi.org/10.1007/978-3-642-24025-6_14
15. Weaver, V.M., et al.: Measuring energy and power with PAPI. In: 2012 41st International Conference on Parallel Processing Workshops, pp. 262–268 (2012)
16. Wrinkler, F.: Redesigning PAPI's high-level API. Technical report, ICL-UT-20-03, Innovative Computing Laboratory, University of Tennessee (2020)

Leveraging HPC Profiling and Tracing Tools to Understand the Performance of Particle-in-Cell Monte Carlo Simulations

Jeremy J. Williams[1]([✉]), David Tskhakaya[2], Stefan Costea[3], Ivy B. Peng[1], Marta Garcia-Gasulla[4], and Stefano Markidis[1]

[1] KTH Royal Institute of Technology, Stockholm, Sweden
jjwil@kth.se
[2] Institute of Plasma Physics of the CAS, Prague, Czech Republic
[3] LeCAD, University of Ljubljana, Ljubljana, Slovenia
[4] Barcelona Supercomputing Center, Barcelona, Spain

Abstract. Large-scale plasma simulations are critical for designing and developing next-generation fusion energy devices and modeling industrial plasmas. BIT1 is a massively parallel Particle-in-Cell code designed for specifically studying plasma material interaction in fusion devices. Its most salient characteristic is the inclusion of collision Monte Carlo models for different plasma species. In this work, we characterize single node, multiple nodes, and I/O performances of the BIT1 code in two realistic cases by using several HPC profilers, such as perf, IPM, Extrae/Paraver, and Darshan tools. We find that the BIT1 sorting function on-node performance is the main performance bottleneck. Strong scaling tests show a parallel performance of 77% and 96% on 2,560 MPI ranks for the two test cases. We demonstrate that communication, load imbalance and self-synchronization are important factors impacting the performance of the BIT1 on large-scale runs.

Keywords: Performance Monitoring and Analysis · PIC Performance Bottleneck · Large-Scale PIC Simulations

1 Introduction

Plasma simulations are a key asset and tool for improving current and next-generation plasma-based technologies, such as fusion devices, and industrial applications, such as plasma lithography for chip production, to mention a few examples. The Particle-in-Cell (PIC) methods are the most widely used numerical technique to plasmas from first principles. BIT1 is a massively parallel PIC code for studying complex plasma and their interaction with materials [11]. Its main feature is modelling plasma bounded between two conducting walls with an applied external circuit and inclusion of collisions. This work's primary focus

D. Zeinalipour et al. (Eds.): Euro-Par 2023 Workshops, LNCS 14351, pp. 123–134, 2024.
https://doi.org/10.1007/978-3-031-50684-0_10

is investigating, characterizing and understanding the performance of BIT1. To achieve this, we use several profiling and tracing tools and analyze the results. The main contributions of this work are the following:

- We identify the most computationally intensive parts of the BIT1 code, which are amenable for performance optimization, and analyse the performance of running BIT1 on a single node.
- We apply profiling and tracing techniques to evaluate the MPI communication cost, load balancing, parallel efficiency and I/O performance in strong scaling tests.

2   PIC/Monte Carlo BIT1 Simulation Code

In its first inception, the BIT1 code is a 1D3V PIC code: this means that simulations are performed in one-dimensional space using three dimensions for the particle velocities. While particles are only allowed to move in one direction, particles have three components for the velocities.

The PIC method is one of the most widely used simulation techniques for plasma simulation. At its heart, it consists of calculating the particle trajectories for million particles in a field consistent with the density and current distributions, e.g., that satisfy the Maxwell's equations. BIT1 uses an explicit formulation of the PIC method. Figure 1 shows the basic algorithm of the BIT1 code. First, we initialize the simulation by setting up the computational grid and particle (of different species, such as electrons and ions) position and velocity. Then a computational cycle is repeated several times to update the field (the Electric field) and particle position and velocity. BIT1 includes sophisticated Monte Carlo techniques to mimic collisions and ionization processes. At this end, BIT1 can simulate considerably realistic configurations relevant to plasmas in the laboratories, including fusion machines.

A few distinctive phases are carried out in each simulation time step (typically, there are a hundred thousand steps).

As shown in Fig. 1, the computational cycle consists of five phases: (i) plasma density calculation using particle to grid interpolation (ii) a density smoother to remove high-frequency spurious frequencies iii) a field solver using a liner system (iv) calculation of particle collisions and interaction with the walls using a Montecarlo technique (v) a particle mover to advance in time the particle positions and velocities.

Together with these five phases, there is an I/O phase occurring only for specific time steps (for instance, only every 1,000 cycles), enabling diagnostics and providing checkpointing and restart capabilities.

BIT1 is a successor of the XPDP1 code, developed by Verboncoeur's team at Berkeley [13]. It comprises approximately 31,600 lines and is entirely written in the C programming language. Currently, BIT1 is not relying on numerical libraries but natively implements solvers for the Poisson equation, particle mover, and smoother.

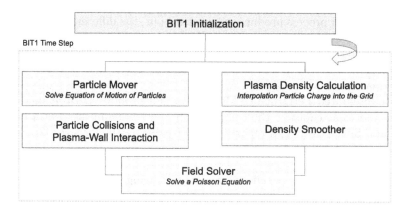

Fig. 1. A diagram representing the algorithm used in BIT1.

The main BIT1 feature is the data layout for storing the particle information, as explained in Ref. [12]. While in the typical, simple PIC formulation, the data of i-th particles are stored as an array A[s][i], where A is the particle property (like coordinate, or velocity components) and s is the particle species, BIT1 associates the particles with the cells they are located in and stores the particle information as A[s][k][i], where k is the cell number where the particle is at a given time. As we know k, then A[s][k][i] can represent the relative position inside the k cell (and we can also use single-precision floating points). This particle data layout has the advantage that particles neighbouring in space are also neighbours in memory, increasing the possibility of having cache hits. Another advantage of this approach is that it allows for easier development of Montecarlo collision models.

However, one of the disadvantages of this approach is the fact that the particles needs to be sorted: for each particle, we need to *i)* check the new position of the particle, and *ii)* if a given particle has left its cell, update its corresponding address accordingly. The function responsible for this in BIT1 is called arrj.

BIT1 uses a domain decomposition for parallelization and MPI for parallel communication. The one-dimensional grid is divided across different MPI processes, and MPI point-to-point communication is used for halo exchange for the smoother, Poisson solver and particles (exiting the domain). BIT1 uses point-to-point non-blocking communication.

3   Methodology and Experimental Setup

This work aims to understand the BIT1 performance bottleneck and potential improvements. We use several performance analysis tools, such as profilers and tracers, to achieve this. In particular, we use the following tools:

- gprof is an open-source profiling tool that gathers information on the execcution time and reports the relevant functions used most often by the processor.

Since each MPI process produces a `gprof` output, the different profiling information is reduced to one containing all statistics.

- `perf` is a low-level profiler used to gather hardware performance counters. In particular, we use `perf` to characterize the cache and memory system, performance.
- IPM or Integrated Performance Monitoring is a profiling performance monitoring tool that captures the computation and communication of a parallel program. Specifically, IPM reports on MPI calls and buffer sizes [2]. We use IPM to understand the parallel and MPI performance and evaluate the impact of workload imbalance.
- `Extrae` & `Paraver` are parallel performance tracing and profiler tools, developed by the Barcelona Supercomputing Center (BSC) [9]. Specifically, `Extrae` is used to instrument the code and Paraver to post-process the `Extrae` output and visualize it.
- `Darshan` is a performance monitoring tool, specifically designed for analysing serial and parallel I/O workloads [10]. We use `Darshan` to evaluate the I/O performance of BIT1 in terms of write bandwidth.

3.1 BIT1 Test Cases

We monitor and analyse BIT1 performance on two test cases that differ in problem size and BIT1 functionalities. We consider two cases: *i)* a relatively straightforward run simulating neutral particle ionization due to interaction with electrons, and *ii)* formation of high-density sheath in front of so-called *divertor* plates in future magnetic confinement fusion devices, such as the ITER and DEMO fusion energy devices. More precisely, the two cases are as followed:

- **Neutral Particle Ionization Simulation**. In this test case, we consider unbounded unmagnetized plasma consisting of electrons, D^+ ions and D neutrals. Due to ionization, neutral concentration decreases with time according to $\partial n/\partial t = nn_eR$, where n, n_e and R are neutral particles, plasma densities and ionization rate coefficient, respectively. We use a one-dimensional geometry with 100K cells, three plasma species (e electrons, D^+ ions and D neutrals), and 10M particles per cell per species. The total number of particles in the system is 30M. Unless differently specified, we simulate 200K time steps. An important point of this test is that it does not use the Field solver and smoother phases (shown in the diagram of Fig. 1). The baseline simulation for this test case uses one node of the Dardel supercomputer with a total of 128 MPI processes.
- **High-Density Sheath Simulation**. We consider a double bounded magnetized plasma layer between two walls. Initially the system is filled by a uniform plasma consisting of electrons and D^+ Deuterium ions. During the simulation, plasma is absorbed at the walls initiating recycling of D neutrals and plasma sheath is forming. We use a one-dimensional geometry with three million cells, three plasma species (e electrons, D^+ ions and D neutrals), and 200M particles per cell per species. The total number of particles in the

system is approximately 2.2B. Unless differently specified, we simulate 100K time steps. The baseline simulation for this test case uses five nodes of the Dardel supercomputer with a total of 640 MPI processes, since this simulation cannot fit in the memory of one node.

3.2   Hardware and Software Environment

We simulate and evaluate the performance of PIC/MC BIT1 on two systems:

- **Greendog** is a workstation with an i7-7820X processor (8 cores), 32 GB DRAM, and one NVIDIA RTX2060 SUPER GPU. The processor has a L1 cache 256 KiB size, L2 cache 8 MiB size and L3 cache (LLC) 11 MiB size.
- **Dardel** is a HPE Cray EX supercomputer, with 554 compute nodes with 256GB DRAM and two AMD EPYC Zen2 2.25 GHz 64 core processors per node. The nodes are interlinked with a HPE Slingshot network using a Dragonfly topology and currently with a bandwidth of 100 GB/s. Each processor has a L1 cache 32 KiB size, L2 cache 512 KiB size and L3 cache (LLC) 16.38 MiB size. The storage employs a Lustre file system.

4   Performance Results

As a first step of this work, we analyse the impact of different compiler automatic optimization using flags -O0, -O2 and -O3 respectively.

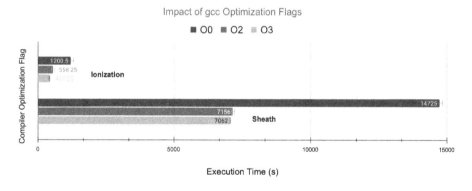

Fig. 2. Impact of the `gcc` optimization flags for the Ionization and Sheath test cases.

Figure 2 shows the execution time for BIT1 codes compiled with different compiler flags for the two test cases in the baseline configuration on the Dardel supercomputer. The -O2 and -O3 flag leads to an impressive performance improvement of more than 50%. This is largely due to vectorization in the particle mover phase, where particle coordinates and velocities can be calculated in SIMD fashion thanks to the auto-vectorization. However, it's important to note that in some cases, -O3 optimizations may introduce subtle bugs or unexpected behavior due to the aggressive transformations applied to the code. Although such cases are rare, using the -O2 optimization is generally considered more stable. Therefore, for the remaining tests, we will use the -O2 optimization flag as -O3 optimization might be too aggressive. As probably the most important part of the performance analysis, we identify which functions take most of the computing time. Figure 3 shows the distribution of computational time in the two test cases using baseline configurations on Dardel. For the two test cases, the function taking most of the time is `arrj` (in the yellow color): `arrj` takes 75.5% and 51.1% of the total execution time, for the ionization and sheath test baseline cases on Dardel, respectively.

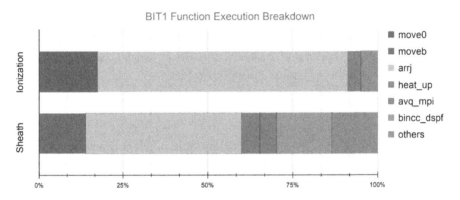

Fig. 3. Percentage breakdown of the BIT1 functions where most of the execution time is spent for the Ionization and Sheath baseline cases. The `arrj` sorting function (in yellow colour) is the function that takes most of the time. The `gprof` tool have been used.

> **Observation I:** The BIT1 serial execution time is dominated by the sorting function `arrj` characterized by many memory transfers and little to no computing. BIT1 in the current implementation and data layout might not benefit from the usage of GPUs (given the low arithmetic intensity of the `arrj` function) but will improve when adding high-bandwidth memories.

To further investigate the BIT1 performance dependence on the memory system, we study the hardware profile counters using `perf` on the `Greendog` workstation (as we have root privileges on the machine). Table 1 shows the L1 and Last Level Cache (LLC) load misses percentage. For this investigation, we use a baseline case with 10K time-steps for the Ionization case; we then reduce the problem size by 10%, e.g. the number of cells and particles-per-cell parameter are decreased by a factor of ten, and then again by 20% (the number of cells and particles-per-cell reduced by a factor of 20). The reason for that is, we want to analyze the impact of problem size on the usage of the cache system. In addition to our `perf` investigation, we perform additional profiling with a `cache-test` [3] code that is known to have good cache performance and we take it as a reference point.

Table 1. BIT1 L1 & LLC load misses percentages.

Baseline Size	10% Reduction Size	20% Reduction Size	`cache-test`
L1 Load Misses	L1 Load Misses	L1 Load Misses	L1 Load Misses
3.43%	2.51%	2.17%	5.53%
LLC Load Misses	LLC Load Misses	LLC Load Misses	LLC Load Misses
99.07%	52.25%	47.51%	18.95%

While high L1 performance (low L1 miss rate) is observed for all our tests, the LLC performance for BIT1 is poor for the baseline case (99% of the load are misses!). However, as soon as the problem becomes smaller and fits the LLC, we start observing an acceptable performance of the LLC.

Observation II: The BIT1 performance considerably depends on the problem size and effective LLC usage. In serial runs, the BIT1 is a highly memory-bound code.

4.1 Parallel Performance

We analyze first the communication pattern using Extrae/Paraver, which allows us to trace the communication pattern precisely. Figure 4 shows a communication phase in BIT1. We note that the MPI communication is non-blocking point-to-point (`MPI_Isend` / `MPI_Irecv`) and only involves neighbouring processes (this is halo exchange in a one-dimensional domain-decomposition). The important point is that MPI rank 0 starts the communication late, e.g., it has more computation than other processes or is slower. Faster neighbour processes (MPI ranks 1 and 7) must wait for MPI rank 0 to proceed. A simple tracing reveals that there is a potential imbalance situation.

Observation III: The trace of the parallel BIT1 communication shows the rise of workload imbalance, with the MPI rank 0 being the slowest and other neighbor MPI processes waiting for it as they are locally synchronized by the `MPI_Wait` call.

We then perform a strong scaling study of the two simulation scenarios on Dardel. These are strong scaling tests as we fix the problem size and increase the number of cores in use. Figure 5 shows the scaling of up to 19,200 cores. The Ionization simulation stops scaling at 2,560 cores, e.g., the problem size per MPI process is too small, and the communication cost takes large part of the simulation time: for instance, for the run on 19,200 cores, the communication takes 57% of the total time with a large increase of the simulation! On 2,560 MPI processes, the relative parallel efficiency is 77% and 96% for the Ionization and Sheath test cases, respectively. One important aspect of a strong scaling test is that BIT1 exhibits a superlinear speed-up [8] for both test cases. In particular, for the larger problem of the Sheath test case, when using more than 2,560 MPI processes, we always observe superlinear relative speed-up when comparing the speed-up to the five-node performance. The superlinear speed-up is because the problem size per MPI process decreases as the number of processes increases. As soon as the problem becomes small enough to fit into LLC, the performance vastly improves, leading to a superlinear speed-up.

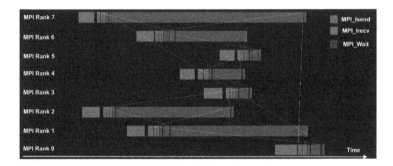

Fig. 4. The MPI communication pattern is obtained, using `Extrae`/`Paraver`, with BIT1 using eight MPI processes on Dardel. The trace shows that MPI communication is non-blocking point-to-point and only involves neighboring processes. The MPI Rank 0 is the slowest. MPI ranks 1 and 7 wait for it, leading to a load imbalance.

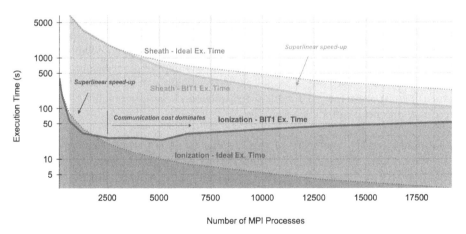

Fig. 5. BIT1 strong scaling test execution times on Dardel supercomputer for the Ionization (blue line) and Sheath (yellow line). (Color figure online)

> **Observation IV:** BIT1 parallel performance shows a superlinear speed-up because increasing the number of MPI processes makes the problem size per process smaller and fits into LLC.

As the last part of the analysis of parallel communication, we study the load imbalance, as we suspected by analysing Fig. 4, in the largest simulation we performed in the strong scaling test: 19,200 MPI processes on 150 nodes, using the Sheath test case.

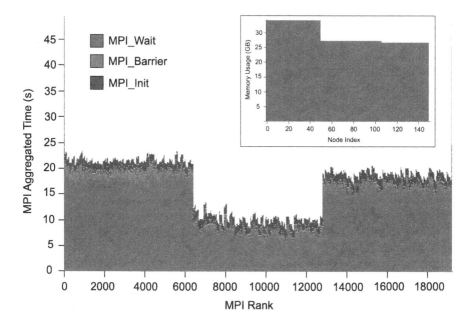

Fig. 6. MPI aggregated communication time for the BIT1 Sheath simulation on 19,200 cores. The insert shows the usage of memory per compute node (this plot shows an imbalance in memory usage).

We present these results in Fig. 6, where we have the cumulative time of MPI functions per rank. The MPI ranks at the domain boundaries (ranks 0 and 19199) take more than double the time in MPI operations. The MPI time is dominated by the MPI_Wait (in red color) synchronization function, showcasing a problem with load imbalance [5], as we have stated before. In addition, by inspecting Fig. 6, we can see that, excluding the boundary MPI processes, there are three large groups of MPI processes, which are *self-synchronized*: two groups have an aggregated MPI call time of approximately 20 s, while one group has an aggregated MPI call time of approximately 10 s. The self-synchronization is due to the presence of idle waves [4] [7] in a memory-bound MPI application with a simple communication pattern [1]. In the Fig. 6 insert, we show the amount of memory consumed per node. Part of the computing nodes has a more considerable use of the nodes, approximately 23% more: the largest usage of memory per node is approximately 34 GB while the smallest is approximately 26 GB.

Observation V: The IPM performance results confirm the workload imbalance issue with some processes spending more (MPI processes relative to domains at the boundaries) than double the time in MPI calls with respect to other MPI processes. At large number of MPI processes, BIT1 is subject to a self-synchronization process, degrading the overall parallel performance.

4.2 I/O Performance

Finally, we investigate the I/O performance when the diagnostics are activated. To better understand I/O performance, we use a simulation of 1,000 time steps. We have diagnostics output (with BIT1 I/O flags `slow` for plasma profiles and distribution functions, `slow1` for self-consistent atomic collision diagnostics, generating the required `.dat` files) every 100 cycles and checkpointing files (so-called `.dmp` files) every 333 cycles. The read operations are limited to read the simulation input files. We focus only on analysing the performance of the write operations. BIT1 performs serial I/O, e.g. each MPI process writes its own diagnostics and checkpointing files. Figure 7 presents the write bandwidth results, measured with `Darshan` for the increasing number of MPI processes (up to 12,800 MPI processes) in the two test cases. By studying the two plots, we observe that write bandwidth increases with the number of MPI processes, and then it saturates, for both the test cases. The write bandwidth saturates approximately at 300 MiB/s and 70 GiB/s for the Ionization and Sheath test cases, respectively. The peak I/O write bandwidth depends on the problem size. After the peak I/O is reached, the performance degrades as the metadata writing cost increases.

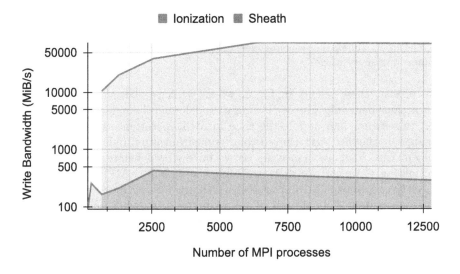

Fig. 7. BIT1 I/O Write Bandwidth, measured in MiB/s

> **Observation VI:** BIT1 performs serial I/O. The write bandwidth increases for a small number of MPI processes until the peak bandwidth is reached. For a large number of MPI processes, the I/O write bandwidth decreases as the cost associated with metadata write increases.

5 Discussion and Conclusion

In this article, we presented the BIT1 code performance results and analysis, understanding the bottleneck and identifying optimization opportunities. We showed that BIT1 is a memory-bound code, and its performance is highly dependent on the problem size (that might fit or not to the different memory hierarchy capacities). Our scaling tests showed a superlinear speed-up that can be explained by better usage of LLC on a very large number of cores.

We have found that the main performance bottleneck is a highly memory-bound sorting function that depends on cache usage and available memory bandwidth. Future optimizations targeting the BIT1 performance must target the optimization of this function and consider the dependency on memory performance. At this end, using high-bandwidth memories [6] will likely increase considerably the BIT1 performance without any further code optimization.

The dependency of the code performance on the arrj sorting function (with many memory transfers and little to no computing) does not make BIT1 a good candidate to port to GPU systems. For porting BIT1 to GPU systems and achieving high performance, the BIT1 sorting code algorithm, or the data layout should be likely reformulated to reduce the memory traffic and increase the computational intensity to use GPUs effectively.

Another performance bottleneck is the imbalance that slows the simulation because of the synchronization of MPI point-to-point communication. We have found that MPI processes at the domain boundaries (dealing with the boundary conditions to the simulations) are considerably slower than other MPI processes. However, other processes must wait for the processes at the domain boundaries as they are bound to local synchronization of the message passing. Additionally, we have found that when utilizing a large number of cores, BIT experiences self-synchronization issues, leading to a degradation in overall parallel performance. Future MPI communication optimization strategies must address this issue and de-synchronize the MPI processes.

Finally, BIT1 would benefit from the usage of parallel I/O communication (such as utilizing MPI I/O or HDF5 parallel I/O libraries) to reduce the cost of metadata writing (as thousands of files are written at each I/O cycle) and enhance the I/O performance. Another possibility is to provide BIT1 with in-situ visualization and data analysis via ADIOS-2 and Kitware Catalyst libraries to reduce the overall cost of I/O and post-processing.

Acknowledgments. Funded by the European Union. This work has received funding from the European High Performance Computing Joint Undertaking (JU) and Sweden, Finland, Germany, Greece, France, Slovenia, Spain, and Czech Republic under grant agreement No 101093261.

References

1. Afzal, A., Hager, G., Wellein, G.: Analytic modeling of idle waves in parallel programs: communication, cluster topology, and noise impact. In: Chamberlain, B.L., Varbanescu, A.-L., Ltaief, H., Luszczek, P. (eds.) ISC High Performance 2021. LNCS, vol. 12728, pp. 351–371. Springer, Cham (2021). https://doi.org/10.1007/978-3-030-78713-4_19

2. Fuerlinger, K., et al.: Effective performance measurement at petascale using IPM. In: 2010 IEEE 16th International Conference on Parallel and Distributed Systems, pp. 373–380. IEEE (2010)

3. KTH: Cachetest (2023). https://gits-15.sys.kth.se/jjwil/BIT-Code-Tests, updated: 2023-05-04

4. Markidis, S., et al.: Idle waves in high-performance computing. Phys. Rev. E **91**(1), 013306 (2015)

5. Peng, I.B., et al.: The cost of synchronizing imbalanced processes in message passing systems. In: 2015 IEEE Cluster, pp. 408–417. IEEE (2015)

6. Peng, I.B., et al.: Exploring application performance on emerging hybrid-memory supercomputers. In: 2016 IEEE International Conference on High Performance Computing and Communications), pp. 473–480. IEEE (2016)

7. Peng, I.B., et al.: Idle period propagation in message-passing applications. In: 2016 IEEE 18th International Conference on High Performance Computing and Communications, pp. 937–944. IEEE (2016)

8. Ristov, S., et al.: Superlinear speedup in HPC systems: Why and when? In: 2016 FedCSIS, pp. 889–898. IEEE (2016)

9. Servat, H., et al.: Framework for a productive performance optimization **39**(8), 336–353 (2013)

10. Snyder, S., et al.: Modular HPC I/O characterization with Darshan. In: 2016 5th Workshop on Extreme-Scale Programming Tools (ESPT), pp. 9–17. IEEE (2016)

11. Tskhakaya, D., et al.: PIC/MC code BIT1 for plasma simulations on hpc. In: 2010 18th Euromicro, pp. 476–481. IEEE (2010)

12. Tskhakaya, D., Schneider, R.: Optimization of PIC codes by improved memory management. J. Comput. Phys. **225**(1), 829–839 (2007)

13. Verboncoeur, J., et al.: Simultaneous potential and circuit solution for 1d bounded plasma particle simulation codes. J. Comput. Phys. **104**(2), 321–328 (1993)

Performance Prediction for Sparse Matrix Vector Multiplication Using Structure-Dependent Features

Konstantin Pogorelov[1], James Trotter[1], and Johannes Langguth[1,2]

[1] Simula Research Laboratory, Oslo, Norway
{konstantin,james,langguth}@simula.no
[2] University of Bergen, Bergen, Norway

Abstract. Sparse matrix-vector multiplication (SpMV) is one of the most important kernels in high-performance computing, with numerous applications in scientific computing, machine learning, and many other fields. Consequently, it has been studied extensively in the past decades, and many ideas for optimizing and predicting SpMV performance have been proposed. Unlike dense matrix operations, where performance is mostly determined by the floating-point capabilities of the system, the performance of sparse kernels like SpMV can vary widely for each combination of algorithm, the matrix itself, and hardware architecture. And while these performance differences can be puzzling, it is widely understood that the reuse of the data elements is a crucial determinant of SpMV performance. This in turn means that a simple reordering of a matrix using methods such as the Cuthill-McKee algorithm can have a massive impact on the SpMV performance.

However, performing such a reordering is costly and not all sparse matrices benefit from reordering. Therefore, it would be desirable to predict whether reordering a matrix will benefit SpMV performance. Most existing systems for SpMV performance prediction are not suitable for this purpose since they only use order-invariant features such as the relative length of the rows. Consequently, they are incapable of predicting the performance of a reordered matrix.

In this work we present a machine learning system based on order-dependent features that is capable of such predictions. We perform an experimental evaluation for large instances on multiple modern CPU architectures, showing that our system is capable of predicting reordering benefit with 94% accuracy.

This work was supported by the European High-Performance Computing Joint Undertaking under grant agreement No. 956213. The research presented in this paper has benefited from the Experimental Infrastructure for Exploration of Exascale Computing (eX3), which is financially supported by the Research Council of Norway under contract 270053.

D. Zeinalipour et al. (Eds.): Euro-Par 2023 Workshops, LNCS 14351, pp. 135–146, 2024.
https://doi.org/10.1007/978-3-031-50684-0_11

1   Introduction

The multiplication between a sparse matrix and a dense vector is a recurring operation in many different domains, and it often turns out to be a performance bottleneck for these applications. In scientific computing, many iterative solvers for finite element or finite volume computations make use of it, and via the *High Performance Conjugate Gradient* (HPCG) benchmark, it has become a standard benchmark for evaluating supercomputers [8]. SpMV is also widely used in machine learning, e.g., in Graph Neural Networks [22], and similar kernels play an important role in many other domains such as network analysis, with Page Rank [16] being a prominent example. While they may differ from SpMV, they exhibit very similar data access patterns. Therefore, optimizing data accesses for SpMV can increase the performance of a wide variety of applications.

Due to its immense importance, SpMV performance has been studied intensely for more than 20 years. Since the kernel has a very low arithmetic intensity, its performance generally depends on the speed of accessing the matrix and vector entries, which, in turn, depends on the speed of the memory subsystem as well as the reuse of vector elements in cache.

A common approach for optimizing SpMV performance lies in developing storage formats that exploit structures common to many matrices. Optimized formats can lower the storage space required for sparse matrices, as well as optimize data access and execution patterns. Depending on the instance and architecture, the performance difference between formats can be very high, especially on GPUs [2,7]. However, the cost of changing the storage format is also high, and thus it is desirable to perform a cheap prediction of the optimum format before performing a conversion.

Several machine learning methods have been proposed in order to predict SpMV performance for different formats [23,24]. They generally fall into two classes. Methods of the first class typically use gradient boosting algorithms, such as XGBoost [4], which learn on the basis of predefined features. The other class uses *Convolutional Neural Networks* (CNN), which are fed a downscaled image of the matrix.

While CNNs can provide high accuracy on test sets such as *Suitesparse* [6], they perform poorly for larger matrices [7]. The reason for this is that the majority of matrices in Suitesparse are relatively small, combined with the fact that downsampling introduces a loss of accuracy. For small matrices, a pixel in the downsampled image may represent a small submatrix, but for very large matrices, a $10^5 \times 10^5$ submatrix might be represented by a single pixel that contains no information about the structure inside that block. Although this could be counteracted by using CNNs that take much larger images as inputs, the cost of both training and inference would become prohibitively high.

On the other hand, while the feature-based methods work well for larger matrices, their features are typically structure-independent. Thus, by design, they are unable to predict the change in performance when the structure of a given matrix changes, e.g., by reordering the rows or columns.

This limitation is important because matrix reordering is a crucial technique for improving SpMV performance. By grouping nonzero elements tightly together, e.g., in blocks along the main diagonal, cache reuse can be improved. Although matrix entries are used only once per SpMV iteration, most vector elements are read and used multiple times. The more often the entry is read from a location that is high (i.e. close to the core) in the memory hierarchy, the less time is spent on the read. Thus, more frequent cache reuse generally leads to higher performance, which motivates reordering the matrix in a way that increases cache reuse [21].

A common method for finding improved orderings is the Reverse Cuthill-McKee (RCM) algorithm for heuristic bandwidth minimization [5]. An alternative approach is to create dense blocks along the main diagonal using graph partitioning software such as KaHip [20].

Since many matrices in the SuiteSparse collection [6] are relatively small, repeated SpMV iterations on these matrices run entirely out of cache on modern architectures, and thus have very different performance characteristics than large instances, which do not fit in the last level of cache. Therefore, aggregating results over large test sets may not represent the true challenges of SpMV performance prediction for large instances.

For this reason, in this paper we study the SpMV performance of sparse matrices having at least 10^8 nonzeroes, comparing SpMV performance for the original and RCM reordered versions of these matrices. We then introduce structure-dependent features along with a model that can predict whether performing an RCM reordering will lead to a performance gain. Our paper thus makes the following contributions:

- We introduce structure-dependent features for SpMV performance prediction and test their utility.
- We show how these features can be used to design a machine learning model that can predict the SpMV performance of RCM reordered matrices.
- We perform extensive experiments on multiple CPU platforms using reordered and non-reordered instances. The results show that the benefits of reordering are instance and architecture dependent, making informed choices mandatory.
- We test the model using these experimental results and obtain an accuracy of 94%. We also show that it is capable of guiding SpMV execution to attain more than 99% of the achievable performance in this setting.

2   Background and Related Work

While SpMV is a trivial linear time algorithm in the RAM model, it was observed more than two decades ago that the irregularity of the matrix, combined with the cache hierarchies of CPUs, can cause major differences in the performance of different SpMV instances [21].

An additional challenge for the efficiency of SpMV codes on multicore CPUs is load balancing. For the CSR format, a naive shared memory multicore implementation using **OpenMP** typically uses `#pragma omp parallel for` with `static` scheduling while looping over the rows. This can be described as a one-dimensional (1D) partitioning of the rows. It introduces load imbalance if the number of nonzeroes per row differs.

A solution to this problem is to use SpMV implementations that can split rows and thus obtain a perfect load balance with respect to the number of nonzeroes per thread. We refer to them as 2D methods. Several such codes have been proposed in recent years. Out of these, we use the merge-based CSR code by Duane and Garland [14]. It was implemented for both GPUs and CPUs and works well on both devices.

Note that a perfect load balance with respect to the number of nonzeroes per thread may not be optimal if the cache locality differs in different parts of the matrix and thus in different threads. In a typical *compressed sparse row* (CSR) matrix with four byte indices and eight byte values, SpMV consumes little more memory bandwidth than 12 bytes per nonzero when all vector values are cached. If instead one cache line must be fetched for every vector value, the memory bandwidth requirement increases to 76 bytes on a typical CPU, thus causing a slowdown of more than 6× in the extreme case. Memory access latency may make this effect even worse [12].

Thus, RCM or other reordering algorithms that improve cache locality can also indirectly improve load balance. While RCM minimizes the bandwidth of a matrix (i.e., the maximum distance between the main diagonal and any nonzero element), which is not the same as maximizing the cache reuse, in many scientific computing applications, low-bandwidth reorderings correlate with high SpMV performance. For this reason, Reverse Cuthill-McKee reorderings remain popular for SpMV. Note that bandwidth minimization is NP-hard [17]. Thus, all practical approaches can only provide approximations or heuristic solutions. In this paper, we only predict SpMV performance of RCM reordered matrices, but the same techniques can be applied to matrices reordered by other algorithms.

As mentioned above, when using 1D SpMV algorithms, reordering for cache reuse can also cause load imbalance. This happens with matrices that have a widely varying number of nonzeroes per row and a relatively even distribution of longer and shorter rows among the cores. A typical example are Kronecker graphs which are generated for the Graph500 benchmark [15]. In this case, a random ordering of the rows generally ensures a good load balance for 1D algorithms. However, this load balance will typically disappear when applying an RCM reordering, since the bandwidth minimization does not consider load balance and may, e.g., cluster denser rows.

This effect explains why RCM reordering can reduce SpMV performance for some matrices, an effect that was frequently observed in previous work [19]. Note that 2D methods do not suffer from this problem. Furthermore, matrices arising from scientific computing methods such as finite volume or finite elements typically have little variance in the number of nonzeroes per row, and can be processed efficiently in the CSR or ELLPACK formats using 1D methods. Here, reorderings can provide substantial increases in performance without creating additional challenges [11].

3   SpMV Performance Evaluation

We test SpMV performance in the CSR format on six shared memory architectures using OpenMP. We test both a standard 1D implementation from Intel MKL as well as the 2D merge based algorithm [14], using the code provided in the paper. We use the standard 64 bit double precision floating point for the matrix and vector values, and 32 bit integers for the indices. As a result, some large matrices cannot be tested since the number of nonzeroes exceeds the 32 bit limit. While this could be easily fixed by using 64 bit integer indices, doing so would produce values that are incomparable to older reported results.

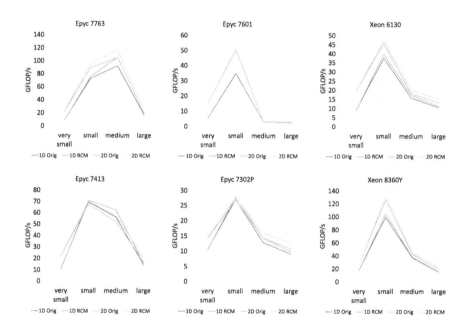

Fig. 1. Performance in GFLOP/s of the 1D and 2D SpMV algorithm by matrix size for original and RCM reordering on each tested architecture.

We compiled the codes with *gcc* 11.2.0 on the AMD processors and with Intel *icc* version 2020.19.1.3 on the Xeons. We use MKL version 2020.4.304. We measure performance after a "warm start", i.e. after 100 iterations of SpMV. In this manner, we ensure that all experiments can benefit equally from caches. The performance results are then computed as the average of 100 additional iterations. In some cases the 100 iterations contained outliers which are typically the result of operating system interference. In this case the entire computation for the matrix is repeated. All runs use one OpenMP thread per core, with *numactl* and *OMP_PROC_BIND* ensuring thread placement.

Our first test set is taken from the Suitsparse collection [6]. Since reordering affects caching behaviour and the last-level caches of modern CPUs are very large, it has a very different effect if the entire problem is small enough to fit in cache. As a consequence, we split the test set by the number of nonzeroes into four groups: *very small* matrices having less than 10^6 nonzeroes, *small* with 10^6 to 10^7, *medium* with 10^7 to 10^8 nonzeroes, and *large* matrices having more than 100 million nonzeroes. The latter are the primary focus of this paper. However, since only a few matrices in the Suitesparse collection exceed 10^8 nonzeroes, we use additional matrices to enhance the test set. Nine of these instances are large graphs from the KONECT network library [9], while 8 are based on meshes of the human cardiac ventricle [10,11].

For each architecture we test both the 1D and the 2D algorithm on the original and the reordered matrix. Average results weighted by matrix size for each group are shown in Fig. 1.

On the large instances which exceed 10^8 nonzeroes, performance is limited by DRAM bandwidth for all architectures since the matrices no longer fit in cache. Since Epyc 7763, Epyc 7413, and Xeon 8360Y have the same memory configuration, their performance is quite similar. For the large matrices, the gain from the 2D algorithm is somewhat higher than the gain from RCM.

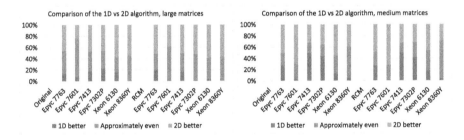

Fig. 2. Number of large (left) and medium (right) instances in which the 1D or 2D algorithm performs significantly better. *Approximately even* means a performance difference of less than 5%.

Figure 1 uses average performance, which is susceptible to outlier values. To gain a more robust insight, we also count the number of times in which the 1D and 2D algorithm is measurably better, which we define as having at least 5% higher performance.

Results for large instances are shown in Fig. 2 on the left. Clearly, the 1D algorithm is faster only in a small number of cases, which shrinks even further when using RCM. This means that for the reordered matrices, the 2D approach is especially useful. In most cases, this is due to the fact that 2D is impervious to the load imbalance that can be induced by RCM. As a consequence, we only use the 2D algorithm for the prediction experiments in the rest of the paper. Note that for medium matrices shown on the right, the advantage of the 2D algorithm is significantly smaller. For Epyc 7413 and Epyc 7302P, which both have a small number of cores, the 1D algorithm is, in fact, better.

4   Structure-Dependent Features

As discussed in Sect. 1, the features that are commonly used for SPMV prediction tasks such as format selection are not sensitive to the order of the matrix. Thus, they are not usable when predicting the effects of matrix reorderings. Instead, we propose two new order-dependent features based on simplified simulations of the cache: the *group reuse rate* and the *cache reuse rate*. Both are relatively simple and, unlike CNNs, can be computed efficiently. Furthermore, they do not lose information with increasing matrix size.

4.1   Single Cache Line Reuse

The *group reuse rate* feature attempts to capture spatial locality through a simple single-line cache model for a straightforward SpMV algorithm. We assume that the single available cache line consists of N consecutive elements, which are always loaded simultaneously from memory. We also assume that matrix nonzeros are accessed in row major order. For the first nonzero of the matrix, a load is triggered which moves N consecutive vector elements into cache, starting with the element corresponding to the position of the nonzero. For each subsequent nonzero, if the corresponding vector element is in cache, a reuse event is triggered, and we move on to the next nonzero. Otherwise, a new load event is triggered, as described above. For simplicity, our model of the group reuse rate does not assume that cache lines begin and end at multiples of the cache line size N. Although this is different from how CPU caches operate in reality, the model works well enough in practice.

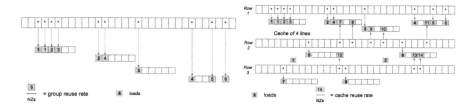

Fig. 3. An example of the group reuse rate (left) and the cache reuse rate (right).

After all nonzeros have been accessed, the group reuse rate is obtained by simply dividing the number of reuse events by the number of nonzeros in the matrix. Since a cache line has one load and can have up to $NZ - 1$ reuse events, the best possible reuse rate is $(NZs - 1)/NZs$.

4.2   Multiple Cache Line Reuse

We introduce a second type of feature which we call *cache reuse rate*. It represents a simplified multi-line cache access simulation implemented for a simple SpMV algorithm. As with the *group load and reuse rates*, a cache line consists of N elements, but now there are M cache lines organized in an ordered list. Again, the nonzeros in the matrix are accessed consecutively and the first element triggers a load event.

For each subsequent nonzero, if the corresponding vector element is currently present in any of the already loaded cache lines, a reuse event is triggered, and the cache line that contained the cached element is moved to the top of cache line access list. If the vector element is not currently in cache, a load event will be triggered, loading another cache line which is placed on top of the cache line access list. If at least M cache lines have been loaded, the line at the bottom of the access list must be evicted before a new cache line can be loaded. This is part of a single load event. In this manner, we simulate a simple fully associative least recently used (LRU) policy.

Once the simulation is finished, the cache reuse rate is obtained by dividing the number of reuse events by the number of nonzeros in the matrix. An example of both features is shown in Fig. 3(b). We compute this feature with N set to 64 and M to 65536.

5   Performance Prediction

5.1   Performance Prediction Model

Based on the structure-dependent features presented in the last section, we develop a qualitative performance prediction model in order to determine whether a given matrix can be reordered to increase SpMV performance. Thus, we have to solve a classification problem with two classes. To do so, we first extract the group and cache reuse rate from the matrices, along with the row length statistics which include mean row length, standard deviation, skewness and variance, and the number of rows, columns, and non-zero elements. These features are then used to train the classifier. We use the performance data presented in Sect. 3 to determine the ground truth (i.e. whether the original or the reordered version had better performance).

We use a standard Random Forest classifier [3] from the WEKA data mining system [13] and the scikit-learn machine learning library [18] in Python. Due to a shortage of available data for training the model, we perform multiple rounds of the additive model training process using 10-fold cross-training with artificially added random noise performed until the model continued to converge.

The Random Forest classifier not only performs well for small datasets, but it can also handle input features of different scales without pre-normalization of the feature values. Since the number of available large instances is very low, we do not have enough data to train a separate model for each architecture. However, the resulting model has a high accuracy. This is expected, since the fundamental reason for high performance is the same for all architectures: frequent data reuse. Still, given more training data, the result could be improved further by training CPU-specific models.

We trained an additional model for medium sized matrices. Training a single model by combining both size classes is also possible, but it leads to lower accuracy due to the strong effect the cache has on the performance of smaller instances.

5.2 Performance Prediction Experiment

To verify the accuracy of our classifiers, we show the standard classification performance metrics in Table 1 on the left. The classifier for large matrices shows a very good accuracy. However, for the medium size matrices classification performance is lower. One important reason for this is that the classifier makes an architecture-independent prediction, but due to the difference in cache size, performance as well as optimum reordering strategy vary more among the medium sized matrices, and reordering a given matrix is often beneficial for some architectures but not for others.

Table 1. Prediction quality of the random forest classifier for medium and large instances. Left: performance metrics. Right: Percentage of maximum performance reached by the different reordering strategies.

	large	medium		Prediction	Always RCM	Never RCM
True positives	159	457	Large			
True negatives	26	9	Epyc 7763	99.38	96.77	73.23
False positives	11	95	Epyc 7601	99.27	97.65	77.15
False negatives	0	2	Epyc 7413	99.78	96.07	72.34
			Epyc 7302P	99.08	94.19	79.02
Accuracy	0.94	0.83	Xeon 6130	99.07	94.8	78.78
Precision	0.94	0.83	Xeon 8360Y	99.97	99.28	79.29
Sensitivity	1	1	Medium			
Specificity	0.7	0.09	Epyc 7763	84.42	84.16	74.8
F1 score	0.97	0.9	Epyc 7601	97.4	98.19	89.08
			Epyc 7413	83.67	82.3	71.98
			Epyc 7302P	96.54	97.4	83.5
			Xeon 6130	96.87	97.23	79.16
			Xeon 8360Y	98.35	98.06	90.93

In Table 1, right side, we show the effect of applying the predictions. We weight every matrix by the number of nonzeroes in order to reflect that mispredictions on larger matrices are more costly. Clearly, RCM is beneficial for most, but not all matrices, and the classifier correctly predicts this in almost all cases. Furthermore, applying RCM when it is not needed is very costly. While we used a slow sequential code, based on the fastest parallel implementation of RCM [1], reordering takes roughly as much time as 300 SpMV iterations. About 14% of the instances do not benefit from RCM, and in these cases, using our system saves this cost. These savings could be increased further by training the classifier to suggest the original ordering if the gain from RCM is very small.

We provide detailed individual performance and prediction data for the large matrices in Table 2. The results show that even in case of mispredictions, the performance loss is rarely more than 10%.

Table 2. Size, prediction, and performance in GFLOP/s for all large instances used in the experiments. The better of the original/RCM performance is marked in green (prediction correct), blue (prediction wrong but performance difference is less than 5%), or red (prediction wrong and higher difference).

Matrix	Rows/Columns	Nonzeroes	Prediction	Epyc 7763 ORIG	Epyc 7763 RCM	Epyc 7302P ORIG	Epyc 7302P RCM	Epyc 7413 ORIG	Epyc 7413 RCM	Epyc 7601 ORIG	Epyc 7601 RCM	Xeon 8360Y ORIG	Xeon 8360Y RCM	Xeon 6130 ORIG	Xeon 6130 RCM
Suitesparse															
mycielskian17	98,303	100,245,742	RCM	25.25		3.77		21.89		17.51	16.86	22.14		27.38	
delaunay_n24	16,777,216	100,663,202	RCM	10.80		2.31		7.14		4.49		6.33		15.93	
europe_osm	50,912,018	108,109,320	RCM	7.59		1.23		5.55		3.09		4.89		10.35	
ML_Geer	1,504,002	110,686,677	RCM	32.72		3.67		24.55		19.45		23.21	21.91		27.14
hollywood-2009	1,139,905	113,891,327	RCM	23.63		3.81		25.81		13.57		16.29		26.62	
Flan_1565	1,564,794	114,165,372	RCM	1.84		0.45		1.11		2.18		2.68		4.44	
kmer_V2a	55,042,369	117,217,600	RCM	31.82	31.53	3.69	3.68	23.88		19.47		19.61		26.59	26.53
Cube_Coup_dt0	2,164,760	124,406,070	RCM	26.10		3.62		22.67		14.89		18.81		25.3	25.02
Cube_Coup_dt6	2,164,760	124,406,070	RCM	29.48		3.67		24.82		19.01		21.58		26.28	
rgg_n_2_23_s0	8,388,608	127,002,786	RCM	30.04	29.21	3.68	3.67	24.92		19.12		20.93		26.39	26.39
Bump_2911	2,911,419	127,729,899	RCM	24.07		3.67		25.38		19.05	18.90	22.19		26.12	
vas_stokes_4M	4,382,246	131,577,616	RCM	26.61	26.09	3.65	3.64	26.38		16.80		19.15	18.96	25.76	
kmer_U1a	67,716,231	138,778,562	RCM	1.70		0.43		1.13		2.08		2.61		4.39	
mawi_201512020030	68,863,315	143,414,960	RCM	10.15		1.56		8.58		5.22		5.40		11.90	
kron_g500-logn21	2,097,152	182,082,942	RCM	28.68		2.00		23.47		6.07		10.39		26.34	
indochina-2004	7,414,866	194,109,311	ORIG	25.65	26.24		3.64	25.57	26.66		16.95	20.97	21.04	25.31	
nlpkkt160	8,345,600	225,422,112	RCM	29.51		3.61		26.57	22.72	17.6	17.54	20.57		25.62	25.53
com-Orkut	3,072,441	234,370,166	RCM	27.8	27.61	1.32		23.11		3.49		8.89		25.49	25.35
rgg_n_2_24_s0	16,777,216	265,114,400	RCM	29.73	29.32	3.64		25.49		14.26		20.73	18.92	25.15	24.97
mawi_201512020130	128,568,730	270,234,840	RCM	9.41		1.56		8.96		5.20		5.36		12.15	
HV15R	2,017,169	283,073,458	RCM	28.27		3.71		27.28	26.79	19.43		23.30	21.85	26.58	26.52
kmer_P1a	139,353,211	297,829,984	RCM	1.85		0.46		1.91		2.23		2.44		4.05	
uk-2002	18,520,486	298,113,762	ORIG		25.78		3.55	22.83	27.84		13.88		17.40		23.98
mycielskian18	196,607	300,933,832	RCM	26.82		3.89		25.08	25.63	17.36	16.66	20.31		26.81	
Queen_4147	4,147,110	316,548,962	RCM	29.81		3.71		27.00	25.48	19.33		22.07	20.52	26.29	
stokes	11,449,533	349,321,980	RCM	27.20		3.62	3.59	21.71		16.36	16.15	19.53	17.61	25.70	
kmer_A2a	170,728,175	360,585,172	RCM	1.97		0.45		2.22		2.20		2.49		4.14	
nlpkkt200	16,240,000	440,225,632	RCM	27.47		3.67	3.67	25.69		17.37		20.86	19.73	25.63	25.57
kmer_V1r	214,005,017	465,410,904	RCM	4.30		0.78		3.82		3.15		2.85		5.46	
mawi_201512020330	226,196,185	480,047,894	RCM	9.83		1.59		8.76		5.04		5.31		11.29	
arabic-2005	22,744,080	639,999,458	ORIG		27.09		3.65	24.23	25.23		16.22	18.70			24.89
nlpkkt240	27,993,600	774,472,352	RCM	27.15	27.07	3.66		25.57	23.83	17.37		20.86	20.66	25.61	25.56
mycielskian19	393,215	903,194,710	RCM	28.13		3.94		26.06	19.88	17.21	16.29	18.70		26.51	
uk-2005	39,459,925	936,364,282	ORIG		23.51		3.54		14.20		14.18	16.25		24.22	
webbase-2001	118,142,155	1,019,903,190	ORIG		17.22		2.61	19.28	26.43		9.18	11.11		22.42	20.95
it-2004	41,291,594	1,150,725,436	ORIG		25.57		3.62		3.76		16.04	18.52		25.35	
GAP-twitter	61,578,415	1,468,364,884	RCM	2.45		0.60		1.43		2.19		3.23		5.73	
twitter7	41,652,230	1,468,365,182	RCM	2.49		0.62		1.47		2.18		3.26		5.99	
GAP-web	50,636,151	1,930,292,948	ORIG		25.23		3.58		24.33		12.68	17.17			24.90
sk-2005	50,636,154	1,949,412,601	ORIG		25.10		3.59		13.13		12.99	16.17			24.88
Heart meshes															
heart05_dt0100_fv	7,205,076	107,994,304	RCM	26.90		3.51		24.71		14.12		18.73	18.11	24.53	
Lynx68	6,811,350	111,560,826	RCM	10.13		0.82		7.51		3.32		4.70		20.39	
Lynx144	14,430,318	238,881,092	RCM	3.11		0.71		2.70		2.16		3.80		8.92	
heart06_dt0100_fv	23,595,379	357,427,713	RCM	27.56	27.33	3.47	3.44	23.33		13.80		17.27		24.44	
Lynx297	29,731,110	495,532,182	RCM	2.39		0.65		1.37		2.21		3.42		6.15	
heart07_dt0100_fv	55,603,164	846,710,472	RCM		25.18	3.45	3.42	24.00		13.78		16.46		24.41	
Lynx649	64,950,632	1,087,205,422	RCM	1.94		0.65		1.14		1.98		3.18		5.26	
Lynx1151	115,187,228	1,934,489,424	RCM	1.89		0.63		1.09		2.23		3.04		4.93	
Graphs															
graph500-scale22-ef16	1,243,072	126,926,600	RCM	22.03		3.96	3.83	26.97	25.77	9.97		13.15		26.71	26.16
graph500-scale22-ef16	2,393,285	256,388,016	RCM	28.51		2.95		26.16		8.16		12.65		26.71	26.44
delicious-ti	33,777,768	301,183,605	RCM	3.51		0.86		1.97		2.50		3.41		7.03	
delicious-ui	33,778,221	301,186,579	RCM	6.47		1.29		4.81		4.47		5.32		10.94	
delicious-ut	4,512,099	301,186,579	RCM	28.25		3.70		23.78		12.17	10.98	16.59		25.44	
bag-pubmed	8,200,000	483,450,157	RCM	28.77	28.23	3.90	3.88	26.71	25.76	17.93	16.81	18.70		26.75	26.64
graph500-scale23-ef16	4,606,314	517,002,820	RCM	26.34		2.23		22.97		6.44		11.25		26.22	26.00
graph500-scale24-ef16	8,860,450	1,041,047,372	RCM	19.98		1.75		14.72		5.58		10.03		24.52	
graph500-scale25-ef16	17,043,780	2,093,869,792	RCM	12.58		1.50		9.63	8.15	4.95		7.78		18.75	

6 Conclusions

We have presented a set of order-dependent features which complement existing order-invariant features that have previously been introduced in SpMV performance prediction. We used these features to design a highly accurate classifier and tested it on a set of large instances.

Since there is substantial synergy between 2D SpMV algorithms and RCM reorderings, for most instances, using both yields the best performance. This effect is due to the potential load imbalance caused by RCM, which does not affect the 2D method. Thus, the largest gains are not so much in choosing the faster reordering option but in avoiding expensive RCM computations when they are not needed.

Our analysis has only targeted CPUs. However, high quality reorderings have been shown to be at least as important for SpMV performance on GPUs since their caches tend to be smaller and the memory access latency tends to be higher [12]. Since our system can be used to make predictions for GPUs as well, we will evaluate the accuracy of the system on a variety of GPU architectures in the future.

References

1. Azad, A., Jacquelin, M., Buluç, A., Ng, E.G.: The reverse Cuthill-McKee algorithm in distributed-memory. In: 2017 IEEE International Parallel and Distributed Processing Symposium (IPDPS), pp. 22–31. IEEE (2017)
2. Bell, N., Garland, M.: Efficient sparse matrix-vector multiplication on CUDA. Technical report, Citeseer (2008)
3. Breiman, L.: Random forests. Mach. Learn. **45**(1), 5–32 (2001)
4. Chen, T., Guestrin, C.: XGBoost: a scalable tree boosting system. In: ACM SIGKDD International Conference on Knowledge Discovery and Data Mining, pp. 785–794 (2016)
5. Cuthill, E., McKee, J.: Reducing the bandwidth of sparse symmetric matrices. In: Proceedings of the 1969 24th National Conference. ACM '69, pp. 157–172. Association for Computing Machinery, New York, NY, USA (1969). https://doi.org/10.1145/800195.805928
6. Davis, T.A., Hu, Y.: The University of Florida sparse matrix collection. ACM Trans. Math. Softw. **38**(1), 1:1–1:25 (2011)
7. Dhandhania, S., Deodhar, A., Pogorelov, K., Biswas, S., Langguth, J.: Explaining the performance of supervised and semi-supervised methods for automated sparse matrix format selection. In: 50th International Conference on Parallel Processing Workshop, pp. 1–10 (2021)
8. Dongarra, J., Luszczek, P., Heroux, M.: HPCG technical specification. Sandia National Laboratories, Sandia Report SAND2013-8752 (2013)
9. Kunegis, J.: KONECT - The Koblenz network collection. In: Proceedings of International Conference on on World Wide Web Companion, pp. 1343–1350 (2013). http://dl.acm.org/citation.cfm?id=2488173
10. Langguth, J., Arevalo, H., Hustad, K.G., Cai, X.: Towards detailed real-time simulations of cardiac arrhythmia. In: 2019 Computing in Cardiology (CinC), p. 1. IEEE (2019)

11. Langguth, J., Sourouri, M., Lines, G.T., Baden, S.B., Cai, X.: Scalable heterogeneous CPU-GPU computations for unstructured tetrahedral meshes. IEEE Micro **35**(4), 6–15 (2015)
12. Langguth, J., Wu, N., Chai, J., Cai, X.: Parallel performance modeling of irregular applications in cell-centered finite volume methods over unstructured tetrahedral meshes. J. Parallel Distrib. Comput. **76**, 120–131 (2015). https://doi.org/10.1016/j.jpdc.2014.10.005
13. Markov, Z., Russell, I.: An introduction to the WEKA data mining system. ACM SIGCSE Bull. **38**(3), 367–368 (2006)
14. Merrill, D., Garland, M.: Merge-based sparse matrix-vector multiplication (SpMV) using the CSR storage format. In: ACM SIGPLAN Symposium on Principles and Practice of Parallel Programming (2016)
15. Murphy, R.C., Wheeler, K.B., Barrett, B.W., Ang, J.A.: Introducing the graph 500. Cray Users Group (CUG) **19**, 45–74 (2010)
16. Page, L., Brin, S., Motwani, R., Winograd, T.: The PageRank citation ranking: bringing order to the web. Technical report, Stanford InfoLab (1999)
17. Papadimitriou, C.H.: The NP-completeness of the bandwidth minimization problem. Computing **16**(3), 263–270 (1976)
18. Pedregosa, F., et al.: Scikit-learn: machine learning in Python. J. Mach. Learn. Res. **12**, 2825–2830 (2011)
19. Pichel, J.C., Singh, D.E., Carretero, J.: Reordering algorithms for increasing locality on multicore processors. In: 2008 10th IEEE International Conference on High Performance Computing and Communications, pp. 123–130. IEEE (2008)
20. Sanders, P., Schulz, C.: Think locally, act globally: highly balanced graph partitioning. In: Bonifaci, V., Demetrescu, C., Marchetti-Spaccamela, A. (eds.) SEA 2013. LNCS, vol. 7933, pp. 164–175. Springer, Heidelberg (2013). https://doi.org/10.1007/978-3-642-38527-8_16
21. Toledo, S.: Improving the memory-system performance of sparse-matrix vector multiplication. IBM J. Res. Dev. **41**(6), 711–725 (1997)
22. Wu, Z., Pan, S., Chen, F., Long, G., Zhang, C., Philip, S.Y.: A comprehensive survey on graph neural networks. IEEE Trans. Neural Netw. Learn. Syst. **32**(1), 4–24 (2020)
23. Zhao, Y., Li, J., Liao, C., Shen, X.: Bridging the gap between deep learning and sparse matrix format selection. In: ACM SIGPLAN Symposium on Principles and Practice of Parallel Programming, pp. 94–108 (2018)
24. Zhao, Y., Zhou, W., Shen, X., Yiu, G.: Overhead-conscious format selection for SpMV-based applications. In: IEEE International Parallel and Distributed Processing Symposium, pp. 950–959, May 2018

Analyzing One-Sided Communication Using Memory Access Diagrams

Olaf Krzikalla[1]([envelope]), Arne Rempke[1], and Ralph Müller-Pfefferkorn[2]

[1] German Aerospace Center, Dresden, Germany
{olaf.krzikalla,arne.rempke}@dlr.de
[2] Technische Universität, Dresden, Germany
ralph.mueller-pfefferkorn@tu-dresden.de

Abstract. In recent years, one-sided communication has emerged as an alternative to message-based communication to improve the scalability of distributed programs. Decoupling communication and synchronization in such programs allows for more asynchronous execution of processes, but introduces new challenges to ensure program correctness and efficiency. The concept of memory access diagrams presented in this paper opens up a new analysis perspective to the programmer. Our approach visualizes the interaction of synchronous, asynchronous, and remote memory accesses. We present an interactive tool that can be used to perform a postmortem analysis of a distributed program execution. The tool supports hybrid parallel programs, shared MPI windows, and GASPI communication operations. In two application studies taken from the European aerospace industry we illustrate the usefulness of memory access diagrams for visualizing and understanding the logical causes of programming errors, performance flaws, and to find optimization opportunities.

Keywords: One-Sided Communication · PGAS Programming Models · Memory Access Analysis

1 Introduction

Today, distributed applications can create a shared global address space across nodes of an HPC system by using asynchronous, one-sided memory accesses to remote memory. This global address space has given rise to new programming models like one-sided MPI or GASPI [1], which allow new ways to develop powerful applications, but also introduces new challenges to ensure program correctness and efficiency.

In a one-sided communication model a process can directly access memory areas of another target process. For the target process, such accesses are transparent, leading to a decoupling of data transfer and process synchronization. In addition, these accesses can even be asynchronous to the executing process, allowing an overlap of computation and communication. However, the potential interaction of direct, asynchronous and remote memory accesses to the same memory region increases the software complexity. The software developer must ensure race free memory accesses across the entire process space. On the other

© The Author(s), under exclusive license to Springer Nature Switzerland AG 2024
D. Zeinalipour et al. (Eds.): Euro-Par 2023 Workshops, LNCS 14351, pp. 147–159, 2024.
https://doi.org/10.1007/978-3-031-50684-0_12

hand, process synchronization must not be stricter than necessary, otherwise the performance and scalability benefits of one-sided communication will be lost.

The paper contributes to the systematic understanding of parallel distributed applications that use one-sided, asynchronous communication. The introduced visualization concept opens up a new analysis perspective to the programmer. We present an interactive visualization tool for the memory access analysis of GASPI programs with an extension for MPI shared windows. Our tool supports the analysis of hybrid parallel programs, i.e. programs combining distributed and shared-memory parallelization. Two application studies on the analysis of industrial codes from the European aerospace industry complete the paper.

2 Terms, Operations, and Execution Model

Throughout this paper, we distinguish between two types of memory accesses. A *direct memory access* is executed synchronously by a thread, usually by a CPU instruction. It always accesses process-local memory. An *asynchronous memory access* is caused by a one-sided communication operation and is usually part of a data transfer between processes. It can access local memory as well as remote memory. In addition, we use the term *remote memory access* for asynchronous memory accesses to the local memory of one process caused by a communication operation of another process.

A one-sided communication operation copies data from the memory of one process to the memory of another process. It is usually accompanied by synchronization operations. For example, the `write_notify` operation specified by the GASPI standard copies data from local source memory to target remote memory. It also sets a notification flag on the remote side signaling the completion of the data transfer. Source and remote memory reside in dedicated regions. In GASPI these regions are called *segments*, in MPI *windows*. Asynchronous memory accesses can only occur to these regions.

We model a program execution as a *task graph*. A task executed by a thread represents either a direct memory access or a communication operation. We compute the synchronization relations between threads and processes using a replay algorithm. This algorithm replays the recorded synchronization operations in an arbitrary order respecting the synchronization relations of the operations. As proved in [7] this leads to a logically sound task graph, which includes all happens-before relations across threads and processes.

In addition, the task graph is extended with *virtual* tasks. Virtual tasks are not assigned to a thread and therefore run in parallel to all threads. However, they are forked by thread tasks or other virtual tasks and eventually joined by thread tasks. Figure 1 shows a task graph of a `write_notify` operation initiated by process 1, that writes data to the memory of process 2. The `write_notify` call is modeled as the task WN. It forks three virtual tasks R_L, W_R, and W_F. R_L represents the asynchronous read from the local memory. W_R represents the remote writing to the memory of process 2. Due to the data dependency, we model R_L as happening before W_R. The third virtual task forked by `write_notify` is the

notification task W_F. It sets a flag on the remote process signaling the completion of the write access. So W_R happens before W_F. The task WT represents a
call to an operation waiting for the completion of the local asynchronous read.
Note that this task waits only for the local read task, but not for the remote write
task. The remote side waits for the data to arrive. The corresponding operation
is modeled by the NW task. This task is triggered, when the flag is set by W_F.

Virtual tasks can be used to model all kinds of one-sided communication and
synchronization operations. Many examples for the modeling of MPI, GASPI,
and openShmem operations are given in [6]. Virtual tasks play a central role
in our analysis approach, because they abstract from concrete APIs while accurately modeling the logical relationships of events.

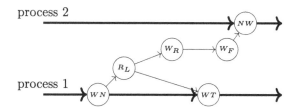

Fig. 1. Virtual tasks of a `write_notify` operation.

3 Visualization Concept and Realization

In programs with one-sided communication, the interactions between direct
memory accesses and remote memory accesses form the central element of communication between processes. In order to analyze these interactions we have
developed a visualization concept based on memory access diagrams.

A memory access diagram is a two-dimensional Cartesian coordinate system.
It represents the course of the memory accesses related to the execution of a
particular thread. The x-axis denotes the program time of the visualized thread
as logical time steps. A logical time step is either a direct memory access or
another event represented in the task graph (e.g. a synchronization operation).
The y-axis denotes the local address space of the process to which the visualized
thread belongs. Each direct memory access is represented as a vertical line, which
marks the access interval at the time of the access. The access type is determined
by color: read accesses are marked green and write accesses red (Fig. 2).

Figure 2 illustrates this visualization concept. It displays the direct memory
accesses to the **source** and **target** arrays as they happen over time. During
each logical time step one direct memory access is performed.

Asynchronous memory accesses, like direct memory accesses, have an address
interval and an access type. However, unlike direct memory accesses, such a memory access has a potentially very large address interval. A single memory access
to individual data words within this interval is not represented by our diagrams.

```
1    int* source = 0x10;
2    int* target = 0x20;
3    for (int i=0; i<4; ++i)
4    {
5       target[i] = source[i];
6    }
```

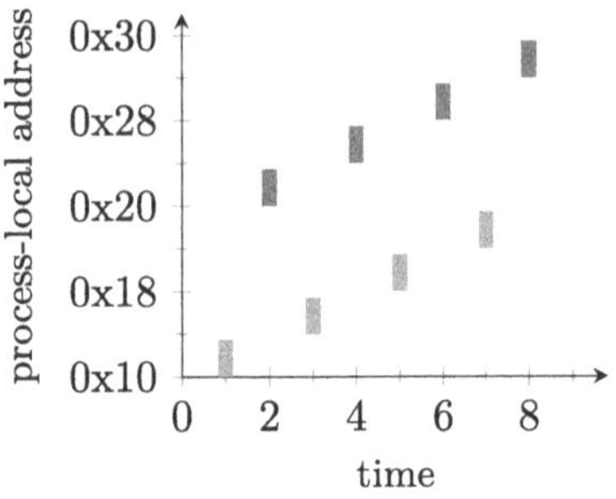

Fig. 2. Visualization of direct memory accesses in a memory access diagram. (Color figure online)

Instead, each memory access by a communication operation is always represented as access to the entire address interval. This interval is plotted directly on the y-axis of the diagram.

Specifying a concrete logical time for such a memory access from the point of view of the visualized thread is usually not possible, since it occurs asynchronously to the thread execution. However, both the earliest time at which the access can take place and the latest time at which the access can take place can be specified. Thus, our diagrams draw asynchronous memory accesses as rectangles. The width of the rectangle represents the time range, at which the shown memory access can happen. The height represents the address range, and the color of the rectangle represents the access type again.

Figure 3 illustrates this concept. The vertical sequence of tasks in the task graph are executed by a thread. The first task represents a loop similar to the one of Fig. 2. It performs four direct memory writes to address 0x10-0x20. The second task is a write operation, which transfers the data just written to another process. This operation initiates an asynchronous read access – the virtual task R – to the local memory at address 0x10-0x20. Depending on R is the asynchronous write access W (see also Fig. 1). Asynchronous accesses initiated by GASPI operations are specified by the GASPI segment id seg, an offset o into seg, and a byte size sz. For remote accesses the target rank r is added. The third task of the thread again represents a loop, this time writing to address 0x0-0x10. The fourth task represents a wait operation, which synchronizes with the local read of the former write operation. The final task again represents a loop, this time reading from address 0x0-0x10. The green rectangle in the associated memory access diagram represents the asynchronous read access from the perspective of the thread. This access starts with the execution of the write operation, and it lasts until the wait operation is executed. During that time, all memory locations inside the rectangle can be read by the asynchronous read access. The representation as a rectangle corresponds to the usual specifications of one-sided communication operations, since these specifications neither specify any access order nor further timing constraints.

In order to visualize all kinds of asynchronous memory accesses in the described way we have generalized the computation of the time range of the

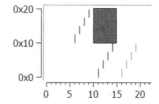

Fig. 3. Task graph and corresponding memory access diagram of a thread. (Color figure online)

access as seen by a particular thread based on the task graph of the program execution. An asynchronous memory access starts with the latest thread task, which has a happens-before relation to the corresponding virtual task. And it ends with the first thread task, to which this virtual task has a happens-before relation.

Figure 4 visualizes both an asynchronous local read access and a remote write access of process 1. Two processes, each consisting of one thread, exchange data via `write_notify`. The virtual notification tasks are specified by the target rank r, the target segment s and the flag id f. Both processes have organized its memory in the same way: the region from 0x0-0x10 is only locally accessed, the region from 0x10-0x20 is locally written and then sent to the remote process, and the region from 0x20-0x30 acts as receive buffer, from which the data received is later read. The green rectangle in the memory access diagram represents the local asynchronous read access similar to Fig. 3. The red rectangle represents the remote write access, which is caused by the other process. The red arrow in the task graph outlines how this remote access is timed in relation to process 1. From the point of view of process 1 the remote write access can occur as soon as the barrier before the data exchange is entered (`barrier(E)`). And it is not finished until the corresponding notification flag is received by the `notify_reset` operation, which corresponds to the NW task in Fig. 1.

process 1   process 2

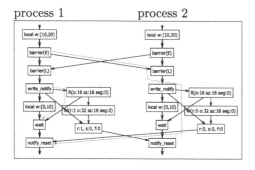
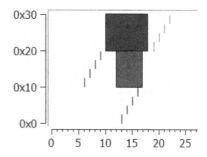

Fig. 4. Representation of a local asynchronous read access and a remote write access to the memory of process 1. (Color figure online)

The tool presented in this paper consists of two components. The recording tool traces a program execution. The analysis and visualization tool evaluates the recorded program execution after its completion.

The recording tool is implemented on top of the dynamic instrumentation API PIN [10]. We trace function calls including the values of their arguments and the return result, and we use the fine-grained instrumentation capabilities of PIN to record the addresses of direct memory accesses. With our implementation, practical applications are slowed down by a factor of 2–10 due to instrumentation and recording, and a native 10-second run of a CFD program on 24 processes over a typical mesh, for example, will generate a total of 10 GB of analysis data [5]. However, memory access patterns do not usually depend on the length of the program run. Also, the number of processes usually does not affect the interaction between local computation and communication, only the amount of data exchanged. Therefore, when applying our analysis, one should limit oneself to a rather short program run with few processes. In our experience, this is also perfectly sufficient to obtain the desired insights.

The second component of our tool suite is the analysis and visualization tool. It reads a recorded program execution and displays a task graph for all threads of all processes. The task graph provides a global view of the program execution, including its synchronization relationships. From there, a user can select a thread and view its memory access diagram. The memory access diagram provides a view of the process-local memory as observed by the selected thread. The user may zoom in, and hide address ranges. By default, address ranges without accesses are hidden. Moreover, our tool automatically checks for data races. A memory access diagram is well suited for visualizing such a race, since races are intuitively recognizable as an overlap of multiple memory accesses.

Figure 5 shows a case very similar to Fig. 3. The only difference is that the direct memory accesses in the third task have been shifted by 8 bytes. In this case the memory from address 0x10-0x18 is written by direct memory accesses, while at the same time the write operation reads data from this region. This constitutes a data race, which can also be recognized by the two direct write accesses inside the green rectangle.

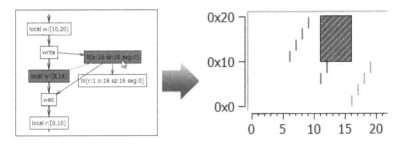

Fig. 5. Selection of a task representing an asynchronous memory access that causes a data race. (Color figure online)

Figure 5 also demonstrates the interactive capabilities of our tool to understand the relationships between program synchronization and memory access patterns. All tasks involved in data races are marked red in the task graph display. Red lines are drawn to the tasks representing conflicting memory accesses. The user can click on such a task to switch to the memory accesses diagram. The selected memory access is then shown hatched. Thus, a user who clicks on the mouse pointer position shown in the task graph of Fig. 5 will see the right memory access diagram with the hatched asynchronous read access.

The interaction also works the other way around. A user can select an asynchronous memory access in the diagram to see its temporal embedding in the displayed thread. The left part of Fig. 6 shows a memory access diagram of a stencil code using double buffering. Clicking at the shown mouse pointer position in the remote write access leads to the task graph on the right side. In this case, not only is the access event highlighted in gray in the task graph, but also the paths to those tasks are marked blue, that lead to the logical time limit of the memory access with respect to the displayed thread. This allows you to analyze asynchronous memory accesses not only in the context of other memory accesses, but also in the context of the triggering and synchronizing functions.

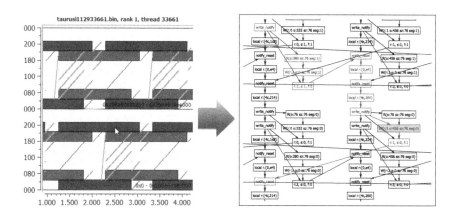

Fig. 6. Selection of a remote memory access – the causal relationship to the operations of the thread associated with the memory access diagram (here: the left thread) becomes clear. (Color figure online)

4   Application Studies

Case studies on the application of memory access diagrams to small and commonly used code patterns are explained in [5]. In this paper we describe the analysis of two industry codes that we have evaluated using our trace and visualization tools. Both codes originate from the European aerospace industry.

4.1 Checking Correctness and Performance During Development - Spliss

Spliss [8] is a linear solver library, which supports a wide range of linear operators typically used in computational fluid dynamics (CFD) applications. This includes sparse block matrices of variable block sizes and different scalar types as well as matrix-free operators. It is actively developed at the German Aerospace Center (DLR) and used by various research institutions and industry partners.

Since a key design goal of Spliss is HPC efficiency and scalability, a one-sided asynchronous communication strategy using GASPI was implemented. During the development we used memory access diagrams to ensure, that the communication patterns behave as intended, and to spot optimization opportunities.

Figure 7 shows the memory access diagram of a Jacobi solver run in Spliss. Only accesses to the memory area of the halo segment of the vectors were traced, since the local part is never accessed by asynchronous or remote memory accesses. Before timestamp ~230 some initialization accesses occur. At ~230 the first Jacobi iteration starts. From then on, a regular pattern is visible with alternating direct and remote accesses.

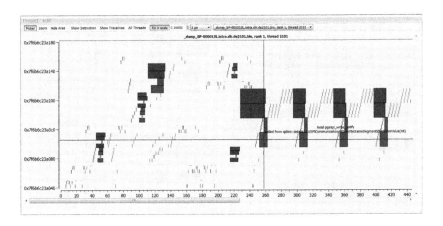

Fig. 7. Memory access diagram of the halo segment of a Jacobi solver run in Spliss.

What stands out during the iterations is the rather short duration of asynchronous read accesses and the large temporal gaps from those accesses to the following direct write accesses. This points to a very tightly coupled synchronization pattern. By clicking in one of the rectangles representing such an asynchronous read access (in the figure the cross-hair is already in the right place) the user can switch to the task graph view to examine the reason for the synchronization pattern (Fig. 8). In the task graph view the task representing the clicked read access is marked gray and the synchronization relations to the formerly watched thread are highlighted by blue arrows.

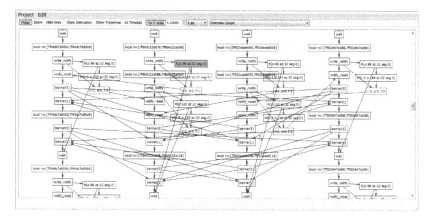

Fig. 8. Task graph for a Jacobi solver run in Spliss showing the blue marked synchronization path of an asynchronous memory access. (Color figure online)

The actually intended synchronization task for the examined read access is the `wait` task at the very bottom of the task graph view (the one which is directly connected to the gray marked read task). However, the blue synchronization path joins the watched thread already before the next direct memory access due to a global barrier (`barrier(E)`: enter barrier, `barrier(L)`: leave barrier). It turned out, that this particular barrier was not necessary during the solver loop. After we removed it, the memory access pattern changed as depicted in Fig. 9. In this diagram the temporal gaps have disappeared. On the other hand there are still no overlaps of direct and asynchronous memory accesses proofing that the change doesn't cause a data race.

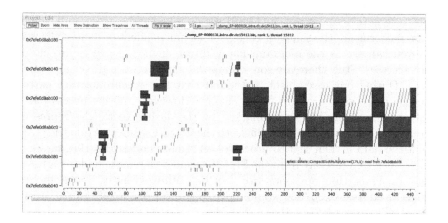

Fig. 9. Memory access diagram of the halo segment of a Jacobi solver run after the removal of a gratuitous barrier.

This case demonstrates one strategy to utilize our memory access diagrams to find optimization opportunities. The developer can look for temporal gaps between asynchronous and direct memory accesses to the same addresses. By closing such gaps communication operations get more time to finish before a process actually waits for the corresponding data. Thus, the program becomes more asynchronous and hence can scale better.

In the explained example the optimization improved the performance of the solver loop by up to 30% even for few processes, since an entire global barrier could be removed. However, for this kind of optimization one should usually expect measurable improvements especially for many processes. For instance, a similar optimization approach of a stencil code only significantly increased the parallel efficiency above 256 processes [4]. A method for automatically finding such temporal gaps is also described there. To reduce the search space, such gaps are only searched for along the critical path.

4.2   Assessing Memory Accesses of an Established Code - HYDRA

Rolls-Royce's CFD solver framework HYDRA [9] uses a pure distributed parallelization scheme. Our task was to assess an evaluation version, which uses a one-sided communication scheme. In that version node-local communication is organized by shared MPI windows. Therefore, we have extended our tool suite to handle direct memory accesses to remote process memory. We have done this by mapping tasks for direct memory accesses to shared MPI windows to the process address space of the just visualized thread and handle them as virtual tasks. In this way, the synchronization relationships to other tasks are preserved.

Figure 10 shows a memory access diagram of a sample HYDRA run. Data in the GASPI segment memory is sent and received by processes from remote nodes. Data in the SHAN segment memory is directly read and written by other processes running on the same node. Those accesses still appear as rectangles similar to remote accesses to the GASPI segment, since the access and synchronization patterns are the same for each process independent of its node location.

As you can see in the diagram, many direct memory accesses are close to remote accesses. Still, there are some temporal gaps between direct and remote accesses. During our assessment, we found that the synchronization patterns that cause these gaps are difficult to change. However, another access pattern caught our attention. The spots marked by the dashed rectangles represent a copy operation from the SHAN segment to the GASPI segment. From the GASPI segment the data is then sent to processes on remote nodes. But this data could also be transferred directly from the SHAN segment to remote nodes via GASPI operations. Thus, the copy operation can be optimized away. Then the green rectangle at address 0x6d7000 would move to address 0x2ba285fe3020, because the data will be read from there. The diagram also shows, that in this case the GASPI remote access represented by that green rectangle needs a stricter synchronization. This prevents an overlap and hence a data race with the direct write accesses to address 0x2ba285fe3020 starting at timestamp ~140.

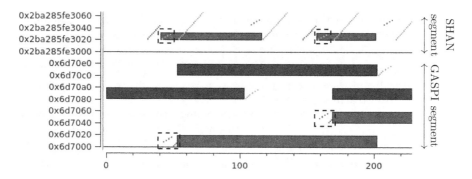

Fig. 10. Memory access diagram of halo segments of a HYDRA run. The dashed rectangles mark a copy operation that can be saved.

As a result of our assessment we have shown, that there are no data races in HYDRA regarding the interaction on direct memory accesses, accesses to shared MPI windows and remote asynchronous accesses. We have also identified several optimization opportunities. The asynchronicity of memory accesses could be increased on several occasions. In addition, a superfluous copy operation in the solver loop has been identified.

5   Related Work

Memory access analysis tools are used for a wide variety of problems. We limit our brief overview to tools targeting distributed platforms and visualization tools.

Data race detection tools that include direct memory accesses in their analysis, are *MC-Checker* [2] and *UPC-Thrille* [11]. *MC-Checker* checks one-sided MPI communication operations; and *UPC-Thrille* checks UPC programs. A performance analysis tool for MPI programs is described in [14], which traces memory accesses and provides a dataflow and dependency graph.

A visualization tool for memory accesses is described in [13]. It focuses on visualizing performance characteristics of direct memory accesses. The space-time diagrams used are very similar to our visualization concept. *MemAxes* [3] uses a radial layout to visualize the performance of direct memory accesses.

To the best of our knowledge, our tool is the only one that combines direct, asynchronous, and remote memory accesses in its visualization and analysis.

6   Conclusion

This paper extends the portfolio of available analysis methods for distributed programs with one-sided communication. The introduced tool offers new possibilities to examine all memory accesses in their respective logical context and draw conclusions about the correctness and efficiency of the program. The interactive integration of memory access diagrams with the task graph model makes it possible to study the logical relationships in a program in detail. The visualization can also contribute to a better understanding of the often complex interrelationships of threads and processes in development meetings, documentation or even in teaching.

Our tool combines the analysis of local memory accesses, accesses via shared MPI windows, and GASPI operations. However, the underlying model is API-independent. One-sided MPI operations can easily be supported and will be integrated as the need arises. We expect the popularity of one-sided communication to continue to grow as a remote completion operation similar to GASPIs `write_notify` is integrated into MPI [12].

The recent addition of shared MPI windows to our tool suggests another improvement. In principle, this method can also be used to examine shared memory programs. The visualization can reveal basically the same information about the access patterns of a shared memory program. Overlaps would still indicate data races, and it would still be important to have as few gaps as possible between memory accesses of the watched thread and the memory accesses from other threads to the same region.

Acknowledgements. We would like to thank the Center for Information Services and High Performance Computing (ZIH) Dresden, esp. Prof. Wolfgang Nagel for supporting this work. We would also like to thank the German Aerospace Center (DLR) and Rolls-Royce for their support and the permission to publish analysis results of their codes.

References

1. Alrutz, T., et al.: GASPI – a partitioned global address space programming interface. In: Keller, R., Kramer, D., Weiss, J.-P. (eds.) Facing the Multicore-Challenge III. LNCS, vol. 7686, pp. 135–136. Springer, Heidelberg (2013). https://doi.org/10.1007/978-3-642-35893-7_18
2. Chen, Z., Dinan, J., et al.: Mc-checker: detecting memory consistency errors in MPI one-sided applications. In: SC14: International Conference for High Performance Computing, Networking, Storage and Analysis. pp. 499–510, November 2014
3. Gimenez, A.A., Gamblin, T., et al.: Memaxes: visualization and analytics for characterizing complex memory performance behaviors. IEEE Trans. Visual. Comput. Graph. 1 (2017)
4. Herold, C., et al.: Optimizing one-sided communication of parallel applications using critical path methods. In: 2017 IEEE International Parallel and Distributed Processing Symposium Workshops (IPDPSW), pp. 567–576, May 2017
5. Krzikalla, O.: Neue Ansätze zur Speicherzugriffsanalyse paralleler Anwendungen mit gemeinsam genutztem Adressraum. Ph.D. thesis, Technische Universität Dresden (2018)
6. Krzikalla, O., Knüpfer, A., et al.: On the modelling of one-sided communication systems. In: Proceedings of the 7th International Conference on PGAS Programming Models. Edinburgh, UK, pp. 41–53, October 2013

7. Krzikalla, O., Müller-Pfefferkorn, R., Nagel, W.E.: Synchronization debugging of hybrid parallel programs. In: Dutot, P.-F., Trystram, D. (eds.) Euro-Par 2016. LNCS, vol. 9833, pp. 37–50. Springer, Cham (2016). https://doi.org/10.1007/978-3-319-43659-3_3

8. Krzikalla, O., Rempke, A., Bleh, A., Wagner, M., Gerhold, T.: Spliss: a sparse linear system solver for transparent integration of emerging HPC technologies into CFD solvers and applications. In: Dillmann, A., Heller, G., Krämer, E., Wagner, C. (eds.) STAB/DGLR Symposium 2020. NNFMMD, vol. 151, pp. 635–645. Springer, Cham (2021). https://doi.org/10.1007/978-3-030-79561-0_60

9. Lapworth, L.: Hydra: a framework for collaborative CFD development. In: International Conference on Scientific and Engineering Computation, Singapore (2004)

10. Luk, C.K., et al.: Pin: building customized program analysis tools with dynamic instrumentation. In: Proceedings of the 2005 ACM SIGPLAN Conference on Programming Language Design and Implementation. PLDI '05, pp. 190–200. ACM, New York, NY, USA (2005)

11. Park, C.S.: Active testing: predicting and confirming concurrency bugs for concurrent and distributed memory parallel systems. Ph.D. thesis, EECS Department, University of California, Berkeley, December 2012

12. Sergent, M., Aitkaci, C.T., et al.: Efficient notifications for MPI one-sided applications. In: Proceedings of the 26th European MPI Users' Group Meeting. EuroMPI '19. Association for Computing Machinery, New York, NY, USA (2019)

13. Servat, H., Llort, G., González, J., Giménez, J., Labarta, J.: Low-overhead detection of memory access patterns and their time evolution. In: Träff, J.L., Hunold, S., Versaci, F. (eds.) Euro-Par 2015. LNCS, vol. 9233, pp. 57–69. Springer, Heidelberg (2015). https://doi.org/10.1007/978-3-662-48096-0_5

14. Subotic, V., Ferrer, R., Sancho, J.C., Labarta, J., Valero, M.: Quantifying the potential task-based dataflow parallelism in MPI applications. In: Jeannot, E., Namyst, R., Roman, J. (eds.) Euro-Par 2011. LNCS, vol. 6852, pp. 39–51. Springer, Heidelberg (2011). https://doi.org/10.1007/978-3-642-23400-2_5

The 1st International Workshop on Urgent Analytics for Distributed Computing (QUICKPAR 2023)

International Workshop on Urgent Analytics for Distributed Computing (QuickPar)

Workshop Description

Urgent Analytics refers to a category of time-sensitive scientific applications that utilize distributed data sources to accelerate the making of critical decisions. The overarching objective of managing urgent analytics, also known as Urgent Computing, is to foresee the outcome of scenarios early enough to prevent or mitigate the negative effects of critical situations. Abstractions and software stacks that can support data-driven reactive behaviors, i.e. determining what, where, and when data is collected and processed across the edge/cloud/HPC computing continuum, are lacking. The development of data-driven applications also necessitates programming abstractions and runtime systems that account for platform heterogeneity and the extreme unpredictability of data availability and quality. Such contributions have the potential to resolve the grand challenges in science, engineering, and society that face the world today.

QuickPar is a venue for scientific contributions that leverage the Computing Continuum to support urgent analytics applications. The standard use cases for this field are data-driven dynamic procedures that integrate knowledge from multiple data sources with distributed, large-scale computational models on demand.

The inaugural workshop (QuickPar 2023) was conducted in Limassol, Cyprus, for a half-day on August 28. This workshop was organized alongside the Euro-Par annual international conference. A pioneer of Urgent Computing delivered the workshop's keynote address, which was followed by three technical presentations. The program committee (PC) consisted of ten members with expertise in diverse facets of distributed systems, cyberinfrastructures, and urgent computing. The first edition of the workshop attracted an average of 15 enthusiastic participants.

This year, we received four articles for review from four different countries. Each submission received at least three single-blind from PC members. After a comprehensive peer-reviewing process, three articles (75 percent acceptance rate) were chosen for presentation at the workshop. The review process centered on the content of the papers, their innovative ideas, and their relevance to the field of urgent computing.

The accepted articles covered a wide variety of subjects, techniques, and applications, clearly demonstrating the breadth, depth, and expansion of the urgent computing discipline. Performance optimization for intelligent IoT applications, quantum computation applied to streaming data, and dynamic adaptation of urgent applications on heterogeneous systems were among the topics covered.

Finally, we thank the QuickPar 2023 Program Committee for their tireless efforts to ensure the success and high quality of this workshop. In addition, I would like to appreciate Euro-Par for hosting our community and the Euro-Par workshop chairs Dora Blanco Heras and Demetrius Zeinalipour for their assistance and support.

Organization

Program Chairs

Daniel Balouek   Inria, France
Manish Parashar   University of Utah, USA

Program Committee

Nick Brown	University of Edinburgh, UK
Helene Coullon	IMT Atlantique, Inria, France
Philip Davis	University of Utah, USA
Nicola Ferrier	Argonne National Laboratory, USA
Shadi Ibrahim	Inria, France
Georges Markomanolis	AMD, France
George Pallis	University of Cyprus, Cyprus
Patricia Stolf	IRIT, France
Christian Sicari	University of Messina, Italy
Remous-Aris Koutsiamanis	IMT Atlantique, Inria, France

.

A Framework for Performance Optimization of Internet of Things Applications

Osama Almurshed[1,2]($\boxtimes$), Souham Meshoul[3], Asmail Muftah[4],
Ashish Kumar Kaushal[5], Osama Almoghamis[6], Ioan Petri[1], Nitin Auluck[5],
and Omer Rana[1]

[1] Cardiff University, Cardiff, UK
almurshedo@cardiff.ac.uk,o.almurshed@psau.edu.sa
[2] Prince Sattam Bin Abdulaziz University, Al-Kharj, Kingdom of Saudi Arabia
[3] Princess Nourah Bint Abdulrahman University, Riyadh, Kingdom of Saudi Arabia
[4] Azzaytuna University, Tarhuna, Libya
[5] Indian Institute of Technology Ropar, Rupnagar, India
[6] King Saud University, Riyadh, Kingdom of Saudi Arabia

Abstract. A framework to support optimised application placement across the cloud-edge continuum is described, making use of the Optimized-Greedy Nominator Heuristic (EO-GNH). The framework can be employed across a range of different Internet of Things (IoT) applications, such as smart agriculture and healthcare. The framework uses asynchronous MapReduce and parallel meta-heuristics to support the management of IoT applications, focusing on metrics such as execution performance, resource utilization and system resilience. We evaluate EO-GNH using service quality achieved through real-time resource management, across multiple application domains. Performance analysis and optimisation of EO-GNH has also been carried out to demonstrate how it can be configured for use across different IoT usage contexts.

Keywords: Cancer Classification · Edge Computing · Industrial IoT · IoT Management · Meta-heuristics · Precision Agriculture · System Resilience

1 Introduction

An increasing demand for Internet of Things (IoT) technologies across various sectors, including agriculture, healthcare and industry, has heightened the necessity for effective data communication and processing. While cloud computing provides significant benefits, challenges persist in ensuring low latency and data privacy in IoT applications, particularly where bandwidth and power/energy are restricted. Edge computing provides a potential solution, extending cloud capabilities to embedded hardware systems such as single-board computers or user-owned (computational) acceleration devices.

As the IoT ecosystem evolves, there is an increasing demand for platforms that can handle complex applications, particularly those incorporating artificial intelligence (AI) and machine learning (ML). The integration of AI/ML

© The Author(s), under exclusive license to Springer Nature Switzerland AG 2024
D. Zeinalipour et al. (Eds.): Euro-Par 2023 Workshops, LNCS 14351, pp. 165–176, 2024.
https://doi.org/10.1007/978-3-031-50684-0_13

into IoT applications enhances their potential for optimizing processes utilising data acquired at the edge of a data network. This paper explores the use of an AI-based scheduling approach for managing intelligent IoT applications. An optimisation algorithm is used to reduce execution time and improve resource utilisation, referred to as the Enhanced Greedy Nominator Heuristic (EO-GNH). Integrated within the proposed IoT application management framework, EO-GNH aims to provide non-dominant solutions across delay, cost and risk factors. This strategy focuses on advancing one objective without compromising others.

Is EO-GNH adaptable to cross-domain characteristics and infrastructure configurations of IoT applications? We investigate this question within an IoT application landscape, forming the key contribution of this work. This paper is organized as follows: Sect. 2 discusses related work, providing context for our research. Section 3 describes our proposed Adaptive Platform for Edge-Cloud infrastructure. Section 4 explores the use of this framework within specific applications. Section 5 presents an evaluation of our proposed solution with concluding comments in Sect. 6.

2   Greedy Nominator Heuristic and Extensions

The Greedy Nominator Heuristic (GNH) is an optimization algorithm that addresses infrastructure deployments involving IoT, fog, and cloud computing environments [2]. GNH consists of several key components: a similarity function, max-heap, mappers, reducers, system controllers, and workers (described below). The similarity function, derived from TOPSIS [10], utilizes a context-dependent distance measure for comparing solutions derived from various optimization algorithms.

In GNH, mappers are assigned to specific nodes (labeled as *locations*), that process workflow functions and generate decision variables. When a placement request is made, mappers nominate potential nodes for deployment. A reducer then evaluates these nominations and selects the best nodes. This selection is repeated until the entire workflow is deployed. A greedy approach is applied in both the mapper and reducer stages, where the Euclidean distance similarity function is used as a heuristic to compare solutions to the ideal one. GNH adjusts to a variety of similarity functions, including cosine similarity [15] and fuzzy measures [17], so long as they can quantify the similarity between the ideal and explored solutions. To manage these solutions, a max-heap is employed. The max-heap is advantageous and allows quicker, more streamlined retrieval and removal of the solutions stored within it.

Max-heap is a binary tree structure which stores results from mappers and the reducer, ensuring that the maximum value is always at the root. Mappers calculate the similarity to an ideal solution for all locations using the norm-2 (euclidean distance) measure. The reducers then consolidate these results to select optimal deployment locations. Both mappers and reducers loop through the search space and update the max-heap.

The GNH system comprises a controller, which functions as the reducer, and workers that act as mappers, monitoring network performance and available computing resources at various locations, while the controller selects deployment locations from these options. This is implemented using Parsl [5], an asynchronous parallel programming library in Python, which can support execution on both high performance computing and edge resources.

The GNH has been used in intelligent IoT applications across diverse environments. For instance, in smart city applications, GNH demonstrated its capacity by autonomously deploying virtual functions across edge and cloud environments. This resulted in optimized resource usage, superior execution performance and significant cost reduction [3]. Further extending its use, GNH was successfully implemented in federated learning within a rural environment (with limited network connectivity). It was used to efficiently balance resource efficiency and performance across diverse IoT applications [1]. However, it became evident that GNH could not guarantee resource availability, underlining the need for further refinement in the optimization algorithm.

The EO-GNH framework is an enhanced GNH variant – each module of this framework is described in Almurshed et al. [2]. EO-GNH also integrates asynchronous parallel computing and machine learning models for meta-heuristic selection. Simulation-based evaluation has been used to develop EO-GNH, allowing assessment of system performance under various IoT conditions and failure scenarios [1–3].

Despite the merits of GNH [2], it has limited efficiency in supporting Pareto-optimal solutions. EO-GNH was created to address this challenge, and uses asynchronous MapReduce and parallel meta-heuristics to reduce execution time of the optimisation algorithm, avoiding local optima and ensuring service availability. It modifies the jMetalPy framework [7] using Parsl [5] for more efficient optimization, making it suitable for real-time IoT applications.

An important characteristic of EO-GNH is its ability to produce non-dominant solutions from the Pareto front, a crucial aspect of multi-objective optimization. It also simplifies the scalarization process [20] for a more dynamic and faster optimization.

3   Adaptive Framework for Edge-Cloud

This section describes the system components of our optimisation framework that makes use of EO-GNH, including properties of this algorithm. A description of software libraries used to realise EO-GNH is provided, identifying its use across a range of different application use cases.

3.1   System Components

The framework makes use of: Parsl, a Python library for parallel programming [5]; the Integer Linear Programming (ILP) model for adaptive decision-making [2]; and heuristic and meta-heuristic scheduling via jMetalPy [7]. Parsl provides efficient service function execution, while the ILP model aids in optimal decision-making. As illustrated in Fig. 1, the *controller*'s adaptive components

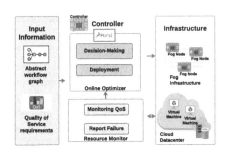

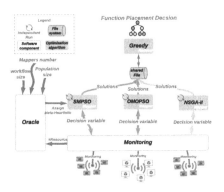

Fig. 1. Proposed adaptive controller architecture

Fig. 2. Asynchronous MapReduce performs EO-GNH, initiated by the Oracle.

consist of a *Resource Monitor* and an *Online Optimizer*. The Resource Monitor measures QoS and reports failures for use by the Online Optimizer. The decision-making process of the Online Optimizer uses ILP modeling to optimize the placement plan, employing heuristics such as GNH and EO-GNH. Furthermore, the Online Optimizer utilizes the Parsl library to accelerate decision-making and perform function deployments.

3.2   Enhanced-Optimized Greedy Nominator Heuristic (EO-GNH)

EO-GNH refines the GNH algorithm by incorporating Asynchronous MapReduce and meta-heuristics to determine optimal locations for redundant deployments. Figure 2 shows the workflow used in the EO-GNH framework. Mappers employ meta-heuristics to explore decision variables, while the Reducer, acting as a control fog node, chooses the most suitable locations. In contrast to GNH, EO-GNH utilizes meta-heuristics to generate a Pareto-front of solutions, giving the Reducer more flexibility when selecting resources, based on the similarity function. EO-GNH operates asynchronously, not requiring the Reducer to wait for all Mappers to complete their meta-heuristic iterations before making placement decisions. Each Mapper maintains a file of current optimal solutions accessible to the Reducer, facilitating instant decision-making, regardless of the solution's quality. The optimization algorithm employs nature-inspired meta-heuristics sourced from the jMetalPy library [7]. These meta-heuristics provide multiple solutions during runtime, each being an approximation of the best discovered Pareto-front.

The Oracle, a software module in EO-GNH, determines the compatibility of meta-heuristics with the application or infrastructure setup. Using decision tree models, it conducts preference-based sorting and assigns meta-heuristics to Mappers. Our approach dynamically selects one of jMetalPy's meta-heuristic algorithms for optimization. Depending on specific application requirements, it chooses among the available Particle Swarm Optimization algorithms such as OMOPSO or SMPSO, or Genetic Algorithms such as GDE3, HYPE, IBEA, MOCell and NSGAII. This dynamic algorithm selection provides a unique perspective on optimisation not available in approaches.

Solution encoding in EO-GNH involves the transformation of meta-heuristic data into a processable form. The solution, initially represented as an array of integers in the jMetalPy framework, is converted into a data model compatible for the Reducer, ensuring the efficiency of the EO-GNH workflow.

EO-GNH relies on an asynchronous MapReduce mechanism initiated by the Oracle. Each Mapper runs a meta-heuristic chosen by the Oracle, based on attributes learned during the training phase. The Reducer's heuristic is selected manually as greedy.

4   Applications

We developed three IoT applications to inspect the EO-GNH across them. The workflow description highlights RPi 4B execution times and shows real-world functionality.

4.1   Federated Learning (FL) Application

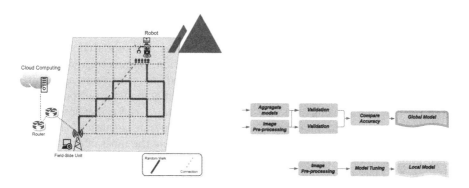

Fig. 3. Robot performs a random walk, affecting the connection to a field-side unit.

Fig. 4. Workflows for federated learning online training

Precision farming employs data-centric technologies and holds immense potential to improve farming productivity and outcomes [6]. Among its varied applications, automated weed control is a commonly discussed use case. By precisely identifying and handling weeds, this application can enhance farm yield, reduce labour expenses and decrease pesticide use, thereby promoting efficient and sustainable farming practices. With the intent of supporting farm autonomy, this application leverages federated learning as a secure alternative to conventional machine learning approaches [19]. Federated learning enables model creation with locally sourced data, eliminating the need for centralised data storage, ensuring each farm is able to manage its own data, whilst still sharing good practice with nearby farms. Rural areas, due to their limited network infrastructure, present unique challenges for implementing precision farming. Conventional machine learning algorithms might face difficulties under these conditions, potentially affecting network reliability and service availability. Hence, this scenario necessitates a solution that can operate effectively within this constrained network environment, ensuring consistent and effective precision farming practices. In this context, the scenario involves deploying Federated Learning-enabled mobile robots to mitigate these challenges. Serving as edge devices, these robots enhance field coverage and data collection, contributing to a global model without sharing raw data [1] The path of a robot are guided by a truncated random walk method to ensure efficient field coverage and task accuracy [14]. Significantly, the robot's distance from computing resources symbolises network latency in mobile edge devices, which can affect the quality of data communication (as shown in Fig. 3).

Workflow. Fig. 4 shows the federated learning workflow used in precision farming. The descriptions for each function utilized in this workflows are provided below: *(1) Image pre-processing:* This task makes color mode alterations, image resizing, data formatting and pixel value scaling to prepare images for machine learning models. The processed images and their associated labels are then stored. *(2) Model tuning:* the model weights are adjusted on a new dataset to improve the performance of an existing neural network. The updated weights are saved separately for future use. *(3) Model aggregation:* parameters (weights) of several trained models are combined (e.g. averaged) to create one aggregated model. *(4) Validation:* the trained machine learning model's performance is tested on new data, using loss and accuracy metrics – these metrics are also returned along with the model. *(5) Accuracy comparison:* accuracy/ loss function across different models are compared to determine the most effective model – returning the best performing model. The average execution on RPi's for the following 5 functions are: *0.33 s, 178.16 s, 22.33 s, 37.16 s, and 0.10 s* respectively.

4.2   Recurrent Neural Network (RNN) Inference Application

Food production, marked by intricate processes and strict food safety regulations, calls for innovative solutions to maintain high standards [4]. Notably, climate-controlled storage units play a crucial role in preserving food batches. IoT-based temperature monitoring systems (Fig. 5) offer real-time tracking of temperature, ensuring optimal storage conditions, and regulatory adherence. A food processing facility employing a smart energy cluster for improved energy efficiency is used as another case study. The facility integrates a Recurrent Neu-

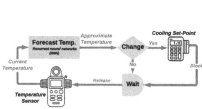
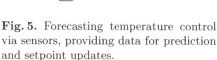

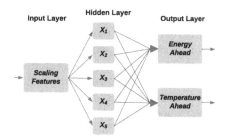

Fig. 5. Forecasting temperature control via sensors, providing data for prediction and setpoint updates.

Fig. 6. Workflow of neural network for energy-saving applications

ral Network (RNN) specifically designed for energy conservation. By forecasting room temperature and energy consumption, adjusting temperature setpoints automatically, the RNN facilitates precise energy and temperature forecasts. The RNN implementation is divided into several service functions, depicted in Fig. 6. This workflow management approach optimizes resource utilization. The RNN architecture comprises a pre-processing layer for data preparation, a hidden layer for prediction and output layers to yield predicted energy use and temperature values.

Workflow. Figure 6 depicts the workflow of the neural network for energy-saving applications. The functions used in the workflow include: *(1) Scaling features:* involving normalization of the input data, such as current readings of the chamber's settings, power, capacity and the current season. The data is transformed into a standard scale compatible with the RNN, to support subsequent model-based predictions. *(2) Neurons X_1 to X_5:* These are the middle-layer neurons in the RNN, which apply weights to inputs and process them through a Hyperbolic Tangent (tanh) activation function. The output of the Scaling Features function is adjusted for combining the weight value passed through the activation output. *(3) Energy ahead and temperature ahead:* these functions predict energy and temperature respectively. They consist of an output layer, unscaling layer and a bounding layer. The output layer calculates the sum of the outputs from the X_j layers, adjusted by the output layer weights. The result is then scaled back to original units (kWh for energy and degrees Celsius for temperature) in the unscaled layer. The average execution time on RPi's for these 3 functions are: *1.29 s, 0.44 s, and 0.07 s, 0.06 s* respectively.

4.3   Cancer Diagnosis

Prostate Cancer (PCa) is the second most prevalent cancer among men worldwide, with 1.4 million new cases detected in 2020 [18]. Precise disease classification, assisted by AI, is critical for optimal treatment and risk reduction [13]. Cancer research has made remarkable progress over the last century, leading to innovative diagnostic and treatment methods, especially for PCa [9]. This progress has led to a large amount of cancer-related data. Nonetheless, precise cancer detection still remains a difficult challenge. Currently, machine learning techniques are being utilized, demonstrating profound effectiveness in deciphering complex patterns and predicting cancer types [11]. The current ProstateX dataset, a derivative of the Cancer Imaging Archive (TCIA) dataset, includes retrospective prostate MR studies [12]. It addresses limitations within the TCIA dataset by providing lesion masks and information, facilitating research in medical image analysis and computer-aided diagnosis for prostate cancer [8].

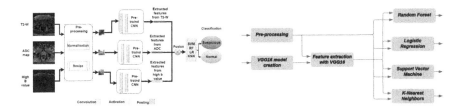

Fig. 7. Intelligent decision support system for prostate cancer diagnosis

Fig. 8. Workflow for prostate cancer classification using Machine Learning

Workflow. Figure 8 shows the training workflow for machine learning in prostate cancer classification. The workflow comprises the following functions: *(1) Pre-processing Data:* involves fetching data from a specified location and performing initial cleaning and formatting. *(2) Creating a VGG16 Model:* involves the application of transfer learning via the use of VGGNet, a broadly recognized 16-layer architecture. The model is pre-trained on ImageNet's database, an extensive repository containing more than 10M natural images across 1000 object categories [16]. *(3) Extracting Features from Magnetic Resonance Imaging (MRI) modalities with VGG16:* involves passing the loaded data through the VGG16 model, to extract the features, the first 2 blocks of the VGG model are used. We extract the features from each MRI modality alone, and then fuse the features. *(4) Creating, Training, and Testing Machine Learning Models:* This task sets up, trains, and evaluates Random Forest, Logistic Regression, Support Vector Machine, and K-Nearest Neighbors models from the Scikit-learn library on the RPi. The models are trained using extracted features and labels, and their performance is evaluated with unseen data. The average execution on RPi's for these 4 functions are: *0.47 s, 1.53 s, 10.23 s, and 2.99 s, 28.09 s, 39.98 s, 7.65 s* respectively.

5   Evaluation

5.1   Experimental Setup

Evaluation was carried out through simulation, as outlined in Sect. 2, by dynamically modifying simulation parameters across the three scenarios: precision agriculture, the intelligence cooling system, and machine learning for Prostate Cancer classification. For these simulations, we utilized RPi benchmark data from Sect. 4. An important feature of this evaluation was the assessment of the EO-GNH under various mapper configurations, from EO-GNH-1 to EO-GNH-4 (representing 1 to 4 mappers respectively). The experiment also incorporated results from a basic greedy approach without replicas, as well as the original GNH approach. Each scenario involved using a unique set of parameters. The number of Raspberry Pis (RPis) implemented was a key parameter, with most scenarios employing 1000 RPis, except the agriculture scenario which utilized 100 RPi resources. Simulation was chosen for its affordability, scalability, and failure control.

The Mean Time to Repair (MTTR) measures the average repair duration: 20–100 seconds for the Agriculture and the Cooling System scenarios; 5–15 seconds for the Prostate Cancer Classification scenario. The Mean Time to Failure (MTTF) measures the average duration between failures: 250–500 seconds in the Agricultural and Cooling System scenarios, and 50–100 seconds in the Prostate Cancer Classification scenario. By adjusting these parameters for each scenario within the simulated environment, the experiments offered detailed insights into the system's performance and resilience under differing conditions. This enables comparison across multiple scenarios, such as greedy approach without replicas and the original GNH approach.

5.2   Results

The evaluation of the EO-GNH framework on the above three scenarios considers the following metrics: *(1) Success rate:* this represents the likelihood of completing a task within the deadline. Together with risk (the probability of not meeting the deadline), it forms a proactive mechanism to minimize service disruptions. *(2) Makespan:* this refers to the total execution time of a workflow across distributed resources. The scheduler's primary objective is to optimize this, aiming for the shortest makespan possible. *(3) Utilized location (Cost):* this is defined by the number of resources used in a workflow. The goal is to balance resource use, minimize network congestion, and manage the risk-cost trade-off of redundant deployments.

As shown in Fig. 9 (RNN forecasting, 100 RPis) and Fig. 10 (RNN forecasting, 1000 RPis), the EO-GNH configurations employ MapReduce with a varying number of mappers, consistently outperforming other algorithms across all measured metrics: success rate, makespan, and utilized locations. Specifically, EO-GNH-3 and EO-GNH-4 yield the best results for 100 RPi and 1000 RPi configurations, respectively.

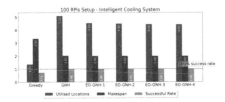

Fig. 9. RNN Forecasting with 100 RPis (average values)

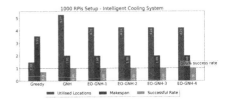

Fig. 10. RNN Forecasting with 1000 RPis (average values)

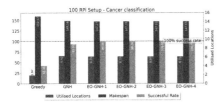

Fig. 11. ML Pipeline with 100 RPis (average values)

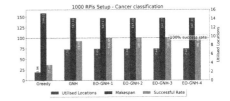

Fig. 12. ML Pipeline with 1000 RPis (average values)

The ML pipeline results for prostate cancer classification is shown in Figs. 11 (100 RPis) and 12 (1000 RPis). Results show that EO-GNH configurations demonstrate superior efficiency across all metrics, with EO-GNH-4 being the top performer in both configurations. The longer makespan when transitioning from 100 to 1000 RPi setup indicates that the current task is more computationally intensive than RNN forecasting. In spite of this, EO-GNH configurations maintains a 100 percent success rate, indicating robust performance across a variety of distributed computing scenarios.

Examining the results of the tuning model for robotic agriculture using a federated learning approach (Fig. 13) reveals a notable difference from previous patterns. While EO-GNH configurations continue to perform well, the makespan disparities between them become more pronounced. This result may indicate that the number of mappers utilized in the MapReduce implementation is more crucial in this particular context. The GNH algorithm also exhibits significant performance enhancement in this configuration, although it does not surpass results of EO-GNH configurations.

The global model aggregation results (Fig. 14) confirm previous findings, with all EO-GNH configurations achieving a 100 percent success rate. The variation in makespan and utilized locations between EO-GNH configurations suggest that adjusting the number of mappers can affect execution speed and resource utilization.

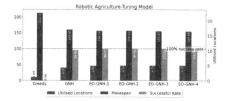

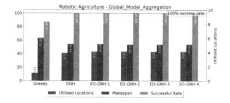

Fig. 13. Federated Learning - Model Tuning (average values)

Fig. 14. Federated Learning - Global Model Aggregation (average values)

6 Conclusion

We describe the Enhanced Optimized-Greedy Nominator Heuristic (EO-GNH), outlining how it can be used across various IoT applications. Using asynchronous MapReduce and parallel metaheuristics, EO-GNH can be used to support dynamic resource allocation, by adjusting the number of mappers in the MapReduce component of this algorithm.

EO-GNH's adaptability and inherent hierarchical meta-heuristics approach, which is by definition problem-independent, allows it to overcome slow convergence by exploring multiple Pareto front approximations. This opens up its potential use beyond IoT task placements, including feature selection and hyperparameter optimization in machine learning, thereby improving accuracy, reducing overfitting and training time, and simplifying large-scale search problems. In deep learning, EO-GNH could be used to search for the optimal architecture, potentially enhancing Neural Architecture Search methods. All these areas are potential venues to be explored in the future. Additional investigation of potential EO-GNH research areas holds promise for future projects.

In conclusion, we note that EO-GNH effectively manages AI-driven IoT applications and its hierarchical meta-heuristics approach promises a wealth of possibilities for future research. By applying this algorithm to different domains, we may continue to uncover new strategies for optimization in a variety of contexts.

References

1. Almurshed, O., et al.: Adaptive edge-cloud environments for rural ai. In: 2022 IEEE International Conference on Services Computing (SCC), pp. 74–83. IEEE (2022)
2. Almurshed, O., Rana, O., Chard, K.: Greedy nominator heuristic: virtual function placement on fog resources. Conc. Comput. Pract. Exper. **34**(6), e6765 (2022)
3. Almurshed, O., et al.: A fault tolerant workflow composition and deployment automation iot framework in a multi cloud edge environment. IEEE Internet Comput. (2021)
4. Alzahrani, A., Petri, I., Rezgui, Y.: Analysis and simulation of smart energy clusters and energy value chain for fish processing industries. Energy Rep. **6**, 534–540 (2020)
5. Babuji, Y.N., et al.: Parsl: scalable parallel scripting in python. In: IWSG (2018)
6. Balducci, F., Impedovo, D., Pirlo, G.: Machine learning applications on agricultural datasets for smart farm enhancement. Machines **6**(3), 38 (2018)

7. Benitez-Hidalgo, A., Nebro, A.J., Garcia-Nieto, J., Oregi, I., Del Ser, J.: jmetalpy: a python framework for multi-objective optimization with metaheuristics. Swarm Evol. Comput. **51**, 100598 (2019)
8. Cuocolo, R., Stanzione, A., Castaldo, A., De Lucia, D.R., Imbriaco, M.: Quality control and whole-gland, zonal and lesion annotations for the prostatex challenge public dataset. Eur. J. Radiol. **138**, 109647 (2021)
9. Hanahan, D., Weinberg, R.A.: Hallmarks of cancer: the next generation. Cell **144**(5), 646–674 (2011)
10. Hwang, F., Chen, S.J., Hwang, C.L.: Fuzzy multiple attribute decision making: methods and applications. Springer, Berlin/Heidelberg (1992). https://doi.org/10.1007/978-3-642-46768-4
11. Kourou, K., Exarchos, T.P., Exarchos, K.P., Karamouzis, M.V., Fotiadis, D.I.: Machine learning applications in cancer prognosis and prediction. Comput. Struct. Biotechnol. J. **13**, 8–17 (2015)
12. Litjens, G., Debats, O., Barentsz, J., Karssemeijer, N., Huisman, H.: Prostatex challenge data. Cancer Imaging Archive (2017). https://doi.org/10.7937/K9TCIA.2017.MURS5CL
13. Noguerol, T.M., Paulano-Godino, F., Martín-Valdivia, M.T., Menias, C.O., Luna, A.: Strengths, weaknesses, opportunities, and threats analysis of artificial intelligence and machine learning applications in radiology. J. Am. Coll. Radiol. **16**(9), 1239–1247 (2019)
14. Pang, B., Song, Y., Zhang, C., Yang, R.: Effect of random walk methods on searching efficiency in swarm robots for area exploration. Appl. Intell. **51**(7), 5189–5199 (2021)
15. Radouche, S., Leghris, C.: Network selection based on cosine similarity and combination of subjective and objective weighting. In: 2020 International Conference on Intelligent Systems and Computer Vision (ISCV), pp. 1–7. IEEE (2020)
16. Russakovsky, O., et al.: Imagenet large scale visual recognition challenge. Int. J. Comput. Vision **115**(3), 211–252 (2015)
17. Samriya, J.K., Kumar, N.: An optimal sla based task scheduling aid of hybrid fuzzy topsis-pso algorithm in cloud environment. Mater. Today: Proc. (2020)
18. Sung, H., et al.: Global cancer statistics 2020: globocan estimates of incidence and mortality worldwide for 36 cancers in 185 countries. CA: Cancer J. Clin. **71**(3), 209–249 (2021)
19. Yang, Q., Liu, Y., Cheng, Y., Kang, Y., Chen, T., Yu, H.: Federated learning. Synth. Lect. Artifi. Intell. Mach. Learn. **13**(3), 1–207 (2019)
20. Zeleny, M.: Compromise programming. Multiple criteria decision making (1973)

Streaming IoT Data and the Quantum Edge: A Classic/Quantum Machine Learning Use Case

Sabrina Herbst[(✉)], Vincenzo De Maio[ID], and Ivona Brandic[ID]

Vienna University of Technology, Vienna, Austria
e11807863@student.tuwien.ac.at, {vincenzo,ivona}@ec.tuwien.ac.at

Abstract. With the advent of the Post-Moore era, the scientific community is faced with the challenge of addressing the demands of current data-intensive machine learning applications, which are the cornerstone of urgent analytics in distributed computing. Quantum machine learning could be a solution for the increasing demand of urgent analytics, providing potential theoretical speedups and increased space efficiency. However, challenges such as (1) the encoding of data from the classical to the quantum domain, (2) hyperparameter tuning, and (3) the integration of quantum hardware into a distributed computing continuum limit the adoption of quantum machine learning for urgent analytics. In this work, we investigate the use of Edge computing for the integration of quantum machine learning into a distributed computing continuum, identifying the main challenges and possible solutions. Furthermore, exploring the data encoding and hyperparameter tuning challenges, we present preliminary results for quantum machine learning analytics on an IoT scenario.

1 Introduction

IoT data and machine learning have recently become the keystone of urgent computing [1,2]. Data from IoT devices can be processed by machine learning models to improve simulations of different scientific phenomena [3]. However, machine learning applications require a huge amount of data for training. While data are streamed from IoT devices, they need to be transferred, stored and processed under strict response time constraints [4], which requires a huge amount of storage, computational and network resources. Therefore, training of machine learning is often performed inside HPC facilities.

However, we recently entered the Post-Moore era, which faces the scientific community with the challenges of scaling computing facilities beyond current limits, which are codified by Moore's law and Dennard scaling. As a consequence, current HPC facilities struggle to scale with the increasing amount of data available, pushing the scientific community towards research in Post-Moore Computing to address this issue. Among different possibilities, quantum computing clearly stands out due to theoretical speedups and increased space efficiency. This is particularly true for quantum machine learning, whose potential benefits

D. Zeinalipour et al. (Eds.): Euro-Par 2023 Workshops, LNCS 14351, pp. 177–188, 2024.
https://doi.org/10.1007/978-3-031-50684-0_14

are (1) increased speed, (2) increased predictive performance, and (3) reduced amount of data needed for training [5].

Quantum machine learning requires adapting data from the classical to the quantum domain before training and inference, following a process that is often referred to as *data encoding*. The choice of data encoding method can significantly affect the performance and accuracy of a quantum machine learning model [6]. Also, the choice of hyperparameters is of capital importance for the performance and accuracy of trained models.

In this work, we expand our idea of the Quantum Edge [7] by investigating the possibilities of applying Edge computing methodologies to enable fast and efficient quantum machine learning on hybrid systems. After defining the problem, we present our idea of the Quantum Edge and describe how it can be applied to the target scenario. We identify challenges and possible solutions, and provide some preliminary results of our work towards the goal of Quantum Edge, tackling data encoding and hyperparameter selection.

We perform training and inference of quantum machine learning models based on a bike sharing dataset, publicly available at the UCI Machine Learning repository[1] [8], which is representative of typical IoT data. We use IBM Qiskit [9] and Aer simulators to perform training and inference of quantum machine learning models, evaluating the predictive performance and runtime of different hyperparameters configurations.

The paper is organized as follows: first, we introduce preliminary notions about quantum computing and machine learning in Sect. 2. Related work is described in Sect. 3. Afterwards, we describe our motivational scenario in Sect. 4, and identify challenges of the target scenario in Sect. 5. In Sect. 6, we discuss possible solutions, while in Sect. 7 we provide some preliminary results of our work, and we conclude our paper in Sect. 8.

2   Background

2.1   Quantum Computing

Quantum computing relies on different quantum phenomena, such as *superposition*, *entanglement*, and *quantum parallelism*. The basic entities of quantum computing are quantum-bits, also known as *qubits*. While classic bits can only be in two states, i.e., either 0 or 1, a single qubit ψ is in a linear *superposition* of the two *orthonormal basis* states, $|0\rangle = [1,0]^T$ and $|1\rangle = [0,1]^T$, namely, $|\psi\rangle = c_0 |0\rangle + c_1 |1\rangle$, where c_0 and c_1 are the *probability amplitudes*, which determine the probability that $|\psi\rangle$ will collapse in $|0\rangle$ or $|1\rangle$ when measured. We define $c_0, c_1 \in \mathbb{C}$, and $|c_0|^2 + |c_1|^2 = 1$.

A set of n qubits taken together forms a *quantum register*. Quantum computation is performed by manipulating qubits within a quantum register. As a consequence, while a n-bit classic register can store one of 2^n values, a $n-$qubit

---

[1] https://archive.ics.uci.edu/ml/datasets/Seoul+Bike+Sharing+Demand.   Accessed: 21.03.2023.

quantum register can store 2^n values at the same time, resulting in a higher space efficiency. When measured, the quantum register will collapse into one single value i. The probability of collapsing into state i depends on the value of the complex amplitude c_i. As a consequence, quantum computations are repeated several times, and the most frequent result will be the returned as the final result.

There are different models for quantum computation. In this work, we refer to the *quantum circuit model*, where computation consists of the manipulation of qubits by applying a set of *quantum gates*, similar to classical logical gates, and *measurement* operations. Users prepare a high-level description of a quantum circuit [9], that is transpiled to be executed on target quantum hardware.

2.2 Quantum Machine Learning

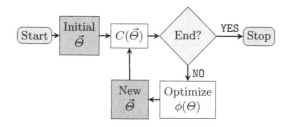

Fig. 1. Variational Quantum Algorithms.

Quantum machine learning (QML) aims at increasing time and space efficiency of machine learning tasks [10] by exploiting properties of quantum computing. We identify two main areas of QML: Quantum Classification and Quantum Regression. In this work, we focus on quantum regression.

We focus on Variational Quantum Algorithms (VQAs)-based regression, whose execution is summarized in Fig. 1. The idea behind VQAs is to minimize a cost function ϕ that represents a specific property of a physical system (e.g., its ground state). The state of the physical system is modeled by a Parametrized Quantum Circuit C, which is a quantum circuit whose state is determined by a set of parameters $\vec{\Theta}$. The main idea is to minimize $\phi(\vec{\Theta})$ to achieve the optimal set of parameters $\vec{\Theta}^*$, which models the solution to our target problem.

3   Related Work

First applications of hybrid classical/quantum systems are described by [11], focusing on the integration of quantum computers in HPC infrastructures. Similarly, [7] provides a proof of concept for hybrid molecular dynamics workflows. Applications of Edge computing for the integration of Non-Von Neumann architectures in the computing continuum have been discussed in [12]. VQAs are surveyed in [13].

The authors in [14] provide a great overview of recent advances in QML, such as a hybrid implementation of the perceptron algorithm on current quantum hardware in [15] which achieves an exponential advantage in storage. Furthermore, a quantum support vector machine was implemented in [16], which scales logarithmically in terms of feature dimension and data samples.

In [17], hidden quantum Markov models are investigated, showing that they manage to model the same classical data but with less hidden states.

Abbas et al. [18] investigate the capacity of VQAs for ML and compare the capacity of classical and quantum models, showing that some VQAs have desirable characteristics, allowing for a better expressivity and trainability, especially if the data encoding employed is difficult to simulate on classical hardware.

Finally, the results from [17] show how QML can provide valuable insights both for quantum and classical computing [14].

4   Motivational Use Case: Quantum Edge Analytics

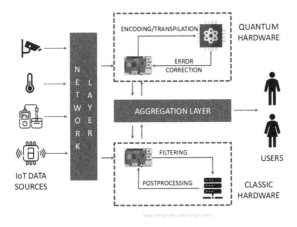

Fig. 2. The Quantum Edge Analytics.

Following from Sect. 2.2, we identify three main hyperparameters in quantum regression: the *encoding* of the input into a quantum state, the structure of the *quantum circuit*, encoding the problem, and the *optimizer* that is applied to identify the optimal set of parameters. Moreover, efficient execution of VQAs requires fast communication between classic and quantum systems, and eventually offloading some parts of the computation (i.e., optimization and encoding) for load balancing. We consider Edge computing to address these issues.

Edge computing is a paradigm where data are processed in lower layers of the network, i.e., closer to data sources, such as sensors or edge nodes. Processing and storage at the Edge results in lower response time and enhanced data processing, which makes edge analytics suitable for near real-time analytics, such as traffic safety applications [19], environmental monitoring [20], smart buildings [21], and scientific computing [22]. Edge Computing will constitute an additional layer between classical and quantum machines, performing necessary tasks such as (1) encoding of streaming data, (2) performing small-scale simulations to reduce the load on quantum machines, (3) the transpilation of quantum circuits for the target quantum machine, or (4) the execution of classic optimizer.

Figure 2 summarizes the concept of Quantum Edge Analytics. First, data coming from different IoT sources are streamed through the network to the Edge. At the Edge, resources of Edge nodes can be used (1) for encoding data into a quantum state, (2) for the transpilation of the quantum circuit, and (3) to apply error correction to the output of the computation. Also, Edge nodes can act as an aggregation layer between the quantum and classic layer. In the next sections, we describe the challenges of enabling our vision.

5   Challenges

5.1   Fast Data Encoding

Data encoding is the process of translating classical data into a quantum state. Different methods are available in the literature [6]. In QML, the most popular encoding is Feature Map Based Encoding [23,24], which is also what we consider in this work. In Feature Map Based Encoding, classical data are encoded employing a quantum feature map, i.e., a unitary function that maps the input data into a quantum feature space, where feature vectors are quantum states.

Data encoding is a computationally expensive process, that requires deep knowledge of (1) the input problem, (2) the target hardware where data will be processed, and (3) the algorithm employed for data processing. Data encoding is one of the keys for an efficient quantum computation, since inefficient data encoding could hinder speedups provided by QML.

5.2   Automatic Hyperparameter Tuning

QML models, and in general VQAs, are influenced by different hyperparameter settings, such as (1) the structure of the parametrized quantum circuit (which includes hyperparameters such as the qubit entanglement and the circuit repetitions), (2) the classical optimizer, (3) the termination condition, (4) the cost function, and others [13]. As shown by [7], hyperparameter selection strongly affects both accuracy and the runtime of VQAs.

The main issue with the selection of hyperparameters is that they strongly depend on the input problem and the target quantum machine, which makes it difficult to select them a-priori. Also, the high heterogeneity of quantum hardware, together with the wide spectrum of applications requiring Edge analytics, makes finding a "one-size-fits-all" solution infeasible. As a consequence, to enable Quantum Edge Analytics, it is of paramount importance to design methods for the automatic selection of hyperparameters, based on the available quantum hardware and target applications.

5.3 Edge Error Mitigation

Current quantum computing hardware is referred to as Noisy Intermediate Scale Quantum (NISQ) [25] technology, i.e., they are sensitive to the environment in which they are deployed and subject to quantum decoherence. As a consequence, different error correction methods need to be applied to the output of the quantum execution, while other approaches focus on exploiting noise to improve the performance of QML models [26]. Since Edge nodes are supposed to act as an aggregation layer between classical and quantum nodes, the application of error mitigation methods at the Edge is necessary to enable efficient data exchange.

However, typical quantum error mitigation methods rely on computationally intense artificial neural networks [27,28] and deep learning approaches [29], which cannot be executed on typical Edge devices, i.e., Raspberry Pi [30].

6 Quantum Edge Pre/Post Processing

6.1 Fast Data Encoding

Considering the high rate at which IoT data are streamed over the network [4], enabling Quantum Edge analytics requires that data are encoded at a speed that allows data to be quickly transferred to the quantum hardware to be encoded as a quantum state. Typical data encoding methods [6] require performing complex algebraic operations, such as computing unitary functions and complex matrix operations, which is computationally intensive for typical Edge nodes.

To enable fast data encoding, our suggested solution is to increase heterogeneity at the Edge, by enabling the use of a wider spectrum of accelerators that can perform data encoding at a higher speed, i.e., GPUs, FPGAs or ASICs [31] such as Nvidia Jetson Nano, or Edge Spartan 6, which are already available off-the-shelf. Another possibility is to exploit Edge preprocessing to apply different techniques, such as symbolic data representation, to reduce the size of data that needs to be forwarded to quantum nodes, or enable distributed data encoding at the Edge, exploiting multiple Edge devices to perform the required calculations.

6.2 Automatic Hyperparameter Tuning

Hyperparameter tuning can affect both the predictive performance and runtime of QML models, and it is inherently correlated to (1) the input data coming from IoT devices, (2) the target problem, and (3) the available quantum hardware. Since Edge nodes act as an intermediate layer between data sources and classic/quantum hardware, they have access to this information. Therefore, it must be their responsibility to determine the ideal setting of hyperparameters to perform QML, with minimum or no human intervention in the process.

Our suggestion is to enable Edge nodes to perform hyperparameter tuning techniques, such as Bayesian Optimization or Grid Search [32], based on data available from previous executions of QML models. Interplay between Cloud and Edge resources, as it is common in Edge AI [33], represents another possibility to cope with the limited resources available at the Edge.

6.3 Edge Error Mitigation

The output of QML inference must be postprocessed at the Edge before being forwarded to users due to the amount of noise in modern NISQ hardware. However, typical techniques for error mitigation rely on complex ML models, which are not suitable for execution at the Edge.

Enhancing Edge devices with specific accelerators, such as TPUs or FPGAs allow us to speed up the execution of error correction methods. Another promising techniques is to downsize ML models, i.e., running a reduced size model for error correction, optimized for specific quantum hardware, while training is performed at the HPC layer.

7   Preliminary Results

In this section, we perform first preliminary evaluation on Quantum Regression of IoT streaming data. We focus on Feature Map based encoding, and hyperparameter configurations. We use the Seoul Bike Sharing Dataset [34,35], which is available at the UCI Machine Learning Repository[2] [8], since its features include data similar to those in IoT sensors (i.e., temperature, humidity, wind speed).

7.1   Experimental Setup

We use the Python programming language and the open source package Qiskit [9] for our experiments. We employ Quantum simulators from Qiskit Aer, which provide the possibility of simulating 'perfect' quantum computers, without the noise that is present in current hardware.

Our dataset has 13 attributes, an integer target and $8,760$ instances. The goal is to predict bike sharing demands for every hour of the day, based on weather conditions and seasonal information. We normalize the target into the range $[0,1]$, as Qiskit's VQR function does not allow predicting bigger values.

We perform an exhaustive search over all hyperparameter configurations, summing up to 672 configurations. We use principal component analysis (PCA) to reduce the dimensionality to seven. This was done to ensure that the experiments could be run on IBM quantum computers as well, as they offer seven qubit machines for free.

We limited our experiments to 400 data points for training and 250 for evaluation to ensure a reasonable runtime. Table 1 summarizes the top five configurations in terms of Mean Square Error (MSE), Mean Absolute Error (MAE) and running time. More configurations are described in the following sections.

We conducted experiments on a Debian/GNU Linux 11 computer, featuring an Intel(R) Xeon(R) CPU E5-2623 v4 (16 cores @ 2.60 GHz) and 128 GB RAM.

---

[2] https://archive.ics.uci.edu/ml/datasets/Seoul+Bike+Sharing+Demand.   Accessed: 21.03.2023.

Table 1. Top Five Configurations

Ansatz	Optimizer	Feature Map	Entanglement	MSE	MAE	Time
EfficientSU2	SPSA	ZFeatureMap	circular	0.0209	0.1074	23993 s
RealAmplitudes	SPSA	ZFeatureMap	full	0.0219	0.1113	27585 s
TwoLocal	SPSA	ZFeatureMap	sca	0.0227	0.1172	22055 s
EfficientSU2	SPSA	ZFeatureMap	full	0.0229	0.1161	31995 s
TwoLocal	SPSA	ZFeatureMap	linear	0.0245	0.1209	21314 s

7.2   Evaluation

Data Encoding. Figure 3 summarizes the results of data encoding. Data encoding defines how classical data is mapped into a quantum state. An example is *Basis Encoding*, where a number, i.e. 5, is transformed into binary 101 and the bits are directly mapped into qubits $|101\rangle$. We employ a more space efficient feature map, that is estimated to be difficult to reproduce on a classical computer, i.e. the PauliFeatureMap [23]. It uses a feature map to map the data into a quantum state and two concrete implementations are derived in Qiskit, i.e., ZFeatureMap and the ZZFeatureMap. Since a qubit entanglement strategy can be specified for ZZFeatureMap, we experiment with 'full' entanglement (all qubits are entangled with all other ones), 'linear' (q_i with $q_{i+1}, i \in [0, N - 2]$, N being the number of qubits), 'circular' (linear plus q_{N-1} with q_0), 'pairwise' (in even layers, qubit q_i is entangled with q_{i+1}, in uneven ones with q_{i-1}) and 'sca'. In 'sca' entanglement, the target and control qubit are swapped in every iteration, and the entanglement between qubit q_{N-1} and q_0 is shifted in every iteration, i.e. in the first repetition it is the first entanglement operation, in the second it is shifted into the second position and q_0 and q_1 are entangled first.

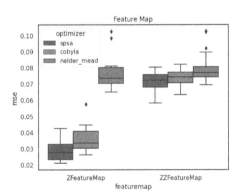

Fig. 3. MSE of Training w.r.t. Feature Map

Figure 3 shows the performances of different feature maps, highlighting the optimizers used. It can be seen that ZFeatureMap works significantly better than

ZZFeatureMap does, however the advantage is not independent of the optimizer. Our results show that choosing the feature map carefully can significantly impact the results. Nonetheless, a good feature map cannot make up for a bad optimizer.

Circuit Hyperparameter Tuning. Figure. 4a summarizes the results for the Ansatz selection. EfficientSU2, TwoLocal, RealAmplitudes and PauliTwoDesign are commonly used ansatzes available in Qiskit. They all use rotations around the X, Y and Z axis of the Bloch sphere, which is a way to geometrically represent a qubit, with a trainable angle θ. Furthermore, entanglement strategies can be employed for all except PauliTwoDesign, analogously to the ZZFeatureMap.

Figure 4b summarizes results for selection of different optimizers. We select COBYLA [36], SPSA [37], and Nelder-Mead [38], because they have diverse characteristics, which allows to gain insights on which class of optimizers could work well for VQAs. COBYLA and Nelder-Mead are gradient-free methods which use trust regions and the simplex algorithm, respectively, to find an optimization path. SPSA calculates the loss function using only two measurements and is often recommended in noisy environments[3]. We can see that the ansatzes perform similarly in mean, however, for all except PauliTwoDesign, some configurations that perform a lot better can be found. Furthermore, the range that the PauliTwoDesign configurations form is a lot more narrow than for the other ansatzes.

When analyzing the optimizers, we see that SPSA makes up the best configurations, however, there are several good COBYLA ones as well. Despite taking a long time to optimize, Nelder-Mead is significantly outperformed by all other optimizers. Furthermore, the SPSA runtime is usually higher than COBYLA, which makes COBYLA better in case of runtime constraints.

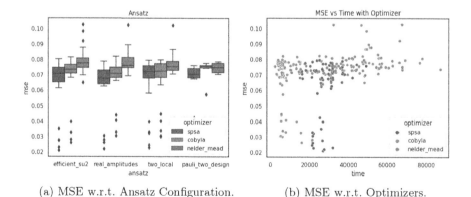

(a) MSE w.r.t. Ansatz Configuration.   (b) MSE w.r.t. Optimizers.

Fig. 4. Ansatz and Optimizer

---

[3] https://qiskit.org/documentation/stubs/qiskit.algorithms.optimizers.SPSA.html. Accessed 17.06.2023.

8   Conclusion and Future Work

In this work, we investigate the possibility of applying QML on streaming IoT data. First, we describe the concept of the Quantum Edge, i.e., applying Edge computing as an integration layer between classic and quantum hardware. We describe challenges of enabling our vision and identify possible solutions. Finally, we provide some preliminary results on the feasibility of applying QML for streaming IoT data.

In the future, we plan to investigate applications of QML to different application scenarios, which will help data scientists in the application of QML on IoT data. Also, we will further investigate the Quantum Edge, addressing challenges of integration of classic and quantum hardware by means of Edge computing.

Acknowledgements. This work has been partially funded through the Rucon project (Runtime Control in Multi Clouds), Austrian Science Fund (FWF): Y904-N31 START-Programm 2015, by the CHIST-ERA grant CHIST-ERA-19-CES-005, Austrian Science Fund (FWF), Standalone Project Transprecise Edge Computing (Triton), Austrian Science Fund (FWF): P 36870-N, and by Flagship Project HPQC (High Performance Integrated Quantum Computing) # 897481 Austrian Research Promotion Agency (FFG). We acknowledge the use of IBM Quantum services for this work. The views expressed are those of the authors, and do not reflect the official policy or position of IBM or the IBM Quantum team.

References

1. Heidari, A., Navimipour, N.J., Unal, M., Toumaj, S.: Machine learning applications for covid-19 outbreak management. Neural Comput. Appl. **34**(18), 15313–15348 (2022)
2. Shafaf, N., Malek, H.: Applications of machine learning approaches in emergency medicine; a review article. Arch. Acad. Emerg. Med. **7**(1), 34 (2019)
3. Løvholt, F., Lorito, S., Macias, J., Volpe, M., Selva, J., Gibbons, S.: Urgent tsunami computing. In: 2019 IEEE/ACM HPC for Urgent Decision Making (UrgentHPC), pp. 45–50 (2019)
4. De Maio, V., Bermbach, D., Brandic, I.: TAROT: spatio-temporal function placement for serverless smart city applications. In: 15th IEEE/ACM International Conference on Utility and Cloud Computing, UCC 2022, Vancouver, WA, USA, December 6–9, 2022, pp. 21–30. IEEE (2022)
5. Mensa, S., Sahin, E., Tacchino, F., Barkoutsos, P.K., Tavernelli, I.: Quantum machine learning framework for virtual screening in drug discovery: a prospective quantum advantage. Mach. Learn. Sci. Technol. **4**(1), 015023 (2023)
6. Weigold, M., Barzen, J., Leymann, F., Salm, M.: Data encoding patterns for quantum computing. In: Proceedings of the 27th Conference on Pattern Languages of Programs, pp. 1–11 (2020)
7. De Maio, V., Aral, A., Brandic, I.: A roadmap to post-moore era for distributed systems. In: Georgiou, C., Schiller, E.M., Ali-Eldin, A., Iosup, A., (eds.), ApPLIED 2022: Proceedings of the 2022 Workshop on Advanced Tools, Programming Languages, and PLatforms for Implementing and Evaluating Algorithms for Distributed systems, Salerno, Italy, 25 July 2022, pp. 30–34. ACM (2022)

8. Dua, D., Graff, C.: UCI Machine Learning Repository (2017)
9. Qiskit contributors. Qiskit: An open-source framework for quantum computing (2023)
10. Biamonte, J., Wittek, P., Pancotti, N., Rebentrost, P., Wiebe, N., Lloyd, S.: Quantum machine learning. Nature **549**(7671), 195–202 (2017)
11. Schulz, M., Kranzlmüller, D., Schulz, L.B., Trinitis, C., Weidendorfer, J.: On the inevitability of integrated HPC systems and how they will change HPC system operations. In: Proceedings of the 11th International Symposium on Highly Efficient Accelerators and Reconfigurable Technologies, HEART 2021, New York, NY, USA, 2021. Association for Computing Machinery (2021)
12. Cranganore, S.S., De Maio, V., Brandic, I., Anh Do, T.M., Deelman, E.: Molecular dynamics workflow decomposition for hybrid classic/quantum systems. In: 18th IEEE International Conference on e-Science, e-Science 2022, Salt Lake City, UT, USA, October 11–14, 2022, pp. 346–356. IEEE (2022)
13. Cerezo, M., et al.: Variational quantum algorithms. Nat. Rev. Phys. **3**(9), 625–644 (2021)
14. O'Quinn, W., Mao, S.: Quantum machine learning: recent advances and outlook. IEEE Wirel. Commun. **27**(3), 126–131 (2020)
15. Tacchino, F., Macchiavello, C., Gerace, D., Bajoni, D.: An artificial neuron implemented on an actual quantum processor. NPJ Quant. Inf. **5**(1), 26 (2019)
16. Rebentrost, P., Mohseni, M., Lloyd, S.: Quantum support vector machine for big data classification. Phys. Rev. Lett. **113**(13), 130503 (2014)
17. Srinivasan, S., Gordon, G.J., Boots, B.: Learning hidden quantum Markov models. In: International Conference on Artificial Intelligence and Statistics (2017)
18. Abbas, A., Sutter, D., Zoufal, C., Lucchi, A., Figalli, A., Woerner, S.: The power of quantum neural networks. Nat. Comput. Sci. **1**(6), 403–409 (2021)
19. Lujic, I., De Maio, V., Pollhammer, K., Bodrozic, I., Lasic, J., Brandic, I.: Increasing traffic safety with real-time edge analytics and 5g. In: Ding, A.Y., Mortier, R. (eds.) EdgeSys@EuroSys 2021: 4th International Workshop on Edge Systems, Analytics and Networking, Online Event, United Kingdom, April 26, 2021, pages 19–24. ACM (2021)
20. Aral, A., De Maio, V., Brandic, I.: ARES: reliable and sustainable edge provisioning for wireless sensor networks. IEEE Trans. Sustain. Comput. **7**(4), 761–773 (2022)
21. Lujic, I., De Maio, V., Brandic, I.: Resilient edge data management framework. IEEE Trans. Serv. Comput. **13**(4), 663–674 (2020)
22. De Maio, V., Kimovski, D.: Multi-objective scheduling of extreme data scientific workflows in fog. Future Gener. Comput. Syst. **106**, 171–184 (2020)
23. Havlíček, V., et al.: Supervised learning with quantum-enhanced feature spaces. Nature **567**(7747), 209–212 (2019)
24. Goto, T., Tran, Q.H., Nakajima, K.: Universal approximation property of quantum machine learning models in quantum-enhanced feature spaces. Phys. Rev. Lett. **127**(9), 090506 (2021)
25. Preskill, J.: Quantum computing in the NISQ era and beyond. Quantum **2**, 79 (2018)
26. Domingo, L., Carlo, G., Borondo, F.: Taking advantage of noise in quantum reservoir computing. arXiv preprint arXiv:2301.06814 (2023)
27. Kim, C., Park, K.D., Rhee, J.-K.: Quantum error mitigation with artificial neural network. IEEE Access **8**, 188853–188860 (2020)
28. Bennewitz, E.R., Hopfmueller, F., Kulchytskyy, B., Carrasquilla, J., Ronagh, P.: Neural error mitigation of near-term quantum simulations. Nat. Mach. Intell. **4**(7), 618–624 (2022)

29. Kim, J., Oh, B., Chong, Y., Hwang, E., Park, D.K.: Quantum readout error mitigation via deep learning. New J. Phys. **24**(7), 073009 (2022)
30. Steffenel, L.A., Pinheiro, M.K., Souveyet, C.: Assessing the impact of unbalanced resources and communications in edge computing. Pervasive Mob. Comput. **71**, 101321 (2021)
31. Hu, Y., Liu, Y., Liu, . A survey on convolutional neural network accelerators: GPU, FPGA and ASIC. In: 2022 14th International Conference on Computer Research and Development (ICCRD), pp. 100–107. IEEE (2022)
32. Wu, D., Sun, B., Shang, M.: Hyperparameter learning for deep learning-based recommender systems. IEEE Trans. Serv. Comput. **16**, 2699–2712 (2023)
33. Cao, L.: Decentralized AI: edge intelligence and smart blockchain, metaverse, web3, and DESCI. IEEE Intell. Syst. **37**(3), 6–19 (2022)
34. Sathishkumar, V.E., Jangwoo, P., Yongyun, C.: Using data mining techniques for bike sharing demand prediction in metropolitan city. Comput. Commun. **153**, 353–366 (2020)
35. Sathishkumar, V.E., Yongyun, C.: A rule-based model for Seoul Bike sharing demand prediction using weather data. Eur. J. Remote Sens. **53**(sup1), 166–183 (2020)
36. Powell, M.J.D.: A direct search optimization method that models the objective and constraint functions by linear interpolation. In: Gomez, S., Hennart, J.P. (eds.) Advances in Optimization and Numerical Analysis, pp. 51–67. Springer, Dordrecht (1994). https://doi.org/10.1007/978-94-015-8330-5_4
37. Spall, J.: An overview of the simultaneous perturbation method for efficient optimization. J. Hopkins APL Tech. Dig. **19**(4), 482–492 (1998)
38. Nelder, J.A., Mead, R.: A simplex method for function minimization. Comput. J. **7**(4), 308–313 (1965)

Dynamic Adaptation of Urgent Applications in the Edge-to-Cloud Continuum

Daniel Balouek[(⊠)] and Hélène Coullon

IMT Atlantique, INRIA, LS2N, UMR CNRS 6004, 44307 Nantes, France
`daniel.balouek@inria.fr, helene.coullon@imt-atlantique.fr`

Abstract. The integration of Urgent Computing is essential in order to adhere to stringent time and quality constraints of emerging distributed applications, hence facilitating efficient decision-making processes in numerous fields. Adaptation of such applications to produce outcomes within the desired confidence range and defined time interval can be of great benefit, especially in distributed and heterogeneous execution contexts. This study provides a justification for the necessity of dynamic adaptation in applications that are time-sensitive. Furthermore, we present our viewpoint on time-sensitive applications and undertake a thorough analysis of the underlying principles and challenges that need to be resolved in order to accomplish this goal. This research aims to provide a comparative analysis of our suggested vision for adaptation in contrast to the existing literature. We provide a comprehensive explanation of the architectural framework that we plan to construct, and conclude with discussing some on-going challenges.

Keywords: Urgent Computing · Computing Continuum · Dynamic Adaptation · Decentralized System

1 Introduction

Recent years have witnessed an increase in global emergencies, from pandemics that claim lives and livelihoods to risks of flooding and food harvesting challenges brought on by climate change. Society at large is wrestling with these pressing challenges, which warrant for solutions guided by science [26]. Advanced information and communication technologies, such as IoT, Artificial Intelligence, big data analytics, and super computers (*e.g.,* Clouds, High Performance Computing), have been proven to be more and more helpful in predicting scenarios' outcomes early enough to prevent disastrous situations or lessen their harmful effects. During the COVID-19 pandemic, supercomputers and data systems have worked together with unprecedented efficiency, from understanding the structure of the SARS-CoV-2 virus to modeling its spread, from therapeutics to vaccines, from medical response to managing the virus's impacts [3,17]. Similarly, the

ⓒ The Author(s), under exclusive license to Springer Nature Switzerland AG 2024
D. Zeinalipour et al. (Eds.): Euro-Par 2023 Workshops, LNCS 14351, pp. 189–201, 2024.
https://doi.org/10.1007/978-3-031-50684-0_15

VESTEC European FET project fuses super computers and real-time data for urgent decision-making [11].

Urgent computing aims at facilitating scientific applications that leverage distributed data sources to support critical decision-making in a timely manner. Overall, urgent applications consist of the identification of events from distributed data sources and the triggering of appropriate reactions to accelerate response [19,24]. The time scales of the underlying processes vary from days in case of social unrest events, to hours in flood protection systems, to minutes in ship safety, and to seconds in earthquakes or tsunamis [10]. The time available for decision support therefore varies in different application domains. An urgent application is typically modeled as a workflow of components exchanging discrete or continuous flows of data.

Low-latency connections and distributed servers, illustrated by the Edge-to-Cloud Continuum (Computing Continuum, or Continuum for short), are demonstrating new potential for urgent computing. Running applications on an aggregation of resources spanning the edge of the network, where data are generated, to the cloud and HPC resources at the network's core, is an opportunity for steering computations and numerical models to help reduce latency while increasing flexibility [7,22]. For example, the Tactile Internet is expected to enable the matching of specific needs in one physical location with the best skill in another location. Building on 5G-like connectivity and haptic encoders, this technology will require an end-to-end latency below 1ms with minimal outage [2,30]. Due to these requirements, the Computing Continuum is an excellent enabler for urgent applications due to its holistic approach that exploits end-users, resources, and services at the logical extreme of the network and throughout the data path [6] [9].

The realization of urgent applications presents specific requirements and constraints due to the nature and distribution of the data, the complexity of the models involved, the stringent error thresholds, and the strict time constraints. Identifying and mapping various user concerns (such as functional and non-functional requirements, restrictions for response time, solution quality, data resolution, cost, energy use, etc.) against a heterogeneous and dynamic environment warrant the design of adaptation mechanisms. Examples of such adaptations are choosing suitable workflow components and services, modifying application parameters, modifying the connections between components of the workflow, changing the required constraints when provisioning resources (e.g., CPU, RAM, network, etc.) Such mechanisms must be able to address cost/benefit trade-offs of the application.

This paper proposes a vision of how adaptation mechanisms can be natively handled when designing urgent applications across the Continuum. The remainder of the paper is organized as follows: Sect. 2 gives a motivating use-case for our vision with an Early Earthquake Warning (EEW) workflow, which combines data streams from geo-distributed seismometers and high-precision GPS stations to detect large groundmotions; Section 3 presents our vision of urgent applications through the modeling of both the development and management aspects; Sect. 4 presents elements of solutions and open challenges around our vision, and finally, Sect. 5 concludes this work.

2   Motivating Use Case

In this section, we introduce the Earthquake Early Warning use case that motivated this work. We also discuss the challenges associated with executing distributed applications on the Computing Continuum.

Earthquakes are among the most destructive natural disasters. Networks of distributed seismic instruments on various scales are used for earthquake detection. *Earthquake Early Warning* (EEW) systems provide earthquake alerts before the shaking damage of a seismic event reaches sensitive areas, giving governments and communities a time window of seconds to minutes to take protective actions.

EEW can be described as a *classification problem* in which high-frequency seismic data stream from multiple sensors are processed to infer classes indicating the magnitude of the seismic event in a timely manner. Related efforts include novel algorithms recently developed to locate earthquakes and to calculate their magnitudes using P- and S-wave energy [31]. Recently, ShakeAlert proposed detecting and disseminating EEW alerts using smartphones, relying on the fact that they have become ubiquitous to the public [21,28].

EEW is a workflow typically composed of four components: (1) the *preprocessing* component that collects and cleans raw data obtained from sensors; (2) the *classification* component that relies on window-based processing to gather measurements streamed by each sensor, and performs classification on this streamed data; (3) the *prediction* component that filters and aggregates the data streams by regions using a bag-of-words representation to calculate the final prediction of eventual seismic events; (4) the *alert* component that is responsible for broadcasting alerts based on class predictions (normal activity, medium earthquake, or large earthquake). Some of these components may run continuously somewhere in the Continuum, but when initial seismic waves are detected, this complete workflow has to be deployed in a timely manner.

Traditionally, EEW is executed in a fully centralized fashion with data from sensors being sent to clouds (private or public) which is compatible with a static way of designing the application. However, this vision of EEW will not withstand potential destruction or unavailability of the infrastructure (fault tolerance), and thus is not reliable. Instead, we would like to leverage heterogeneous geographically distributed resources across the Continuum, which requires applications to adapt dynamically their codes, communication protocols, etc. According to the dynamically chosen hosting resource. For instance, if deployed within the Cloud, the *prediction* component can leverage heavy stream processing frameworks such as Flink, whereas if deployed at the Edge on small devices, low-level C libraries and MPI would be preferable.

In previous work [8,16] we proposed moving part of the sensor data processing toward the Edge to speed up detection and enhance fault tolerance. Figure 1 illustrates this static Edge deployment. However, if we have shown that different versions of the application running on different parts of the Continuum may have different behaviors, we did not address the automatic and dynamic adaptation of the application.

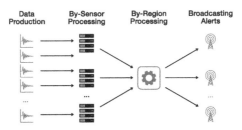

Fig. 1. An illustration of Distributed MultiSensor Earthquake Early Warning use-case (DMSEEW), previously proposed in [7]. Seismic sensors located in the Edge send measurements to gateways in the network which preprocess that data. Those preprocessed data are sent to cloud servers which complete that data processing and eventually broadcast earthquake alerts.

We use Fig. 2 (extracted from [8]) to further illustrate the need for adaptation in this use-case. Figure 2 presents the latency resulting from processing one seismic event in a previous evaluation of our EEW implementation [8]. Using the *gros* cluster on the Grid'5000 experimental testbed, we deployed a prototype of the application under different network configurations: a 10Gb link between the Edge and Fog layers, and different links (2G, 3G, 10 Gb) between the Fog and the Cloud layers. *Edge* designates that each component is executed on a separated layer of the Continuum whereas *Cloud-only* means all components are executed on the Cloud. Of course, when running in the Edge or at the Cloud level, the components also have to be adapted (*e.g.,* libraries, frameworks, etc.).

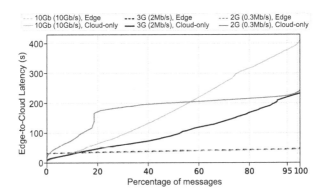

Fig. 2. Latency resulting from processing one seismic event under different applications and infrastructure scenarios, extracted from [8].

The performance of the application is influenced by two factors: the network and the bottlenecks resulting from the interaction between the different libraries (in the context of the current paper, *components*). The different values were obtained in separated experiments to understand the behavior of the application under different conditions. Currently, there is no mechanism to switch from one configuration to another based on availability of the infrastructure and the events occurring in the system, but also there is a need to consider the cost and feasibility of the operations when such reconfiguration is needed, which motivates the need for adaptation mechanisms.

3   Our Vision of Urgent Computing

First, we see the Continuum as an external infrastructure offered by a provider. We consider that we do not have to handle this Continuum but instead that the Continuum is offering APIs to ask for resources (*e.g.*, virtual or physical machines). In particular, we think that, in addition to the usual Cloud APIs that provides a type of resource as well as specific features (RAM, CPU, GPU etc.), one can also provision specific geographical locations in the Continuum.

Definition 1. *We model an urgent application as a pair $(\mathcal{D}, \mathcal{M})$, where $\mathcal{D}$ is specified by the application developers (functional and nonfunctional developers), and $\mathcal{M}$ is specified typically by DevOps engineers or system administrators to manage the application deployment and life-cycle (i.e., adaptation).*

This vision follows the one presented in [15], a survey on component-oriented reconfiguration.

3.1   Development Part of an Urgent Application

Definition 2. *The development of an urgent application $\mathcal{D}$ is a tuple (C, P, m, p_i, p_c) with:*

- *C the set of software components available for the application, some of them being produced by the current developer, others being made available from the community;*
- *P the set of patterns or strategies of service assemblies;*
- *m a labeled finite state machine that indicates from which to which pattern in P the application may switch at runtime and under which conditions;*
- *p_i the initial pattern in P;*
- *p_c the current pattern in P.*

Definition 3. *A pattern $p \in P$ is defined as an assembly of components (C_p, L_p) where $C_p \subseteq C$ is the set of component instances in the pattern, and L_p is the set of connections or links between components.*

In urgent applications, the nature of the connections is typically data-driven, and thus the assembly of components can be considered as a dataflow or a workflow. However, we want to add configurations to the links between components, under the form of connectors in the CBSE literature [15], or service-mesh approaches [18,25]. For example, we may want to redirect 50% of data to one component or another dynamically according to events. Hence, a link is configurable in our vision of urgent components (Fig. 3).

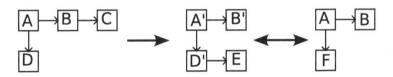

Fig. 3. An illustration of m, an object (state machine) modeling from which to which pattern the urgent application can switch. The pattern on the left is the initial pattern. In this example the initial pattern cannot be reached after a first switch.

Definition 4. *An urgent component $c \in C$ is defined as a tuple $(S_f, S_{nf}, V^c, C_{st}^c)$, where S_f is the set of functional services of the urgent component, S_{nf} is the set of non-functional services of the component, V^c a set of variables to model the state, behavior or parameters of the component, and C_{st}^c is the set of constraints on variables.*

A component is associated with a set of variables V^c to model the component (state, behavior, parameters), thus representing either the static or dynamic knowledge (modeling) on each component. These variables can then be used within constraints C_{st}^c that should be satisfied on a set of variables. One typical constraint that we consider at the level of the component is the geographical location of the component.

A non-functional service is a piece of software responsible for features not related to the functional aspect of the component, for instance how the component communicates (*i.e.,* communication protocol), handles privacy, or energy etc. Services are deployed (instantiated) from types known in advance, and thus one service can be switched to another if compatible. At the level of one component, this catalog of services should be quite small. It is offered by the developer. Both the elements of S_f and S_{nf} are considered as configurable. Functional and non-functional services will typically change their configuration according to the constraints imposed by the infrastructure. For instance, if placed in an IoT device, the urgent component communicates through the LoRa protocol and optimizes the energy consumption rather than the performance. As a consequence the non-functional service responsible for communications may be modified, and the version of the functional service may need to be a downgraded version.

Each service is also associated with a set of variables V^s modeling their parameters, state, behavior, etc., and these variables can then be used within constraints C_{st}^s that should be satisfied on a set of variables. For example, we could have a constraint on the amount of memory required by a service.

Definition 5. *A service is defined as a tuple* (t, V^s, C_{st}^s), *where* t *is the type of the service,* V^s *is the set of variables of the service, and* C_{st}^s *is the set of constraints to satisfy for the service.*

3.2 Management Part of an Urgent Application

The management $\mathcal{M}$ of an urgent application is a complex task responsible for deploying and then adapting the application dynamically at run-time according to events. However, because of scalability and fault tolerance issues when considering urgent cases, the management cannot be considered as a centralized process.

We model the management of the application as a set of controllers C_t, one around each component in C involved in the application. Each controller is responsible for an autonomic infinite loop MAPE-K [20] for its own component: monitoring the component and its environment (through sensors, infrastructure, or application instrumentation); deciding which new configuration should be targeted according to the monitoring knowledge (inference through constraints, by applying rules and policies); planning an adaptation program to move from the current to the targeted configuration (writing a program to modify the state of the component [13,14]); and execute this plan (*i.e.*, program). Controllers, by being local to one component, have the possibility of adapting locally if isolated from the rest of the application, but in a normal context neighbor controllers can collaborate to take better decisions [4].

It is assumed that each controller component operates on its own unique time scale, independent from the others. For example, monitoring can be an ongoing process, whereas analysis of the data that has been acquired most likely occurs only on occasion. Both processes are used to analyze the information that was collected. The planning is done on a consistent basis or in reaction to changes, and the executions are done as a direct result of the planning.

Definition 6. *The management of an urgent application* $\mathcal{M}$ *is a tuple* (C_t, P, m, p_i, p_c) *where* C_t *is the set of controllers,* P, m, p_i, *and* p_c *respectively the same set of patterns, state machine, initial and current patterns as in* $\mathcal{D}$.

Definition 7. *Two controllers are neighbors if their components are connected in the current pattern (graph, assembly)* $p \in P$ *of the urgent application. The neighbors of a controller are denoted* $neighbors(c_t)$.

Definition 8. *A controller* $c_t \in C_t$ *is a piece of software responsible for running an autonomic infinite loop MAPE-K [20] for its own component, denoted* $component(c_t)$.

We denote by X^{c_t} the local projection of any piece of the above knowledge in $(\mathcal{D}, \mathcal{M})$ to a controller $c_t \in C_t$. A local projection contains the information that relates to the local component that is controlled, and the neighbor components in the current pattern $p \in P$ (Fig. 4).

Definition 9. *The local knowledge (K) of each controller c_t is composed of a subpart of the application model $(\mathcal{D}, \mathcal{M})$ as follows:*

- *in $\mathcal{D}$, the local projection of the set of components C^{c_t};*
- *in $\mathcal{M}$, the local projection of the set of controllers $C^{c_t}_t$;*
- *for both $\mathcal{D}$ and $\mathcal{M}$, the local projection of the set of patterns P^{c_t}, and the initial and current patterns $p_i^{c_t}$ and $p_c^{c_t}$;*
- *for both $\mathcal{D}$ and $\mathcal{M}$, the labeled state machine m.*

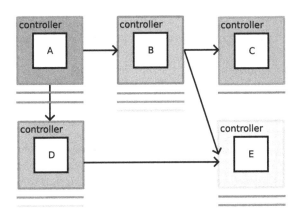

Fig. 4. An illustration of a pattern with five components and their associated controllers (one color per controller). The colored lines under components represent the local projection of the controller associated with the color, in other words the knowledge of each controller. For instance, the controller of the component B (purple) has knowledge of components A, C and E represented by purple lines.

The local projections of a pattern can be seen as a subgraph of the overall component assembly that contains as vertices

$$component(c_t) \cup neighbors(component(c_t)) \tag{1}$$

As always in distributed systems, we assume that the knowledge shared by controllers is consistent, which is a challenging issue to address. However, to facilitate the global consistency in our modeling, we use a local projection on the local component and its neighbors. The labeled state machine m, which represents the rules under which an urgent application may change its pattern, is the only piece of knowledge that is centralized in this vision. This state machine is given by the developer. However, as will be discussed in the challenges of this paper, it is possible that m change through time, in which case a consistent vision of m is difficult to guarantee.

A controller can adapt many aspects related to an urgent component such as: (1) change the constraints of the component related to the Continuum C_{st}^c; (2) change the versions of the services within the component while respecting the composability (compatibility of output/input data) $(S_f, S_n f)$; (3) change the configuration of the services of a component (t, V^s, C_{st}^s); (4) change the current pattern p_c to another one by following m, thus changing the topology between components and involved components; (5) change the configuration of the link between components; and (6) spawn, or ask for the destruction of a neighbor component. The "urgent" nature of the domain makes adaptation sensitive to time, which will be discussed in the challenges.

4   Elements of Solution and Open Scientific Challenges

As detailed in the previous section, each controller of a component handles a local autonomic loop MAPE-K. However, the loops cannot be strictly local and requires to collaborate with their neighbors so that the overall application does not deviate from a stable state. In particular, the (A), (P) and (E) steps require collaborations between controllers by exchanging some elements of their local knowledge (K) and by reaching a consensus in their decisions [4]. For instance, if deciding locally to apply a switch of pattern, the decision should spread across all the controllers and should be compatible for all controllers. We give some elements of solutions in the rest of this section.

(K)nowledge - In our vision the first element to study is how to concretely model the programming and management of urgent applications. We think we can build our vision on three domains of the literature. First, we think that leveraging modern *workflow engines* based on the FaaS paradigm (Function-as-a-Service), such as Argo workflows[1], or other engines adapted to heterogeneous workflows [12], is an interesting starting point to model urgent applications. Second, this vision of an urgent application as a workflow of components will have to be coupled with the *service-oriented* and *microservices-oriented* trend (*e.g.*, REST, gRPC, GraphQL APIs). In particular, in our vision each component of the workflow is divided into services. Third, we think we will have to model the variability of components and services composing urgent applications with the help of *feature models*. Feature models are used in software engineering to capture the various configurations that can be selected or enabled in a software system. A feature model consists of a set of features, relationships between features, and constraints on their combinations. Features represent distinct functionalities, or behaviors that can be included or excluded in the software system. Coupling these three domains is not trivial and requires a software-engineering-oriented study. For example, coupling feature models with workflows has been studied in the past [1], as well as coupling feature models and micro-services [29], but the three of them together is a new challenge.

---

[1] https://argoproj.github.io/argo-workflows/.

(A)nalysis - The second element to study is how to decide which local config-uration to target according to internal and external events and to some degree of knowledge from neighboring controllers. In particular, if all controllers take a local decision, will the decisions be compatible, and how to make sure of it? We think that the three domains could be combined to handle this aspect. First, we think that distributed algorithms such as consensus, gossip, and leader election algorithms [4,23] could be helpful to reach a convergence between controllers in their decisions. Second, we think that auto-stabilizing versions of these algo-rithms could be important to avoid too many communications but still guarantee the convergence (stabilization) of the overall system [5]. Third, we think that because of the huge variability when adapting urgent application (large search space), and because of the urgent nature of the decisions, machine learning could be of interest. In particular, perhaps reinforcement learning and federated learn-ing could be studied so that decisions become better through time and so that learning models are trained in a distributed fashion among the controllers. We also think that a learning approach could be supplemented with more traditional approaches to solve satisfaction problems such as constraint solvers or SAT/first-order logic solvers to keep a certain level of explainability in the decision.

(P)lanning and the (E)xecution - In order to tackle many controllers, each with its own autonomic loop, we need languages to define adaptation actions (*e.g.,* changing the pattern, changing internal behaviors of components or ser-vices, changing the links between components, etc.), and an associated engine to run these actions in a decentralized fashion. Indeed, if each controller takes its own decision, controllers are not independent because components are connected together, thus requiring some coordination when applying changes. For exam-ple, if updating one component, thus requiring it be interrupted, the components that depend on it have to adapt temporarily their own behavior.

In the literature planning and executing an adaptation is often referred as a reconfiguration problem: a reconfiguration language offers programming support to structure and expresses the actions to perform to change the system state; a reconfiguration engine executes and coordinates actions [13,14]; and a reconfig-uration inference system automatically generates the set of actions to apply (the plan) [27] according to the current and target configurations as inputs. However, existing solutions are mainly centralized in the literature [4,15].

Moreover, the usual reconfiguration systems in the literature do not tackle the reconfiguration of the links between components of the system [15]. For this reason, we think that concepts of service-mesh [18,25] could be of interest to couple with the usual reconfiguration solutions.

5   Conclusion

Urgent applications are of significant interest in the literature due to the increase of global challenges. The availability of data and pervasive computing promise potential for supporting timely decision-making across the Computing Continuum. In this paper, we presented a vision for modeling urgent applications, with a particular focus on adaptation aspects across heterogeneous and geo-distributed resources. Building on an earthquake early warning motivating use-case, we propose an approach based on component-based reconfiguration. We expect the realization of this vision to impact cyber-infrastructures and similar shared sensors platform in a way that will manage time-sensitive applications and associated requirements with few assumptions during the design of applications.

References

1. Acher, M., Collet, P., Lahire, P., France, R.: Managing variability in workflow with feature model composition operators. In: Baudry, B., Wohlstadter, E. (eds.) SC 2010. LNCS, vol. 6144, pp. 17–33. Springer, Heidelberg (2010). https://doi.org/10.1007/978-3-642-14046-4_2

2. Aijaz, A., Dohler, M., Aghvami, A.H., Friderikos, V., Frodigh, M.: Realizing the tactile internet: haptic communications over next generation 5G cellular networks. IEEE Wirel. Commun. **24**, 82–89 (2017)

3. Alashhab, Z.R., Anbar, M., Singh, M.M., Leau, Y.B., Al-Sai, Z.A., Alhayja'a, S.A.: Impact of coronavirus pandemic crisis on technologies and cloud computing applications. J. Electron. Sci. Technol. **19**(1), 100059 (2021)

4. Alidra, A., et al.: SeMaFoR - self-management of fog resources with collaborative decentralized controllers. In: SEAMS 2023 - IEEE/ACM 18th Symposium on Software Engineering for Adaptive and Self-Managing Systems (2023). https://doi.org/10.1109/SEAMS59076.2023.00014

5. Altisen, K., Devismes, S., Dubois, S., Petit, F.: Introduction to Distributed Self-Stabilizing Algorithms. (2019). https://doi.org/10.2200/S00908ED1V01Y201903DCT015

6. Balouek-Thomert, D., Renart, E.G., Zamani, A.R., Simonet, A., Parashar, M.: Towards a computing continuum: enabling edge-to-cloud integration for data-driven workflows. Int. J. High Perform. Comput. Appl. **33**, 1159–1174 (2019)

7. Balouek-Thomert, D., Rodero, I., Parashar, M.: Harnessing the computing continuum for urgent science. ACM SIGMETRICS Perform. Rev. **48**, 41–46 (2020)

8. Balouek-Thomert, D., Silva, P., Fauvel, K., Costan, A., Antoniu, G., Parashar, M.: MDSC: modelling distributed stream processing across the edge-to-cloud continuum. In: Proceedings of the 14th IEEE/ACM International Conference on Utility and Cloud Computing Companion, pp. 1–6 (2021)

9. Beckman, P., Dongarra, J., Ferrier, N., Fox, G., Moore, T., Reed, D., Beck, M.: Harnessing the computing continuum for programming our world. In: Fog Computing: Theory and Practice: Theory and Practice, Wiley (2019)

10. Boukhanovsky, A.V., Krzhizhanovskaya, V.V., Bubak, M.: Urgent computing for decision support in critical situations. Future Gener. Comput. Syst. **79**, 111–113 (2018)

11. Brown, N., et al.: The role of interactive super-computing in using HPC for urgent decision making. In: Weiland, M., Juckeland, G., Alam, S., Jagode, H. (eds.) ISC High Performance 2019. LNCS, vol. 11887, pp. 528–540. Springer, Cham (2019). https://doi.org/10.1007/978-3-030-34356-9_40

12. Cadorel, E., Coullon, H., Menaud, J.M.: Handling heterogeneous workflows in the cloud while enhancing optimizations and performance. In: 2022 IEEE 15th International Conference on Cloud Computing (CLOUD) (2022). https://doi.org/10.1109/CLOUD55607.2022.00021

13. Chardet, M., Coullon, H., Pérez, C.: Predictable efficiency for reconfiguration of service-oriented systems with concerto. In: CCGrid 2020 : 20th IEEE/ACM International Symposium on Cluster, Cloud and Internet Computing (2020). https://doi.org/10.1109/CCGrid49817.2020.00-59

14. Chardet, M., Coullon, H., Robillard, S.: Toward safe and efficient reconfiguration with concerto. Sci. Comput. Program. (2021). https://doi.org/10.1016/j.scico.2020.102582

15. Coullon, H., Henrio, L., Loulergue, F., Robillard, S.: Component-based distributed software reconfiguration: a verification-oriented survey. ACM Comput. Surv. **56**, 1–37 (2023). https://doi.org/10.1145/3595376

16. Fauvel, K., al.: A Distributed multi-sensor machine learning approach to earthquake early warning. In: Proceedings of the Thirty-Fourth AAAI Conference on Artificial Intelligence (2020)

17. Friji, H., Hamadi, R., Ghazzai, H., Besbes, H., Massoud, Y.: A generalized mechanistic model for assessing and forecasting the spread of the COVID-19 pandemic. IEEE Access **9**, 13266–13285 (2021)

18. Ganguli, M., Ranganath, S., Ravisundar, S., Layek, A., Ilangovan, D., Verplanke, E.: Challenges and opportunities in performance benchmarking of service mesh for the edge. In: 2021 IEEE International Conference on Edge Computing (EDGE) (2021). https://doi.org/10.1109/EDGE53862.2021.00020

19. Gibb, G., Nash, R., Brown, N., Prodan, B.: The technologies required for fusing HPC and real-time data to support urgent computing. In: 2019 IEEE/ACM HPC for Urgent Decision Making (UrgentHPC), pp. 24–34. IEEE (2019)

20. Kephart, J., Chess, D.: The vision of autonomic computing. Computer **36**, 41–50 (2003)

21. Kohler, M.D., et al.: Earthquake early warning ShakeAlert 2.0: public rollout. Seismol. Res. Lett. **91**(3), 1763–1775 (2020). https://doi.org/10.1785/0220190245 https://doi.org/10.1785/0220190245

22. Kumar, R., Baughman, M., Chard, R., Li, Z., Babuji, Y., Foster, I., Chard, K.: Coding the computing continuum: fluid function execution in heterogeneous computing environments. In: 2021 IEEE International Parallel and Distributed Processing Symposium Workshops (IPDPSW), pp. 66–75. IEEE (2021)

23. Lamport, L., Shostak, R., Pease, M.: The byzantine generals problem. ACM Trans. Program. Lang. Syst. **4**, 382–400 (1982)

24. Leong, S.H., Kranzlmüller, D.: Towards a general definition of urgent computing. Procedia Computer Science **51**, 2337–2346 (2015)

25. Li, W., Lemieux, Y., Gao, J., Zhao, Z., Han, Y.: Service mesh: challenges, state of the art, and future research opportunities. In: 2019 IEEE International Conference on Service-Oriented System Engineering (SOSE) (2019)

26. Peleg, K., Bodas, M., Hertelendy, A.J., Kirsch, T.D.: The COVID-19 pandemic challenge to the all-hazards approach for disaster planning. Int. J. Disaster Risk Reduction **55**, 102103 (2021)

27. Robillard, S., Coullon, H.: SMT-based planning synthesis for distributed system reconfigurations. In: FASE 2022 : 25th International Conference on Fundamental Approaches to Software Engineering (2022). https://doi.org/10.1007/978-3-030-99429-7_15
28. Rochford, K., Strauss, J.A., Kong, Q., Allen, R.M.: MyShake: using human-centered design methods to promote engagement in a smartphone-based global seismic network. Front. Earth Sci. **6**, 237 (2018)
29. Sousa, G., Rudametkin, W., Duchien, L.: Automated setup of multi-cloud environments for microservices applications. In: 2016 IEEE 9th International Conference on Cloud Computing (CLOUD) (2016)
30. Van Den Berg, D., et al.: Challenges in haptic communications over the tactile internet. IEEE Access **5**, 23502–23518 (2017)
31. Yih-Min, W., Ta-liang, T.: A virtual sub-network approach to earthquake early warning. Bull. Seism. Soc. Am. **92**, 2008–2018 (2002)

The 21st International Workshop on Algorithms, Models and Tools for Parallel Computing on Heterogeneous Platforms (HETEROPAR 2023)

International Workshop on Algorithms, Models and Tools for Parallel Computing on Heterogeneous Platforms (HeteroPar)

Workshop Description

HeteroPar is a forum tailored for the study of diverse aspects of heterogeneity and caters to researchers working on algorithms, programming languages, tools, and theoretical models aimed at efficiently solving problems on heterogeneous platforms. It includes a broad range of topics about high-performance heterogeneous computing from heterogeneous parallel programming paradigms, and algorithms, models, and tools for energy optimization on heterogeneous platforms to fault tolerance of parallel computations on heterogeneous platforms.

The 21st edition of the workshop (HeteroPar 2023) was held on August 28th in Limassol, Cyprus. For the fifteenth time, this workshop was organized in conjunction with the Euro-Par international conference. The format of the workshop included a keynote followed by four sessions of technical presentations. The program committee (PC) comprised 36 members with expertise in various aspects of high-performance heterogeneous computing. The workshop was well-attended, featuring a healthy average of 40 attendees.

We received 19 articles for review this year. Each paper secured three reviews from members of the PC. After a thorough single-blind peer-reviewing process, we selected 12 high-quality articles (an acceptance ratio of 63%) for presentation at the workshop. The review process focused on the quality of the papers, their innovative ideas, and their applicability to the field of high-performance heterogeneous computing. Reflecting the papers' interest, the audience participation was very high and each presenter received at least three questions or remarks during the allotted time for discussions.

I would like to thank the HeteroPar Steering Committee and the HeteroPar 2023 Program Committee for their diligent efforts in ensuring the high quality and continued success of this workshop. I would also like to thank Euro-Par for hosting our community, and the Euro-Par workshop chairs Demetris Zeinalipour and Dora Blanco Heras for their help and support. In particular, I want to thank Terry Cojean for ensuring the smooth workshop implementation on-site in Limassol.

Organization

Steering Committee

Domingo Giménez	University of Murcia, Spain
Alexey Kalinov	Cadence Design Systems, Russia
Alexey Lastovetsky	University College Dublin, Ireland
Yves Robert	École Normale Supérieure de Lyon, France
Leonel Sousa	Universidade de Lisboa, Portugal
Denis Trystram	Grenoble Alpes University, France

Program Chairs

Hartwig Anzt	University of Tennessee, Knoxville, USA
Terry Cojean	Karlsruhe Institute of Technology, Germany

Program Committee

Giovanni Agosta	Politecnico di Milano, Italy
Andrey Alekseenko	KTH Royal Institute of Technology, Sweden
Raja Appuswamy	EURECOM, France
Michael Bader	Technical University of Munich, Germany
Jorge Barbosa	Faculdade de Engenharia do Porto, Portugal
George Bosilca	University of Tennessee, USA
Xing Cai	Simula, Norway
Danial Chitnis	University of Edinburgh, UK
Jan Ciesko	Sandia National Labs, USA
Biagio Cosenza	University of Salerno, Italy
Jorge Ejarque	Barcelona Supercomputing Center, Spain
Toshio Endo	Tokyo Institute of Technology, Japan
Mehdi Goli	Codeplay, UK
Brice Goglin	Inria & University of Bordeaux, France
Alfredo Goldman	São Paulo University, Brazil
Kevin Harms	Argonne National Laboratory, USA
Francisco Igual	Universidad Complutense de Madrid, Spain
Aleksandar Illic	Universidade de Lisboa, Portugal
Joanna Kolodziej	NASK Warsaw, Poland

Leveraging MLIR for Loop Vectorization and GPU Porting of FFT Libraries

Yifei He$^{(\boxtimes)}$, Artur Podobas, and Stefano Markidis

KTH Royal Institute of Technology, Stockholm, Sweden
{yifeihe,podobas,markidis}@kth.se

Abstract. `FFTc` is a Domain-Specific Language (DSL) for designing and generating Fast Fourier Transforms (FFT) libraries. The `FFTc` uniqueness is that it leverages and extend Multi-Level Intermediate Representation (MLIR) dialects to optimize FFT code generation. In this work, we present `FFTc` extensions and improvements such as the possibility of using different data layout for complex-value arrays, and sparsification to enable efficient vectorization, and a seamless porting of FFT libraries to GPU systems. We show that, on CPUs, thanks to vectorization, the performance of the `FFTc`-generated FFT is comparable to performance of `FFTW`, a state-of-the-art FFT libraries. We also present the initial performance results for `FFTc` on Nvidia GPUs.

Keywords: FFTc · Automatic Loop Vectorization · GPU Porting · LLVM · MLIR

1 Introduction

Discrete Fourier Transforms (DFT) and their efficient formulations, called Fast Fourier Transforms (FFT), are a critical building block for efficient and high-performance data analysis and scientific computing. In a nutshell, DFTs allow for transforming a digital signal in time, ingested as an input array, into its components in the spectral domain, typically as a complex-value output array. Among several applications, DFTs are widely used for signal processing, e.g., decomposing a signal into its spectral components, or solving Partial Differential Equations (PDE). For instance, the DFT computation is one of the major computational bottleneck in the Particle-Mesh Ewald calculation of the GROMACS, molecular dynamics code [1].

Because of the central role of FFTs in data analysis and scientific computing, several high-performance FFT libraries have been developed. The Fastest Fourier Transform in the West (`FFTW`) library is among the most used HPC FFT libraries for its performance on serial and parallel systems. In essence, `FFTW` is a source-to-source compiler emitting a C code to express an FFT library optimized for a given system. However, the FFTW core was first designed and implemented with compiler technologies, nowadays outdated and support only multicore CPUs and not GPUs. On the other hand, the open-source compiler

D. Zeinalipour et al. (Eds.): Euro-Par 2023 Workshops, LNCS 14351, pp. 207–218, 2024.
https://doi.org/10.1007/978-3-031-50684-0_16

infrastructure is evolving fast. For instance, LLVM became the industry standard for compiler infrastructure, which is the general Intermediate Representation (IR) and supports many hardware back-ends, including for instance GPU programming. More recently, Multi Level IR (MLIR) introduced the concept of multiple abstraction levels and made it easy to apply high-level domain-specific transformations. All these new efforts in the compiler area can be used to develop a modern FFT libraries that can support heterogeneous computing, multiple hardware backends, including accelerator support.

FFTc is a new Domain-Specific Language (DSL) built on top of MLIR and LLVM to generate high-performance portable FFT libraries [6]. Differently from FFTW, FFTc can leverage new compiler technologies that allows for a seamless usage of vectorization capabilities and GPU porting. In this work, we present and discuss the new FFTc developments on enabling automatic loop vectorization on CPUs and automatic porting to Nvidia GPUs. To enable these functionalities efficiently, a new data layout for complex-value data and an algorithmic formulation using sparse computation (as opposed to previous FFTc dense computation). The work, presented in this paper, makes the following contributions:

- We introduce a methodology to convert the complex data type to a first-class type supported by LLVM and hardware ISA, making it possible to apply target-specific optimizations such as vectorization on complex data in MLIR.
- We discuss the whole compilation transformation pipeline to enable loop vectorization and GPU usage.
- We showcase FFTc portability: FFTc can generate efficient code for exploiting vectorization on CPUs and porting FFT libraries to GPU, with a single input source code.

2   FFTc: An MLIR Dialect for FFT Development

Our goal when designing FFTc is to mask out the hardware details and apply high-level domain-specific optimizations automatically, meanwhile targeting multiple different backends (CPUs/GPUs/etc.) without changes of the source code.

We provide an overview of the FFTc compilation pipeline in Fig. 1. The approach consists a combination of three different components:

1. A declarative DSL that operates on tensors (we formulate the FFT algorithm as a factorization of several matrices) and uses tensor products and matrix multiplications. The framework frontend component is shown in the green blocks of Fig. 1. Alternatively, we can also use the MLIR Python binding to generate MLIR directly.
2. A MLIR dialect with high-level domain-specific FFT semantics, based on Static Single Assignment (SSA) form.
3. A progressive lowering compilation pipeline, which consists of high-level domain-specific optimizations in MLIR and target-specific transformations in MLIR and LLVM. The MLIR dialects and transformations are shown in

the blue boxes of Fig. 1, and the LLVM compilation parts are orange. The detailed description and code examples of FFTc DSL and FFT dialect in MLIR can be found in our prior work [6].

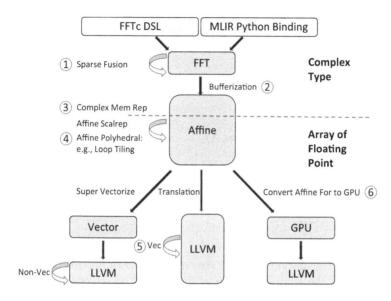

Fig. 1. FFTc Compilation Pipeline

3   FFTc Transformations, Loop Vectorization and GPU Porting

In this paper, we describe the new FFTc developments in the compilation to enable loop vectorization and GPU porting. In FFTc, we use a tensor formalism expressing FFT algorithms as the factorization of the DFT matrix into sparse matrices. This approach is widely used in developing FFT libraries, such as SPIRAL [3] and Lift [7]. For instance, using this formulation, the Cooley-Tukey general-radix decimation-in-time algorithm for an input of size N can be written as:

$$\text{DFT}_N = (\text{DFT}_K \otimes \text{I}_M)\, \text{D}_M^N (\text{I}_K \otimes \text{DFT}_M)\, \Pi_K^N \quad \text{with} \quad N = MK, \tag{1}$$

where Π_K^N is a stride permute operator and D_M^N is a diagonal matrix of *twiddle* factors. We present now the new developments following the compilation pipeline, presented in Fig. 1 as differed numbered phases.

① **FFTc Sparse Fusion Transformation.** The first implementation we demonstrated in the DSL used dense matrix representation and computation [6],

Table 1. Sparse Fusion and Bufferization Transform.

FFTc DSL Pattern	Sparse Fusion	Bufferization
$Y = (A_m \otimes I_n) \cdot X$	FusedMKIV(A, n, X)	for$(i = 0;\ i < n;\ i++)$ $Y[i : n : i + m * n - n] =$ $A*(X[i : n : i + m * n - n])$
$Y = (I_m \otimes A_n) \cdot X$	FusedIKMV(A, n, X)	for$(i = 0;\ i < m;\ i++)$ $Y[i * n : 1 : i * n + n - 1] =$ $A*(X[i * n : 1 : i * n + n - 1])$
$(\Pi_m^{mn} \otimes I_k) \cdot X$	FusedPKIV(m, mn, k, X)	for$(i = 0;\ i < m;\ i++)$ for$(j = 0;\ j < n;\ j++)$ $Y[k * (i + m * j) : 1 : k * (i + m * j)] =$ $X[k * (n * i + j) : 1 : k * (n * i + j)]$
$D_m^n \cdot X$	Mul(TwiddleCoe, X)	for$(i = 0;\ i < m;\ i++)$ $Y[i] = D_m^n[i] * X[i])$
$\Pi_m^{mn} \cdot X$	Permute(m, mn, X)	for$(i = 0;\ i < m;\ i++)$ for$(j = 0;\ j < n;\ j++)$ $Y[i + m * j : 1 : i + m * j] =$ $A*(X[n * i + j : 1 : n * i + j])$

e.g., we perform calculations also for zero matrix entries. In this new FFTc version, we perform the computation in sparse format to achieve the $\mathcal{O}(N \log N)$ complexity of FFT. The FFT dialect closely represents the semantics of the mathematical formula, carrying high-level information about the FFT computation. Also, the FFT dialect works on tensor values that are immutable and without side effects, which brings convenience for compiler analysis and transformations. Therefore, we perform the Sparse Fusion Transform (SFT) on FFT dialect. SFT uses the pattern match and rewriting mechanism in MLIR to fuse several FFT operators into one. As shown in Table 1, the FFT computation pattern $Y = (A_m \otimes I_n) \cdot X$ is fused into one operator `FusedMKIV`. Here M stands for matrix, K for kronecker product, I is identity matrix, and V means vector.

(2) **Bufferization: Lower to Affine and MemRef Dialect.** After the high level transformations on FFT dialect, we apply bufferization, the FFT dialect operations with tensor semantics are lowered down to explicit loops with MemRef semantics. The lowering matches patterns of individual FFT dialect operations, rewriting them with explicit affine loop nests to implement the computations. The scalarized tensor arithmetic operations are performed by corresponding operations in the Complex dialect. The pseudo code of the FFT operations after bufferization, are demonstrate in Table 1. We can see that the computation is already sparsified. We got some inspiration from SPIRAL [3] for the sparse fusion and bufferization work.

(3) **Conversion of Complex Data to an Array of Floating-point.** The FFT algorithms operate on complex numbers and it is critical to have high-performance data access to complex-value arrays. The complex dialect in MLIR

```
 1  From:  %12 = "complex.create" %10, %11 : complex<f64>
 2
 3  To:    %13 = "memref.alloc"() : memref<2xf64>
 4         "affine.store" %14, %13[0] : memref<2xf64>
 5         "affine.store" %15, %13[1] : memref<2xf64>
 6         %16 = builtin.unrealized_conversion_cast %13 :
           memref<2xf64> to complex<f64>
```

Listing 1.1. Converting Complex Dialect Operations

is used to hold complex numbers and perform complex arithmetic operations. The complex data type is more explicit when representing computation workloads, also more convenient for domain-specific transformations since the aggregated complex data is wrapped as a single unit. So we apply all the domain-specific transformations to the complex data type. However, the complex data type is neither a first-class type in LLVM nor widely supported by hardware instructions. Also, in MLIR, some dialects cannot work with the complex data type, e.g., Vector dialect. The Vector dialect is a low-level but still machine-agnostic dialect for virtual vector operations [9]. The virtual vector operations will map closely to LLVM IR and, eventually, hardware vector instructions.

To perform vectorization in MLIR, we convert the complex type to an array of floating point data types. We introduce a conversion pass `fft-convert-complex-to-floating` and a rewriting pass `fft-complex-mem-rep`. These two passes apply conversion patterns to convert the operations of complex dialect and other dialects' operations on complex data to memory access operations on an array of floating point data. For instance, as shown in the Listing 1.1, after conversion the complex data type is eliminated.

We can also change the data layout of the complex array here by setting a flag to the pass: currently, we can switch between the *Interleaved* and *Split* modes. In the *Interleaved* mode, the real and imaginary parts of a complex number are located in consecutive memory locations [10] [2]. On the other hand, the *Split* data format stores the real and imaginary components as two disjoint sequences.

(4) **Polyhedral Transformations in the Affine Dialect.** The Affine dialect is a simplified polyhedral representation designed to enable progressive lowering [8]. We utilize the transformations in the Affine dialect to explore the loop optimization opportunities, such as fusion, tiling, and vectorization. The automatic loop fusion at this stage cannot generate the most optimal fused loops, so we rely on the Sparse Fusion pass, which works on the high-level tensor data. The loop optimization we develop in FFTc are:

- **Loop Tiling.** We need to set the loop tiling size as a hyperparameter to the `affine-loop-tile` pass. There are two ways of setting the tiling size: exact tile size or indicating the target cache volume. We found the latter ones performed better for our FFT code generation.

– **Loop Vectorization.** Affine dialect's `affine-super-vectorize` pass is designed to generate virtual vector operations out of loops. At this stage, the FFT transforms mentioned above have already generated parallel loops without dependencies which may prevent vectorization. The `affine-super-vectorize` needs to determine the most optimal loop dimension and virtual vector size to perform vectorization, either generated automatically by heuristics or set as hyperparameters by the developer. After the naive vectorization, we run the `test-vector-transfer-lowering-patterns` pass to apply optimization patterns on the vector operations.

```
1  for(i=0;i<M;i++)
2    for(j=0;j<N;j++)
3      c[i][j]=
4      a[i][j]+
5      b[i][j];
```

```
1  for(i=0;i<M;i++)
2    for(j=0;j<N;j+=4)
3      c[i][j:j+3]=
4      a[i][j:j+3]+
5      b[i][j:j+3];
```

```
1  for(i=0;i<M;i+=4)
2    for(j=0;j<N;j++)
3      c[i:i+3][j]=
4      a[i:i+3][j]+
5      b[i:i+3][j];
```

(a) Scalar Loop   (b) Inner Loop Vectorized   (c) Outer Loop Vectorized

Fig. 2. Loop Vectorization Example (Vector Length = 4)

3.1 LLVM Loop Vectorizer

After the FFT code is lowered to LLVM IR, we can leverage the LLVM pipeline to further optimization. We specifically explore opportunities in vectorization, one of the most critical optimizations for performance. As shown in Fig. 1, for this case we bypass the MLIR vectorizer.

There are two different vectorizers in the LLVM pipeline: SLP [11] and VPlan [12] vectorizers. From a user's perspective, SLP is a innermost loop vectorizer, as shown in Fig. 2b, and VPLAN vectorizes the outermost loop, demonstrated in Fig. 2c. The current heuristic in LLVM loop vectorizer to choose the vector length will block AVX512 instructions for Intel CPUs, due to the probable frequency drop, which may negate the performance gains, especially for non-computation-intensive workloads. In our FFT computation, wider vectors brings more performance, so we modified the x86 target configuration and `PreferVectorWidth` heuristic in LLVM to enable AVX512 code generation.

(5.1) Interleaved Memory Access and Innermost Loop Vectorizer: SLP.
The complex numbers are stored under interleaved data layout in most cases, such as the complex data type in C++: `std::complex`. Interleaved means that a complex number's real and imaginary parts are stored consecutively in memory. However, this raises a challenge for effective memory access using SIMD instructions. For example, strided load is needed to pack the real/imaginary parts of multiple complex numbers into a SIMD register, which may end up using expensive gather instructions. An example is shown in Fig. 3a.

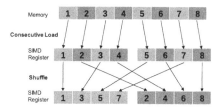

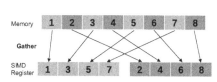

(a) Directly Load Complex Data Using Gather Instructions

(b) Optimized Interleaved Memory Access

Fig. 3. Pack Complex Data into SIMD Registers during Auto-vectorization

An interleaved memory access optimization is available in LLVM's loop vectorizer, and we enable this by explicitly setting the corresponding flag to the loop vectorize pass. After the optimization, two consecutive SIMD loads will be generated, followed by shuffle operations on these two SIMD registers to replace the gather/scatter, as shown in the Fig. 3b. The interleaved memory access optimization can work together with the SLP inner loop vectorizer.

SLP (Superword-Level Parallelism) is the default loop vectorizer in the LLVM optimization pipeline, targeting to combine similar independent instructions in the innermost loop into vector instructions.

(5.2) **Outermost Loop Vectorization: VPLAN.** Outermost vectorization can be beneficial for some cases, e.g., the number of iterations in the innermost loop is small. VPlan is a recently introduced LLVM vectorizer. A current development effort is ongoing to migrate the loop vectorizer to the VPlan infrastructure and support outer loop vectorization in the LLVM loop vectorizer. Currently, VPlan is a temporary vectorization path. For this reason. we need to set `enable-vplan-native-path` option to enable it. Also, VPlan only vectorizes the outermost loop with explicit vectorization annotation, e.g., `#pragma omp simd`. We modified the execution logic to make it run on our FFT loops.

3.2 FFTc GPU Code Generation

As shown in Fig. 1, the progressive lowering above the Affine dialect is hardware target agnostic. Below there are divergent branches to support different hardware targets and heterogeneous computing. To generate GPU code, we lower down to MLIR GPU dialect [13], the retargetable GPU programming model in MLIR. The MLIR GPU dialect can further lowering down to different hardware targets, such as NVIDIA and AMD GPUs. We demonstrate the subsequent GPU code generation using the NVIDIA compilation pipeline.

(6.1) **Preparation: Partial Lowering Affine Memory Operations.** We generate the GPU kernel from Affine loops using the *convert-affine-for-to-gpu* pass. However, the current implementation of the pass does not support memory access using Affine load/store. For this reason, we introduce a partial lowering pass to convert the Affine memory access to corresponding ones in the Memref dialect, e.g., `memref.load/store`. Also, we need to register all the Memref used in GPU kernel using `gpu.host_register`, to access it from the device.

(6.2) **Convert Affine Loops to GPU Kernel.** The *convert-affine-for-to-gpu* pass converts each Affine loop nest into a GPU kernel. This pass collects the loop nest's ranges, bounds, steps, and induction variables, then uses them to calculate the grid and block sizes for the GPU kernel.

(6.3) **CUDA Binary Code Generation.** In the generated code with GPU dialect, the CPU (host) and GPU (device) codes are embedded in a single IR. However, the GPU kernel code is wrapped into specific functions to separately run compilation passes. The GPU device code is lowered to platform-specific dialects, such as the Nvidia NVVM, a compiler IR for CUDA kernels based on LLVM IR. As the last step, the CUDA binary code is generated. Returning to the host side, we lower the host side GPU code to LLVM, then go through the LLVM code generation pipeline. We support both Just-in-Time (JIT) and Ahead-of-Time (AoT) compilation modes for the GPU code generation.

4   Experimental Setup and Evaluation

We evaluate the CPU performance of the FFTc-generated FFT on the Tetralith supercomputer, located at the National Supercomputer Centre in Linköping, Sweden. The Tetralith computing nodes have a dual-socket Intel Xeon Gold 6130 CPU, 96 GB of RAM. For GPU tests, we use the Alvis supercomputer in Chalmers, Sweden. Each Alvis' computing node has 4xA40 NVIDIA GPUs, the CUDA version is 12.0.0. The LLVM we use to embed the FFTc was forked from the LLVM main branch on 2022/08/11.

We run the FFT kernels 1,000 times and calculate the average execution time. We develop a Python script to generate the implementation of the FFT algorithm using our FFTc DSL. The other option is using MLIR Python binding to generate MLIR directly. Albeit our script can generate different FFT algorithm implementations, in this paper, we mainly present the results of the Stockham algorithm.

We evaluate our compiler on double-precision complex-to-complex FFT. Currently, we do not support mixed radix algorithms and the runtime decomposition of DFT as FFTW does. For this reason, in this study, the FFT sizes are all powers of two. We precompile our FFT kernels into a static library and then call it in a C++ file using a similar API as FFTW. The input/output data type for MLIR library code is the member data type, which describes a structured multi-index pointer into memory. To convert it to an externally-facing function and call in C/C++, we use `llvm.emit_c_interface` function to generate wrapper functions that convert a Memref augment to a pointer-to-struct argument. A

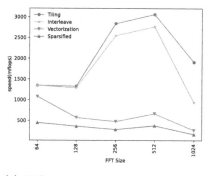

(a) Different and combined optimizations on CPU.

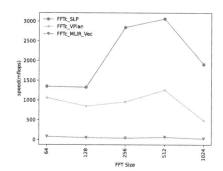

(b) Different vectorizers approaches on CPU.

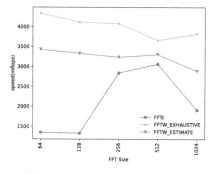

(c) FFTc compared with FFTW on the CPU.

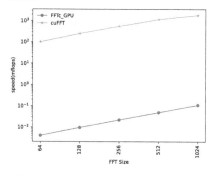

(d) FFTc (naive) compared with cuFFT on GPU.

Fig. 4. Performance Results of FFTc. CPU performance is tested on on Tetralith compute node with Intel Xeon Gold 6130 CPU. GPU performance on Alvis compute node with NVIDA A40 GPU.

wrapper on C++ array pointer is also provided to generate the pointer-to-struct structure equivalent to MLIR Memref when lowering down to LLVM IR.

Results. As the first step of our work, we verify the correctness of FFTc implementation. The test takes random input vectors as input, with different FFT sizes: the input sizes are the powers of two, from 16 to 4,098. We call the FFTc library from the C++ test case and compare the results with FFTW. The error is calculated as $\frac{|result_{DSL} - result_{Numpy}|}{FFT_{size}}$. In all our runs, the error is smaller than 1e−7.

In Fig. 4a, we report performance attained by different optimizations. We run it on FFT sizes of power of two and avoid large FFT sizes since we do not support a runtime planner like FFTW to decompose the FFT into smaller problems, nor support random-sized FFT. We apply the same optimization pipeline and hyperparameters to all different FFT sizes. Performance is demonstrated in MFLOPs/s. The MFLOPs are calculated as $5(N \log_2(N))$, where N is the number of input data points. The compiler transforms with low or detrimental performance are not reported, and we report only the ones with performance gains. In Fig. 4a, the red bottom line stands for the FFT code after sparse fusion. This optimization leads to up to 1,000x performance improvement compared with the dense computation before sparsify and significantly reduces the compilation time [6]. The dense computation is implemented through dense matrix multiplication, which requires $\mathcal{O}(N^2)$ operations: in this case, the MFLOPS/s needed for specific FFT sizes are different, so we do not compare them with the sparsified ones. The green line represents the sparsified code with SLP vectorization; it achieves approximately 2x speed-ups for most cases. The most significant performance gain comes from the interleaved memory access optimizations: up to 5x speed up is achieved. Finally, we can gain additional performance with loop tiling, especially for large FFT sizes. In Fig. 4b, we present the performance with different vectorizers. The green bottom line stands for the MLIR vectorizer. Although it successfully vectorized the code (on virtual vector abstraction), the subsequent lowering passes failed to generate optimal target-specific vector instructions, e.g., in our cases, the memory access instruction vector.transfer_read/write is scalarized when lowering down. In the current implementation of the MLIR pipeline, only some memory access patterns are efficiently mapped to vector instructions. Further customization and fine-tuning of the vectorizer are needed to generate high-performance code. The other path is to lower the scalar MLIR code to LLVM and utilize LLVM's vectorizers. We can see that the innermost loop vectorizer SLP with interleaved memory access optimization outperforms the outermost loop Vectorizer VPlan. VPlan cannot work with interleaved memory access optimization and generates gather/scatter instructions.

In Fig. 4c, we compare our implementation with the state-of-art library FFTW. We test FFTW with different planner flags, which control the planning process and, therefore, the overall FFTW performance. We choose FFTW_ESTIMATE and FFTW_EXHAUSTIVE out of all the options. To pick an optimal plan, FFTW_ESTIMATE uses a simple heuristic, which requires the least compilation time. While FFTW_EXHAUSTIVE performs an exhaustive search, it is the most time-consuming option: it will compute several FFTs and measure the execution time and select the algorithm with the best performance.

There is a large performance gap for certain sizes, such as 64 and 128. Part of the reason is that currently, we cannot support mixed radix FFT algorithms, so we cannot decompose the random FFT size into radix sizes that match the memory hierarchy capacities. For instance, size-128 FFT is calculated using radix-2 kernels, which is not optimal for memory access and vectorization. The other reason would be that we did not apply aggressive unroll on small-size kernels. The performance difference between FFTc and FFTW is relatively small for the FFT sizes, which we can decompose into vectorization and memory access-friendly radix sizes. An example is size-256 FFT, which can be split into radix-16 kernels. Figure 4d demonstrates the GPU performance result compared with the Nvidia FFT library. The primary purpose is to show FFTc's portability, that we can support multiple hardware targets with a single source code. We have not investigated performance optimization on GPU: currently, the performance difference between cuFFT and FFTc is considerable. In FFTc, each affine loop nest of FFT code is mapped into a GPU kernel: at this point, the Affine loop nest is not optimized to map efficiently to the hierarchical hardware parallelism (grid/block) of a GPU. We plan to do this in the near future, together with other optimizations, e.g., vectorization and memory promotion, to utilize the hierarchical (shared/private) memory in GPU.

5 Related Work

The most widely used open-source FFT library, FFTW [5], is essentially an FFT compiler. FFTW is written in Objective Caml to generate Directed Acyclic Graphs (DAG) of FFT algorithms and perform algebraic optimization. FFTW uses a planner at runtime to recursively decompose the DFT problem into sub-problems. This sub-problems are solved directly by optimized, straight-line code generated by a special-purpose compiler called genfft [4]. Another successful library using compiler technology is SPIRAL [3], which uses a mathematical framework for representing and deriving numerical and scientific algorithms, including FFTs. SPIRAL applies pattern match and rewriting to generate optimal FFT formulation for different hardware, such as SIMD and multicore systems. Then, SPIRAL maps the matrix formula to high-performance C code. A similar approach to our methodology is used in the Lift framework [7] that uses compiler technologies and a mathematical formulation to generate FFT libraries for different hardware, including accelerators. Differently from all these approaches, in our work we build our framework on the top of the recent LLVM and MLIR technologics.

6 Discussion and Conclusion

FFTc is a DSL built upon a series of existing and newly introduced abstractions in MLIR and LLVM. In particular, FFTc allows for decoupling the high-level domain-specific FFT abstractions (tensor operations) and lower-level target-specific abstractions (vector instructions and CUDA primitives).

In this paper, we described the new FFTc features, including automatic support for loop vectorization and the possibility of generating code for execution on GPUs. In order to enable loop vectorization and GPU porting a number of LLVM and MLIR transformation are needed.

While we show that the FFTc performance on CPU is on-par with the performance of FFTW, the performance of the FFTc-generated code is largely suboptimal to the performance of cuFFT. As a priority for future work, we will investigate the MLIR's vectorizer to generate optimized vector code both for GPU and CPU and improve the Affine loops to be efficiently mapped to CPU's Multicore/SIMD and GPU's workitem/group (thread/block) hierarchical parallelism architecture. In addition, similarly to FFTW, we will investigate the development of a compiler runtime to generate and select optimal candidates of FFT formula decomposition plans.

Acknowledgement. Funding for the work is received from the EU HPC Joint Undertaking (JU), Grant Agreement No. 3893 (IO-SEA). The computation resources were provided by NAISS at NSC and C3SE partially funded by the Swedish Research Council through grant 2022-06725. I want to thank Kateryna Morozovska (kmor@kth.se) and Federica Bragone (bragone@kth.se) for their help with the proofread.

References

1. Andersson, M.I., Murugan, N.A., Podobas, A., Markidis, S.: Breaking down the parallel performance of GROMACS, a high-performance molecular dynamics software. In: Wyrzykowski, R., Dongarra, J., Deelman, E., Karczewski, K. (eds.) PPAM 2022. LNCS, vol. 13826, pp. 333–345. Springer, Cham (2022). https://doi.org/10.1007/978-3-031-30442-2_25

2. Andersson, M.I., Markidis, S.: A case study on dace portability & performance for batched discrete Fourier transforms. In: HPC Asia 2023, pp. 55–63 (2023)

3. Franchetti, F., et al.: SPIRAL: extreme performance portability. Proc. IEEE **106**(11), 1935–1968 (2018)

4. Frigo, M.: A fast Fourier transform compiler. ACM SIGPLAN Not. **39**(4), 642–655 (2004)

5. Frigo, M., Johnson, S.G.: FFTW: an adaptive software architecture for the FFT. In: ICASSP'98, vol. 3, pp. 1381–1384. IEEE (1998)

6. He, Y., Podobas, A., Andersson, M.I., Markidis, S.: FFTc: an MLIR dialect for developing HPC fast Fourier transform libraries. In: Singer, J., Elkhatib, Y., Blanco Heras, D., Diehl, P., Brown, N., Ilic, A. (eds.) Euro-Par 2022. LNCS, vol. 13835, pp. 80–92. Springer, Cham (2023). https://doi.org/10.1007/978-3-031-31209-0_6

7. Köpcke, B., Steuwer, M., Gorlatch, S.: Generating efficient FFT GPU code with lift. In: 8th ACM SIGPLAN International Workshop on Functional High-Performance and Numerical Computing, pp. 1–13 (2019)

8. Lattner, C., et al.: MLIR: scaling compiler infrastructure for domain specific computation. In: 2021 IEEE/ACM International Symposium on Code Generation and Optimization (CGO), pp. 2–14. IEEE (2021)

9. MLIR: Case Study Docs on Vector Dialect CPU Codegen (2021). https://discourse.llvm.org/t/case-study-docs-on-vector-dialect-cpu-codegen/1674

10. Popovici, D.T., Franchetti, F., Low, T.M.: Mixed data layout kernels for vectorized complex arithmetic. In: 2017 IEEE HPEC, pp. 1–7. IEEE (2017)

11. Rosen, I., Nuzman, D., Zaks, A.: Loop-aware SLP in GCC. In: GCC Developers Summit. Citeseer (2007)

12. Tian, X., et al.: LLVM compiler implementation for explicit parallelization and SIMD vectorization. In: Proceedings of the Fourth Workshop on the LLVM Compiler Infrastructure in HPC, pp. 1–11 (2017)

13. Vasilache, N., et al.: Composable and modular code generation in MLIR: a structured and retargetable approach to tensor compiler construction. arXiv preprint arXiv:2202.03293 (2022)

Enabling Dynamic Selection of Implementation Variants in Component-Based Parallel Programming for Heterogeneous Systems

Suejb Memeti[✉]

Department of Computer Science (DIDA), Blekinge Institute of Technology,
Karlskrona, Sweden
suejb.memeti@bth.se

Abstract. Heterogeneous systems, consisting of CPUs and GPUs, offer the capability to address the demands of compute- and data-intensive applications. However, programming such systems is challenging, requiring knowledge of various parallel programming frameworks. This paper introduces COMPAR, a component-based parallel programming framework that enables the exposure and selection of multiple implementation variants of components at runtime. The framework leverages compiler directive-based language extensions to annotate the source code and generate the necessary glue code for the StarPU runtime system. COMPAR provides a unified view of implementation variants and allows for intelligent selection based on runtime context. Our evaluation demonstrates the effectiveness of COMPAR through benchmark applications. The proposed approach simplifies heterogeneous parallel programming and promotes code reuse while achieving optimal performance.

Keywords: component-based programming · implementation variant selection · heterogeneous parallel computing systems · source-to-source compilation · performance optimization

1 Introduction

Heterogeneous parallel computing systems, comprising CPUs and GPUs, have emerged as powerful platforms capable of meeting the requirements of compute- and data-intensive applications. However, programming such systems is a challenging task that demands knowledge of various parallel programming frameworks. Multi-core resources, such as CPUs, require frameworks like Pthreads or OpenMP, while many-core resources, such as GPUs, necessitate frameworks like OpenCL or CUDA. Moreover, for many algorithms, multiple implementations exist, written using different programming frameworks or targeting different architectures.

In the era of AI advancements, tools like Github Copilot have revolutionized the development process by suggesting code snippets, functions, and algorithms directly within the editor. This capability enables developers to effortlessly create multiple implementation variants of functions, aligning with the concept of

© The Author(s), under exclusive license to Springer Nature Switzerland AG 2024
D. Zeinalipour et al. (Eds.): Euro-Par 2023 Workshops, LNCS 14351, pp. 219–231, 2024.
https://doi.org/10.1007/978-3-031-50684-0_17

component-based programming. These tools facilitate exploration of different algorithmic approaches and code optimization for heterogeneous systems.

Despite the availability of numerous implementation variants for specific functions, the challenge lies in determining the most suitable one at a given time. Choosing the implementation variant that achieves the best performance relies on the runtime context, including input size, processing capability of available resources, and other system configuration parameters. Therefore, selecting the best implementation variant at compile-time is not feasible.

To address this challenge, this paper proposes an approach that enables developers to easily expose available implementation variants to the runtime system, which can then make informed decisions based on the given context. We introduce compiler directive-based language extensions that allow developers to annotate the source code with implementation variant options. A pre-compiler analyzes these annotations, performs syntax and semantic analysis, and generates the necessary glue code to seamlessly integrate with the StarPU runtime system [1]. The StarPU runtime system takes over the decision-making process at runtime, selecting the most appropriate implementation variant based on the specific runtime context.

Several existing approaches have been proposed to expose multiple variants to runtime systems. For instance, [7] and [3] utilize XML-based descriptors for annotating various components, but these approaches lack seamless integration with the programming language and incur additional overhead for writing and parsing XML descriptors. Another relevant approach is the `declare variant` directive introduced in the recent version of OpenMP. Although it enables the specification of alternate implementations for base functions, it primarily supports single types of functions and lacks extensibility for diverse target architectures. Our proposed solution is inspired by the `declare variant` directive in OpenMP but extends its capabilities to support multiple types of functions and a wide range of target architectures.

The key contributions of this paper include:

- A language extension that enables developers to annotate the source code and expose multiple implementation variants.
- A pre-compiler that performs syntax and semantic analysis and generates the necessary glue code.
- Utilization of the StarPU runtime system for intelligent selection of the most suitable implementation variant at runtime.
- An empirical evaluation of the proposed solution using various benchmark applications.

This paper is structured as follows: Sect. 2 provides an overview of the COMPAR framework and its key components. In Sect. 3 we present an empirical evaluation of the proposed solution using various benchmark applications. Section 4 summarizes, synthesizes, compares, and contrasts the related state-of-the-art. Finally, Sect. 5 concludes the paper and outlines future directions for research and development.

2   COMPAR: Language Extensions for Exposing Multiple Component Implementation Variants to the Runtime System

This section presents the language extensions used in COMPAR to expose multiple component implementation variants to the runtime system. Furthermore, it describes the design aspects, including the syntax and usage of the COMPAR directives; and the implementation aspects, including the source-to-source compiler and the runtime system.

2.1   Design Aspects

Benchmark studies, such as the research conducted by Memeti et al. [8], suggest that programming with OpenMP is considered more straightforward in comparison to other parallel programming models like CUDA and OpenCL. This is primarily due to the level of abstraction provided by OpenMP, which shields programmers from certain low-level details while maintaining performance that is on par with alternative models. It is important to note, however, that this abstraction may limit the level of control available for fine-tuning.

In recent versions of OpenMP [9], the `declare variant` directive was introduced to enable the specification of alternative implementations for specific base functions. This directive, in conjunction with the `match` clause, allows for the explicit definition of the contextual conditions under which each variant should be considered. During runtime, when a function call's context aligns with that of a variant, the variant becomes a potential replacement for the base function. The selection process for determining the most suitable variant involves considering a score-based evaluation among all compatible variants.

The design of the COMPAR language draws inspiration from the OpenMP language, while aiming to expand upon the functionality offered by the `declare variant` directive to support multiple target architectures and programming models.

COMPAR encompasses two primary compiler directives: `method_declare` and `parameter`. The `method_declare` directive is employed to annotate methods that represent implementation variants, while the `parameter` directive is utilized to define the parameters of these methods.

When using the `method_declare` directive for the first implementation variant of an interface (i.e., function), a corresponding `parameter` directive is expected for each parameter. However, for subsequent implementation variants of the same interface, it is unnecessary to use the `parameter` directive since these variants are assumed to have the same method signature.

The syntax of the `method_declare` directive is demonstrated in Listing 1. The directive supports several clauses, including `interface`, `target`, and `name`. The `interface` clause is used to specify the name of the interface (i.e., function) to which the variant corresponds, such as "sort". The **name** clause is utilized to indicate the name of the function that represents the implementation variant, for instance, "**bubble_sort**", "**merge_sort**", and so on. The **target** clause is employed to denote the target programming model in which the variant is written, such as **CUDA, OpenMP, Seq**, or **OpenCL**.

```
#pragma compar method_declare interface(...) name(...) target(...)
```

Listing 1: An example of the COMPAR **method_declare** directive.

The syntax of the **parameter** directive is depicted in Listing 2. The directive supports various clauses, including **name, type, size**, and **access_mode**. The **name** clause is used to specify the name of the parameter. The **type** clause indicates the type of the parameter, such as **int, float, double, char, wchar_t**, and so on. The **size** clause indicates the size of the parameter. It is worth noting that the **size** clause can accept different numbers of parameters: one parameter for vectors, two parameters for matrices, three parameters for 3-dimensional data structures, and four parameters for 4-dimensional data structures. Lastly, the **access_mode** clause corresponds to the access mode of the parameter, such as **read, write**, or **readwrite**.

```
#pragma compar parameter name(...) type(...) size(...) access_mode(...)
```

Listing 2: An example of the COMPAR **parameter** directive.

Listing 3 presents an excerpt from an application that demonstrates the use of the COMPAR framework with the **sort** and **matrix multiplication** functions, each having two implementation variants. Specifically, for both functions there are corresponding CUDA and OpenMP implementation variants.

For the sort function, two parameters are utilized: an array of floats and a scalar integer. In the case of the matrix multiplication interface, four parameters are required: two 2-dimensional float arrays (A and B) with a size of N × M, as well as two scalar integers, N and M.

Within Listing 3, lines 23 and 24 exemplify method calls to the defined interfaces, specifically invoking the **sort** and **mmul** functions, respectively.

Lines 1, 22, and 25 in Listing 3 demonstrate additional COMPAR directives, which are seamlessly translated into their corresponding C/C++ code. For instance, the **#pragma compar include** directive is translated to **#include "compar.h"**, ensuring that the necessary COMPAR functionality is included.

```
1    #pragma compar include
2    ...
3    #pragma compar method_declare interface(sort) target(cuda) name(sort_cuda)
4    #pragma compar parameter name(arr) type(float*) size(N)
5    #pragma compar parameter name(N) type(int)
6    void sort_cuda(float* arr, int N) {...}
7
8    #pragma compar method_declare interface(sort) target(openmp) name(sort_omp)
9    void sort_omp(float* arr, int N){...}
10
11   #pragma compar method_declare interface(mmul) target(cuda) name(mmul_cuda)
12   #pragma compar parameter name(A) type(float*) size(N, M)
13   #pragma compar parameter name(B) type(float*) size(N, M)
14   #pragma compar parameter name(N) type(int)
15   #pragma compar parameter name(M) type(int)
16   void mmul_cuda(float* A, float* B, int N, int M) {...}
17
18   #pragma compar method_declare interface(mmul) target(openmp) name(mmul_omp)
19   void mmul_omp(float* A, float* B, int N, int M) {...}
20
21   int main(int argc, char **argv) {
22      #pragma compar initialize
23      sort(arr, N); ...
24      mmul(A, B, N, M); ...
25      #pragma compar terminate
26   }
```

Listing 3: Source code example of using COMPAR to expose multiple implementation variants of sort and mmul to the runtime system.

Similarly, the #pragma compar initialize directive is translated into a method call, compar_init(), which is defined within the generated compar.h file. Invoking this method call initializes the COMPAR framework, preparing it for utilization within the application. Likewise, the #pragma compar terminate directive is transformed into a method call, compar_terminate(), also defined in the compar.h file, ensuring the proper termination and cleanup of the COMPAR framework at the conclusion of program execution.

It is important to note that all of the COMPAR directives, if not processed by our pre-compiler, do not introduce any changes to the existing code. Thus, the original code would continue to function as intended, ensuring backward compatibility is maintained.

2.2   Implementation Aspects

This section discusses the tools and techniques employed in the implementation of the source-to-source pre-compiler for COMPAR. The pre-compiler is responsible for translating COMPAR pragma directives into the corresponding C/C++ code, including the integration of the StarPU runtime system.

Source-to-Source Compiler. The COMPAR pre-compiler encompasses various phases of a compiler, including lexical, syntax, and semantic analysis (the front-end), and intermediate representation and code generation (the back-end).

For the lexical analysis, the Flex tool (Fast Lexical Analysis Generator, formerly known as Lex) was utilized to define and write the COMPAR language specification. Since COMPAR is a pre-compiler, it only needs to analyze the parts of the program that start with `#pragma compar`. Therefore, the language specification is straightforward.

To perform syntax analysis, the GNU Bison tool (formerly known as Yacc) was employed to define and write the syntax specification for COMPAR language extensions. The syntax analyzer ensures the correct structure and usage of COMPAR directives, validating the values and clauses provided within them. It generates an abstract syntax tree for further processing.

The semantic analysis phase verifies the semantic correctness of the COMPAR directives within their respective contexts. It checks for duplicate interface or parameter definitions and ensures the correct usage of clauses and options. While the current version of COMPAR makes certain assumptions, such as assuming the existence of variable names provided in the clauses, additional analysis steps are needed in a production environment to enforce such requirements.

The current version of COMPAR does not include compile-time optimization. However, as mentioned in the future works section (Sect. 5), optimization techniques could be applied during compilation to reduce the set of implementation variants based on benchmarking results or other criteria.

Assuming no semantic errors are found, the compiler proceeds to the intermediate representation (IR) phase, where the IR is generated, capturing the necessary information for subsequent code generation. The code generator, utilizing template-based techniques, then produces the target code, in this case, the StarPU code and the glue code required to integrate the source code with the StarPU runtime system [1]. It is important to note that StarPU is considered a back-end target tool, and it can be easily replaced with other runtime systems, such as StarSs [2].

Runtime System. COMPAR utilizes the StarPU runtime system [1] to handle the mapping and execution of the various implementation variants on different computational resources, including CPUs and accelerators.

StarPU operates on a task-based model, where applications submit computational tasks, each with multiple potential implementations targeting different heterogeneous processing units. The StarPU runtime system handles the mapping, scheduling, and data transfers required for executing these tasks. The key components in StarPU are codelets and tasks. A codelet in StarPU corresponds to a variant implementation in COMPAR, representing different implementations of the same algorithm targeting various architectures. A task in StarPU, similar to a function interface in COMPAR, represents a set of codelets and the data required to execute them. When a task is executed, a codelet is selected based on the specific architecture and data associated with it.

The COMPAR pre-compiler generates the necessary code to define codelets, input/output data parameters, and task submission for the StarPU runtime

```
1     ...
2     extern void sort_cuda(float* arr, int N)
3     extern void sort_omp(float* arr, int N)
4     void sort_cuda_wrapper(void* buff[], void *_args) {
5       sort_cuda((float*) STARPU_VECTOR_GET_PTR((struct starpu_vector_interface *)buff[0]), ...);
6     }
7     void sort_omp_wrapper(void* buff[], void *_args) {
8       sort_omp((float*) STARPU_VECTOR_GET_PTR((struct starpu_vector_interface *)buff[0]), ...);
9     }
10    ...
11    sort(float* arr, int N) { ...
12      struct starpu_codelet cl = {
13        .cpu_funcs = { sort_opmp_wrapper },
14        .cuda_funcs = { sort_cuda_wrapper }, ...
15      };
16    }
17    starpu_data_handle_t arr_handle;
18    starpu_vector_data_register(&arr_handle, 0, (uintptr_t)arr, N, sizeof(arr[0]));
19    ...
20    struct starpu_task *task = starpu_task_create();
21    starpu_task_submit(task);
```

Listing 4: Excerpt of the COMPAR generated code for StarPU. The generated code corresponds to the example shown in Listing 3

system. For example, in the code excerpt in Listing 4, which corresponds to the example in Listing 3, the generated code integrates the StarPU runtime system. Lines 2–9 declare the external functions for sorting using CUDA and OpenMP and define their corresponding wrapper functions, which are then specified as implementation variants of the StarPU codelet inside the **sort** function (lines 11–16). Lines 17–18 show the code for registering the data handle for the input array **arr**. Lines 20–21 show the code corresponding to the creation and the submission of the task. Note that all data handle(s) associated with the parameter(s) need to be unregistered, which is not shown on the example.

It is important to note that this example showcases the generated code for the **sort** function, while the example in Listing 3 includes another interface named **mmul** for matrix multiplication. However, the corresponding generated code for the **mmul** interface is not presented in the example. COMPAR generates separate code files, similar to the code excerpt in Listing 4, for each defined interface.

3   Evaluation

This section, first, describes the experimentation environment, which includes details related to the hardware configuration, the set of application benchmarks and the used data-sets for the corresponding applications, as well as the evaluation metrics. Afterwards, the results of the empirical evaluation are presented and discussed.

3.1 Experimentation Environment

Table 1 lists the properties of the heterogeneous computing system that was used for experimentation in this paper.

Table 1. Hardware system configuration.

	Multi-core CPU	Many-core GPU
Processor	Intel Xeon E5-2620 v4	NVIDIA GP102 Titan Xp
# cores and core frequency	8 cores, 2.10–3.00 GHz	3840 cores, 1.41–1.58 MHz
Cache size	20 MB Intel Smart Cache	L1: 48 KB per SM; L2: 3 MB
Memory size and bandwidth	96 GB, 68.3 GB/s	12 GB, 547.6 GB/s
Thermal Design Power	85 W	250 W

To empirically evaluate the performance and the programmability effort required to utilize the COMPAR framework, we have selected various benchmarks from the Rodinia benchmark suite, including the hostpot, hotspot3D, lud, nw, and a matrix multiplication application which is not part of the Rodinia benchmark suite.

Table 2 lists the benchmark applications and the different ranges of input that were used during the evaluation. Each of the configuration, i.e. hardware platform selection and input configuration is repeated for 10 times, and the average values are reported.

Table 2. Benchmark applications used to evaluate COMPAR.

Application	Implementation variants	Input parameters[*]	Input range
Hotspot	CUDA, OMP	squared grid size	64–8192
Hotspot3D	CUDA, OMP	rows/cols	64–512
Lud	CUDA, OMP	squared matrix size	64–8192
Nw	CUDA, OMP	max. rows/cols	64–8192
Matrix multiply	BLAS, OMP, CUDA, CUBLAS	squared matrix size	8–8192

[*]Only parameters that are used to scale the application are shown here.

3.2 Results

The evaluation results of the COMPAR framework are presented in Fig. 1, where a comparison is made between CPU-only and GPU-only executions. The CPU-only configuration is controlled by setting the STARPU_NCUDA environment variable to 0, while the GPU-only configuration is controlled by setting the STARPU_NCPU environment variable to 0.

In this specific hardware configuration, where the GPU exhibits significantly higher performance compared to the CPU, most of the benchmark applications (except for matrix multiplication) demonstrate improved performance when executed on the GPU. However, it is important to note that this observation may not hold true for other hardware configurations or applications. The matrix multiplication application serves as an example, as depicted in Fig. 1e. For smaller input sizes (8–128), it is not always clear which implementation variant (BLAS, OPENMP, or CUDA) performs the best. In the case of matrices with dimensions of 4096, the performance of the CUDA implementation surpasses that of the CUBLAS variant. Conversely, when the matrix dimensions are expanded to 8192, CUBLAS demonstrates superior performance. This emphasizes the nontrivial nature of such decisions, suggesting that they should be delegated to the runtime system rather than being hard-coded.

The empirical evaluation of the COMPAR framework, as illustrated in Figs. 1a–1d, reveals that the code generated by COMPAR, when integrated with the StarPU runtime system, consistently opts for the most performance-efficient implementation variant. It is important to highlight that the marginal discrepancies in execution time between COMPAR and a CUDA-only approach can be ascribed to the stochastic variability inherent in performance experiments. Although the CUDA-only implementation frequently exhibits superior performance—likely due to the absence of overheads associated with StarPU's decision-making mechanism—there are specific instances (e.g., in the LUD application) where the COMPAR version outperforms its CUDA-only counterpart.

In relation to the matrix multiplication application, which involves multiple implementation variants, it was observed that the STARPU selection mechanism frequently chose sub-optimal options. For example, while the BLAS implementation is the optimal choice for matrices of size 32, COMPAR—guided by the STARPU runtime—opted for the OPENMP variant. Likewise, for matrix dimensions ranging from 64 to 4096, the CUDA implementation demonstrated superior performance; however, STARPU selected less efficient variants, such as OPENMP and BLAS. Given that the STARPU decision-making process relies on machine learning models, it is reasonable to hypothesize that additional training of these models could lead to more accurate and optimal variant selection.

Table 1f presents findings related to programmer productivity, also referred to as programmability. It is evident that the COMPAR approach necessitates substantially less effort than both the method proposed in [7] and direct usage of StarPU. It should be noted that the metrics for the aforementioned approaches are derived from the study by Dastgeer et al. [7]. Additionally, it is worth mentioning that results for the `hotspot3D` application are absent, as this specific application was not evaluated in the study by Dastgeer et al. [7].

4   Related Work

SYLKAN [12] is a framework that extends the SYCL programming model to utilize the Vulkan graphics API for efficient parallel computing on GPUs and other Vulkan-compatible devices. It aims to provide a Vulkan compute target platform for SYCL. While both SYLKAN and COMPAR share similar goals, they differ in focus and approach. COMPAR emphasizes component-based parallel programming for heterogeneous systems with integration of the StarPU runtime

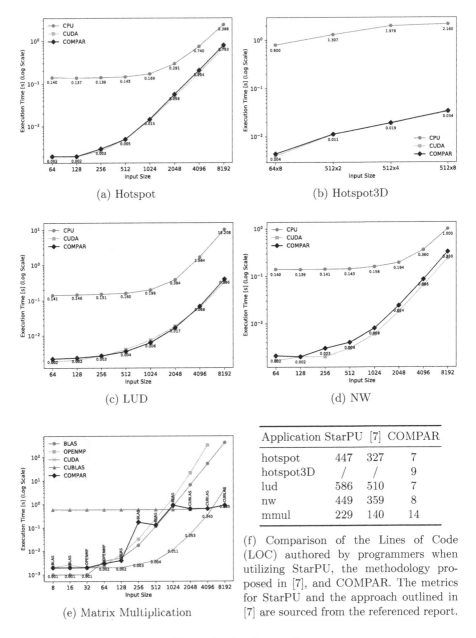

(a) Hotspot

(b) Hotspot3D

(c) LUD

(d) NW

(e) Matrix Multiplication

Application	StarPU	[7]	COMPAR
hotspot	447	327	7
hotspot3D	/	/	9
lud	586	510	7
nw	449	359	8
mmul	229	140	14

(f) Comparison of the Lines of Code (LOC) authored by programmers when utilizing StarPU, the methodology proposed in [7], and COMPAR. The metrics for StarPU and the approach outlined in [7] are sourced from the referenced report.

Fig. 1. Evaluation results

system, while SYLKAN specifically targets Vulkan as the runtime system and extends SYCL to leverage Vulkan's low-level capabilities for parallel computing.

In their work, Österlund and Löwe [10] present an approach for runtime selection of implementation variants based on varying contexts, which shares similar goals as COMPAR. While their focus lies on addressing the optimal variant selection process, our paper shifts the responsibility of selection to the runtime system. Instead, our focus is on facilitating the exposure of implementation variants to both the compiler and the runtime system.

Soudris et al. [11], as part of the EXA2PRO project, propose a framework for exascale systems that utilizes multiple implementation variants. This idea was initially introduced in the PHEPPER project [3, 7]. Like our work, they annotate implementation variants and rely on external runtime systems such as STARPU for selection. However, their approach requires developers to provide XML-based descriptions of the hardware platform, implementation variants, and compilation process. In contrast, our approach utilizes compiler directives for annotation, resembling the OpenMP parallel programming model, and automatically collects details about available computing resources using tools like hwloc.

Compeanu et al. [4] introduce a component-based approach for parallel computing software development on CPU-GPU embedded systems. They propose using APIs to abstract the characteristics of CPUs and GPUs, making the components platform-agnostic. The decision of running components on CPUs or GPUs is deferred to a higher system level. In contrast, our approach focuses on reusing existing components (implementation variants) with minimal modifications. Our pre-compiler ensures compatibility with other compilers, avoiding functionality disruptions if the code is not processed through our framework.

Carvalho et al. [5] introduce the # component model, enabling developers to build software using components. These components utilize Haskell-like parallel programming extensions, allowing for the separation of concerns and emphasizing processing separation from the developer's perspective. The components are synthesized into the desired parallel program by a back-end system. While our paper also focuses on systems built from components, we differ in our objective. Instead of synthesizing a complex application from smaller components, we optimize systems that feature multiple implementations of the same components.

Mani and Kesselman [6] present the Compositional C++ extensions for constructing parallel systems using components. Their focus is on providing extensions and features that facilitate the development of components themselves. In contrast, our work assumes that the components already exist and concentrates on providing mechanisms to effectively expose the multiple implementation variants of these components to both the compiler and the runtime system.

5   Conclusion and Future Work

In this paper, we presented COMPAR, a framework for component-based parallel programming on heterogeneous systems. COMPAR allows developers to annotate multiple implementation variants of components using compiler directives, enabling the runtime system to select the most suitable variant at runtime.

Through evaluation experiments, we demonstrated that COMPAR, in combination with the StarPU runtime system, effectively selects the best implementation variant for different scenarios. Despite the need for further training of the performance models, COMPAR offers a flexible and efficient approach to optimize performance on heterogeneous systems while maintaining compatibility with existing codebases. Future work involves enhancing the training of performance models, exploring integration with other runtime systems, and expanding its applicability to different programming models and architectures.

References

1. Augonnet, C., Thibault, S., Namyst, R., Wacrenier, P.A.: StarPU: a unified platform for task scheduling on heterogeneous multicore architectures. Concurr. Comput. Practic. Exp. **23**(2), 187–198 (2011)
2. Ayguadé, E., Badia, R.M., Igual, F.D., Labarta, J., Mayo, R., Quintana-Ortí, E.S.: An extension of the StarSs programming model for platforms with multiple GPUs. In: Sips, H., Epema, D., Lin, H.-X. (eds.) Euro-Par 2009. LNCS, vol. 5704, pp. 851–862. Springer, Heidelberg (2009). https://doi.org/10.1007/978-3-642-03869-3_79
3. Benkner, S., et al.: The PEPPHER approach to programmability and performance portability for heterogeneous many-core architectures. In: ParCo (2011)
4. Campeanu, G., Carlson, J., Sentilles, S.: Developing CPU-GPU embedded systems using platform-agnostic components. In: 2017 43rd Euromicro Conference on Software Engineering and Advanced Applications (SEAA), pp. 176–180 (2017). https://doi.org/10.1109/SEAA.2017.20
5. de Carvalho Junior, F.H., Lins, R.D., Corrêa, R.C., Araújo, G., de Santiago, C.F.: Design and implementation of an environment for component-based parallel programming. In: Daydé, M., Palma, J.M.L.M., Coutinho, Á.L.G.A., Pacitti, E., Lopes, J.C. (eds.) VECPAR 2006. LNCS, vol. 4395, pp. 184–197. Springer, Heidelberg (2007). https://doi.org/10.1007/978-3-540-71351-7_15
6. Chandy, K.M., Kesselman, C.: Compositional C++: compositional parallel programming. In: Banerjee, U., Gelernter, D., Nicolau, A., Padua, D. (eds.) LCPC 1992. LNCS, vol. 757, pp. 124–144. Springer, Heidelberg (1993). https://doi.org/10.1007/3-540-57502-2_44
7. Dastgeer, U., Li, L., Kessler, C.: The PEPPHER composition tool: performance-aware dynamic composition of applications for GPU-based systems. In: 2012 SC Companion: High Performance Computing, Networking Storage and Analysis, pp. 711–720 (2012). https://doi.org/10.1109/SC.Companion.2012.97
8. Memeti, S., Li, L., Pllana, S., Kołodziej, J., Kessler, C.: Benchmarking OpenCL, OpenACC, OpenMP, and CUDA: programming productivity, performance, and energy consumption. In: Proceedings of the 2017 Workshop on Adaptive Resource Management and Scheduling for Cloud Computing, ARMS-CC 2017, New York, NY, USA, pp. 1–6. Association for Computing Machinery (2017). https://doi.org/10.1145/3110355.3110356
9. OpenMP Architecture Review Board: OpenMP 5.0 Specification, November 2018 (2018)
10. Österlund, E., Löwe, W.: Self-adaptive concurrent components. Autom. Softw. Eng. **25**(1), 47–99 (2018). https://doi.org/10.1007/s10515-017-0219-0

11. Soudris, D., et al.: EXA2PRO programming environment: architecture and applications. In: Proceedings of the 18th International Conference on Embedded Computer Systems: Architectures, Modeling, and Simulation, SAMOS 2018, New York, NY, USA, pp. 202–209. Association for Computing Machinery (2018). https://doi.org/10.1145/3229631.3239369
12. Thoman, P., Gogl, D., Fahringer, T.: Sylkan: towards a Vulkan compute target platform for SYCL. In: IWOCL 2021, New York, NY, USA. Association for Computing Machinery (2021). https://doi.org/10.1145/3456669.3456683

MassiveClicks: A Massively-Parallel Framework for Efficient Click Models Training

Skip Thijssen[1](✉) , Pooya Khandel[1], Andrew Yates[1] ,
and Ana-Lucia Varbanescu[1,2]

[1] University of Amsterdam, Amsterdam, The Netherlands
skip.thijssen@student.uva.nl
[2] University of Twente, Enschede, The Netherlands

Abstract. *Click logs* collect user interaction with information retrieval systems (e.g., search engines). Clicks therefore become implicit feedback for such systems, and are further used to train *click models*, which in turn improve the quality of search and recommendations results. Click models based on expectation maximization (EM) are known to be effective and robust against various biases.

Training EM-based models is challenging due to the size of click logs, and can take many hours when using sequential tools like PyClick. Alternatives, such as ParClick, employ parallelism and show significant speed-up. However, ParClick only works on single-node multi-core systems. To further scale up and out, in this work we introduce MassiveClicks, the first massively parallel, distributed, multi-GPU framework for EM-based click-models training. MassiveClicks relies on efficient GPU kernels, balanced data-partitioning policies, and distributed computing to improve the performance of EM-based model training, outperforming ParClick by orders of magnitude when using GPUs and/or multiple nodes. Additionally, the framework supports heterogeneous GPU architectures, variable numbers of GPUs per node, allows for multi-node multi-core CPU-based training when no GPUs are available.

Keywords: massively-parallel training · multi-node multi-GPU · click models training · expectation-maximization models

1 Introduction

The primary goal of an Information Retrieval (IR) system, such as a search or recommendation engine, is to return results that satisfy users' information needs: users submit *queries* and receive *documents* in response to their query. Assessing the relevance of the documents (as answers to the query) is essential for the further development of IR systems. While domain experts can run such assessments, this approach does not scale with the number of IR applications and queries. Instead, Radlinski et al. [21] demonstrate that user interactions, such as *clicks*, may quantify users' satisfaction and serve as a proxy for relevance assessments. Thus, clicks are collected in *click logs* and further analysed.

D. Zeinalipour et al. (Eds.): Euro-Par 2023 Workshops, LNCS 14351, pp. 232–245, 2024.
https://doi.org/10.1007/978-3-031-50684-0_18

However, click logs are not perfect: user clicks suffer from various types of biases, such as position or popularity bias [7]. To mitigate biases, many click models have been developed, based on probabilistic graphical model (PGM) [7,18] and neural networks [3,19,24], and trained with users' click logs over time. In general, the PGM-based approaches are more explainable, more compact, and perform well, and are common for applications focusing on improving ranking models for web search [1,14,22,23].

While PGM-based click models are known to be effective, their training efficiency and scalability are not well studied, despite the immense volume of available search data - e.g., Google processes 1.2 trillion searches per year[1]. Scalability is essential to process increasingly large datasets, while efficiency is essential in light of raising concerns about the CO_2 footprint of big data applications [15]. Recently, Khandel et al. [16] introduced ParClick, a scalable algorithm for training Expectation-Maximization (EM)-based click models that enables multi-core training of PGM-based models, and demonstrates significant speed-up over previous methods. But ParClick's applicability is limited to multi-core shared-memory machines (basically, single-node CPU-only systems), and its performance is limited by the available number of cores.

In this work, we advance state-of-the-art with MassiveClicks , a framework that uses multi-scale, heterogeneous distributed systems for efficient EM-based training of click models. Our proposed framework supports the most common click models: Position-Based Model (PBM) [8], Click Chain Model (CCM) [13], User Browsing Model (UBM) [9], Dynamic Baysian Network Model (DBN) [6], and enables their training on heterogeneous system configurations, efficiently scales up to multiple nodes with multiple GPU devices, and, in the absence of GPU devices, can switch to CPU-based parallelism in a multi-node manner.

We measure the efficiency of MassiveClicks through extensive experiments using different mixes of CPUs and GPUs, and large-scale datasets. We find that MassiveClicks does use large-scale heterogeneous systems efficiently, and it can outperform ParClick by a factor larger than 850× when using 14 nodes with multiple GPUs.

This paper makes the following contributions:

- We design, implement, and analyze highly-efficient generic GPU kernels for training EM-based click models.
- We introduce MassiveClicks , the first framework that can be deployed to train click models using multi-node, multi-GPU, heterogeneous machine configurations.
- We demonstrate MassiveClicks provides orders-of-magnitude improvement over state-of-the-art in terms of training performance.
- We provide the open-source implementation of MassiveClicks.

---

[1] https://www.internetlivestats.com/google-search-statistics.

2   Background and Related Work

2.1   EM-Based Click Models

Click models are developed to address the bias in logged users' clicks over time. Formally, given a click model M, the probability of a click on the document d given the query q, will be calculated as follows [7]: $P(C_d) = P(E_d = 1) \cdot P(A_d = 1)$, where $P(E_d = 1)$ is the examination probability of document d, i.e., the probability that a user will scan this document on search engine results page (SERP) and $P(A_d = 1)$ is the attractiveness probability of d, i.e., the probability that user finds this document relevant for the input query. Various probabilistic graphical model (PGM)-based click models designed in the last decade differ in their assumption of user behavior while scanning the SERP, which in turn leads to specific formulations for the examination and attractiveness probabilities.

It follows that each model consists of a few examinations and a large number of attractiveness parameters. Their values can be estimated by employing the Expectation-Maximization (EM) algorithm through an iterative process where all parameters are initialized at the beginning, and new estimates are calculated based on user click logs at each iteration. This process continues for a certain number of iterations, such that the estimated parameters reach a convergence point for click probability calculation.

The primary challenge with EM-based click models training is that for every existing combination of query-document pairs, one attractiveness parameter exists; thereby, the number of attractiveness parameters scales with the size of the click log, and standard sequential training becomes too slow and inefficient. In this work, we propose to address this inefficiency by using all resources available in heterogeneous distributed systems.

2.2   Programming Models

In this work, we consider a heterogeneous node to combine a CPU and one or more GPUs. A distributed heterogeneous system is therefore a cluster of heterogeneous nodes, with potentially different architectures. For the remainder of this work, we use NVIDIA GPUs; however, our approach works without modification on, for example, AMD GPUs. The code, however, is not directly portable, but can be converted using, for example, the `hipify` tool[2].

To program distributed heterogeneous systems, we use a combination of CUDA (for GPUs), multi-threading (for CPUs), and MPI (for communication). Our framework is therefore usable on any multi-node multi-GPU cluster where CUDA and MPI are available.

2.3   Related Work

Click models were chiefly designed based on PGMs [7], and more recently, based on neural networks [3]. In the context of PGMs, Craswell et al. [8] introduced

---

[2] https://docs.amd.com/bundle/HIPify-Reference-Guide-v5.4/page/HIPify.html.

PBM that assumes the probability of clicking on a document in SERP highly relies on its position and is independent of the rest of the documents in the same SERP. In contrast, in CCM [13], the probability of clicking for a document is affected if the documents in higher rank within a SERP are clicked. Several other click models [7,12] are introduced as extensions of these models to improve their capabilities in addressing various biases in users' clicks, such as UBM [9] or DBN [6] click models. Our work is orthogonal to these approaches, as they only focus on the effectiveness of click models, while we focus on training efficiency and scalability aspects, but as they are trained with EM, our proposed framework is applicable for training them.

In contrast to click models' effectiveness, their training efficiency and scalability are not well studied. [20] focus on large-scale training of the Bayesian browsing model though it does not generalize with the rest of EM-based click models. Recently, [16] was introduced as a generic algorithm that can be applied for EM-based click models training; however, it is only limited to multi-core shared-memory machines. In our work, we aim to address the limitations of existing approaches, and we introduce the first general framework applicable to diverse machine configurations that can efficiently scale up when more (heterogeneous) resources are added.

Finally, there are several runtime systems - e.g., OmpSS, StarPU, IRIS, PARSEC or LAMA [2,4,5,11,17] - and many heterogeneous programming models [10]. However, our application is very specific in terms of computation to communication to synchronization ratios: the processing and code are very simple, and most design decisions are related to data structures, balanced data distribution, and synchronization. To the best of our knowledge, none of these systems could have better automated this design process. Therefore, we developed MassiveClicks as a prototype starting from the ParClick[3] method and code, and chose native programming models. However, for portability, one can easily port MassiveClicks to use different programming models or runtime systems.

3   Framework Design

Our goal is to design and prototype MassiveClicks as a general framework for training EM-based click models using distributed heterogeneous systems. The framework must support multi-GPU configurations (ranging from single-node/single-GPU to multi-node/multi-GPU), heterogeneous GPU architectures and memory sizes, and if/when a node does not have access to GPUs, the framework must run correctly on CPUs only. The framework must enable the users to partition the training dataset using several strategies, thus taking into account load balancing and processor compute capability. Finally, the framework must support four different click models: PBM, CCM, UBM, and DBN.

---

[3] https://github.com/uva-sne/ParClick.

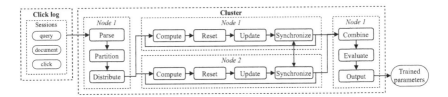

Fig. 1. The training process from start to finish.

A high-level design of MassiveClicks , complying with these requirements, is presented in Fig. 1. The training process is initiated by parsing the click log dataset, which includes queries, documents, and clicks on the documents, on a single machine. The dataset is then sorted internally and partitioned according to a user-specified partitioning scheme, with each partition being sent to a separate node in the cluster. A node receives the incoming partition and starts the training process by repeatedly carrying out the following four steps: (1) Estimating the click model parameters (*Compute*), (2) Clearing the previous iteration's results (*Reset*), (3) Copying the new iteration's results to the previous results (*Update*), and (4) Synchronizing the results with other nodes (*Synchronize*).

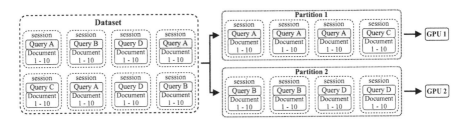

Fig. 2. Dataset distribution for separate GPUs, according to a partitioning scheme. Sessions are grouped by their search query into the same partition.

Upon completion of the designated number of training iterations, the node sends the trained parameters to the root node to evaluate the effectiveness (accuracy) of the trained click model.

4   Implementation Details

The implementation of the framework[4] utilizes multiple nodes, possibly with several GPUs per node, to train a click model using a click log dataset. The click log comprises search engine result pages (SERPs) - also referred to as sessions - and the clicks that occur on these pages. Each session is a personalized response

---

[4] MassiveClicks is open-source and available here https://github.com/skip-th/MassiveClicks.

generated by a search engine for a user's search query and contains a number of documents (search results) and the clicks on these documents.

Click models mainly use two types of parameters: (1) parameters common to documents with similar search queries from different sessions, and (2) parameters shared across all documents. The combination of these parameters allows for the estimation of the probability of a user clicking on a document given a certain query. Click models are trained precisely to estimate these parameters, where the estimation process requires calculations with different parameters on each document in the click log. Given the large number of documents, the application should be a well-suited workload for GPUs.

4.1 Data Distribution

We scale out MassiveClicks by using multiple GPUs (possibly on multiple nodes). To divide the click log among the multiple GPU devices, we propose four partitioning strategies, aiming to match different hardware configurations. These strategies aim to assign multiple sessions with the same search query to a single GPU device, as shown in Fig. 2, thereby eliminating the need for communication between nodes when estimating the parameters.

1. *Round-robin:* Assign groups of sessions to each device in a cyclic manner. It is suitable for test cases with smaller click logs, where slight imbalances in the workload per device do not significantly impact the performance.
2. *Maximum-Utilization:* Distribute, evenly, the number of sessions to all devices by continuously assigning groups of sessions to each GPU in turn. This strategy is useful for homogeneous (i.e., same-performance) GPUs.
3. *Proportional Maximum-Utilization:* Assign a number of sessions proportional to each device's memory size; devices with less memory receive fewer sessions, but have the same percentage of their memory occupied. This strategy is recommended when the size of a device's memory is an indicator of its performance.
4. *Newest Architecture First:* Prioritize assigning sessions to GPUs with the highest Compute Capability. Once these GPUs are "full", sessions are sent to less recent GPUs. This strategy is appropriate when there is a significant performance difference between older and newer GPUs in the system.

To minimize the memory footprint of the click log on the GPU, only the clicks on each document are included; the session, query, and document IDs are excluded during the transfer process.

4.2 GPU-Based Parameter Estimation

The estimation of the parameters for the click model is performed through iterative Expectation-Maximization (EM), which combines clicks on each session's documents and parameters from the previous iteration, stored in global GPU memory. An EM iteration has four phases: (1) *Computing* the parameters, (2)

Resetting the original parameters, (3) *Updating* the original parameters, and (4) *Synchronizing* the result. The first iteration is initialized with a default value of $\frac{1}{2}$, as per the PyClick implementation[5].

Compute. The GPU processes one session per thread, with multiple threads handling sessions with the same search queries. Each thread handles all ten documents in a session sequentially. This granularity is a trade-off between the degree of parallelization and thread independence. A more fine-grained approach, with a single document per thread, would increase communication between threads, while assigning a group of sessions with a similar query to a single thread would decrease communication, but increase load imbalance, as groups may vary in size.

Each thread uses its ID to access the click log and retrieve the documents for its session. The parameters associated with a document are also stored in the click log and indexed for quick access. This index is precomputed on the host machine. The parameters are stored in the click log because different sessions processed by separate threads can contain documents belonging to the same search query and, thus, require the same parameters (such as attractiveness in the PBM click model). Estimating the parameters for these query-document (QD) pairs involves reading and writing to the same memory location, which is addressed by storing the parameter index alongside each document in the click log. Unfortunately, this approach does not coalesce memory accesses, but is the only currently viable solution.

The use of shared parameters by different GPU threads can result in race conditions, where one thread writes changes to a parameter before another thread has had a chance to read its original value. To prevent such errors, each thread writes its results to a unique intermediate parameter in global memory.

Update. The intermediate parameters are then combined into a single original parameter in the Update phase for use in the next iteration. This process starts by *resetting* the original values to the default value of $\frac{1}{2}$. A reset of the original parameters is necessary to ensure that the previous iteration's parameters do not influence the results of the next iteration twice. During the Update phase, there are two types of parameters being reduced: (1) the parameters that are unique to a group of similar-query sessions (such as attractiveness in PBM), and (2) the parameters that are shared by all threads (such as examination in PBM).

To update the unique intermediate parameters, each thread atomically writes the intermediate values to the corresponding original parameters, which are identified using the index stored in the click log. The intermediate shared parameters are also written atomically to the original parameters. However, writing all intermediate shared parameters simultaneously with all threads to the same small set of shared original parameters can cause a significant delay due to the large number of threads awaiting their turn to write. To reduce this delay, each thread

---

[5] https://github.com/markovi/PyClick/blob/master/pyclick/click_models/Param.py.

block performs a local reduction operation on each of its threads' intermediate shared parameters. The reduced results are then atomically written to the original parameters in global memory by a single thread. This writing thread also starts with the shared parameter whose index is equal to its thread block index, further reducing the number of atomic writes to the same memory location.

4.3   Communication and Synchronization

The *synchronization* of parameters between GPUs occurs once a GPU has finished updating all its parameters. For the shared parameters to be communicated between iterations and workers, they are transferred to the host machine. The aggregation of shared parameters happens first at node level, using only the parameters received the local GPUs. The node-level (combined) shared parameters are subsequently sent to the other nodes using an MPI `Allgather` routine. Each node then repeats the aggregation operation and copies the result to all its GPUs. A new iteration can then start.

4.4   Dealing with Heterogeneity

The framework integrates two programming models: CUDA and MPI, to perform the click model training. The two models are separated into distinct tasks, with CUDA handling the parallel computation on GPUs and MPI managing the communication and coordination between multiple nodes. The heterogeneity of combining CUDA and MPI is managed through C++ as the main programming language. In the framework, high performance is achieved by CUDA providing the parallel computing power required for training large click models, and MPI allowing for the distribution of work across multiple nodes, increasing scalability.

4.5   CPU-Based Parameter Estimation

Each click model is designed to run both on the CPU and the GPU, with instructions for host-side computation and device-side computation, respectively. The data partitioning strategies remain unchanged, with the data passed to each machine being the size of the corresponding (i.e., CPU or GPU) memory.

To train the click model, the nodes locally sort their assigned data partition into groups based on search query and distribute the groups evenly among the specified number of threads. This sorting helps to minimize communication between threads by reducing concurrent access to the same parameters. Further, the CPU-based approach assigns entire groups to a single thread (while the GPU-based approach assigns each session to its own thread to balance the load). Thus, the CPU-based approach can process the documents within a group of sessions sequentially, allowing for direct writes to the parameters unique to that group without the need for intermediate parameters as in the GPU-based approach. Parameters shared across all sessions still require atomic writes to retrieve the final result.

Each thread uses a local copy of the shared parameters to estimate their values; the original shared parameters are updated with the local copies when all threads have completed their work. Finally, the results are synchronized among multiple nodes using the same scheme as in the GPU-based training.

4.6 Limitations

The current implementation of MassiveClicks is limited by the size of the input machine's memory, which must contain the full click log. This is necessary because our data distribution requires that each GPU receives a set of sessions with "unique" queries - i.e., that do not occur on another GPU. This approach allows GPUs to compute the parameters for the session separately until the final synchronization step, when some parameters must be synchronized.

Currently, the input machine reads the entire click log, and groups same-query sessions together on the same GPU, according to the chosen partitioning scheme. The distribution of sessions to GPUs is performed only after reading the entire click log, so the size of each group of sessions is known to prevent the session groups from being assigned to GPUs with insufficient memory.

Assigning sessions to GPUs on separate nodes while reading the click log, in order to not be limited by the input machine's memory, requires the grouping of sessions located on different nodes. This operation is currently not supported.

The limitation can be circumvented by sorting the click log beforehand with sessions of the same query grouped together. The click log can then be processed in separate chunks that individually fit into the input machine's memory. The few parameters shared between all sessions can be combined afterward manually.

5   Evaluation

Our evaluation focuses on MassiveClicks's ability to use multi-node multi-GPU systems, its scalability, and its efficiency in using various heterogeneous configurations[6]. For all our experiments, *training time* is the main metric of interest, and we also report speed-up versus state-of-the-art (to quantify advancements in performance) and memory footprint (to assess feasibility for large datasets).

Table 1. Training time, speed-up, and ACE for **PBM** and **CCM** for different datasets and **NVIDIA RTX A4000 GPUs** compared to ParClick on an **AMD EPYC 7402P CPU** with **48 threads**.

GPUs	D10						D25						D50					
	Training [s]		Speed-up		ACE [%]		Training [s]		Speed-up		ACE [%]		Training [s]		Speed-up		ACE [%]	
	PBM	CCM	PBM	CCM	PBM	CCM	PBM	CCM	PBM	CCM	PBM	CCM	PBM	CCM	PBM	CCM	PBM	CCM
1	4.0	6.1	10.1	73.1	14.7	42.4	10.1	15.7	10.5	70.1	14.0	41.4	21.8	31.9	9.7	66.3	13.5	40.5
2	1.9	3.3	20.9	137.6	10.4	41.7	5.8	8.5	19.2	129.5	12.9	39.8	12.1	17.4	17.5	121.8	12.8	39.0
4	1.1	1.6	37.5	272.2	13.7	39.6	2.8	4.1	39.4	267.5	13.1	39.2	6.1	7.6	34.5	280.0	7.1	24.5
8	0.6	0.9	67.1	488.8	12.4	36.2	1.7	2.2	66.4	494.1	10.1	36.2	3.0	4.4	71.2	482.0	12.9	36.3
14	0.4	0.5	110.1	850.4	12.2	37.2	1.0	1.4	110.0	794.0	10.8	33.4	1.9	2.7	112.1	790.7	11.6	34.6

---

[6] Additional evaluation data and plots are available at https://bit.ly/HP23-extra.

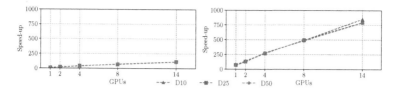

Fig. 3. MassiveClicks's speedup over ParClick for PBM (left) and CCM (right) using 10, 25, and 50 million sessions. ParClick runs on an AMD EPYC 7402P CPU with 48 threads, and MassiveClicks uses NVIDIA RTX A4000 GPUs.

5.1 Experimental Setup

The Platform. For all our experiments, we use DAS-6[7], a cluster comprising compute nodes with one CPU (AMD EPYC 7402P or Intel E5-2630 v3) and various NVIDIA GPUs (e.g., Titan X, Titan-X Pascal, A6000, A4000), interconnected using 100 Gbit/s Ethernet and managed by SLURM. The nodes run CUDA v11.5.119 on the Red Hat 8.5.0-3 operating system. We measure GPU (kernel) performance using NVIDIA Nsight Compute NVIDIA[8], and we measure the CPU performance with simple code instrumentation.

The Data. All our models are trained and tested with the Yandex dataset[9]. For all experiments, we divide the dataset into two parts: the first 80% forms a training set, and the last 20% forms a test set. Because the trained click-model only provides relevant parameters for search results contained within the training set [7, p.53], we filter the test set to only include sessions from the training set. To do so, we follow ParClick's approach of *filtering on sessions* [16].

5.2 The GPU Impact

Speed-Up. To assess the performance gain due to GPU acceleration, we analyze the speed-up of MassiveClicks on up to 14 GPUs compared to ParClick running on a 24-core AMD EPYC 7402P CPU. We use PBM and CCM as representatives of a less and more complex click model, respectively. Speed-up is calculated as the ratio of ParClick's training time to MassiveClicks's training time. We also measure the **A**verage **P**ercentage of **C**omputation Time spent within the parameter estimation stage per it**E**ration (ACE - introduced in [16]), to indicate parameter synchronization overhead.

---

[7] https://www.cs.vu.nl/das/.

[8] https://developer.nvidia.com/nsight-compute.

[9] https://www.kaggle.com/competitions/yandex-personalized-web-search-challenge/data.

Table 1 shows the training time, speed-up, and ACE, for 10, 25, and 50 million sessions. We observe that a single GPU already improves training performance up to 10x for PBM and 73x for CCM. When using 14 GPUs, MassiveClicks shows speed-ups as high as 850x for the smallest dataset, and as high as 790x for the largest log. However, the stages unrelated to parameter estimation, measured with ACE, take up a considerable part of the total training time. Consequently, the maximum speed-up in training time observed in Table 1 differs significantly between click models, as also seen in Fig. 3: PBM achieves a significantly lower maximum speed-up compared to CCM, due to the lower computation intensity of the former. As expected, higher computational intensity indicates more efficient GPU acceleration, and thus higher speed-up.

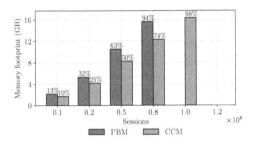

Fig. 4. MassiveClicks memory footprint for **PBM** and **CCM** using an **NVIDIA RTX A4000 GPU** with 16.7 GBs of memory and up to 120M sessions.

Memory Footprint. Figure 4 shows that the memory footprint linearly increases with the number of sessions, albeit with different slopes. The PBM and CCM click models cut off at 75 and 100 million sessions, respectively, when the GPU's memory becomes too small to hold the entire click log and parameters.

5.3 Scalability

We measure the scalability of MassiveClicks by comparing speed-up and training time PBM and CCM for an increasing number of NVIDIA RTX A4000 GPUs computing up to 120 million sessions, the maximum size of the Yandex dataset.

Figure 5 shows that even for very large click logs, our framework significantly reduces training time. The addition of multiple GPUs further reduces training time to several seconds for even the largest dataset sizes. These performance improvements through scaling the number of GPUs also apply to the less complex PBM click model. Furthermore, the speed-up shows that the overhead of scaling to multi-GPU multi-node configurations has minimal impact on the final training time. Each click log size scales close to the ideal scaling factor for both the complex CCM and less complex PBM click model.

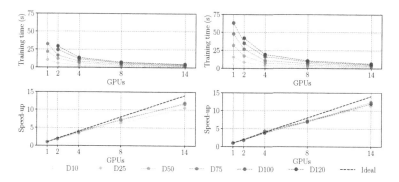

Fig. 5. MassiveClicks training time (top) and scalability (bottom) for **PBM** (left) and **CCM** (right) using 14 **NVIDIA RTX A4000 GPUs** with up to 120M sessions.

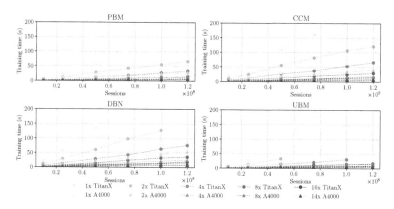

Fig. 6. MassiveClicks training time for **PBM, CCM, DBN**, and **UBM** on up to 16 NVIDIA TITAN X (red) and 14 A4000 (blue) GPUs for dataset sizes of D10 to D120. (Color figure online)

5.4 Putting It All Together

We demonstrate the framework's full capability by testing various combinations of click models computed on multiple nodes with different GPU devices; the achieved performance is summarized in Fig. 6. The results indicate a significant difference in training time when comparing the older NVIDIA TITAN X GPU to the newer A4000 model: A4000 performs the training significantly faster. However, the TITAN X does still provide significant performance improvements and is capable of reducing training time, even for the largest dataset, to seconds.

These results show that multi-GPU training of EM-based click models with our proposed framework can significantly reduce training time. Moreover, the performance benefits of GPUs are more significant for models like the CCM and DBN, which are more complex models than PBM and UBM.

6   Conclusion

User clicks can be used as implicit feedback to IR systems such as search and recommendation engines, but they suffer from various types of biases. Click models are trained to avoid such biases, but they can be slow and inefficient., with the notable exception of ParClick [16], the first parallel, shared-memory solution for training these models. As ParClick is fundamentally limited in scale, we propose MassiveClicks , a framework for training EM-based click models on heterogeneous systems of any scale. MassiveClicks supports heterogeneous, multi-node and multi-GPU systems, but can be also used with CPU-only clusters. We also support multiple partitioning schemes.

Our empirical analysis demonstrates that MassiveClicks can speed-up training by more than $850\times$ when compared with ParClick. The framework is open-source and can be executed on any distributed heterogeneous system using NVIDIA GPUs, where CUDA and MPI are available.

In the future, we plan to improve the heterogeneity of training by employing CPU and GPU resources simultaneously, a task that is particularly challenging in determining the best partitioning of user clicks among processors. We aim to also extend the framework by implementing more efficient data ingestion and data distribution mechanisms.

References

1. Agarwal, A., et al.: Estimating position bias without intrusive interventions. In: WSDM'19, pp. 474–482 (2019)
2. Augonnet, C., et al.: StarPU: a unified platform for task scheduling on heterogeneous multicore architectures. In: CCPE Special Issue: Euro-Par 2009 23, 2 February 2011, pp. 187–198. https://doi.org/10.1002/cpe.1631
3. Borisov, A., et al.: A neural click model for web search. In: WWW '16, pp. 531–541 (2016)
4. Bosilca, G., et al.: PaRSEC: exploiting heterogeneity to enhance scalability. Comput. Sci. Eng. **15**(6), 36–45 (2013). https://doi.org/10.1109/MCSE.2013.98
5. Bueno, J., et al.: Productive programming of gpu clusters with OmpSs. In: IEEE IPDPS'12, pp. 557–568 (2012). https://doi.org/10.1109/IPDPS.2012.58
6. Chapelle, O., Zhang, Y.: A dynamic Bayesian network click model for web search ranking. In: ACM WWW '09, pp. 1–10. Association for Computing Machinery (2009)
7. Chuklin, A., et al.: Click Models for Web Search. Morgan & Claypool, San Rafael (2015)
8. Craswell, N., et al.: An experimental comparison of click position-bias models. In: ACM WSDM '08, pp. 87–94 (2008)
9. Dupret, G.E., Piwowarski, B.: A user browsing model to predict search engine click data from past observations. In: ACM SIGIR '08, pp. 331–338 (2008)
10. Fang, J., et al.: Parallel programming models for heterogeneous many-cores: a comprehensive survey. CCF Trans. High Perform. Comput. **2**(4), 382–400 (2020). ISSN 2524-4930. https://doi.org/10.1007/s42514-020-00039-4

11. Fraunhofer SCAI: LAMA - development of fast and scalable software. https://www.scai.fraunhofer.de/en/business-research-areas/high-performance-computing/products/lama.html
12. Grotov, A., Chuklin, A., Markov, I., Stout, L., Xumara, F., de Rijke, M.: A comparative study of click models for web search. In: Mothe, J., et al. (eds.) CLEF 2015. LNCS, vol. 9283, pp. 78–90. Springer, Cham (2015). https://doi.org/10.1007/978-3-319-24027-5_7
13. Guo, F., et al.: Click chain model in web search. In: ACM WWW'09, pp. 11–20 (2009)
14. Joachims, T., et al.: Unbiased learning-to-rank with biased feedback. In: ACM WSDM '17, pp. 781–789 (2017)
15. Jones, N., et al.: How to stop data centres from gobbling up the world's electricity. Nature **561**(7722), 163–166 (2018)
16. Khandel, P., et al.: ParClick: a scalable algorithm for EM-based click models. In: ACM Web 2022.WWW'22, pp. 392–400. Virtual Event, Lyon, France: ACM (2022). ISBN 9781450390965. https://doi.org/10.1145/3485447.3511967
17. Kim, J., et al.: IRIS: a portable runtime system exploiting multiple heterogeneous programming systems. In: IEEE HPEC'21, pp. 1–8 (2021). https://doi.org/10.1109/HPEC49654.2021.9622873
18. Koller, D., Friedman, N.: Probabilistic Graphical Models: Principles and Techniques - Adaptive Computation and Machine Learning. The MIT Press, Cambridge (2009)
19. Lin, J., et al.: A graph-enhanced click model for web search. In: ACM SIGIR '21, pp. 1259–1268. New York, NY, USA (2021)
20. Liu, C., et al.: BBM: Bayesian browsing model from petabyte-scale data. In: ACM KDD'09, pp. 537–546. Paris, France (2009)
21. Radlinski, F., et al.: How does clickthrough data reflect retrieval quality? In: ACM CIKM'08, pp. 43–52. New York, NY, USA: ACM (2008)
22. Vardasbi, A., et al.: Cascade model-based propensity estimation for counterfactual learning to rank. In: ACM SIGIR'20, pp. 2089–2092. Association for Computing Machinery (2020)
23. Wang, X., et al.: Position bias estimation for unbiased learning to rank in personal search. In: ACM WSDM'18, pp. 610–618 (2018)
24. Yu, H.-T., et al.: A rank-biased neural network model for click modeling. In: CHIIR '19 (2019)

Sparse Matrix-Vector Product
for the bmSparse Matrix Format in GPUs

Gonzalo Berger$^{(\boxtimes)}$, Ernesto Dufrechou, and Pablo Ezzatti

Instituto de Computación, Universidad de la República, J. H. y Reissig 565,
11300 Montevideo, Uruguay
{gberger,edufrechou,pezzatti}@fing.edu.uy

Abstract. Historically, the sparse matrix-vector product (SpMV) acceleration concentrated the central part of the research efforts devoted to sparse linear algebra kernels. Lately, other fundamental sparse operations have gained considerable attention. A remarkable example is the SpGEMM (sparse matrix-matrix product) operation, for which several routines and specific sparse formats have been proposed in the last few years. One of these storage formats, the bitmap-based *bmSparse*, shows promising performance on the SpGEMM kernel over massively parallel hardware platforms and storage advantages that could benefit other operations. In this work, we study and develop an SpMV kernel for the *bmSparse* format. The experimental results show that the implementation can reach up to a 4× speedup over cuSPARSE's CSR implementation, suggesting that this format is an interesting alternative for a potentially broad range of sparse matrix applications.

Keywords: Tiled sparse storage formats · SPMV · GPU

1 Introduction

The sparse matrix-vector product (SpMV) is an essential operation of sparse numerical linear algebra. It is the core of many numerical methods, such as solving sparse linear systems using Krylov subspace solvers. Therefore it has fired the interest of the High-Performance Computing (HPC) community for decades [10], resulting in realizations of this kernel for almost all major HPC platforms. In particular, given the disruptive evolution of GPUs in the HPC landscape, the research dedicated to developing efficient implementations for these devices is abundant [3,4,9].

Several other sparse operations have gained relevance accompanying the explosion of machine-learning-related research in recent years. A remarkable example is the SpGEMM, for which several recent efforts have produced efficient GPU kernels and storage formats [14,16,22]. One of the main challenges of the SpGEMM is its irregular memory access, given that the nonzero pattern of the inputs establishes that of the output. To mitigate this irregularity, which severely harms the performance of the kernel, Zhang and Gruenwald proposed

© The Author(s), under exclusive license to Springer Nature Switzerland AG 2024
D. Zeinalipour et al. (Eds.): Euro-Par 2023 Workshops, LNCS 14351, pp. 246–256, 2024.
https://doi.org/10.1007/978-3-031-50684-0_19

the *bmSparse* format [23]. This format aggregates the nonzeros of the matrix in sparse blocks of 8×8, and uses bitmaps to store the nonzero pattern of such blocks. In previous work, we proposed improvements to the SPGEMM algorithm using this format and produced highly optimized GPU routines capable, among other things, of leveraging Nvidia's Tensor Cores. Although *bmSparse* was conceived to perform well in the SPGEMM, the format presents interesting characteristics in other aspects. For example, the layout is highly compact, taking less storage than mainstream formats in many situations. A more lightweight storage format can also imply fewer data movements from the memory to the processors, which is the main bottleneck in this operation.

The above facts are encouraging and make *bmSparse* attractive as a general-purpose sparse storage format. However, to be general-purpose, it is mandatory to prove a competitive performance for the SPMV kernels, at least for implementations over massively parallel hardware platforms.

This work proposes two GPU implementations of the SPMV for the *bmSparse* format, comparing their performance with the implementation for the CSR format of CUSPARSE library, which is the standard reference in the field. The results show that our kernels' performance is competitive with CUSPARSE, even reaching considerable speedups for matrices of specific characteristics.

The rest of the article is structured as follows. Section 2 describes the main aspects of the *bmSparse* format. Next, Sect. 3 provides a brief review of related work. Our proposal to implement the SPMV leveraging *bmSparse* is detailed in Sect. 4, followed by the experimental evaluation in Sect. 5. Finally, Sect. 6 offers concluding remarks and discusses lines of future work.

2 The *bmSparse* Format

The *bmSparse* format [23] is similar to the Coordinate Format (COO) [2], except it is a coordinate list of non-empty blocks instead of nonzero scalars. The blocks are of size 8 × 8, and only the nonzero values of each block are explicitly stored. The format uses a bitmap, represented as a 64-bit integer, to store the position of each nonzero in the sparse matrix. This bitmap has a 1 in each position inside the block with a nonzero value. The bitmap is arranged in row-major order. Unlike in COO, the *bmSparse* format compresses block coordinates into a 64-bit integer, where the first 32 bits store the row number and the second store the column number. These integers are called *keys* in *bmSparse* terminology.

The memory structure of *bmSparse* is designed to simplify the intermediate operations of the sparse matrix multiplication. For example, the required memory and the block pattern to store the output of a sparse-matrix product can be computed using only the keys and bitmaps of the inputs.

Another central idea underlying the format is to multiply blocks as dense matrices. To this end, dense blocks are reconstructed in the scratchpad memory of the GPU using bitwise operations such as shifts and __*popcll*.

In summary, the data structure of *bmSparse* contains four vectors: the vector of *keys*, which stores the keys of the blocks in block-row-major order; the *bitmap* vector stores each block's bitmap; the *values* vector stores the nonzero values ordered by block, and then in row-major order, and the *offsets* vector stores the starting position of each block in the *values* vector.

3   Related Work

One of the most relevant early works on accelerating the SpMV in GPUs is probably [3]. There, the authors propose two implementations for the CSR format (*scalar* and *vector*), and also the COO, DIA, ELL, and HYB formats.

After this seminal work, several authors proposed a myriad of domain-specific sparse formats and implementation of SpMV in GPUs. The new sparse storage formats aim to alleviate the volume of communications between the cores and the DRAM by rearranging the data of the matrix (values and indices) so that threads can access it with high parallelism and locality.

Some of these formats, such as CSR5 [15], BCSR [11], BELLPACK [7], BCOO and BRO [19] use tiled computing patterns, rearranging the nonzeros into tiles adequate for SIMD processors, or exploiting in some way the 2D spatial locality of the nonzeros of the matrix. Recently, a format called TiledSPMV has been proposed [18]. In that work, the authors develop several warp-level SpMV kernels for seven basic formats, CSR, COO, ELL, HYB, Dense, Dense Row, and Dense Column, optimized to multiply small (16×16) sparse matrix tiles. They also provide a method to analyze the sparse matrix and obtain the tiled representation, storing each tile in the most convenient format.

Unlike the above formats, *bmSparse* was conceived to regularize the memory access in the SpGEMM operation. The original proposal of SpGEMM for the *bmSparse* format [23] consists of two main stages: constructing an intermediate structure called the *task list* and the multiplication stage. A *task* is the product of two blocks from the input matrices A and B, contributing to a block of the matrix C (the output).

In [5, 6, 16], we proposed several enhancements to different stages of the SpGEMM in this format, such as avoiding the multiplication of blocks that result in a null block, computing the bitmap of the output block using the bitmaps of the input blocks, enhancing the sorting of the task list, and leveraging the Tensor Cores of modern Nvidia GPUs in the multiplication stage.

Other authors have also addressed the acceleration of the SpGEMM leveraging bitmap-based sparse formats [20–22]. The same applies to the SpMV operation, where some authors have evaluated using bitmap-based sparse formats to implement this kernel [12,13]. However, up to our knowledge, the performance of the *bmSparse* format for the SpMV in modern GPUs has not been studied yet.

4   CUDA Implementations

4.1   Baseline Version

Probably the most straightforward alternative to multiply a matrix in *bmSparse* format by a vector is to process each block independently, multiplying it by the corresponding segment of the input vector and adding the results to the output vector. This last addition needs atomic operations to avoid race conditions in the access to the output vector, which can cause severe contention and carry a high-performance penalty. To avoid using atomic operations, we assign a block of threads to a row of matrix blocks and process those blocks sequentially, as in the naive variant of the parallel SPMV.

The *bmSparse* format, as proposed in [23], does not specify a data structure to access the beginning of each row of blocks directly. As efficient access to the beginning of each row of blocks is crucial to implement the second approach, we compute the corresponding structure before the multiplications. Therefore, the proposed SPMV routine has a preprocessing stage that needs to be executed only once for each matrix. This stage processes the vector of *keys* of the *bmSparse* format and finds the index of the first block of each row of blocks in such vector. This process is performed in three steps. First, a vector of ones, with an entry for each block, is allocated in the GPU memory. Second, we perform a Thrust *reduce_by_key* operation, using the row index as the key. This process gives a vector containing an entry with the number of blocks for each row of blocks. Finally, we perform a *scan* operation on that vector to obtain the beginning of each row of blocks in the vector of keys.

After the preprocessing, the second stage multiplies each row of blocks with an independent CUDA thread block. Each thread block uses the vector computed in the preprocessing stage to obtain the first and last block to process and then proceeds to load each block from global memory iteratively, convert it to a dense 8×8 block, and multiply it by the corresponding segment of the input vector. The product is performed using two warps for each block, dividing the warp into sections of 4 threads that process each block row. The threads accumulate the partial sums of the entries they multiply, and the final result of each section of the warp is obtained through a reduction performed using *warp shuffle* operations.

Listing 1.1 shows the CUDA code corresponding to the main kernel. The sparse matrix is stored in the arrays A_keys, A_val, A_bmps, and A_off. The kernel also receives the array bl_rw_ptr computed in the preprocessing stage, containing the start index of each row of blocks in the array of keys.

The grid of CUDA threads is launched so that there are enough blocks of 64 threads to span the rows of A (approximately $n/8$ blocks). After the initializations, the loop between lines 16 and 31 processes the row of blocks corresponding to the CUDA block determined by blockIdx.x. In line 19, each thread shifts the bitmap to check for a nonzero in the block's position corresponding to its thread index. Later, after line 23, if the selected bit is a 1, the thread counts the number of 1's to the left of its bit to obtain the offset of the value in the A_val array, shifting the bitmap to the right the appropriate number of bits and using the *popcll* function.

The index of the value in the input vector is computed in line 24 by shifting the key of the block, which contains its column index in the 32 least significant bits. The product between the matrix coefficient and the value in the input vector is accumulated in a register. At the end of the loop, each set of 8 contiguous threads in the warp contains partial values corresponding to one position of the output vector. We reduce the partial values using a *shuffle down* primitive with a parameter that enables four parallel 8-element reductions per warp.

In the current implementation, we store the value to multiply in registers. In some contexts, storing the dense block in shared memory would be helpful. For example, if a low precision is acceptable, the Tensor Cores can multiply the dense block by the corresponding segment of the input vector or, in a SpMM scenario, a block of the dense input matrix. In that case, the Tensor Core primitives require the data to reside in shared memory. We use registers in this implementation because it is slightly faster. However, it is simple enough to adapt the code to enable the use of Tensor Cores.

Listing 1.1. CUDA code of the baseline kernel.

```
1   template <class VIN, class VOUT> __global__
2   void spmv_kernel_new( uint64_t* bl_rw_ptr, uint64_t* A_keys,
3                         VIN* A_val, uint64_t* A_bmps, uint64_t* A_off,
4                         VIN* v, VOUT* u, int n)
5   {
6       VOUT res = 0;
7
8       const int lane_id = threadIdx.x % 64,
9                 row_idx = blockIdx.x*8+ threadIdx.x/8;
10
11      if (row_idx >= n) return;
12
13      uint64_t first = bl_rw_ptr[blockIdx.x],
14               last = bl_rw_ptr[blockIdx.x+1];
15
16      for(uint64_t bl_idx = first; bl_idx < last; bl_idx++ ){
17
18          uint64_t bmp = A_bmps[bl_idx];
19          uint64_t my_bit = bmp & (uint64_t(1) << 64 - 1 - lane_id);
20
21          VIN mat_coef = 0, valv = 0;
22
23          if (my_bit) {
24              int col_idx = ((A_keys[bl_idx] << 32) >> 32)*8+threadIdx.x%8;
25              int pos = __popcll(bmp >> (64 - lane_id));
26              mat_coef = A_val[A_off[bl_idx]+pos];
27              valv = v[col_idx];
28          }
29
30          res+= (VOUT) (mat_coef*valv);
31      }
32
33      for (int i=4; i>=1; i/=2)
34          res += __shfl_down_sync(__activemask(), res, i, 8);
35
36      if((lane_id % 8) == 0)
37          u[row_idx] = res;
38  }
```

4.2 Batched Variant

The baseline variant presents a direct mapping between the 8×8 matrix blocks and the 64-thread CUDA blocks. This mapping has some advantages, as being straightforward, producing a relatively simple kernel code, and achieving a coalesced memory access to the matrix, as the values accessed by a warp are contiguous in memory. However, the sequential processing of matrix row blocks is a potential performance pitfall. As it happens in the naive parallel SPMV algorithm, there can be a significant load imbalance between the blocks associated with different rows of matrix blocks. Moreover, the maximum theoretical number of parallel operations that can be achieved in the processing of each row of blocks is 64, which can be low for certain matrices.

We propose a variant to our original procedure that processes each row of matrix blocks in batches of 4. This allows using CUDA blocks of 8×32 threads to process each row of blocks, which theoretically increases the potential parallelism regarding the baseline version. In other words, 8 warps process each row of blocks, instead of 2.

Unlike before, in this new variant the threads of a warp are mapped to data lying in different blocks of the matrix but in the same row. This way, after the loop that processes the row of blocks in batches of 4 finishes, the partial values residing in the registers of a warp can be reduced to a obtain a single value in the output vector.

The new variant can be obtained with relatively small modifications to the kernel code. The main changes are in the main loop, which now processes the blocks in batches of 4, in the final reduction and in the computation of index variables such as *lane_id, bl_idx, row_idx,* and *col_idx.*

A consequence of the new mapping of threads to values of the matrix is that in the global memory access of line 26, each warp spans four blocks of the matrix, which means that the accessed data is not contiguous in memory. However, in modern CUDA devices, a memory operation of a warp is always divided into as many transactions of 32 Bytes are needed to satisfy the request of each thread to mitigate the effect of uncoalesced global memory accesses. As the data access by each of the four groups of 8 threads of the new scheme is contiguous (belongs to a row of the same matrix block) it is likely that the request of each warp can be satisfied with a similar number of memory transactions.

5   Experimental Evaluation

This section describes the experimental evaluation of our proposal. It presents the hardware, software, and test cases used in the experiments and discusses our main results.

5.1   Evaluation Hardware Platform

The hardware platform used in the experiments consists of a single-GPU server equipped with an Intel(R) Core(TM) i7-6700 CPU @ 3.40 GHz, 64 GB of RAM, using Linux as OS. The accelerator is an NVIDIA GeForce GTX 3090 Ti GPU (*Ampere*). We used version 11.4 of the CUDA Toolkit (including Thrust and cuSPARSE [1] libraries).

5.2   Test Cases

The instances selected to validate the proposal are 1455 sparse matrices of the *SuiteSparse Matrix Collection* [8]. The set is intended to be as diverse as possible, presenting matrices of different sizes and nonzero patterns, as seen in the left of Fig. 1. However, the plot on the right shows how, on average, the dataset tends to have a predominance of very sparse blocks, which, in principle, does not favor the bmSparse format. Single-precision floating-point numbers (*floats*) are used.

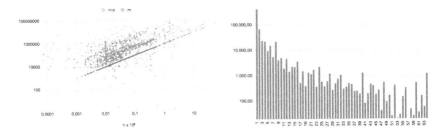

Fig. 1. Characteristics of the set of matrices used for testing. Number of nonzeros and columns of the matrices plotted against their number of rows (left), and average number of bmSparse blocks with 1 to 64 nonzero elements (right). In both plots the *y*-axis is in log scale.

5.3   Experimental Results

In this section, we evaluate the performance of our implementations and validate our proposal by comparing it with the implementations of cuSPARSE library for the CSR [17] format. The routines of cuSPARSE library are highly optimized for Nvidia GPUs and have been improved constantly through many years. Therefore, they establish a reasonable baseline to analyze the performance of the new format.

Both cuSPARSE's SpMV and our routines imply a light preprocessing. In the case of cuSPARSE, it is necessary to call the functions `cusparseSpMV_bufferSize` and `cudaMalloc` before performing the actual multiplication with `cusparseSpMV`. In our case, it is necessary to compute the array of pointers to the start of each row of blocks in the matrix. We focus the evaluation on the multiplications kernels of both routines, neglecting the preprocessing time. The reason is that, in several scenarios, the preprocessing is performed once. At the same time, many calls to the SpMV kernel are required, and therefore the computation time of the kernel strongly dominates.

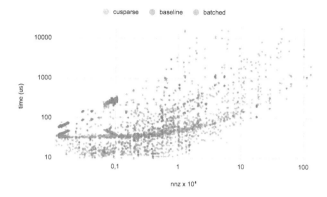

Fig. 2. Execution time (in μs) of the two *bmSparse*-based variants and cuSparse. The matrices are presented in increasing *nnz* order. The *x*-axis is in log scale.

Figure 2 shows the execution times of the two *bmSparse*-based variants and the cuSparse merge-based SpMV. The first observation is the contrast between the regularity of cuSparse's times, which depend almost exclusively on *nnz*, and the execution times of the *bmSparse*-based variants, which present a substantial variability.

Before analyzing this variability, we compare our two variants' performance. Figure 3 shows the ratio between the execution times of the baseline (*bmsp_base*) and batched (*bmsp_batch*) versions of the *bmSparse* SpMV. As seen in the figure, the performance of *bmsp_batch* variant consistently outperforms the *bmsp_base* variant. The harmonic mean of the acceleration is 1.38 in favor of *bmsp_batch*, although there are matrices where *bmsp_batch* is 3× faster than the *bmsp_base*. Moreover, *bmsp_base* is better for only 60 out of 1445 matrices, and its most significant performance gain is 72% regarding *bmsp_batch*.

As the above results position *bmsp_batch* as the best variant, we use it for the following comparison with cuSparse. Figure 4 shows the execution times of cuSparse divided by those of *bmsp_batch* for each matrix, presenting the results in increasing order of *nnz* and in increasing order of average number of *nnz* per *bmSparse* block (right). Analyzing the figures, it is possible to conclude that both the *nnz* and the average number of nonzeros per block significantly influence the advantage of *bmsp_batch* over cuSparse. In particular, *bmsp_batch* is consistently outperformed by cuSparse for matrices with less than 500,000 nonzero elements. Some exceptions are matrices such as *bcsstk33*, which has 393810 nonzeros but has 14.72 nonzeros per block, and for which *bmsp_batch* is more than 4× faster than cuSparse. The harmonic mean of the speedups for matrices with more than 31 nonzeros per block is 1.62 in favor of *bmsp_batch*. This is not surprising because, in these cases, the *bmSparse* format is expected to effectively reduce the memory reads of indexing data. However, it is also remarkable that the harmonic mean of the speedups is 0.97 for matrices with more than nine nonzeros on average. Although, as it appears in the plots, it is not the typ-

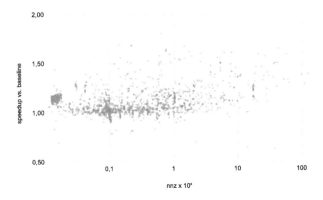

Fig. 3. Execution time of the baseline variant divided by the execution time of the batched variant (values above 1 favour the batched variant). The results are presented in increasing *nnz* order. The *x*-axis is in log scale.

ical case in the SuiteSparse matrix collection, this means that the *bmSparse* format can be competitive in a potentially broad spectrum of situations.

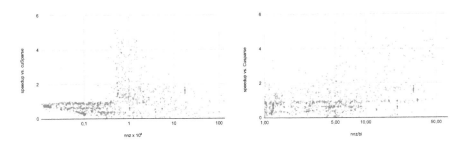

Fig. 4. Acceleration obtained by *bmsp_batch* regarding CUSPARSE presented in increasing order of *nnz* (left) and increasing order of average number of *nnz* per *bmSparse* block (right). The *x*-axis is in log scale.

6   Final Remarks and Future Work

The usual path in sparse numerical linear algebra has been to propose new storage layouts capable of exploiting the computing power of modern parallel architectures on certain operations or use cases. That is the case of *bmSparse*, a format that emerged to provide an adequate layout to perform the SPGEMM on GPUs. In this work, we transit the path in the opposite direction. Acknowledging the strengths of *bmSparse* for the SPGEMM, we explore its performance on the SPMV, proposing two GPU kernels for that operation. The experimental results show that the second kernel proposed is consistently better than the first one.

The comparison with CUSPARSE's CSR implementation, a variant of the Merge-Path SPMV, shows interesting speedups in some cases. Specifically, the *bmSparse* SPMV is competitive with CUSPARSE for matrices with more than nine nonzeros per *bmSparse* block in average, reaching speedups of up to 3× for some matrices.

For future efforts, we plan to revisit the design of the algorithm to mitigate the effect of highly sparse blocks. For these blocks, it is possible that too many computing resources are wasted in the current proposal. One alternative is to analyze the matrix and determine a different mapping of threads for highly sparse blocks or rows of blocks.

Acknowledgment. The researchers were supported by Universidad de la República, specially with the CAP-UdelaR Grant of Gonzalo Berger. We acknowledge also the ANII - MPG Independent Research Groups: "Efficient Heterogeneous Computing" with the CSC group and the PEDECIBA.

References

1. cuSPARSE library. https://developer.nvidia.com/cusparse. Accessed 21 Jun 2022
2. Barrett, R., et al.: Templates for the Solution of Linear Systems: Building Blocks for Iterative Methods. Society for Industrial and Applied Mathematics (1994)
3. Bell, N., Garland, M.: Implementing sparse matrix-vector multiplication on throughput-oriented processors. In: Proceedings of the Conference on High Performance Computing Networking, Storage and Analysis, SC 2009. Association for Computing Machinery, New York (2009). https://doi.org/10.1145/1654059.1654078
4. Benatia, A., Ji, W., Wang, Y., Shi, F.: Sparse matrix partitioning for optimizing SpMV on CPU-GPU heterogeneous platforms. Int. J. High Perform. Comput. Appl. **34**(1), 66–80 (2020)
5. Berger, G., Freire, M., Marini, R., Dufrechou, E., Ezzatti, P.: Advancing on an efficient sparse matrix multiplication kernel for modern GPUs. Concurrency Comput. Pract. Exp. **35**, e7271. https://doi.org/10.1002/cpe.7271, https://onlinelibrary.wiley.com/doi/abs/10.1002/cpe.7271
6. Berger, G., Freire, M., Marini, R., Dufrechou, E., Ezzatti, P.: Unleashing the performance of bmSparse for the sparse matrix multiplication in GPUs. In: 12th Workshop on Latest Advances in Scalable Algorithms for Large-Scale Systems, ScalA@SC 2021, St. Louis, MN, USA, 19 November 2021, pp. 19–26. IEEE (2021). https://doi.org/10.1109/ScalA54577.2021.00008
7. Choi, J.W., Singh, A., Vuduc, R.W.: Model-driven autotuning of sparse matrix-vector multiply on GPUs. In: Proceedings of the 15th ACM SIGPLAN Symposium on Principles and Practice of Parallel Programming, PPoPP 2010 pp. 115–126. Association for Computing Machinery, New York (2010). https://doi.org/10.1145/1693453.1693471
8. Davis, T.A., Hu, Y.: The University of Florida sparse matrix collection. ACM Trans. Math. Softw. **38**(1) (2011). https://doi.org/10.1145/2049662.2049663
9. Dufrechou, E., Ezzatti, P., Quintana-Ortí, E.S.: Selecting optimal SpMV realizations for GPUs via machine learning. Int. J. High Perform. Comput. Appl. **35**(3) (2021). https://doi.org/10.1177/1094342021990738
10. Golub, G.H., Van Loan, C.F.: Matrix Computations, 4th edn. Johns Hopkins Studies in the Mathematical Sciences (2013)

11. Im, E.J., Yelick, K., Vuduc, R.: Sparsity: optimization framework for sparse matrix kernels. Int. J. High Perform. Comput. Appl. **18**(1), 135–158 (2004)

12. Kannan, R.: Efficient sparse matrix multiple-vector multiplication using a bitmapped format. In: 20th Annual International Conference on High Performance Computing, pp. 286–294 (2013). https://doi.org/10.1109/HiPC.2013.6799135

13. Liu, L., Liu, M., Wang, C., Wang, J.: LSRB-CSR: a low overhead storage format for SpMV on the GPU systems. In: 2015 IEEE 21st International Conference on Parallel and Distributed Systems (ICPADS), pp. 733–741 (2015). https://doi.org/10.1109/ICPADS.2015.97

14. Liu, W., Vinter, B.: A framework for general sparse matrix-matrix multiplication on GPUs and heterogeneous processors. J. Parallel Distrib. Comput. **85**(C), 47–61 (2015). https://doi.org/10.1016/j.jpdc.2015.06.010

15. Liu, W., Vinter, B.: Csr5: an efficient storage format for cross-platform sparse matrix-vector multiplication. In: Proceedings of the 29th ACM on International Conference on Supercomputing, ICS 2015, pp. 339–350. Association for Computing Machinery, New York (2015). https://doi.org/10.1145/2751205.2751209

16. Marini, R., Dufrechou, E., Ezzatti, P.: Towards an efficient sparse storage format for the SpMM kernel in GPUs. In: Chaves, R., et al. (eds.) Euro-Par 2021 International Workshops on Parallel Processing Workshops, Euro-Par 2021, Lisbon, Portugal, 30–31 August 2021, Revised Selected Papers. LNCS, vol. 13098, pp. 104–115. Springer, Cham (2021). https://doi.org/10.1007/978-3-031-06156-1_9

17. Merrill, D., Garland, M.: Merge-based sparse matrix-vector multiplication (SpMV) using the CSR storage format. In: Proceedings of the 21st ACM SIGPLAN Symposium on Principles and Practice of Parallel Programming. PPoPP 2016. Association for Computing Machinery, New York (2016). https://doi.org/10.1145/2851141.2851190

18. Niu, Y., Lu, Z., Dong, M., Jin, Z., Liu, W., Tan, G.: TileSpMV: a tiled algorithm for sparse matrix-vector multiplication on GPUs. In: 2021 IEEE International Parallel and Distributed Processing Symposium (IPDPS), pp. 68–78 (2021). https://doi.org/10.1109/IPDPS49936.2021.00016

19. Tang, W.T., Tan, W.J., Goh, R.S.M., Turner, S.J., Wong, W.F.: A family of bit-representation-optimized formats for fast sparse matrix-vector multiplication on the GPU. IEEE Trans. Parallel Distrib. Syst. **26**(9), 2373–2385 (2015). https://doi.org/10.1109/TPDS.2014.2357437

20. Xie, Z., Tan, G., Liu, W., Sun, N.: IA-SpGEMM: an input-aware auto-tuning framework for parallel sparse matrix-matrix multiplication. In: Proceedings of the ACM International Conference on Supercomputing, ICS 2019, pp. 94–105. Association for Computing Machinery, New York (2019). https://doi.org/10.1145/3330345.3330354

21. Xie, Z., Tan, G., Liu, W., Sun, N.: A pattern-based SpGEMM library for multi-core and many-core architectures. IEEE Trans. Parallel Distrib. Syst. **33**(1), 159–175 (2022). https://doi.org/10.1109/TPDS.2021.3090328

22. Zachariadis, O., Satpute, N., Gómez-Luna, J., Olivares, J.: Accelerating sparse matrix-matrix multiplication with GPU tensor cores. Comput. Electr. Eng. **88**, 106848 (2020)

23. Zhang, J., Gruenwald, L.: Regularizing irregularity: bitmap-based and portable sparse matrix multiplication for graph data on GPUs. In: Proceedings of the 1st ACM SIGMOD Joint International Workshop on Graph Data Management Experiences & Systems (GRADES) and Network Data Analytics (NDA). GRADES-NDA 2018, Association for Computing Machinery, New York (2018). https://doi.org/10.1145/3210259.3210263

Power Estimation Models for Edge Computing Devices

Michalis Kasioulis[✉], Moysis Symeonides, George Pallis,
and Marios D. Dikaiakos

Department of Computer Science, University of Cyprus, Nicosia, Cyprus
{mkasio01,msymeo03,pallis,mdd}@ucy.ac.cy

Abstract. The increasing demand for energy-efficient solutions in IoT devices and edge computing calls for novel methodologies to generate accurate power models for diverse devices, enabling sustainable growth and optimized performance. This paper presents a methodology for creating power models for edge devices and their embedded components. The proposed methodology collects power and resource utilization measurements from the edge device and generates both additive and regression models. The methodology is evaluated on a Raspberry Pi 4 device using a smart plug for power monitoring and various benchmarking tools for CPU and network sub-components. The evaluation shows that the generated models achieve low error, demonstrating the effectiveness of the proposed approach. Our methodology can be applied to any edge device, providing insights into the most efficient power consumption model. The heterogeneity of edge devices poses a challenge to creating a global power model, and our approach provides a solution for developing device-specific power models. Our results indicate that the generated models for Raspberry Pi 4 scored a maximum of 8% MAPE.

Keywords: Power Consumption · Power Modeling · IoT · Edge Computing · Edge Benchmarking

1 Introduction

The Internet of Things (IoT) is an ever-growing paradigm that enables a vast number of interconnected devices to communicate and share data. According to [4], the number of IoT and edge devices is expected to reach 6.5 billion devices by 2030, or a three-fold increase since 2020. According to Cisco Annual Internet Report [1], by 2023 50% of all networked communication will account for machine-to-machine communications. Therefore, the energy footprint of those devices needs to be studied, and the estimation of their power consumption is crucial for designing energy-efficient systems and optimizing their operation. Energy-efficient design and operation of edge devices and systems can significantly reduce the need for frequent battery replacement or maintenance.

One of the main challenges in estimating power consumption is the heterogeneity of edge devices [6]. A global model for power estimation is difficult to create, and each device together with its attached peripherals must be individually characterized. As edge computing becomes more prevalent, the energy

D. Zeinalipour et al. (Eds.): Euro-Par 2023 Workshops, LNCS 14351, pp. 257–269, 2024.
https://doi.org/10.1007/978-3-031-50684-0_20

consumption forecasting of edge devices is more crucial. For estimating the cumulative energy footprint of large-scale geo-distributed edge deployments, we need a tailored power model for every edge device. However, most studies on power profiling of IT equipment focus on high-end devices [3]. More work needs to be imposed on edge devices considering the vast amount and the fast pace of increase that calls for efficient ways to estimate their power and carbon footprint.

In this study, we present a methodology for building power consumption models for edge devices, that takes into account the impact of their different hardware sub-components. Our approach involves: (i) the execution of containerized stressing processes dedicated for each hardware sub-component of the edge device as defined by the user, e.g., CPU and Network I/Os, (ii) an end-to-end monitoring sub-system that collects resource utilization and power consumption measurements from the respective device, (iii) a machine learning pipeline, integrated to our monitoring sub-system, capable of training various machine learning models, including linear regression models, random forests, gradient boosting, etc., and (vi) evaluation of the created models by executing real-world Machine Learning (ML) benchmarks and considering well-known evaluation metrics like Mean Squared Error (MSE) and Mean Absolute Percentage Error (MAPE). It should be noted that the users can select to create additive models composed of individual models, each of which is dedicated to a specific hardware sub-component.

The main contributions of the current work are listed below.

1. A device-agnostic methodology that involves an end-to-end pipeline for generating power consumption models for edge devices and can provide insights about the most efficient power consumption models. On top of that, we provide an out-of-the-box procedure for evaluating the most accurate power models with real-world workloads using statistical error indicators.
2. A complete power consumption model for a well-known edge device, namely Raspberry Pi 4, evaluating the applicability and accuracy of our methodology with the results indicating a maximum MAPE of 8% and the models being available to the research community, enabling broader adoption.

The rest of the paper is structured as follows: Sect. 2 provides details about the related work. Section 3 describes our methodology. Section 4 provides technical details about the creation of the power model for an edge device (RPi 4), and a real-world scenario evaluation. Finally, Sect. 5 concludes the paper.

2   Related Work

The process of power consumption modeling is a complex procedure that requires the introduction of various stressors on top of edge devices while at the same time, capturing resource utilization and power consumption measurements of the edge device acting as the system under test (SUT). On top of that, researchers need to build various statistical and ML models based on the captured metrics. Considering the heterogeneity of edge environments, the latter procedure is time-consuming and requires numerous manual configurations during deployment and

ML training. Targeting both power consumption modeling and benchmarking of edge devices, we present the state-of-the-art.

Edge Benchmarking: This is the process of evaluating the performance of an edge device under different workloads and configurations. In the context of edge benchmarking, Kang et al. [9] made use of a Coral Dev Board that is equipped with a Tensor Processing Unit (TPU) and a Jetson Nano that is equipped with a Graphical Processing Unit (GPU) in order to run a set of AI applications over them and evaluate their performance based on their inference speed, accuracy, and power consumption. Similarly, Bekaroo et al. [5] performed a comparative analysis of the power consumption of Raspberry Pi under different utilization levels. In this study, the power consumption of Raspberry Pi was compared against other workstations and results indicated that the power consumption of Raspberry Pi was significantly lower than that of a desktop and a laptop and higher than that of a smartphone and a tablet. Although the aforementioned studies provide some key insights into the power consumption behavior of edge devices, *no further modeling of power consumption for those devices was performed.*

Power Consumption Modeling: A power model is a mathematical representation of how much power a device or system consumes under various operating conditions. It takes as input a set of parameters related to the device load, and outputs an estimate of the device's power consumption. Focusing on single-board edge devices, Paniego et al. [11] created a power estimation model for Raspberry Pi 3. The authors made use of a set of performance counters that reflect the resource utilization of CPU and memory. Even if the evaluation results indicated an average percentage error less than 5%, the authors did not consider the power that is consumed by the network sub-components. On the contrary, Kaup et al. [10] created power estimation models for various edge devices considering both processing and network sub-components. They highlighted that the power consumption of a single-board edge device can be described by multiple models dedicated to the underlying hardware sub-components. Unfortunately, the latter efforts *do not offer a general way for the creation of power consumption models, leaving it up to the users to perform the device's stressing, monitor the sub-components utilization, and tune the parameters of the models.*

3   Methodology

The generation of power consumption models for edge devices requires the installation and deployment of multiple software tools, their configuration, a set of repeatable actions for stressing specific underlying components, the selection of the proper ML or mathematical models and their parameters, the evaluation of the generated models, and, generally, a lot of manual and time-consuming steps. The main goal of this work is to abstract the generation of power consumption models of diverse edge devices. To achieve the latter, we propose a set of well-defined steps in our methodology workflow as shown in Fig. 1.

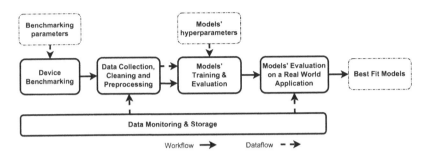

Fig. 1. Workflow for Power Models Generation & Evaluation.

First, we created a monitoring and storage solution that captures both resource utilization metrics from the edge device under test and power consumption metrics as provided by the power reporting tools. We achieved the latter by providing abstract interfaces for user-defined monitoring probes and using containerization as our deployment strategy. To obtain a representative dataset, our pipeline executes a set of repeatable benchmark workloads that utilize different components of the device, such as the CPU and network. In order for our pipeline to execute the set of stressors in any compute node, the device benchmarking sub-module executes them in a containerized environment. The module executes repeatable stressing workloads under various configurable utilization levels to ensure the statistical significance of the measurements.

Before the training of the models, our workflow pre-processes the collected data in order to "clean" them. The pre-processing step includes the outliers detection and removal. When the dataset is marked ready, the workflow propagates it to the Model Generation module. This module is responsible for the generation of the selected models and auto-tunes their parameters based on the user's configurations. The output of the Models Generation module is a set of ML and mathematical models capable of predicting the power consumption of an edge device based on its resource utilization metrics.

Finally, in this evaluation step, the workflow deploys real-world containerized workloads on the examined edge device and monitors its resource utilization. The best-fit models are selected based on the accuracy reported when applied to the collected results from the workload execution period.

3.1   Implementation Aspects

Data Monitoring and Storage. The deployment overview is illustrated in Fig. 2 where the running services are presented next to each device involved in the deployment stack. A monitoring agent is deployed on the edge device under test. Specifically, we use the containerized version of Netdata, which is a lightweight monitoring agent reported to have less than 1% CPU computational footprint, a few hundred of MiB RAM requirements, and minimal disk usage [2]. When the agent is deployed, it continuously collects the underlying resource utilization and

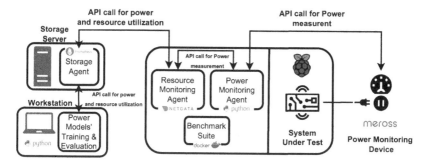

Fig. 2. Deployment Overview.

other monitoring metrics like CPU temperature by directly making use of the host's OS mechanisms reporting real-time metrics (cgroups, pseudofiles, etc.). As a utilization metric for the CPU board, we chose to use the percentage of the total CPU utilization based on the full capacity. For the network boards, we use the kilobits sent or received per second (kb/s). For the accurate collection of the resource utilization metrics, we rely on the underlying monitoring system which monitors CPU utilization by measuring the percentage of time the CPU has actually been executing machine code. The monitoring system can also monitor the CPU frequency at runtime which can be taken into account when creating power models for machines whose CPU architecture supports the Dynamic Voltage and Frequency Scaling (DVFS) mechanism.

Moreover, we created a background process with extensible interfaces that acts as a probe for the power consumption metering external system. It should be noted that the edge device under test and the power meter should have a common communication channel, e.g. both to be connected to the same WiFi network. In our prototype, we integrated Meross[1] Smart WiFi plug to our system under test, and we extended the respective connector interface to perform periodically a remote call to the smart plug API retrieving real-time power measurements and disseminating them to the monitoring agent. The periodicity of monitoring is configurable with its default value being 1 s, providing more fine-grained data to the next step. The results are then transmitted to a remote monitoring storage server via HTTP requests. The monitoring storage utilizes a time series database[2] allowing fast time range queries and is placed on a remote virtual machine (VM) that provides ample processing and storage capacity.

Device Benchmarking. To test the separate components independently, we encapsulate various benchmarks each of which is tailored to a specific component. For the CPU, we use the stress Linux command[3], which allows us to stress the CPU at various utilization levels. The stress command has an optional

---

[1] http://bit.ly/3LvNO76.
[2] http://prometheus.io.
[3] http://linux.die.net/man/1/stress.

parameter that runs all the stressors sequentially for a specified period of time as defined by the user, with each stressor being executed by a separate CPU thread. Therefore, we ran the stressors sequentially using 1...N CPU threads, where N is the maximum number of threads that the specified CPU can run in parallel. Following this approach, allowed us to capture different CPU utilization states at different time scales. It is worth mentioning that during the CPU stressing, the rest of the device components are going through low utilization with minimal power overhead that does not affect the overall performance of the device.

For the network interfaces, the iperf tool[4] was integrated to transmit packages between the edge device and another device acting either as a client or server, that is connected to the same local network via either wired or wireless communication channels. For the purposes of this test, in one case the device under test acted as a client, sending network packets at a specified rate while measuring outward traffic. In the second case, the device acted as a server receiving packets at a specified rate while monitoring inward traffic. For the automation of the stressing procedure, the stressor gradually increases the bandwidth speed and runs each iteration for a total of 15 min in the case of WiFi which has limited bandwidth availability and 10 min in the case of Ethernet by default.

Data Collection, Cleaning and Preprocessing. Our method measures power consumption by first determining the idle power consumption of the system when all components are idle and monitoring services are active. The device collects power measurements from the power monitoring device via the WiFi channel and communication with the storage agent is done via the Ethernet. Once idle power consumption is obtained, we collect CPU benchmarking results using relevant timestamps. For network power estimation, we execute network benchmarks and gather network and CPU utilization statistics, as well as the overall power consumption of the device. To estimate power consumption specific to network components, we subtract idle power consumption and CPU-related power consumption using the generated CPU power model. Due to asynchronous data collection, a minimal number of outliers are observed. By default, outliers are defined as points more than 3 standard deviations from the mean and are removed prior to the training procedure for both training and evaluation data.

Models' Training and Evaluation. In the models' generation step, the users can specify the type of models they want to create, including additive models consisting of separate models for each of the individual device's sub-components, multiple regression models that take as input the set of input variables representing resource utilization metrics in this case, or ensemble models like Random Forests, along with their parameters for training and tuning. Users can also select specific monitoring metrics from the device's sub-components to be included in the modeling procedure. Since our methodology is agnostic to ML and mathematical models, users can make use of different libraries and model types including among others Random Forest, Linear Regression, or even Deep Learning (DL) methods. With the models, possible parameters, and input defined, the

---

[4] http://iperf.fr/.

next step is the training of the selected models. Once the training procedure is complete, the generated models are returned to the user along with the respective performance indicators, such as MSE and MAPE. Before evaluating the models that were found to be more accurate, users can fine-tune the parameters of the respective models with the use of any tools dedicated to hyperparameters' auto-tuning. An example parameter is the number of estimators used in the construction of a random forest. This flexibility allows users to generate power models tailored to edge devices, adjusting the models' parameters and optimizing their accuracy.

Except for the simple or more advanced ML approaches, the Model Generation module allows users to create an additive power model. Equation 1 defines an additive power model for CPU and network sub-components where $P_{CPU}(u)$ represents the CPU's power consumption when it is in use at a certain utilization rate u in %, $P_{eth,dn}(r), P_{eth,up}(r), P_{wifi,up}(r), P_{wifi,dn}(r)$ represent the power consumption of Ethernet and WiFi download and upload links when in use at a certain rate r in kb/s, and P_{idle} the idle state power consumption in Watts.

$$P_{system} = P_{CPU}(u) + P_{eth,dn}(r) + P_{eth,up}(r) + P_{wifi,up}(r) + P_{wifi,dn}(r) + P_{idle} \quad (1)$$

Models' Evaluation on a Real World Application. Our methodology supports the evaluation of models using containerized workloads, offering flexibility, and abstracting the underlying device's heterogeneity, without resource overhead [8]. By default, our approach utilizes two popular ML inference workloads [7]. The first is the Image Classification and Detection (ICD) workload [12], part of the MLPerf benchmark suite, which includes real-world ML applications for inference. Users can customize workload parameters such as image count, inference model, and ML backend. Our example configuration in Sect. 4 employs 1000 images for inference with the resnet50 model[5]. The ML backend, like TensorFlow, provides tools and APIs for ML model building and training. To ensure compatibility with ARM-based edge devices, we made the necessary adjustments to the Dockerfile of the selected workload. Our second workload involves a lightweight Python server[6] exposing an API for a simple yet realistic ML inference service. A workload generator disseminates images over the network for inference. The edge device under test runs the service, while the image workload generator acts as a client, loading images into memory and sending them for inference over the network. The devices are interconnected via Ethernet and WiFi networks. The user applies the most accurate power models from the model generation step to the collected data during workload execution, comparing estimated and actual power consumption. The output includes error metrics and plots demonstrating model performance on independent workloads.

---

[5] http://bit.ly/45Dzbr0.
[6] http://flask.palletsprojects.com.

4   Real World Use Case

4.1   Experimental Setup

The experimental setup is comprised of a Raspberry Pi 4 that serves as the System Under Test (SUT) and is powered by the Meross Smart Plug. The device is equipped with a quad-core ARM Cortex-A72 CPU, 4GB of RAM, and a 32GB SD card for storage. Raspberry Pi 4 is considered an edge device that can be used by a variety of edge applications including ML applications. The SUT is equipped with a Gigabit Ethernet interface with a bandwidth of 1 Gbps and an integrated dual channel (2.4 GHz and 5 GHz) wireless antenna. The device's idle power consumption was found to be 3.10W.

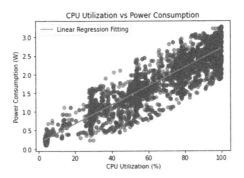

Fig. 3. Distribution of CPU utilization and power consumption with fitted line.

4.2   Generated Models

For the purposes of this study, we created i) an additive model that is composed of CPU and network models and two regression models, ii) a random forest with two hyperparameters (number of estimators and max depth) for which we applied hyperparameter tuning using the Ray framework[7], and iii) a linear regression model. Both regression models take as input the set of parameters and as output the estimated power consumption of the device. The training of the two regression models was performed using scikit-learn[8], by applying cross-validation, splitting input dataset at 80% training and 20% test data. For the additive models, we fitted polynomials with multiple degrees, using the numpy polyfit function[9] and we selected the ones with the lowest MSE and MAPE.

CPU: Figure 3 shows the distribution of CPU utilization and power consumption of the SUT. The set of points is distributed across all the CPU utilization

---

[7] https://ray.io/.

[8] https://scikit-learn.org/.

[9] https://bit.ly/3HE06ZK.

values. The red line represents the regression line that was fitted to the data to represent the linear relation of the CPU utilization relevant to the respective power consumption. It was found that the linear regression model had an MSE of 0.098 and a MAPE of 17% when applied to the collected data. It can also be observed that the maximum power drawn by the CPU component is just above 3 W. The linear regression model for CPU utilization and Power Consumption in Watts ($P_{CPU}(u)$) is represented in the equation Eq. 2 below, where parameter u represents the CPU utilization (%).

$$P_{CPU}(u) = 0.025u + 0.17 \text{ W} \tag{2}$$

Network: In Fig. 4, we provide the distribution of Ethernet and WiFi utilization rates relevant to the respective power consumption along with a red line that represents the polynomial regression model fitted to the data in each case. The observed gaps on all the diagrams are due to the scaling we perform for sampling for rates above 100 Mbps in order to obtain an even distribution of sample rates. In the case of WiFi we were able to achieve a rate of a maximum of 25 Mbps for download and 50Mbps for upload links.

In the case of Ethernet, it was found that the best fit was a third-degree model with an MSE of 0.0035 and 0.004, which correspond to 2.95% and 4.61% MAPE for download and upload links respectively. For low values of network utilization, the estimated power overhead is negative due to the error that exists in the

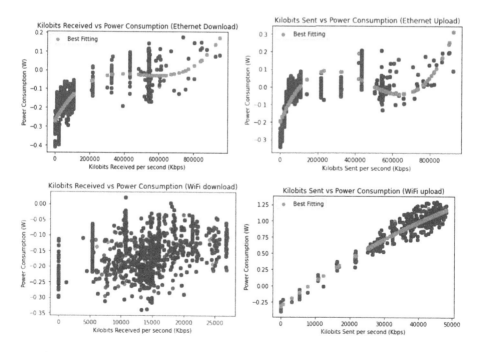

Fig. 4. Distribution of Network Resource Utilization and Power Consumption.

estimation of CPU power overhead that overestimates the power consumption in some cases where CPU utilization is low. Overall, we conclude that the Ethernet power overhead is minimal even in the case that the link is undergoing full utilization in which case the increase of power consumption is relatively low. Another thing that is important to note here, is that packet loss is observed during the transmission of packets through the Ethernet channel, especially at high rates where the loss can reach up to 3.5% of the total packages. This can add some noise to the data. On average the maximum allowed stable bandwidth we could achieve was at 600Mbps. From the top plots in Fig. 4, we can observe that in the case of upload, there is a deviation downwards at 500 Mbps while in the case of upload, there is a flattening up to the same rate before the power consumption is increased again. One intuitively understands that the system follows an optimization strategy when sending and receiving data over the link.

In the case of WiFi, due to the high amount of packet loss that exists on the network link, we have not been able to identify a proper distribution in the case of the receiver which was acting as the iperf server so we decided to omit it from our additive model since the power overhead was minimal and close to idle value. Also, the available bandwidth was significantly lower than in the case of Ethernet. This was mainly caused by the weakness of the onboard WiFi antenna to perform well at higher speeds. The usage of an external WiFi module would possibly fix this limitation although it would cost an extra overhead for powering it on. One thing that is noticeable in the case of WiFi is the power consumption that is imposed in the case of heavy load during upload that accounts for a non-negligible 1.5W marginal power. The best fit for WiFi upload is a second-degree polynomial with an MSE of 0.0054 and a MAPE of 0.015%.

The generated polynomial models for network interfaces are provided below where r represents the network utilization rate at kilobits sent or received per second and functions $P_{eth,dn}, P_{eth,up}, P_{wifi,up}$ the respective power consumption in Watts for Ethernet download, Ethernet upload and WiFi upload links.

$$P_{eth,dn}(r) = 2.39 \cdot 10^{-18} \cdot r^3 - 3.51 \cdot 10^{-12} \cdot r^2 + 1.65 \cdot 10^{-6} \cdot r - 1.7 \cdot 10^{-1} \text{ W} \quad (3)$$

$$P_{eth,up}(r) = 5.04 \cdot 10^{-18} \cdot r^3 - 6.82 \cdot 10^{-12} \cdot r^2 + 2.55 \cdot 10^{-6} \cdot r - 1.96 \cdot 10^{-1} \text{ W} \quad (4)$$

$$P_{wifi,up}(r) = -2.03 \cdot 10^{-10} \cdot r^2 + 4.06 \cdot 10^{-5} \cdot r - 3.16 \cdot 10^{-1} \text{ W} \quad (5)$$

4.3   Evaluation of the Results

Inference over WiFi: Figure 5 presents the experimental results after applying our models to the set of data collected during the execution of the inference workload over WiFi. The linear regression equation is included in the legends of the graphs where X represents CPU utilization (%) and Y the network utilization rate (Kb/s). The number of data points retrieved from the storage agent for both the sender and the receiver was totaled at 5400 in order to ensure a good sample size while avoiding missing important information. The red line represents the perfect prediction where the estimated value equals the actual value.

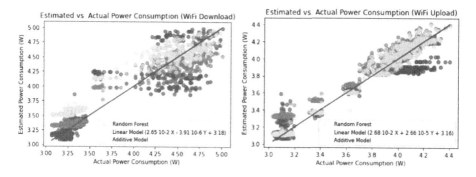

Fig. 5. Actual vs estimated power consumption for inference over WiFi.

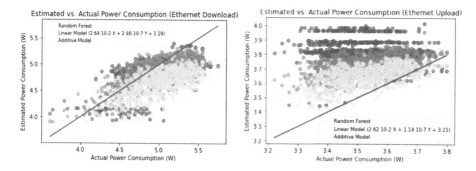

Fig. 6. Actual vs estimated power consumption for inference over Ethernet.

In the case of the sender, the additive model performed better than the rest with an MSE of 0.0035 and a MAPE of 1.15%, while in the case of the receiver, the linear regression model outscored the rest with an MSE of 0.0288 and MAPE of 3.44%. In terms of the estimated energy, the additive model reported a total of 36469.02 J while the actual reported energy was 36310.92 J and the linear regression model reported a total of 38538.44 J compared to the total actual consumption of 38244.78 J. This is due to the high error that is observed for the additive model for low power consumption values. Also, for high power consumption values, the Random Forest cannot perform as expected. This might be due to the linear relationship between CPU utilization and power consumption which can make it difficult to be accurately captured by the Random Forest. To this end, CPU utilization is the main contributor to the system's power consumption which is better captured by the additive and linear regression models.

Inference over Ethernet: The relevant results for the execution of the inference workload over Ethernet are presented in Fig. 6. The same number of samples as in the case of WiFi was collected, for the same reason. In the case of download over Ethernet, all the models tend to underestimate the predicted value while in the case of upload, they tend to overestimate it in most of the cases.

The reported results indicated that the additive model was by far the most efficient for estimating the power for images loaded and sent over Ethernet with a recorded MSE of 0.0227 and a MAPE of 3.65% while on the other side for the receiver performing the inference, the Linear Regression model recorded the lowest error with an MSE of 0.0739 and 4.33% MAPE. The energy consumption values of the aforementioned models were estimated to be 36744.10 J and 48712.32 J in the cases of the sender and the receiver while the actual reported energy consumption was found to be 35552.26 J and 49887.45 J respectively.

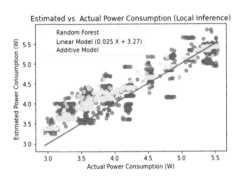

Fig. 7. Actual vs estimated power consumption for inference on the device.

Inference on the Device: For local inference, the experiment was repeated at different CPU utilization levels by limiting the CPU utilization of the container in each iteration at a scale of 10%. As we lower the CPU utilization, the execution time increases and that is why the majority of data points lie in the area between 3 and 4 W. The total number of points collected in this case was 10800, due to the multiple iterations performed. The additive and linear regression models return the same results since there is no network overhead. Evaluation results for this scenario are illustrated in Fig. 7. One thing to point out is the fact that the linear model performs really well at high values where utilization is high while slightly overestimating the values close to idle resource utilization. In this case, the MSE and MAPE were 0.1003 and 8.06%, respectively and the generated models estimated a total of 87254.52 J while the total reported energy consumption based on the power meter readings was 81363.12 J.

5   Conclusion

This work presented a methodology for generating and evaluating power consumption models for edge devices. Our methodology can generate both additive and regression models, and we highlighted its effectiveness by creating accurate power consumption models for a Raspberry Pi 4, and by performing ML inference from a real-world application. Our methodology is useful for creating and evaluating power models for a wide range of edge devices, enabling better energy efficiency and sustainability. Future work includes the creation of an automated tool adopting the pipeline of the proposed methodology, and making use of it for more devices and attached components, like cellular communication. Moreover, we plan to conduct an evaluation of the power consumption of edge applications by integrating power consumption models with evaluation tools like emulators.

References

1. Cisco annual internet report (2018–2023). Tech. rep., Cisco (2018)
2. How to optimize the netdata agent's performance (2023). https://learn.netdata. cloud/guides/configure/performance
3. Alan, I., Arslan, E., Kosar, T.: Energy-performance trade-offs in data transfer tuning at the end-systems. Sustain. Comput. Inform. Syst. (2014)
4. Alsop, T.: Number of edge enabled internet of things (iot) devices worldwide from 2020 to 2030, by market. Tech. rep. (2022). www.statista.com/statistics/1259878/ edge-enabled-iot-device-market-worldwide/
5. Bekaroo, G., Santokhee, A.: Power consumption of the raspberry pi: a comparative analysis. In: IEEE International Conference on Emerging Technologies and Innovative Business Practices for the Transformation of Societies (EmergiTech), pp. 361–366 (2016)
6. Delicato, F., Pires, P., Batista, T., Delicato, F., Pires, P., Batista, T.: The resource management challenge in iot. Resource Manag. Internet of Things (2017)
7. Earney, S.: What is edge computer vision, and how does it work?. http://xailient. com/blog/what-is-edge-computer-vision-and-how-does-it-work/
8. Georgiou, J., Symeonides, M., Kasioulis, M., Trihinas, D., Pallis, G., Dikaiakos, M.D.: Benchpilot: repeatable & reproducible benchmarking for edge micro-dcs. In: IEEE ISCC (2022)
9. Kang, P., Jo, J.: Benchmarking modern edge devices for ai applications. IEICE Trans. Inform. Syst. **104**, 394–403 (2021)
10. Kaup, F., Hacker, S., Mentzendorff, E., Meurisch, C., Hausheer, D.: The progress of the energy-efficiency of single-board computers. Tech. rep, Netsys (2018)
11. Paniego, J., et al.: Unified power modeling design for various raspberry pi generations analyzing different statistical methods. In: Computer Science-CACIC 2019: 25th Argentine Congress Of Computer Science, CACIC 2019, pp. 53–65 (2020)
12. Reddi, V., et al.: Mlperf inference benchmark. In: ACM/IEEE ISCA (2020)

A Performance Analysis of Leading Many-Core Technologies for Cellular Automata Execution

Alessio De Rango[1] [ID], Donato D'Ambrosio[2([envelope])][ID], Alfonso Senatore[1] [ID],
Giuseppe Mendicino[1] [ID], Kumudha Narasimhan[3] [ID], Mehdi Goli[3] [ID],
and Rod Burns[3] [ID]

[1] Department of Environmental Engeneering, University of Calabria, Rende, Italy
[2] Department of Mathematics and Computer Science, University of Calabria,
Rende, Italy
donato.dambrosio@unical.it
[3] Codeplay Software Ltd. "an Intel company", Edinburgh, UK

Abstract. We extend the panorama of performance analyses of CUDA, OpenCL and SYCL for the execution of Cellular Automata. To this end, we apply the SciddicaT landslide model to a real event by considering two complex topographic surfaces of different granularity, thus resulting in two simulations of different computing loads. For each technology, we developed a global memory and two tiled implementations of SciddicaT by adopting the Nvidia nvcc compiler for CUDA, the Nvidia implementation of the OpenCL standard and the CUDA back-end of the Intel DPC++ compiler for SYCL. The experiments, performed on three Nvidia accelerators, point out from good to optimal performances of SYCL compared to CUDA according to the newer device's architecture. The carried-out Roofline analysis evidences high cache effects, pointing out greater advantages of tiled implementations for older architectures.

Keywords: Cellular Automata · Data-Parallel Structured-Grid · Fluid-Flow Simulation · CUDA vs OpenCL vs SYCL · Roofline

1 Introduction

In recent years, we have seen a proliferation of new shared memory data-parallel architectures, with Graphics Processing Units (GPUs) and many-core accelerators imposing as mainstream devices in the High-Performance Computing (HPC) field [22]. Nvidia proposed CUDA in 2008 [21]. Rapidly it was, and still is, adopted in the HPC field due to the competitive performance/cost ratio of NVIDIA devices (see, e.g., [1,7,8]). Khronos Group released the vendor-agnostic OpenCL specifications in 2009 [27], making it possible to target heterogeneous devices like CPUs and GPUs, beside others (see, e.g., [5,19]). One of the most recent and promising shared memory data-parallel technologies is SYCL, a set of specifications by Khronos Group defining a C++ compiler-embedded abstraction layer for data-parallel programming. The programming approach is similar to

© The Author(s), under exclusive license to Springer Nature Switzerland AG 2024
D. Zeinalipour et al. (Eds.): Euro-Par 2023 Workshops, LNCS 14351, pp. 270–281, 2024.
https://doi.org/10.1007/978-3-031-50684-0_21

CUDA, and last specifications allow for different back-ends other than the original OpenCL one, among which CUDA [26]. The interest in SYCL has become very high and its adoption is growing (see, e.g., [9,15,25]). Being quite recent, the computational performance of SYCL needs to be better assessed. Indeed, in certain cases it was sensibly slower than CUDA (see, e.g., [4,23]), while quite competitive in others (see, e.g., [3,12]) on Nvidia GPUs. Moreover, in most cases, SYCL performance assessments rely on classical algorithms (e.g., [3]), even though examples of scientific numerical codes can be found (see, e.g., [12]). Applications to fluid-flows based on the John von Neumann's Cellular Automata (CA) computational paradigm [20] are missing, at best of our knowledge.

To better investigate the performance of SYCL compared to CUDA and OpenCL on a real CA scientific application, we developed several implementations of the ScidddicaT landslide simulation model [2], a simple, though representative, example of a fluid-flows model able to simulate real landslides on complex topographic surfaces, already adopted as a mini-application benchmark in [6,10,13,14,24]. For the experiments, we simulated a real landslide occurred in Italy on two digital elevation models differing in spatial granularity. This choice is motivated by the fact that different levels of SYCL performance were observed depending on the problem size (see, e.g., [3]).

Algorithm 1: ScidddicaT *minimization algorithm of the differences.*

$m \leftarrow h(0) - p_\epsilon$
if $m \not> 0$ **then**
$\quad elim(0:4), again \leftarrow False$
$\quad u(0:4), n, avg \leftarrow 0$
$\quad u(0) = z(0) + p_\epsilon;$

$\quad$ **foreach** $i \in \{1, \ldots, 4\}$ **do**
$\quad\quad$ $u(i) = z(i) + h(i)$

$\quad$ **do**
$\quad\quad$ $again \leftarrow False$
$\quad\quad$ $avg \leftarrow m$
$\quad\quad$ $n \leftarrow 0$
$\quad\quad$ **foreach** $i \in \{0, 1, \ldots, 4\}$ **do**
$\quad\quad\quad$ **if** $elim(i) = False$ **then**
$\quad\quad\quad\quad$ $avg \leftarrow avg + u(i)$
$\quad\quad\quad\quad$ $n \leftarrow n + 1$

$\quad\quad$ **if** $n \neq 0$ **then**
$\quad\quad\quad$ $avg \leftarrow avg/n$
$\quad\quad$ **foreach** $i \in \{0, 1, \ldots, 4\}$ **do**
$\quad\quad\quad$ **if** $avg \leq u(i) \wedge elim(i) = False$ **then**
$\quad\quad\quad\quad$ $elim(i), again \leftarrow True$

$\quad$ **while** *again*

$\quad$ **foreach** $i \in \{1, \ldots, 4\}$ **do**
$\quad\quad$ **if** $elim(i) = False$ **then**
$\quad\quad\quad$ $f(i) \leftarrow (avg - u(i)) \, p_r$

else
$\quad$ **foreach** $i \in \{1, \ldots, 4\}$ **do**
$\quad\quad$ $f(i) \leftarrow 0$

In this work, we: (i) Developed one global memory and two shared memory implementations of SciddicaT for each many-core technology considered; (ii) Conducted a performance analysis based on two case study simulations of different computing loads on the Titan Xp, V100 and A100 Nvidia accelerators; (iii) Performed a Roofline analysis to assess kernels bounds and cache effects.

In the following, Sect. 2 describes the SciddicaT model; Sect. 3 describes the case-study simulations and presents the achieved results; Sect. 4 illustrates the Roofline analysis; Sect. 5 eventually concludes the paper with a general discussion, by outlining possible future developments.

2   The SciddicaT Model

SciddicaT is example of simulation model based on the *minimization algorithm of the differences* [16]. The algorithm is applied in its non-inertial form to simulate a slow landslide on a real topographic surface. The domain is represented by a two-dimensional grid subdivided in square cells. The model evolves by local interactions defined over the von Neumann neighborhood, made by the central cell and its adjacent cells located to the North, East, West and South directions, respectively. The state of each cell is defined by the following state variables: z is the topographic altitude (i.e., the elevation a.s.l.) [m]; h is the fluid width (or thickness) [m]; f^4 are the outflows [m] from the central to the four adjacent cells of the von Neumann neighborhood. The cell's state transition function is defined by the following two kernels:

fc: (*flows computation*) - computes the outflows from the central cell to the four neighboring ones by applying the *minimization algorithm of the differences*, shown in Algorithm 1. Preliminarily, the amount of mass that can flow out the cell is computed as: $m = h(0) - p_\epsilon$, being $h(0)$ the flow thickness in the central cell, and p_ϵ a model parameter representing the adherence effect. If $m > 0$, the remaining part of the neighborhood is considered unmovable. To this end, the local array u is defined as $u(0) = z(0) + p_\epsilon$, $u(i) = z(i) + h(i)$ $(i = 1, \ldots, 4)$. An iterative procedure then begins that computes the average altitude, avg, over the u array and eliminates those cells whose value is greater than avg. The iterative process ends when no cells are eliminated. Let $p_r \in \,]0, 1]$ be a dumping factor, the resulting outflows are given by:

$$f(i) = \begin{cases} 0, & \text{if } m \leq 0 \\ (a - u(i)) \cdot p_r, & \text{if } m > 0 \end{cases} \quad \forall i \in \{1, \ldots, 4\} \quad (1)$$

wu: (*width update*) - updates the cell debris thickness h by considering mass exchange in the cell neighborhood:

$$h^{t+1}(0) = h^t(0) + \sum_{i=1}^{4} (f_{in}(i) - f(i)) \quad (2)$$

Here, $h^t(0)$ and $h^{t+1}(0)$ are the mass thickness inside the cell at the t and $t + 1$ computational steps, respectively, while $f_{in}(i)$ represents the inflow from the ith neighboring cell.

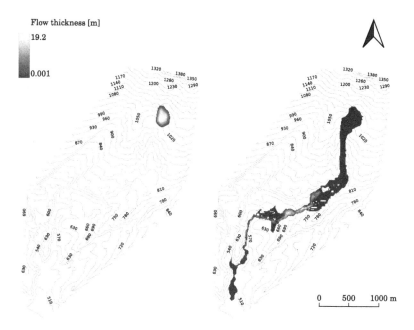

Fig. 1. SciddicaT simulation of the Tessina (Italy) landslide: landslide source on the left; final landslide path on the right.

3   Experiments, Computational Results and Discussion

The initial condition of the system is defined by the Digital Elevation Model (DEM) of the topographic surface, and by a raster map defining the mass thickness in each cell of the flow source. The Neumann no-flow condition is considered at boundaries. The evolution of the system is obtained by applying the cell's transition function to each domain cell for an arbitrary number of steps. Refer to [2] for a detailed definition of SciddicaT and *minimization algorithm.*

We developed several implementations of SciddicaT, both straightforward (global memory-only) and tiled, with and without halo cells (both global and shared memory) [17], for each many-core technology considered. The complete code repository is freely available on GitHub [11]. CUDA and OpenCL codes were compiled using NVIDIA compiler and libraries. The SYCL compiler adopted is the Intel DPC++ (llvm fork from Intel at https://github.com/intel/llvm, commit hash 68b089f), which has back-end support to CUDA.

In this work, we applied SciddicaT to the simulation of the Tessina landslide, happened in the Tessina valley between altitudes of 1220 m and 625 m a.s.l., with a longitudinal extension of nearly 3 km and a maximum width of about 500 m. As in [2], we set the p_ϵ and p_r parameters to 0.001 [m] and 0.5 [-], respectively. We considered two DEMs, resulting in two simulations. The first one (standard

DEM) has 610 rows by 496 columns, with cells of 10 m side; The second one (extended DEM) has 2440 rows by 1984 columns, whit a cell of 2.5 m sides. The simulation performed using the standard DEM (standard simulation) required 4000 steps to obtain the final configuration of the landslide, while the simulation performed using the extended DEM (extended simulation) required 64.000 steps. Both the source and the final configuration of the landslide are shown in Fig. 1.

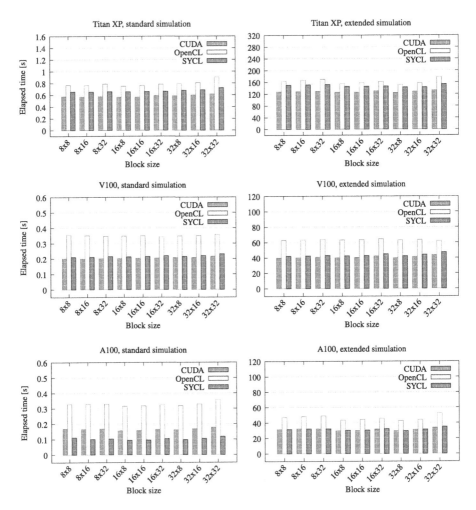

Fig. 2. Elapsed times of the straightforward implementations of SciddicaT on the Titan Xp, V100 and A100 accelerators.

The computational results obtained by the straightforward implementations are reported in Fig. 2. As regards the Titan Xp, CUDA and SYCL performances are pretty close to each other for the standard simulation, with CUDA showing a slight advantage. The gap affecting the OpenCL implementation is sensible

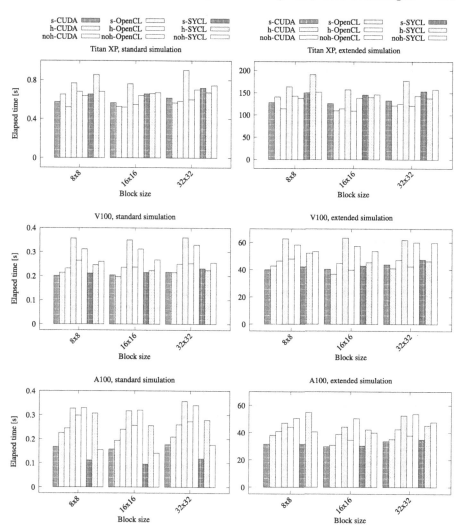

Fig. 3. Elapsed times of the tiled implementations of SciddicaT on the Titan Xp, V100 and A100 accelerators. Key label prefixes s-,h-, and noh- refer to the SciddicaT versions, namely straightforward, tiled with halo and tiled without halo cells, respectively. The suffix refers to the many-core technology adopted. Only square blocks are shown for better readability.

though limited. The trend is similar on the V100, even though CUDA evidences a reduced advantage to SYCL, while the gap affecting OpenCL is increased. The SYCL implementation ran faster than the native CUDA one on the A100, while OpenCL registers the worst performance.

The computational results of the tiled implementations are shown in Fig. 3. The CUDA and OpenCL tiled implementations generally perform better than the straightforward one on the Titan Xp, with SYCL running faster on the 32×32 block. A similar behavior is observed for the extended simulation, with SYCL slightly showing an advantage of tiled implementations also on the 16×16 block. The scenario is less favorable on the V100, with CUDA and SYCL tiled implementations meanly performing slower than the straightforward one. Conversely, the OpenCL tiled implementations perform faster. Only the CUDA implementation with halo cells has a slight advantage to the straightforward one on the extended simulation. Conversely, both OpenCL tiled implementations of the tiled algorithms perform well on the extended simulation. Eventually, the scenario is even less favourable for the tiled algorithms on the A100 for both simulations. CUDA and SYCL never take advantage of the tiled implementations, while the advantage of OpenCL is still present but sensibly reduced.

4   Performance Analysis Through Roofline Model

To understand the impact of the cache effect, which can reduce the advantage of tiled algorithms, besides assessing possible limiting factors of kernels' performance, we conducted a comprehensive analysis by referring to the well-known Roofline model [28]. Considering the results of the experiments described in Sect. 3, we restricted the analysis to the CUDA and SYCL implementations, which achieved the best performance. Initially proposed for multi-threads CPUs, the Roofline model was subsequently extended to the realm of GPUs in [29,30]. This latter version is applied in this work.

We preliminary assessed the peak performance of the devices used, namely double-precision peak computing performance (since this is the kernels' predominant type of computation), besides DRAM and shared memory/L1 cache bandwidths by the *gpumembench* GPU benchmark tool [18] and the *Empirical Roofline Toolkit* [30]. Profiled parameters are the same of those considered in [30] and [29]. Results are shown in Fig. 4.

As regards the standard simulation on the Titan Xp, we appreciate a significant cache effect, as the kernels' performance is considerably above the DRAM bandwidth bound in all cases. Independently of the many-core technology used for the implementation, the width update kernels are L1-bounded, while the flow computation kernels are compute-bound. The kernels' performance is close to the double precision (No-FMA) computing peak, meaning that the kernels are near to their best performance due to hardware computing limitations of the GPU. The same behaviour is observed for the extended simulation. Similar considerations apply to the V100. As regards the standard simulation, we observe a pronounced cache effect, being the achieved performance generally above the DRAM bandwidth bound. As a further insight, the Roofline points out how, due to the low operational intensity (OI) values, the L1/shared memory bandwidth bounds all the analyzed kernels. As regards the extended simulation, the general behaviour of the standard simulation is confirmed. Nevertheless, the performance of the analyzed kernels is generally higher, confirming what already observed on the Titan Xp. As regards the standard simulation executed on the

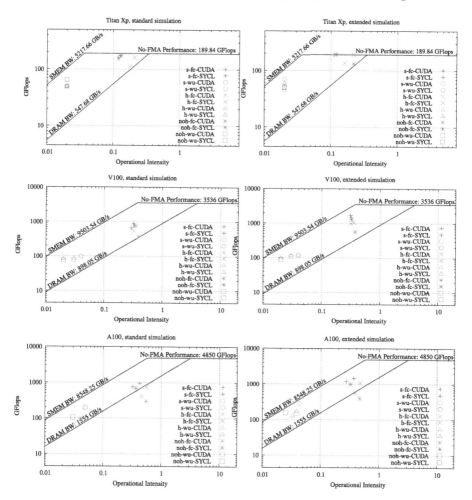

Fig. 4. Roofline analyses of standard and extended simulations on the Titan Xp, V100 and A100 accelerators. Label prefixes s-,h-, and noh- refer to the ScddicaT version, namely straightforward, tiled with halo and tiled without halo cells. Second level prefixes fc-, and wu- refer to the ScddicaT kernels analyzed, namely flow computation (fc) and width update (wu). The suffix refers to the many-core technology adopted.

Ampere A100, we still appreciate a marked cache effect. However, while the width update kernels are above the DRAM bound, not all the flow computation kernels perform above the same bound. Nevertheless, a relevant general cache effect is observed. As regards kernels' characterization, they are all bandwidth bounded due to low OI values. The same consideration of the standard simulation apply to the extended one, though we register a better performance for all the analyzed kernels. The width update kernels approach the shared memory bound, as well as the flow computation kernels (even though some of them still remain under the DRAM bound). The general cache effect registered is therefore even higher than on the standard simulation.

5   Conclusions and Future Outlooks

In this paper, we assessed the effectiveness of the current leading many-core technologies, namely CUDA, OpenCL and SYCL, for Cellular Automata-based fluid-flow numerical simulations based on the *minimization algorithm of the differences*. Regarding SYCL, we focused our analysis on the DPC++ CUDA backends featured compiler, while we referred to Nvidia compilers and libraries for CUDA and OpenCL. We developed several implementations of the SciddicaT benchmark. For the experiments, we considered two study case simulations, differing one from the other for the domain extent to analyse different computational loads, and three Nvidia many-core devices, namely a Titan Xp, a V100 and a A100.

While the CUDA global memory implementation performed mainly better than the SYCL one on the Titan Xp, CUDA and SYCL provided a comparable performance on the V100 and A100 devices, with SYCL outperforming CUDA in certain cased. OpenCL provided non-optimal performance compared to CUDA and SYCL. The tiled implementations, provided slightly better performance in most cases, though the small neighborhood of the simulation model. Nevertheless, we analyzed the cache effect to understand its impact on performance by Roofline analysis, which evidenced a general super DRAM effect. All the kernels resulted L1 bounded on the A100 and V100 devices. The width update kernels was L1 bounded, while the flow computation kernels compute bounded on the Titan Xp.

Overall, global memory-only implementations were already highly performing due to the small stencil (a known limiting performance factor for stencil-based tiled algorithms) and the high cache effect. Nevertheless, tiled implementations were able to speed up the computation further in many cases. Regarding the devices adopted, results confirmed the A100 and V100 as the best choices for executing double precision CA-based numerical codes for both CUDA and SYCL, while the Titan Xp resulted quite inadequate as the flow computation kernels pushed the performance close to the computational bound of the device. According to similar analyses (e.g., [30]), Kernels' performance can be considered satisfying on each device. Best results were registered in the case of the domain-extended simulation, arguably due to a better latency hiding mechanism due to the higher number of threads required by the simulation.

Based on our experience, we can assert the goodness of both CUDA and SYCL many-core technologies in executing stencil-based structured grid numerical code on Nvidia many-core devices, while OpenCL resulted in non-optimal performance. This result is particularly relevant for SYCL, especially if we consider that the CUDA back-end engine of the DPC++ compiler we adopted is still experimental. By merging the single source development approach of CUDA with the possibility to take advantage of the modern C++ facilities, and the ability to target a wide variety of devices like OpenCL, SYCL emerges in the current Parallel Computing panorama as one of the most exciting technologies. As a confirmation, its adoption is constantly growing, even among the Top500 supercomputers.

Possible future developments of this work could regard the study of how the performance of state-of-the-art SYCL compilers like ComputeCpp and hipSYCL, besides the DPC++ adopted in this work, are affected by several factors, among which kernel code complexity (e.g., in terms of nested loops and branches), operational intensity, and computational domain dimension.

Acknowledgements. This work has been supported by the Italian Ministry of Universisty and Research (Tech4You Project, PNRR call n. 3277 - December 30, 2021).

References

1. Arca, B., Ghisu, T., Trunfio, G.A.: GPU-accelerated multi-objective optimization of fuel treatments for mitigating wildfire hazard. J. Comput. Sci. **11**, 258–268 (2015)
2. Avolio, M., et al.: Simulation of the 1992 Tessina landslide by a cellular automata model and future hazard scenarios. Int. J. Appl. Earth Obs. Geoinf. **2**(1), 41–50 (2000)
3. Baratta, I., Richardson, C., Wells, G.: Performance analysis of matrix-free conjugate gradient kernels using SYCL. In: International Workshop on OpenCL. IWOCL'22, Association for Computing Machinery, New York, NY, USA (2022)
4. Castaño, G., Faqir-Rhazoui, Y., García, C., Prieto-Matías, M.: Evaluation of Intel's DPC++ compatibility tool in heterogeneous computing. J. Parall. Distrib. Comput. **165**, 120–129 (2022)
5. Cercos-Pita, J.: AQUAgpusph, a new free 3D SPH solver accelerated with OpenCL. Comput. Phys. Commun. **192**, 295–312 (2015)
6. D'Ambrosio, D., et al.: The open computing abstraction layer for parallel complex systems modeling on many-core systems. J. Parall. Distrib. Comput. **121**, 53–70 (2018)
7. D'Ambrosio, D., Filippone, G., Marocco, D., Rongo, R., Spataro, W.: Efficient application of GPGPU for lava flow hazard mapping. J. Supercomput. **65**(2), 630–644 (2013)
8. D'Ambrosio, D., Filippone, G., Rongo, R., Spataro, W., Trunfio, G.: Cellular automata and GPGPU: an application to lava flow modeling. Int. J. Grid and High Perform. Comput. **4**(3), 30–47 (2012)
9. D'Ambrosio, D., Terremoto, G., De Rango, A., Furnari, L., Senatore, A., Mendicino, G.: First SYCL implementation of the three-dimensional subsurface XCA-Flow cellular automaton and performance comparison against CUDA. In: Proceedings of the International Conference on Applied Computing 2022 and WWW/Internet 2022, Lisbon, Portugal, 8–9 November, 2022, pp. 47–54 (2022)
10. D'Ambrosio, D., et al.: A general computational formalism for networks of structured grids. In: Sergeyev, Y.D., Kvasov, D.E. (eds.) Numerical Computations: Theory and Algorithms, pp. 243–255. Springer, Cham (2020). https://doi.org/10.1007/978-3-030-39081-5_22
11. De Rango, A., D'Ambrosio, D.: Github repository of developed software. https://github.com/alessioderango/CUDA_OpenCL_SYCL_Perfomance_Assessment

12. Deakin, T., McIntosh-Smith, S.: Evaluating the performance of HPC-style SYCL applications. In: IWOCL '20. Association for Computing Machinery (ACM), United States (2020), international Workshop on OpenCL, IWOCL; Conference date: 27-04-2020 Through 29-04-2020
13. Giordano, A., De Rango, A., D'Ambrosio, D., Rongo, R., Spataro, W.: Strategies for parallel execution of cellular automata in distributed memory architectures. In: 2019 27th Euromicro International Conference on Parallel, Distributed and Network-Based Processing (PDP), pp. 406–413 (2019)
14. Giordano, A., De Rango, A., Rongo, R., D'Ambrosio, D., Spataro, W.: Dynamic load balancing in parallel execution of cellular automata. IEEE Trans. Parallel Distrib. Syst. **32**(2), 470–484 (2021)
15. Goli, M., et al.: Towards cross-platform performance portability of DNN models using SYCL. In: Proceedings of P3HPC 2020: International Workshop on Performance, Portability, and Productivity in HPC, Held in conjunction with SC 2020: The International Conference for High Performance Computing, Networking, Storage and Analysis, pp. 25–35 (2020)
16. Gregorio, S.D., Serra, R.: An empirical method for modelling and simulating some complex macroscopic phenomena by cellular automata. Futur. Gener. Comput. Syst. **16**, 259–271 (1999)
17. Kirk, D.B., Mei, W., Hwu, W.: Chapter 7 - parallel patterns: convolution: an introduction to stencil computation. In: Kirk, D.B., Mei W. Hwu, W. (eds.) Programming Massively Parallel Processors (Third Edition), pp. 149–174. Morgan Kaufmann, third edition (2017)
18. Konstantinidis, E., Cotronis, Y.: A Quantitative performance evaluation of fast on-chip memories of GPUs. In: 2016 24th Euromicro International Conference on Parallel, Distributed, and Network-Based Processing (PDP), pp. 448–455 (2016)
19. Macri, M., De Rango, A., Spataro, D., D'Ambrosio, D., Spataro, W.: Efficient lava flows simulations with OpenCL: a preliminary application for civil defence purposes. In: Proceedings of the 10th International Conference on P2P, Parallel, Grid, Cloud and Internet Computing, 3PGCIC 2015, pp. 328–335 (2015)
20. von Neumann, J.: Theory of Self-Reproducing Automata. University of Illinois Press, Champaign, IL, USA (1966)
21. Nickolls, J., Buck, I., Garland, M., Skadron, K.: Scalable parallel programming with CUDA: Is CUDA the parallel programming model that application developers have been waiting for? Queue **6**(2), 40–53 (2008)
22. Owens, J., et al.: A survey of general-purpose computation on graphics hardware. Comput. Graph. Forum **26**(1), 80–113 (2007)
23. Peccerillo, B., Bartolini, S.: PHAST - a portable high-level modern C++ programming library for GPUs and multi-cores. IEEE Trans. Parall. Distrib. Syst. **30**(1), 174–189 (2019)
24. Rango, A.D., Spataro, D., Spataro, W., D'Ambrosio, D.: A first multi-GPU/multi-node implementation of the open computing abstraction layer. J. Comput. Sci. **32**, 115–124 (2019)
25. Reguly, I., Owenson, A., Powell, A., Jarvis, S., Mudalige, G.: Under the Hood of SYCL - an initial performance analysis with an unstructured-mesh CFD application. In: Proceedings - International Supercomputing Conference (ISC21) (2021)
26. Reyes, R., Brown, G., Burns, R., Wong, M.: SYCL 2020: more than meets the eye. In: Proceedings of the International Workshop on OpenCL. IWOCL '20, Association for Computing Machinery, New York, NY, USA (2020)
27. Stone, J., Gohara, D., Shi, G.: OpenCL: a parallel programming standard for heterogeneous computing systems. Comput. Sci. Eng. **12**(3), 66–72 (2010)

28. Williams, S., Waterman, A., Patterson, D.: Roofline: an insightful visual performance model for multicore architectures. Commun. ACM **52**(4), 65–76 (2009)
29. Yang, C.: Hierarchical roofline analysis: how to collect data using performance tools on intel CPUs and NVIDIA GPUs (2020). https://arxiv.org/abs/2009.02449
30. Yang, C., Kurth, T., Williams, S.: Hierarchical roofline analysis for GPUs: accelerating performance optimization for the NERSC-9 Perlmutter system. Concurr. Comput.: Pract. Exper. **32**(20), e5547 (2020)

An Approach to Performance Portability Through Generic Programming

Andreas Hadjigeorgiou[1], Christodoulos Stylianou[2(✉)], Michèle Weiland[2],
Dirk Jacob Verschuur[3], and Jacob Finkenrath[1]

[1] The Cyprus Institute, Nicosia, Cyprus
{a.hadjigeorgiou,j.finkenrath}@cyi.ac.cy
[2] EPCC, University of Edinburgh, Edinburgh, UK
c.stylianou@ed.ac.uk, m.weiland@epcc.ed.ac.uk
[3] Delft University of Technology, Delft, The Netherlands
d.j.verschuur@tudelft.nl

Abstract. The expanding hardware diversity in high performance computing adds enormous complexity to scientific software development. Developers who aim to write maintainable software have two options: 1) To use a so-called data locality abstraction that handles portability internally, thereby, performance-productivity becomes a trade off. Such abstractions usually come in the form of libraries, domain-specific languages, and run-time systems. 2) To use generic programming where performance, productivity and portability are subject to software design. In the direction of the second, this work describes a design approach that allows the integration of low-level and verbose programming tools into high-level generic algorithms based on template meta-programming in C++. This enables the development of performance-portable applications targeting host-device computer architectures, such as CPUs and GPUs. With a suitable design in place, the extensibility of generic algorithms to new hardware becomes a well defined procedure that can be developed in isolation from other parts of the code. That allows scientific software to be maintainable and efficient in a period of diversifying hardware in HPC. As proof of concept, a finite-difference modelling algorithm for the acoustic wave equation is developed and benchmarked using roofline model analysis on Intel Xeon Gold 6248 CPU, Nvidia Tesla V100 GPU, and AMD MI100 GPU.

Keywords: HPC · Performance · Portability · Generic Programming

1 Introduction

The diversity of computer architectures in High Performance Computing (HPC) has evolved remarkably in the past two decades. During this period, HPC systems advanced from *single-core* processing units (PUs), to *many-core* PUs. In other words, performance scaling has been achieved, to a big extend, with additional parallelism at PU-level. However, parallelism comes in different forms.

D. Zeinalipour et al. (Eds.): Euro-Par 2023 Workshops, LNCS 14351, pp. 282–293, 2024.
https://doi.org/10.1007/978-3-031-50684-0_22

Briefly, CPUs and GPUs dominate the HPC landscape today. At the same time, even PUs that fall within the same category, e.g. CPU, may pose differences in their architecture based on how cores are physically placed on chips, e.g. NUMA regions, etc. This evolution has dramatic consequences on the software development side. A single optimized C or FORTRAN code that has been considered a performance portable solution in the past is neither sufficient nor fully-portable at all nowadays. As a result, during the past decade efforts were made for the development of abstraction layers, such as Kokkos [3] and RAJA [2], that enhance the development of portable HPC applications. At the same time, these efforts aim to increase productivity, by easing the development effort. The outcomes from these efforts come in the form of programming models that provide a set of *memory spaces, execution spaces & policies, iteration ranges, data layouts,* and other concepts, which serve as building blocks for the development of parallel *single-source* code that is performance portable to one degree or another [4].

Performance critical software is always developed using low-level verbose programming tools, which expose to the developers ways to optimally map code to the target hardware [11]. On top of this, performance optimization usually requires considerable changes in the software design. Therefore, performance should be considered in the design phase of the software, a step that is usually underestimated in computational science [6,8]. This work is not an attempt to provide an alternative programming model equivalent to the performance portability layers described in the previous paragraph, despite the fact that it is inspired from them. Rather, we discuss a design approach that allows developers to achieve performance and portability by separating two concerns: the algorithm as a multi-step process that evolves in-time, and its actual code implementation details. This separation is achieved through static polymorphism using metaprogramming techniques based on C++ templates, which falls under the broad category of *generic programming* [9].

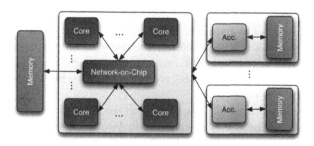

Fig. 1. Host-device computer architecture as an *abstract machine model* [1].

The host-device model introduced as an *abstract machine model* towards exascale computing [1], refers to a machine that has a multi-core processor (host), which is coupled with one or more discrete accelerators (devices). Each accelerator has a local, high throughput, and physically separated memory as illustrated in Fig. 1. The model represents accurately the node architecture of most super-computing systems nowadays. The discussed design approach allows to integrate low-level programming techniques into high-level abstractions in order to target in a performance portable manner host-device computer architectures.

By no means we support this is a silver bullet approach to solve the perfor-mance portability challenge, or that alternative approaches might not be proven equally well. It is however, a robust and simple approach to achieve performance and portability, and good software engineering practises to be incorporated in the development process, such as: separation of concerns, extensibility, ease of testing, and memory safety. As a proof of concept (POC), a two-dimensional Finite-Difference (FD) modelling scheme for the acoustic wave propagation is developed and made publicly available[1] on GitHub. We select this POC appli-cation since its stencil-based nature represents well enough a range of existing applications and at the same time it is simple and broadly understood by the general audience of HPC.

2   Performance Portability by Design

From the science point of view, code is seen as an asset that allows scientists to do more in terms of simulations, analyses, visualization, etc. However, from the software engineering point of view, code is debt. The larger the code-base it is, the more difficult is to manage. Software design, is what allows it to be manageable and grow without collapsing from its own weight. These concepts have been of great concern in the broad computer science domain since long time ago [7]. For scientific computing, the challenge introduced from the emerging hardware diversity in HPC makes this necessity even more apparent. To our experience, the major problem in many scientific applications is usually not the effort itself that is needed for re-writing some part of the code for portability to another architecture. It is rather that by design the applications have architecture-specific code to all their extent and silent assumptions about the location of data, thus, the transition becomes a redundant, not well defined, and as a consequence erroneous procedure. All these problems, become even more apparent due to the lack of a regression test framework in most cases. Developing applications for heterogeneous computer architectures requires radical rethinking of the scientific software development approach.

For the development of HPC applications we came across two approaches. On the one hand, is the use of so-called data locality abstractions [13] (DLAs) that come in the form of libraries, domain-specific languages, or run-time sys-tems with common theme the increase of productivity. Portability is handled internally from the DLAs, thus, the developer does not require hardware specific knowledge. On the other hand, is the use of meta-programming techniques [11] that allow integrating verbose programming tools into generic interfaces with

---

[1] https://github.com/ahadji05/pp-template/.

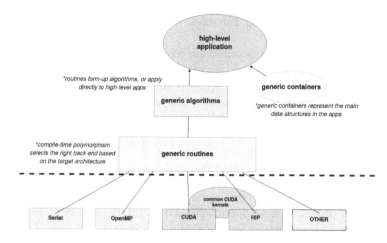

Fig. 2. Software design for performance and portability through generic programming.

common theme the increase of performance. Portability is expanded by integrating more programming models under the generic interface. In practice, portability is easier following the first approach, however, the performance boundary can be pushed further following the second one. The approach described in this work is in the direction of the second. Using C++ templates and meta-programming techniques, we discuss the development of generic containers, routines, and algorithms. The term generic denotes *template-with-respect-to* two types/concepts: Memory-Space and Execution-Space. These serve as the core types that allow to form a generic approach to target host-device computer architectures.

Figure 2 illustrates the software design that we describe in this work. The dashed horizontal line demonstrates the separation of two concerns: 1) the development of generic building-blocks, 2) the implementation details. In this case, generic denotes architecture-agnostic, whereas details denotes architecture-specific. The end goal is to develop building-blocks in the form of *containers, routines*, and *algorithms*, which allow the development of applications that are transferable across architectures. Then, based on compile-time choice, the behaviour of the building-blocks is resolved according to the implementation details we select. Finally, the behaviour has two aspects: first, the location of the data, second, the access pattern.

This design assumes that host is always a CPU that is programmable with C++, and the device could be either the host itself, or an accelerator programmable with a low-level programming tool that is supported in the back-end. In our case the back-end is developed using OpenMP, CUDA and HIP. Serial is the sequential processing back-end that serves as reference for testing. At the same time, the application is extensible to any other back-end we may want to develop in the future. As long as a future implementation adheres to the interface that is already in-place, all code on top of is reused without any additional change.

3   Concern 1: Building Blocks

The core concepts we identify as minimum requirement for separating the implementations details from the generic algorithms are two: Memory Space and Execution Space. The role of Memory Space is to define the location of the data, whereas the Execution Space selects the right back-end that provides the implementation details. In fact, this allows to leverage the type system of the language in order to develop compile-time rules that impose memory safety.

The Memory Spaces are concrete classes that provide five basic memory management operations: `allocate`, `release`, `copy`, `copyFromHost`, and `copyToHost`. These operations are implemented as static methods so they are bound to their class name. Thus, a Memory Space passed as template parameter to other generic classes provides these operations. The right hand side of Fig. 3, illustrates the three Memory Spaces proposed and developed in our case. The default is the host memory space, namely `MemSpaceHost`. For this particular space, the three copy operations have the same underlying implementation; copy data within host memory space. They diverge only for the other two memory spaces `MemSpaceCuda` and `MemSpaceHip`. On the left hand side in Fig. 3, the Execution Spaces, are concrete classes as well that are being used for explicit specialization of routines based on the *tag-dispatching* idiom that is discussed in Sect. 4. Moreover, each Execution Space has one type-trait that defines the accessible Memory Space. This allows the development of type-rules to ensure that the accessible data are on the right location.

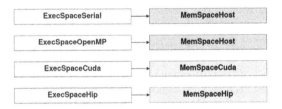

Fig. 3. Execution spaces and their corresponding Memory Spaces for targeting CPU and GPU architectures.

For the development of architecture-agnostic applications we identify three generic building blocks: containers, routines, and algorithms. They are generic in the sense that their type is *to-be-specified* according to template parameters. The two template parameters that define them are: Memory Space and Execution Space. In essence, the containers hold the data that are processed during run-time in a suitable location, processing comes from the routines that act on the containers with a suitable access pattern, and finally, the algorithms are collections of routines and containers.

Containers are generic C++ data-structures, e.g. class or struct, with one template parameter that resolves to a valid Memory Space. The scope of the Memory

Space is to determine the location of the container's data by providing the five basic memory management operations that we mentioned earlier. Containers represent the main entities in our application. For example, for the finite-difference scheme that we developed as POC app, we developed the `ScalarField<Mem>` container to represent velocity and wave fields. Containers may have metadata explicitly on host that serve control-flow and run-time assertions. The data related to the processing done during the simulation are located on the provided Memory Space (see template parameter `Mem`) so they are directly accessible from the routines.

Routines are generic `C++` functions with two template parameters: An Execution and a Memory space. The routines operate on the containers and provide the processing steps that our application involves. The Memory Space determines the location of data in the containers that are passed as parameters to the function. The Execution Space is used as a tag parameter that dispatches the routine to a back-end implementation. This approach leverages the function overloading feature of `C++`. The Execution Space and the Memory Space need to be compatible, otherwise the application could crash due to an invalid memory access. The language's type system allows to develop rules, e.g. using `std::enable_if`, in order to let the compiler inspect this compatibility. This allows to capture with a meaningful message an invalid implementation at compile-time, instead of having to debug an invalid memory access that occurs out of the blue.

Algorithms are generic `C++` classes with a single template parameter representing the Execution Space. The Execution Space provides its accessible Memory Space as a type-trait, which is used internally in the body of the class. The algorithms are collections of containers and routines in the sense that they have containers as member variables and their methods apply operations on them through one or more routines. The class provides no information whether and how the computation is parallelised, and if data reside on the CPU or the GPU, or so. All these concerns resolve to the implementation that is a separate part of the code. The scope of the algorithm as a meta-program is first, to make sure that given an Execution Space, the correct Memory Space is selected based on which the containers allocate their data suitably. Second, based on the Memory Space and the Execution Space the routines dispatch at compile-time to the correct back-end implementation. This design approach adds to the quality of the code in the sense that it makes it more easy to read and understand, reusable across different architectures due to its generic nature, and memory safe. At the same time, since the implementation is decoupled from the interface, we can use any low-level programming tool to develop it efficiently based on the target-hardware without altering the aforementioned.

4 Concern 2: Implementation Details

In Sect. 3, we discussed the development of generic containers, routines, and algorithms based on two template parameters: Memory Space and Execution Space. These serve as the building blocks for the development of performance portable applications. In here, we discuss how we develop the architecture-specific implementations in such way that they adhere to the common abstract interface and can be identified at compile-time through tag dispatching.

As an example, let us consider a generic routine, namely `dosomething`, that applies some processing on a container X. The specializations[2] for `OpenMP` and `CUDA` implementations are shown in Listings 1.1 and 1.2 respectively.

```
template<>
void dosomething(X<MemSpaceHost>& A, ... , ExecSpaceOpenMP tag){
    \\ parallel OpenMP code ...
}
```

Listing 1.1. Specialisation of the OpenMP implementation.

```
template<>
void dosomething(X<MemSpaceCuda>& A, ... , ExecSpaceCuda tag){
    \\ config-launch CUDA kernel ...
}
```

Listing 1.2. Specialisation of the Cuda implementation

Listing 1.1, indicates the function definition for the `OpenMP` back-end. This specialization, receives as parameter, among others, a container X whose data is allocated on host using the corresponding Memory Space. Thus, the data are accessible by a parallel `OpenMP` implementation. In Listing 1.2, the function is launching a `CUDA` kernel, thus, container needs to have the data on device. In that case, this is guaranteed by `MemSpaceCuda`, which is the Memory Space of container X.

Each template specialization is implemented in a different *translation-unit* isolated from others. Alternatively, conditional guards[3] are used to diverge source-code compilation based on which architecture is targeted. More specializations can be developed as long as they adhere to the interface that is provided from the generic routine, and a valid combination of Memory-Execution spaces is used. In that sense, a generic codebase is extensible to other hardware without conflicts with existing parts of the code. As a result, extending portability becomes a well defined procedure that is trivial and memory-safe. At the same time, performance is not compromised or limited by any third party library since it can be specifically implemented with any low-level programming tool of choice.

Based on the design approach that is described in this work, we developed four Execution Space options and three Memory Space options as shown in Fig. 3. The `Serial` and `OpenMP` Execution Spaces are compatible with the `MemSpaceHost`. The `CUDA` and `HIP` Execution Spaces are compatible with the `MemSpaceCuda` and `MemSpaceHip` respectively. These options are sufficient to cover portability on the majority of HPC systems as of today.

---

[2] In `C++` this is so-called explicit (full) template specialization.

[3] `#ifdef`, `#else`, `#endif`, etc.

5   Start and Stop

The discussed design approach targets host-device computer architectures, thus, the start and stop of applications need to pass through the host always for I/O purposes. Thereby, in a program's lifetime, there must coexist one explicit host Memory Space, namely `MemSpaceHost`, and one alias for device Memory Space, namely `memo_space`. By default, `memo_space` can be the host Memory Space itself if no accelerator is targeted.

How an application starts: Applications are organized based on the assumption that there is a host PU whose resources are managed with `MemSpaceHost`, and a device whose resources are managed with `memo_space`. The latter, is defined at compile-time based on the target architecture. All input data are allocated using `MemSpaceHost`, so they are initialized on host. All containers are instantiated using `memo_space`. The, input data are copied into the containers from host using the method `memo_space::copyFromHost`. Once the data are copied into the containers they are directly accessible from the generic routines and algorithms. This approach fits the host-device model, which was introduced in Fig. 1, because it is a unified approach that allows to initialize the generic containers with data, either on host, or the device, using the same interface.

How an application ends: An application ends with output data printed on screen and/or stored in output files. To meet this requirement within the context of the host-device model we follow an analogous to the previous paragraph's approach. The containers have their data managed by `memo_space`, which resolves either to host, or the device memory. Thereby, before output there must be an explicit call for transfer to the host memory. In analogoy to the previous paragraph, this is performed via the method `memo_space::copyToHost`.

6   Testing as an Integral Part

Testing is the proof of correctness and should be an integral part of scientific software. The purpose is to verify in a quantitative manner that the implementation is correct. It applies to individual routines such they are expected to return a specific output given a specific input, so-called *unit-tests*. Additionally, software should be tested in the connectivity between different parts as error may exist in the glue-code, namely *integration-tests*. Testing increases the development curve, however, the returns pay-off the effort and provide a proof that indeed the software behaves exactly as it should. According to Prabhu et al. [10], scientists spend as much as half of their programming effort on finding and fixing errors using "primitive" debugging approaches.

Within the context of our discussion, the development of implementations using different programming tools that provide the same routines and algorithms make the need for testing even more apparent. Ideally, we do not want the effort of developing different architecture-specific implementations to extend the testing effort. This is possible, if the tests are applied to the layer of generic containers, routines, and algorithms. To do so, the tests are developed based on the ideas that we discussed in Sect. 5. We can summarize the procedure in the following steps:

1. the input data are initialised explicitly on Host (`MemSpaceHost`)
2. using `memo_space::copyFromHost` the input data are copied into containers
3. the routine(s) under testing are invoked
4. using `memo_space::copyToHost` the output data are copied back to Host
5. test-assertions are performed on Host .

The `memo_space` is an alias that by conditional compilation resolves to one of the available Memory Spaces from Fig. 3, depending on which backend we want to test against. Based on this approach, all implementations are tested through the same input-output criteria and verify their equivalence. Both unit and integration tests can be effectively implemented based on this approach. Furthermore, this makes code easier and safer to extend in the sense that if a new hardware emerges and we want to develop an implementation to target it, the tests that are already in-place serve as the channels to "pass" through.

7   Proof of Concept

As POC, a finite-difference modelling scheme for the two-dimensional acoustic wave equation:

$$\frac{\partial^2 P(t,x,z)}{\partial t^2} = v(x,z)^2 \left(\frac{\partial^2 P(t,x,z)}{\partial x^2} + \frac{\partial^2 P(t,x,z)}{\partial z^2} \right) + S(t) , \tag{1}$$

has been developed, where P is the pressure amplitude, v is the space-dependent velocity, and S is a time-dependent source. The FD modelling is performed by the `WaveSimulator` algorithm[4], which has been developed based on the discussion for generic building-blocks in Sect. 3. Listing 1.3 is a brief view of the algorithm's interface that shows how the containers and routines that form up the algorithm come together.

```
template<class ExecSpace>
class WaveSimulator {
  public:
    using MemSpace = typename ExecSpace::accessible_space;
    void run(){
        add_source(ScalarField<MemSpace>&P, ..., ExecSpace());
        fd_pzz(ScalarField<MemSpace>&Pzz, ..., ExecSpace());
        fd_pxx(ScalarField<MemSpace>&Pxx, ..., ExecSpace());
        fd_time(ScalarField<MemSpace>&Pnew, ..., ExecSpace());
        swap(Pold, P);
        swap(P, Pnew);
    }
    //...other public methods e.g. set/get
```

---

[4] https://github.com/ahadji05/pp-template/tree/main/include/algorithms.

```
private:
    ScalarField<MemSpace> Pnew, P, Pold, Pxx, Pzz, V;
    d_type _dt, _dh;
    //...other private variables and methods
};
```

Listing 1.3. Generic interface for the Wave simulation algorithm.

Initially, `MemSpace` is the Memory Space that is defined as type-trait from the provided template parameter `ExecSpace`. The member variables Pnew, P, etc. that store wavefields as well the velocity model V are represented by the generic container `ScalarField`, which is defined based on the template parameter `MemSpace`. The algorithm's steps are ordered in the body of the main function, namely `run()`, which invokes the routines that compose it, namely, 1) `add_source`, 2) `fd_pzz`, 3) `fd_pxx`, and 4) `fd_time`. The algorithm as a meta-program is completely agnostic with respect to any target hardware because both the location of the data as well the implementation details are resolved by the template parameters `MemSpace` and `ExecSpace` respectively.

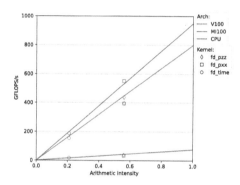

Fig. 4. Roofline-model analysis of individual kernels on CPU and GPU architectures.

Since the implementation details can be developed with any programming model, language, or library of choice we can use a suitable tool for each architecture we target. We use `OpenMP` for threaded parallelism on CPUs, `CUDA` for Nvidia GPUs, and `HIP` for porting CUDA-kernels to AMD GPUs. In Fig. 4, we demonstrate by roofline model analysis that we achieve near optimal performance in all kernels[5] of interest. The architectures that we used for this experiment are: Nvidia Tesla V100 GPU, AMD MI100 GPU, and Intel Xeon Gold 6248 CPU. For each case, the practical main-memory bandwidth is measured using the open-source BabelStream benchmark [5], and plotted on the figure with a different colour. The curve with the highest slope has the highest memory throughput, which in that case is the AMD MI100 GPU. Based on the arithmetic intensity (Flops/Byte), and the achieved performance (GFlops/s), each

---

[5] the `add_source` kernels has no parallelism to exploit, thus, it is neglected.

kernel is marked on the plot. The colour indicates architecture and the symbol indicates the kernel-name. The evaluation shows that all kernels, except from fd_pzz on the MI100 GPU, achieve higher than 90 % efficiency.

8   Discussion

This design approach is powerful because the generic behaviour can be developed without any dependency on external libraries. A C++11 or above compliant compiler is all that is needed. The implementation details that provide the architecture-specific libraries or programming models are needed partially depending on the target hardware. Extensibility is one of the virtues of the described design approach because targeting new hardware becomes a well defined procedure. The first step is to develop the Memory Space that provides the resource management operations. The, second is to develop the Execution Space that is used for tag-dispatching. Once these two classes are developed the back-end for each routine can be implemented in isolation from the others based on two requirements: 1) adhere to the interface, and 2) pass the generic unit-test that is already in place. This strategy allows to implement back-end for a new hardware, e.g. FPGA, or even specialize for specific instruction sets, e.g. AVX, SVE, etc. Furthermore, we argue that productivity does not necessarily come only with the ability to develop code faster. It comes with good separation of concerns so that processes are dissected in small, well defined, understandable pieces that can be developed independently. If a software design is in place and it is understood from the people who develop the different back-ends, productivity is achieved in the most effective way. This work aligns towards this direction. Finally, the discussed design approach is used for the development of preparatory access software within the Delphi Consortium for applications related to seismic wavefield modelling, imaging, and inversion. Similar design approaches were successfully applied in the area of Sparse Linear Algebra through the development of *Morpheus* [14], a library for dynamic sparse matrices and algorithms.

9   Conclusions

In this work, we describe a design approach that allows the development of maintainable scientific software for heterogeneous computing architectures. The design is based on the abstract machine model that represents accurately the majority of HPC systems nowadays. The approach is based on meta-programming techniques using C++ templates, which are used for the development of generic containers, routines and algorithms that serve as building-blocks for the development of performance-portable applications. We identify two concepts necessary for developing the generic building-blocks, the first, is the Memory Space that defines the location of the data, and the second is the Execution Space that distinguishes the implementation details. Our approach allows the integration of any programming model of choice as a back-end that provides the implementation details of the generic high-level application. A FD scheme is developed as proof of concept, and benchmarked using roofline model analysis to demonstrate at least 90 % performance efficiency on modern CPUs and GPUs.

Acknowledgment. This research is funded by Delphi Consortium at Delft University of Technology and the EPSRC project ASiMoV (EP/S005072/1). The experiments have been carried out on the Cyclone HPC system at the Cyprus Institute, and the Isambard 2 UK National Tier-2 HPC Service (http://gw4.ac.uk/isambard) operated by GW4 and the UK Met Office, and funded by EPSRC (EP/T022078/1).

References

1. Ang, J.A., et. al.: Abstract machine models and proxy architectures for exascale computing, Lawrence Berkeley National Laboratory (2014)
2. Beckingsale, D.A., et al.: RAJA: portable performance for large-scale scientific applications. In: IEEE/ACM International Workshop on Performance, Portability and Productivity in HPC (P3HPC), Denver, CO, USA (2019)
3. Carter, H., et al.: Kokkos: enabling manycore performance portability through polymorphic memory access patterns. J. Parall. Distrib. Comput. **74**(12), 3202–3216 (2014)
4. Deakin, T., et al.: Performance portability across diverse computing architectures. In: IEEE/ACM International Workshop on Performance, Portability and Productivity in HPC (P3HPC), Denver, CO, USA (2019)
5. Deakin, T., et al.: Evaluating attainable memory bandwidth of parallel programming models via BabelStream. Int. J. Comput. Sci. Eng. Special issue **17**(3), 247–262 (2018)
6. Hasselbring, W.: Software architecture: past, present, future. In: The Essence of Software Engineering, pp. 169–184. Springer, Cham (2018). https://doi.org/10.1007/978-3-319-73897-0_10
7. Iglberger, K.: C++ Software Design: Design Principles and Patterns for High-Quality Software. O'Reilly Media Inc, 1005 (2022)
8. Johanson, N.A.: Software engineering for computational science: past, present, future. Comput. Sci. Eng. **20**, 90–109 (2018)
9. Lilis, Y., Savidis, A.: A survey of metaprogramming languages. ACM Comput. Surv. **52**(6), 1–39 (2019)
10. Prabhu, P., et al.: A survey of the practice of computational science. In: Association for Computing Machinery, New York, NY, USA, Article 19, 1–12 (2011)
11. Rompf, T., et al.: Go Meta! a case for generative programming and DSLs in performance critical systems. In: 1st Summit on Advances in Programming Languages (SNAPL 2015), Asilomar, CA, USA, May 3–6 (2015)
12. Stroustrup, B.: The C++ Programming Language, Fourth Edition, ch. 17, pp. 481–526. Addison-Wesley (2013)
13. Unat, D., et al.: Trends in data locality abstractions for HPC systems. IEEE Trans. Parall. Distrib. Syst. **28**(10), 3007–3020 (2017)
14. Stylianou, C., Weiland, M.: Exploiting dynamic sparse matrices for performance portable linear algebra operations. In: 2022 IEEE/ACM International Workshop on Performance, Portability and Productivity in HPC (P3HPC). Los Alamitos, CA, USA: IEEE Computer Society, Nov 2022, pp. 47–57 (2022)

Boosting the Performance of Object Tracking with a Half-Precision Particle Filter on GPU

Gabin Schieffer[1](✉), Nattawat Pornthisan[2], Daniel Medeiros[1], Stefano Markidis[1], Jacob Wahlgren[1], and Ivy Peng[1]

[1] KTH Royal Institute of Technology, Stockholm, Sweden
{gabins,dadm,markidis,jacobwah,ivybopeng}@kth.se
[2] Chulalongkorn University, Bangkok, Thailand

Abstract. High-performance GPU-accelerated particle filter methods are critical for object detection applications, ranging from autonomous driving, robot localization, to time-series prediction. In this work, we investigate the design, development and optimization of particle-filter using half-precision on CUDA cores and compare their performance and accuracy with single- and double-precision baselines on Nvidia V100, A100, A40 and T4 GPUs. To mitigate numerical instability and precision losses, we introduce algorithmic changes in the particle filters. Using half-precision leads to a performance improvement of 1.5–2 $\times$ and 2.5–4.6 $\times$ with respect to single- and double-precision baselines respectively, at the cost of a relatively small loss of accuracy.

Keywords: Particle Filter · Half-Precision · Reduced Precision · GPUs

1 Introduction

The particle filter method is a critical algorithm for enabling automatic object or video tracking, e.g., automatically locating one or more moving objects over time using a camera. Today, it is widely used to support and improve autonomous driving and in a wide range of other applications, including video surveillance, sensor networks, signal processing, robot localization, and time-series forecasting [3,10,11]. For its central role in developing emerging technologies, such as autonomous driving, it is crucial to design, and develop high-performance, accelerated, yet accurate, particle filters that can provide real-time or near real-time object tracking capabilities. This research investigates the design and development of accurate particle filters with Graphical Processing Units (GPU) and half-precision data. Ideally, the use of half-precision calculations on CUDA cores could lead to double the performance of the operations in single-precision on Nvidia GPUs and this work studies the challenges, achievable performance and accuracy on half-precision particle filters.

At this heart, the particle filter technique, also known as Sequential Monte Carlo (SMC) method [4], uses random sampling to simulate complex systems,

D. Zeinalipour et al. (Eds.): Euro-Par 2023 Workshops, LNCS 14351, pp. 294–305, 2024.
https://doi.org/10.1007/978-3-031-50684-0_23

such as object movement in a real environment. Particle filters are particularly powerful in cases where the underlying system evolves over time and new observations, potentially affected by an error, become available sequentially, such as in a video stream. Intuitively, the fundamental idea of the particle filter is to approximate the underlying probability density function using a weighted set of samples (the so-called *particles*). At each time step, particles are propagated using the system's transition model, and their weights are updated based on their likelihood to agree with the measurement from the system. After the update, particles with low weights are discarded, and only particles with high weights are re-sampled to create offspring particles for the next time step. Particle filter algorithms are compute-intensive as the propagation, weighting, and resampling calculate for each particle at every time step without significant data movement or synchronization. Previous works of parallelizing particle filters onto parallel computing, e.g., multi-core processors and GPUs [2,3,8], have achieved significant speedup. Recently, GPUs have provided increasing hardware support for low-precision arithmetic operations, motivated by machine learning workloads that are often compute-intensive but resilient to precision loss. In this work, we explore the hardware support for half-precision operations (FP16) on GPU to understand their impact on the performance and accuracy of particle filter algorithms. Differently from previous works [5,9,13], we focus specifically on pure FP16 operations and CUDA cores instead of mixed-precision FP16-FP32 calculations and Tensor Cores.

The main contributions of this work are the following:

- We developed an optimized half-precision particle filter for an object-tracking application on GPUs and associated double- and single-precision baseline implementations.
- We analyzed the numerical instability, performance, pipeline utilization, and accuracy of double-, single-, and two half-precision implementations on Nvidia A100, V100, A40, and Tesla T4 GPUs.
- We identified the performance bottlenecks in the baseline half-precision version and achieved $2 - 6\times$ speedup in the optimized version
- We characterized the impact of the number of threads per block on the particle filter and achieved a further 1.5–1.75× speedup on A100 and V100.

2   Background

The fundamental idea of the particle filter is to approximate the underlying probability density function p using a set of weighted particles at each time step t by

$$p(\mathbf{z}_{1:t} \mid \mathbf{y}_{1:t}) = \sum_{k=0}^{K} \tilde{w}_t^k \delta(\mathbf{z}_{1:t} - \mathbf{z}_{1:t}^k)$$

where y_t is a stochastic observation of the hidden state z_t and $\tilde{w}_t^k$ is the corresponding normalized weights at time t for k th particle [17]. In concrete terms, for object tracking videos, the hidden state z_t can be defined as the actual coordinate of the object in the image after t frame, while y_t is either the color histogram of the pixel in RGB image or the light intensity in monochrome image [11].

Particle filter algorithms are computationally intensive as they must iterate all particles at each time step t. Therefore, GPU is a natural fit for acceleration. Each time step generally goes through three main stages – particle propagation, weighting, and resampling [8,14]. After the initialization, the propagation algorithm creates particle samples from a set of given ancestors using a predefined transition model of the system. Then, the generated samples are incorporated with the observation y_t to recalculate and normalize the particles' weights so that particles with low likelihood to the observation have reduced weights and discarded. Finally, the resampling step selects a set of important particles, i.e., high weight and high likelihood, to generate their corresponding number of offsprings for the next time step. Resampling is a critical step to focus the computational cost on those important samples that are in good alignment with measurements.

Parallelizing the initialization, propagation, and weighting steps is straightforward as they are naturally data parallel. However, resampling requires cumulative operations on all particles, introducing synchronization among threads [3]. Therefore, resampling is the dominant stage in particle filters at a large number of particles.

The IEEE 754-2008 standard defines double, single, and half precision as a binary floating-point number format that occupies 64, 32, and 16 bits, respectively. While double precision, i.e., FP64, is commonly used in scientific computing, popular emerging workloads like neural networks and image processing have achieved significant performance boost from half-precision operations while resilient to precision loss. In this work, we explore half-precision (FP16) on CUDA cores. The IEEE 754 defines that FP16 format has 1 sign bit, 5 exponent bits, and 11 significand bits (10 bits stored), achieving a value range of $\pm 65,504$ and $\log_{10}^{2^{11}} \approx 3.311$ decimal digits.

CUDA provides two FP16 data types, i.e., `half` and `half2`. The former is a scalar data type and the latter is a vector of two elements. Converting a `double` type to `half` type in C++ is straightforward, except that several mathematical functions such as square root and exponential require a special half-precision replacement. Theoretically, the throughput of FP16 operations is twice FP32's throughput. However, on CUDA Cores, hardware arithmetic instructions operate on two 16-bit floating points at a time [6]. Therefore, for high utilization of hardware, operations on two `half` values must be combined into a single operation on `half2`.

3   Related Work

The first implementation of a particle filter on GPU was proposed in [8], which explores parallelization opportunities in the classic particle filter, and propose a GPU-accelerated version. The Metropolis and rejection resampling algorithms

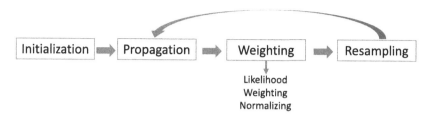

Fig. 1. After the initialization, in each timeframe, the particle filter algorithm iterates over three main phases: propagation, weighting, and resampling.

were evaluated in [14] to avoid the global reduction operation required in standard multinomial, stratified, and systematic resampling algorithms. The authors also evaluated numerical stability and bias in single precision. An approach to further improve the resampling step of the particle filter implementation on GPU was proposed in [16]. The authors evaluate their approach against both the Metropolis method and rejection resampling.

Modern GPU architectures offer tremendous performance in mixed-precision arithmetic. Common challenges of converting a CUDA program from single-precision to half-precision are detailed in [9]. In particular, their findings indicate that the use of the `half2` datatype, which combines two half-precision numbers in one structure, is crucial for performance. We use this technique in our work when converting the particle filter code to use half-precision number representation. In addition, precision loss is an important source of concern when using half-precision. This issue is studied in [13], where the authors provide an analysis of Tensor Cores performance for large matrix multiplication in mixed-precision, and proposes a refinement technique to decrease precision loss. In [5], the authors propose to use an iterative refinement algorithm to improve the solution of their low-precision matrix factorization approach on Tensor Cores.

4   Design, Implementation and Optimization

We design and optimize a particle filter object tracking application to evaluate the effect of half-precision data types on Nvidia GPUs. The application tracks a moving object in a two-dimensional video. The baseline implementation follows the same algorithmic structure as in the Rodinia particle filter [1], but has been improved on the overall organization and extended with single- and half-precision specialization. Figure 1 presents the main workflow, where after the initialization phase, three stages are repeated in each time frame, i.e., an iteration consisting of six kernels – propagation, likelihood, maximum finding, weighting, normalizing, and resampling. For most kernels, their half-precision implementation is algorithmically different from their double- and single-precision counterparts because they have to work with the vector type to improve hardware utilization.

The propagation kernel takes a selected set of ancestors as the input. Propagation means that the next generation of each particle is sampled according to the true distribution of transition conditional density (denoted as $p(\mathbf{z}_{t+1}|\mathbf{z}_t)$), which is a property given on the specific system. Specifically,

$$p(x_t^k \,|\, x_{t-1}^{a_k}) = \mathcal{N}\left(1.0 + x_{t-1}^{a_k}, 5.0^2\right) \tag{1}$$

$$p(y_t^k \,|\, y_{t-1}^{a_k}) = \mathcal{N}\left(2.0 + y_{t-1}^{a_k}, 2.0^2\right) \tag{2}$$

where k is the particle index and a_k is an ancestor index of particle k returned from the resampling kernel in the last time frame. The next generation of particles are sampled from double-precision space, then converted to a target precision if reduced-precision is used because cuRAND is used for the random number generation on GPUs and does not support half-precision value.

The likelihood kernel calculates the log-likelihood of observing the intensity around each particle at time t by

$$log^{likelihood} = L^k = \frac{(I_{ijk} - 100)^2 - (I_{ijk} - 228)^2}{50 \times N}, \tag{3}$$

where the two constants, 100 and 228, represent the mean intensity of the background and foreground, while I_{ijk} refer to the pixel intensity at ith row and jth column at frame k and N refer to a total number of the pixel value to be calculated per particle. The likelihood kernel is parallelized pixel-wise across threads. For example, if the number of particles is set at 512 and there are 10 points around the particle to be evaluated, the kernel will launch a total of $512 \times 10 = 5{,}120$ tasks. Note that the number of tasks is reduced by half on half-precision implementation, as each thread takes care of two pixels simultaneously.

Each particle's weight is re-calculated and normalized at time t. Firstly, the max-finding kernel finds the highest likelihood among the particles by

$$L^k = \left(\frac{I_{ijk} - 100}{\sqrt{50 \times N}}\right)^2 - \left(\frac{I_{ijk} - 228}{\sqrt{50 \times N}}\right)^2. \tag{4}$$

Next, the weighting kernel calculates the unnormalized weight by

$$w_t^k = w_{t-1}^k \exp\left\{L^k - \max_i L^i\right\}, \tag{5}$$

and performs a sum-reduction operation on weights. Then, given the pre-calculated sum, the normalizing kernel normalizes the weights and prepares the cumulative distribution, which is essentially an inclusive-prefix-sum [15], for the next stage.

Resampling selects a set of particles to become the ancestors for the next generation of particles based on their weights and the resampling algorithm. The most straightforward resampling scheme would be multinomial resampling, which is just a categorical distribution with the probability of choosing kth particle as an ancestor equal to its normalized weight. In our case, to be consistent with the original Rodinia implementation, we employ a *systematic resampling* algorithm that divides the normalized space into N partitions, where N is the number of particles and takes one sample from each partition [12]. The parallelization scheme among threads is similar to the other kernels, i.e., in single- and double-precision each thread finds the ancestor for one particle, while in half-precision, each thread finds the ancestors for two particles at a time.

Implementation. For the ease of running experiments, we utilized C++ templates to allow multi-precision support for the kernel. Switching between data types is as effortless as changing a function call, e.g., from `particleFilter<double>` to `particleFilter<half>(...)`. Note that single and double precision use the same kernel implementations, where each thread process one particle, while half-precision kernels change to `half2` datatype and use a different implementation where each thread processes two particles packed into one `half2` element.

Numerical Stability Optimization. First, we analyze the numerical stability in reduced precision and propose our optimizations. In Propagation, the algorithm operates on a low range of values, and thus, there is no significant numerical instability to be concerned. The likelihood kernel can have a numerical overflow when the square operations in Eq. 3 result in large values. Instead of computing Eq. 3 directly, we move the denominator to the square operator too to avoid the problem. In the normalizing kernel, since the exponents can grow arbitrarily large and lead to a particle with infinite weight, the resulted normalized weight can vanish. One way to solve the problem is to employ the log-sum-exp, used in statistical modeling and machine learning. Nevertheless, it requires one more reduction operation to find the maximum likelihood value. On the other hand, the Gumbel-max scheme allows the algorithm to stay on a log space and draw samples from the unnormalized log weight instead, limiting the applicable choice of resampling algorithms to be multinomial resampling only. Given these trade-offs, we decide to use a log-sum-exp scheme to maintain numerical stability and consistency with the existing implementation. For parallelization on GPU, each thread processes each particle in the normalizing step and they jointly perform a reduction operation through a sequential addressing technique proposed by [7]. Half-precision version is similar except that each thread processes two particles at a time. The resampling kernel only involves a series of conditional checks.

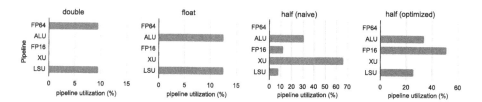

Fig. 2. The pipeline utilization for double-, single-, half-precision implementations on V100.

Performance Optimization. Next, we describe optimizations on hardware pipeline utilization on GPU. The initial implementation of half-precision implementation runs slower than single-precision implementation in our tests, even though it is already processing two packed particles in each `half2` element. Figure 2 presents the profiling results of pipeline utilization obtained from the NVIDIA Nsight Compute. After analysing the instruction mix and hardware pipeline, we find that FP16 pipeline is not as highly utilized as other pipelines like ALU and XU. The utilization of XU pipeline is surprisingly high, reaching 66%. The XU pipeline is responsible for special functions like sin, cos, and reciprocal square root and also int-to-float and float-to-int type conversions. The utilization of ALU pipeline is as expected as conversion between FP32 and FP16 may be included, e.g., NVIDIA Ampere architecture. Also, not all functions in CUDA library supports half-precision, e.g., cuRAND API, and single-precision operations are still used. We optimized the resampling kernel based on these findings, by reducing the computation of reciprocal operations and data casting operations for particles with a saved constant. The optimized half-precision implementation not only removes the bottleneck on XU pipeline but also much improved FP16 utilization, increasing from 10% to 50% as shown in Fig. 2.

5   Experimental Setup and Evaluation

We evaluate our particle filter implementation for three different precisions, namely `double`, `float` and `half` on four different Nvidia GPU testbeds. We summarize the hardware and software environments in Table 1. For reproducible comparison across different precision implementations, the same random number generator seed is used.

Table 1. Nvidia GPUs hardware and software testbeds.

GPU	Compute Capability	CUDA Version	GPU Memory	Peak FP32 (non-Tensor)
Nvidia V100	7.0	11.7	32GB HBM2	14.0 TFLOPS
Nvidia A100	8.0	11.7	40GB HBM2e	19.5 TFLOPS
Nvidia A40	8.6	12.0	48GB GDDR6	37.4 TFLOPS
Nvidia T4	7.5	11.7	16GB GDDR6	8.1 TFLOPS

Verification and Accuracy Results. As the first step of this work, we verify the correctness of our implementations and assess the impact of performing object tracking with lower precision. To achieve this, we execute the particle filter algorithm on a 100-frame video with a resolution of 512×512 pixels, as proposed in the original `Rodinia` particle filter mini-application. This synthetic video represents a circular-shaped object moving in a two dimensional plane xy. The object moves towards the wall at $y = 0$ and bounce back specularly. A single level of pixel intensity is chosen for the background and the foreground. Finally, a Gaussian noise is added to the frame. An example of frame and the tracked trajectories produced by the particle filter with 128 particles and the ground truth trajectory are presented in Figs. 3 and 4.

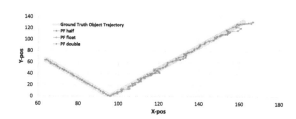

Fig. 3. Object tracking in a 128 × 128 video for evaluation.

Fig. 4. Object tracking using full, single, and half precision particle filter implementations and comparison with the ground truth.

We observe that the baseline double-precision implementation follows accurately the ground truth trajectory. In addition, the predictions obtained with the single-precision implementation exactly match those obtained with the baseline implementation, for all input frames. This first observation indicates that the reduction of precision from double-precision to single-precision did not have any impact on the accuracy of the predictions. The predictions obtained with our half-precision implementation provide comparable accuracy with regard to the ground truth. These results validate the use of lower-precision number representations in the particle filter algorithm, as both single- and half-precision implementations provided accurate tracking of the object in this experiment, and exhibited similar results compared to the baseline double-precision implementation. The results on accuracy confirm that particle filter algorithm and also statistical learning, in general, are resistant to low-precision computation.

Overall Performance. As second step of our study, we evaluate the average execution time for 100 runs of the particle filter at three levels of precision and speed up achieved by using reduced precision. We perform this evaluation for two problem sizes by using either 32k or 64k particles and 128 threads per block. Figure 5 show the results in terms of execution time, along with the speedup provided by our optimized half-precision implementation, over the `double` baseline. For both problem sizes, we consistently observe that the single and half precision implementations outperform the double-precision baseline, on all four GPU architectures. Furthermore, our half precision implementation outperforms the single precision implementation in all test cases. The highest speedup value is reached on the T4 GPU, namely 4.59× and 4.94× for 32k and 64k particles, respectively. While the execution time for the double-precision implementation varies significantly across architectures, the execution time for both single- and half-precision implementations is consistent across all four GPU architectures. We observe that the speedup provided by our half-precision implementation is above 4× on both A40 and T4, while it is close to 2.5× on both V100 and A100. This difference is induced by the low performance observed in double-precision for A40 and T4, compared to the two other GPUs. We explain this difference by the target workloads those GPUs were designed to run. The Tesla T4 GPU is designed primarily for machine learning workloads, which requires higher single-precision performance and relatively low double-precision performance. A40 also follows the same trend, where single- and half-precision performance are favored in GPU design, producing relatively low double-precision performance.

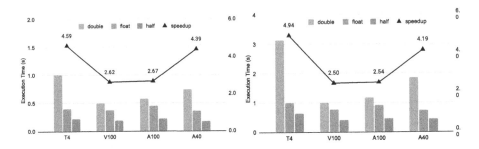

Fig. 5. Execution time and speedup for particle filters with 32k and 64k particles.

Performance Breakdown. Next, we investigate in detail the effect of using lower levels of precision on the execution time of essential kernels. We also include a comparison of the optimized and naive versions of our half-precision implementation, both in terms of kernel runtime, and GPU pipeline utilization. The profiling results of the two major kernels – resampling, and normalizing – are presented in Fig. 6. They were obtained through profiling using NVIDIA Nsight Systems, with 8192 particles, on V100 GPU. In this experiment 100 samples for each kernel are captured, as we run the particle filter on a 100-frame video. Our results show that the introduction of single precision improved the runtime compared to the double-precision baseline, for both the resampling and normalizing kernels, by respectively 16% and 28%. This observation is coherent with the overall runtime improvement observed previously.

The naive version of the half-precision implementation does not provide satisfactory runtime improvement for the resampling kernel. However, the optimized half-precision implementation provided a significant speedup over both the double-precision and single-precision implementations for the resampling kernel, namely ×3.0 and ×2.7, respectively. These observations validate the necessity of our optimization efforts.

To evaluate the effect of the optimizations on the device utilization, we profile the resampling kernel using NVIDIA Nsight Compute to collect statistics on the utilization of computing pipelines. The results for both naive and optimized half-precision implementations are detailed in Fig. 7. We observe that the utilization of ALU, FP16, and LSU pipelines is significantly higher for the optimized version than for the naive one. In particular, the FP16 pipeline, which is responsible for arithmetic operations on half-precision numbers, exhibits a 12% utilization in the non-optimized version, while the optimized version reaches a 51% utilization of this pipeline. Additionally, we observe that the XU pipeline is being heavily utilized in the non-optimized version, while it is not utilized at

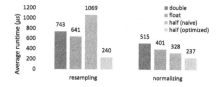
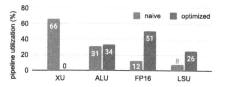
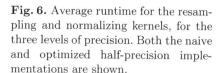

Fig. 6. Average runtime for the resampling and normalizing kernels, for the three levels of precision. Both the naive and optimized half-precision implementations are shown.

Fig. 7. Pipeline utilization for the resampling kernel, for the naive and optimized half-precision implementations, on V100. Pipelines with utilization below 5% are not shown.

all in the optimized version. This indicates precisely where our optimization had effect, and we make the hypothesis that this high utilization of the XU pipeline was limiting the performance, and explains the low FP16 utilization.

Impact of Thread Block Configuration. Finally, we investigate the impact of thread block configuration for several GPU architectures. To perform this evaluation, we execute the three implementations using various numbers of threads per block, between 32 and 1024. The results in terms of speedup over the worst-performing configuration are shown on Fig. 8 for the four GPU models. We observe that decreasing the block size below 1024 threads generally increases speedup up to 128 threads, where it starts to plateau. Both V100 and A100

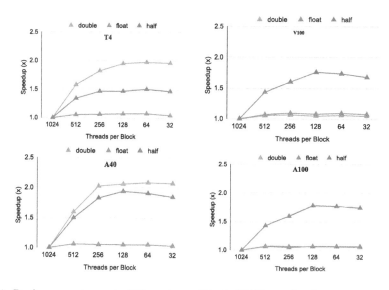

Fig. 8. Performance impact of Threads per Block (TPB) on the three versions on four GPU architectures.

GPUs exhibit similar characteristics, where the speedup for double- and single-precision implementations is below ×1.1 for all block configurations. However, the performance of the half-precision implementation appears to significantly benefit from decreasing the number of threads per block. The maximum speedup for those two GPUs is ×1.8 when using a block size of 128. For A40 and T4 GPUs, the double-precision version is the implementation which benefits the most from decreasing the block size. The maximum speedup of ×2 is reached when using 64 threads per block. To a lower extent, the runtime of the half-precision implementation also improves when reducing the number of threads per block. As for the two other GPUs, the runtime for single-precision is hardly impacted by the block size.

6   Discussion and Conclusion

In this work, we presented a multi-precision implementation of a particle filter on GPU, which supports half-, single-, and double-precision floating points. We showed that Using half-precision leads to a performance improvement of 1.5–2 × and 2.5–4.6 × with respect to single- and double-precision baselines respectively, at the cost of a relatively small loss of accuracy.

Our study shows that algorithm re-design is needed to effectively leverage half-precision operations in particle filter codes on CUDA cores. Our initial porting to half precision has already re-designed algorithms to use intrinsics to pack two FP16 values into one FP32 register using the vector type $half2$ for boosting the utilization of the FP32 pipeline. Still, it did not lead to performance benefits and even caused performance degradation due to the increased conversion instructions causing skewed utilization of hardware pipelines. Also, we note that re-designing large-scale applications to use intrinsics may not always be feasible in practice.

We evaluated the accuracy loss due to reduced precision in an object-tracking application. One limitation of our current design is that up to 64k particles can be used in a particle filter. This is a reasonable assumption because, unlike machine learning, approximate inferences, including particle filters, are relatively small in terms of problem size. Our work focuses on half-precision FP16 operations on CUDA cores, while previous works have shown mixed-precision on Tensor Core could bring even higher throughput but require refactoring algorithms into matrix-multiplication forms, which we plan to explore in future work.

Acknowledgements. This work is funded by the European Union. This work has received funding from the European High Performance Computing Joint Undertaking (JU) and Sweden, Finland, Germany, Greece, France, Slovenia, Spain, and the Czech Republic under grant agreement No 101093261. The computations were enabled by resources provided by the National Academic Infrastructure for Supercomputing in Sweden (NAISS) at KTH, partially funded by the Swedish Research Council through grant agreement no. 2022-06725.

References

1. Che, S., et al.: Rodinia: a benchmark suite for heterogeneous computing. In: 2009 IEEE International Symposium on Workload Characterization, pp. 44–54. IEEE (2009)
2. Chitchian, M., van Amesfoort, A.S., Simonetto, A., Keviczky, T., Sips, H.J.: Adapting particle filter algorithms to many-core architectures. In: 2013 IEEE 27th International Symposium on Parallel and Distributed Processing, pp. 427–438. IEEE (2013)
3. Goodrum, M.A., Trotter, M.J., Aksel, A., Acton, S.T., Skadron, K.: Parallelization of particle filter algorithms. In: Varbanescu, A.L., Molnos, A., van Nieuwpoort, R. (eds.) ISCA 2010. LNCS, vol. 6161, pp. 139–149. Springer, Heidelberg (2011). https://doi.org/10.1007/978-3-642-24322-6_12
4. Gordon, N.J., Salmond, D.J., Smith, A.F.: Novel approach to nonlinear/nongaussian Bayesian state estimation. In: IEE Proceedings F (radar and signal processing), vol. 140, pp. 107–113. IET (1993)
5. Haidar, A., Tomov, S., Dongarra, J., Higham, N.J.: Harnessing GPU tensor cores for fast FP16 arithmetic to speed up mixed-precision iterative refinement solvers. In: Supercomputing 18, pp. 603–613. IEEE (2018)
6. Harris, M.: Mixed-precision programming with CUDA 8 (2016). https://developer.nvidia.com/blog/mixed-precision-programming-cuda-8/
7. Harris, M.: Optimizing parallel reduction in CUDA (2017). https://developer.download.nvidia.com/assets/cuda/files/reduction.pdf
8. Hendeby, G., Karlsson, R., Gustafsson, F.: Particle Filtering: the need for speed. EURASIP J. Adv. Signal Process. **2010**, 1–9 (2010)
9. Ho, N.M., Wong, W.F.: Exploiting half precision arithmetic in NVIDIA GPUs. In: 2017 IEEE HPEC,. pp. 1–7. IEEE (2017)
10. Hsiao, K., Miller, J., de Plinval-Salgues, H.: Particle filters and their applications. Cogn. Robot. 4 (2005)
11. Jaward, M., Mihaylova, L., Canagarajah, N., Bull, D.: Multiple object tracking using particle filters. In: 2006 IEEE Aerospace Conference, p. 8. IEEE (2006)
12. Li, T., Bolic, M., Djuric, P.M.: Resampling methods for particle filtering: classification, implementation, and strategies. IEEE Signal Process. Mag. **32**(3), 70–86 (2015)
13. Markidis, S., Der Chien, S.W., Laure, E., Peng, I.B., Vetter, J.S.: Nvidia tensor core programmability, performance & precision. In: 2018 IEEE International Parallel and Distributed Processing Symposium Workshops (IPDPSW), pp. 522–531. IEEE (2018)
14. Murray, L.M., Lee, A., Jacob, P.E.: Parallel resampling in the particle filter. J. Comput. Graph. Stat. **25**(3), 789–805 (2016)
15. Nguyen, H.: GPU Gems 3. Addison-Wesley Professional (2007)
16. Nicely, M.A., Wells, B.E.: Improved parallel resampling methods for particle filtering. IEEE Access **7**, 47593–47604 (2019). https://doi.org/10.1109/ACCESS.2019.2910163
17. Schön, T.B.: Solving nonlinear state estimation problems using particle filters-an engineering perspective. Linköping University, Linköping, Department of Automatic Control (2010)

Tall-and-Skinny QR Factorization for Clusters of GPUs Using High-Performance Building Blocks

Andrés E. Tomás[1,2(✉)] [iD] and Enrique S. Quintana-Ortí[1] [iD]

[1] Depto. de Informática de Sistemas y Computadores, Universitat Politècnica de València, Valencia, Spain
antodo@upv.es, Andres.Tomas@uv.es
[2] Dpto. de Informática, Universitat de València, Valencia, Spain
quintana@disca.upv.es,

Abstract. We build a message-passing realization of the QR factorization for tall-and-skinny matrices on top of highly parallel linear algebra kernels, such as various types of matrix multiplications and triangular system solves, plus a few small Cholesky decompositions. Our solution, using either the NVIDIA Collective Communications Library (NCCL) or a plain instance of MPI as the message-passing layer, and the implementation of these kernels in linear algebra libraries, can run both on clusters of multicore nodes, possibly accelerated with GPUs, or on multi-GPU platforms.

The experimental evaluation of our parallel algorithm for the QR factorization on a cluster of 8 nodes with NVIDIA A100 boards shows significant acceleration factors over a code from MAGMA, based on Householder reflectors, that provides the same functionality. In addition, the experiments show a fair weak scalability when the problem has many more rows than columns.

Keywords: QR factorization · modified Gram-Schmidt method · high performance computing · graphics processing units (GPUs)

1 Introduction

The (compact) *QR factorization* [9] of a matrix $A \in \mathbb{R}^{m \times n}$ is given by

$$A = QR, \tag{1}$$

where $Q \in \mathbb{R}^{m \times n}$ has orthonormal columns and $R \in \mathbb{R}^{n \times n}$ is upper triangular. This decomposition is a key numerical tool for the solution of many linear algebra problems arising in a variety of scientific applications as well as in data analytics. For example, the QR factorization is employed in the solution of ill-conditioned linear systems and for tackling linear least squares problems. In addition, it is a fundamental component for the solution of eigenvalue problems, in numerical rank computations, and in principal component analysis (PCA) [9].

D. Zeinalipour et al. (Eds.): Euro-Par 2023 Workshops, LNCS 14351, pp. 306–317, 2024.
https://doi.org/10.1007/978-3-031-50684-0_24

When the matrix A is dense, the conventional algorithm to compute (1) applies a sequence of *Householder reflectors* to A from the left, with each transform eliminating the subdiagonal entries of one matrix column, from left to right [9]. For high performance, the Householder-based algorithm is often reformulated to view the input matrix as a collection of column blocks (or panels) of width b, and compute, assemble, and apply the Householder reflectors by blocks [13]. (For simplicity, hereafter we will assume that m, n are both integer multiplies of the algorithmic block size b.)

Unfortunately, when the matrix A is "tall-and-skinny" (that is, it has many more rows than columns; $m \gg n$), the Householder-based algorithms present a serious scalability problem [15]. A potential solution to this issue can be derived from the technique described in [10] to update the QR factorization of an out-of-core matrix in parallel. This work was latter combined with a runtime scheduler in order to exploit task-parallelism in [5,12]. The same ideas lie at the basis of the tall-and-skinny QR (TSQR) and the communication-avoiding QR (CAQR) algorithms for multicore processors and graphics processing units (GPUs) [2,7].

A common problem for all previous algorithms for the QR factorization is that computing the Householder reflectors and assembling them into block reflectors is a fine-grain process that is difficult to accelerate on a GPU. On the positive side, applying the block reflectors boils down to a couple of matrix multiplications, a type of operation that is known to deliver high performance on most current processor architectures, including GPUs.

In this paper we target the efficient, message-passing implementation of the QR factorization, for tall-and-skinny matrices, using highly parallel linear algebra kernels (building blocks) available in libraries for multicore processors and GPUs. In search for a higher scalability than that offered by the TSQR factorization methods, we make the following specific contributions:

- We abandon the Householder-based approach to adopt a double-pass of a blocked variant of the modified Gram-Schmidt (MGS) method with re-orthogonalization for numerical stability, and combine this algorithm with a Cholesky-based QR (CQR) factorization. While these two methods were already known, our work provides the first high performance implementation and evaluation of these combined methods for GPUs.
- We compose the algorithm using existing linear algebra libraries: NVIDIA cuBLAS for GPUs and Intel oneAPI (MKL) for multicore processors. In addition, we extend the codes with MPI (message-passing interface) [14] and the NVIDIA Collective Communication Library (NCCL), obtaining distributed versions that can seamlessly operate on a cluster of multicore nodes equipped with NVIDIA's GPUs as well as multi-GPU platforms.
- We evaluate the performance of the parallel codes on a cluster of eight nodes, each with one NVIDIA A100 GPU, including a comparison in a single-GPU scenario with the code available in MAGMA, based on Householder reflectors, for the same purpose.

The remainder of this paper is organized as follows. In Sect. 2 we describe the new algorithm for the QR factorization based on MGS+CQR and, next, in

Sect. 3, we assess its parallel performance and scalability. In Sect. 4 we close the paper with a short summary.

2   QR Factorization via BMGS and CHOLESKYQR

In this section we describe the algorithms and building blocks underlying our composable, high performance QR factorization. In addition, we offer the most relevant details for its practical implementation on a GPU platform as well as a cluster of GPU-accelerated nodes.

2.1   Gram-Schmidt Method

The MGS method and its classical Gram-Schmidt (CGS) counterpart provide well-known alternatives to compute the QR factorization of a matrix [4]. While both methods consist of a few fundamental, easy-to-parallelize building blocks, CGS offers high parallelism, at the cost of numerical stability, while MGS is intrinsically sequential, but numerically more reliable. To tackle this impasse, MGS can be reformulated into a blocked variant which, as in the case of the blocked Householder-based factorization, proceeds by column blocks, improving its performance while maintaining the numerical properties [6].

In our solution we adopt a double-pass blocked variant of MGS (BMGS) [11] that doubles the computational cost but guarantees that the orthogonal factor satisfies $\|Q^T Q - I\|_2 \approx \epsilon$. A double-pass version of CGS also attains this low bound on orthogonality. However, we prefer MGS because 1) that solution is then easier to integrate into an iterative GMRES-based solver for sparse linear systems, enhancing the composability of our codes; and 2) for the distributed version, BMGS provides more room to overlap computation and communication.

2.2   QR Factorization Using MGS

Our double-pass algorithm for the QR factorization initially applies BMGS to the matrix A (first pass) to obtain

$$A = \hat{Q} S, \tag{2}$$

where $\hat{Q}$ has (quasi-)orthogonal columns and S is upper triangular. Next, to improve numerical stability, it re-orthogonalizes $\hat{Q}$ by means of an additional QR factorization (second pass), computed using BMGS as well, yielding

$$\hat{Q} = Q T, \tag{3}$$

where Q has orthogonal columns, in principle to working precision, and T is upper triangular. As a result,

$$A = \hat{Q} S = (Q T) S = Q (T S) = QR, \tag{4}$$

and it only remains to multiply the two factors T, S in case the triangular factor R is necessary. The procedure is illustrated in Algorithm 1. Note the use of a common algorithmic block size b for all three "stages": the two calls to BMGS and the assembly of R.

Our realization of BMGS computes the factorizations in (2) and (4) by panels of b columns; see Algorithm 2. As corresponds to a blocked generalization of the MGS method, at each iteration of the outermost loop, indexed by j, the procedure orthogonalizes the "current" panel Q_j with respect to the panels to its left; see the innermost loop in the algorithm, indexed by i. The basic matrix operations appearing in BMGS are general matrix multiplications (GEMM) and a QR factorization involving an $m \times b$ block, with $b \ll n$.

Algorithm 1. QR factorization based on MGS.

INPUT: $A \in \mathbb{R}^{m \times n}$, block size b
OUTPUT: $Q \in \mathbb{R}^{m \times n}, R \in \mathbb{R}^{n \times n}$

S1. $[\hat{Q}, S] = $ BMGS (A, b)
S2. $[Q, T] = $ BMGS $(\hat{Q}, b)$
S3. $R = $ BUILDR (S, T, b)

Algorithm 2. BMGS: Block MGS based on CHOLESKYQR.

INPUT: $A \in \mathbb{R}^{m \times n}$, block size b
OUTPUT: $Q \in \mathbb{R}^{m \times n}, R \in \mathbb{R}^{n \times n}$

Partition A, Q into blocks
of b columns $\rightarrow A_j, Q_j$
Partition R into $b \times b$ blocks: $\rightarrow R_{i,j}$
for $j = 1$ to n/b
    $Q_j = A_j$
    for $i = 1$ to $j - 1$
S1. $R_{i,j} = Q_i^T Q_j$ (GEMM)
S2. $Q_j = Q_j - Q_i R_{i,j}$ (GEMM)
    end
S3. $[Q_j, R_{j,j}] = $ CHOLESKYQR (Q_j)
end

Algorithm 3. BUILDR: Assemble triangular factor.

INPUT: $S, T \in \mathbb{R}^{n \times n}$, block size b
OUTPUT: $R \in \mathbb{R}^{n \times n}$

Partition R, S, T into $b \times b$ blocks
    $\rightarrow R_{i,j}, S_{i,j}, T_{i,j}$
for $j = 1$ to n/b
    for $i = 1$ to $j - 1$
S1. $R_{i,j} = S_{i,j} + T_{i,j} S_{j,j}$ (TRMM)
    end
S2. $R_{j,j} = T_{j,j} S_{j,j}$ (TTMM)
end

Algorithm 4. CHOLESKYQR factorization.

INPUT: $A \in \mathbb{R}^{m \times b}$
OUTPUT: $Q \in \mathbb{R}^{m \times b}, R \in \mathbb{R}^{b \times b}$

S1. $W = A^T A$ (GEMM)
S2. $W = R^T R$ (POTRF)
    if not breakdown then
S3. $Q = A R^{-1}$ (TRSM)
    else
S4. $W = A^T A + s I_b$
S5. $W = R_1^T R_1$ (POTRF)
S6 $Q = A R_1^{-1}$ (TRSM)
S7. $W = Q^T Q$ (GEMM)
S8. $W = R_2^T R_2$ (POTRF)
S9. $Q = A R_2^{-1}$ (TRSM)
S10. $R = R_2 R_1$ (TTMM)
    end

To attain higher efficiency, the triangular-triangular matrix multiplication (TTMM) $R = TS$ in (4), to be computed at the end of Algorithm 1, is implemented as a blocked, structure-aware product that decomposes the operation into a collection of triangular-dense matrix multiplications (TRMM) and

TTMM with both types of operations involving $b \times b$ blocks. An additional optimization [3] exploits that the triangular factors to be multiplied come from two "coupled" orthogonalizations to reduce the computational cost of this operation from cubic on the problem dimension n to quadratic; see Algorithm 3.

In our case, the QR factorization appearing in the BMGS algorithm (step S3) is computed using a variant of the SHIFTEDCHOLESKYQR3 procedure from [8], displayed in Algorithm 4. The latter is composed of GEMM, Cholesky decomposition (POTRF), triangular system solves (TRSM) and TTMM. Since we can select $b \ll n$, the particular contribution of the CHOLESKYQR algorithm to the total cost of BMGS can be expected to be small.

Our variant of Algorithm 4 includes only two Cholesky decompositions instead of the three in SHIFTEDCHOLESKYQR3. This is because Algorithm 4 is called twice as part of the re-orthogonalization. The first invocation computes an initial Cholesky decomposition (or two, when a shift is required) while the second invocation computes the second (or third) Cholesky decomposition. In practice, the second invocation does not need to check for a breakdown and, if necessary, apply the shift, but we keep it in the algorithm for simplicity. Moreover, the overhead of the test is negligible as the operations inside the conditional are never executed. The shift s in Algorithm 4 is computed as

$$s = 11\,\epsilon(mn + n^2 + n)\,\|A^T A\|_F^2, \tag{5}$$

which has to be added to the Gram matrix in order to ensure that the Cholesky decomposition succeeds numerically [8].

2.3 Building Blocks from High Performance Libraries

Our realization of the QR factorization based on BMGS is composed of several basic linear algebra kernels such as multiplications involving matrix operands of distinct forms (general, triangular-general, triangular-triangular) and triangular system solves, plus the Cholesky decomposition. In order to compute these basic operations, we rely on NVIDIA's high performance linear algebra routines for GPUs in cuBLAS, except for a few cases. Concretely, due to the complexity of the Cholesky decomposition and TTMM, and the small dimension of their operands, we leverage LAPACK to compute these two kernels on the CPU.

Table 1 specifies 1) the routines employed for the operation at each step of the algorithms and building blocks; 2) the libraries they belong to; 3) the target architecture (GPU, CPU or hybrid); 4) their theoretical costs (in floating point operations, or flops); and 5) the matrix transfers between CPU and GPU.

Computing the QR factorization via Householder transforms requires $2n^2(m - n/3)$ flops to obtain the triangular factor plus $2n^2(m - n/3)$ flops to assemble (the n columns of) the Q factor in the compact QR factorization. For tall-and-skinny matrices, the total cost is thus $4mn^2$ flops, which is about the same as the cost of the QR factorization via (the double-pass) algorithm based on BMGS.

As an additional detail, the computation of BUILDR (Algorithm 3) is performed inside the loops of BMGS (Algorithm 2) as soon as the blocks of R, T

and S are available. This allows to overlap the computations of BUILDR in the CPU with the computations of BMGS in the GPU. In this way, the whole R is stored in the CPU saving some precious workspace on the GPU.

Table 1. Algorithms and building blocks considering A is an $m \times n$ matrix. In the cost expressions, $CA2, CA3, CA4$ respectively return the cost of Algorithms 2 (BUILDR), 3 (BMGS), 4 (CHOLESKYQR) as a function of their parameters.

Algorithm	Step	Algorithm/routine	Library	Target	Cost	Matrix transfers
Algorithm 1	S1/S2	Algorithm 3	–	Hybrid	$CA3(m, n, b)$	
QR fact	S3	Algorithm 2	–	Hybrid	$CA2(n, b)$	
	Total cost:	$2\,CA3(m, n, b) + CA2(n, b) = 4mn^2 + n^2/2$				
Algorithm 2	S1	TRMM	cuBLAS	GPU	$b^3/2$	
BUILDR	S2	TTMM	Custom	CPU	$b^3/3$	
	Total cost:	$\sum_{j=1}^{n/b}\left[\sum_{i=1}^{j-1}(b^2)\right] + b^3/3 \approx n^2/2$				
Algorithm 3	S1	GEMM	cuBLAS	GPU	$2mb^2$	
BMGS	S2	GEMM	cuBLAS	GPU	$2mb^2$	
	S3	Algorithm 4	–	Hybrid	$CA4(m, b)$	
	Total cost:	$\sum_{j=1}^{n/b}\left[\sum_{i=1}^{j-1}(4mb^2) + CA4(m, b)\right] \approx 2mn^2$				
Algorithm 4	S1/S7	GEMM	cuBLAS	GPU	$2mb^2$	
CHOLESKYQR	S2/S5/S8	POTRF	LAPACK	CPU	$b^3/3$	W GPU$\to$CPU
	S3/S6/S9	TRSM	cuBLAS	GPU	mb^2	$R/R_1/R_2$ CPU$\to$GPU
	S4	Sum	–	GPU	b^2	
	S10	TTMM	BLAS	Custom	$b^3/3$	
	Total cost:	$3mb^2 + b^3/3$ in case no breakdown;				
		$6mb^2 + 4b^3/3 + b^2$ otherwise				

2.4 Message-Passing Codes for Clusters

For portability, the distributed-memory version of the BMGS-based algorithm employs MPI as the communication layer. In addition, we developed an alternative version that employs NCCL to improve performance. Given that the target matrices are tall-and-skinny, the $m \times n$ operand A is distributed among the p cluster nodes across the m-dimension, in chunks (i.e., row blocks) of $r = m/p$ rows. (For simplicity, we assume that m is an integer multiple of p.) From this matrix partitioning, we can derive the following workload distribution for the three building blocks that compose the QR factorization based on BMGS:

– For BMGS (see Algorithm 2), each node computes a partial contribution to the result of the GEMM in step S1 by multiplying its local chunks of Q_j^T and Q_i. This is then followed by a global reduction (`Allreduce`) that leaves the result of the multiplication, $R_{i,j}$, replicated in all nodes. In step S2, each node multiplies its local chunk of Q_i with the replicated $R_{i,j}$ to update its local chunk of Q_j.

– For CHOLESKYQR, each node computes a partial Gram matrix followed by a reduction (`Reduce`) to node 0. This node then computes the Cholesky decomposition and broadcasts it to all nodes (`Bcast`). With this result, all nodes update its copy of R and its local chunk of Q.

An alternative that avoids the broadcast is to build the Gram matrix with an `Allreduce` and replicate the computation of the Cholesky decomposition in all nodes. However, this alternative may result in divergence problems as the detection of the breakdown can be skewed by tiny round-off differences among the Cholesky decompositions computed by each node.

– As it is performed inside BMGS, BUILDR does not require any extra communication.

3 Experimental Results

The performance results reported in this section were obtained using IEEE double precision arithmetic, on a cluster of 8 nodes connected via a 200 Gbit/s Infiniband network. Each node comprises two AMD EPYC 7282 16-core CPUs plus an NVIDIA A100 GPU with 40GB of DDR5 RAM. The LAPACK routines are those in Intel oneAPI version 2021.2, while NVIDIA cuBLAS version 11.7 provides the BLAS-level routines for the GPU. The MPI communication routines are provided by the NVIDIA NCCL library. This library does not strictly adhere to the MPI standard, but it provides all the functionality required by BMGSCQR. Besides, the NCCL interface is so close to MPI that our implementation can switch between the two communication layers by just adjusting a pre-processor macro. The compiler and the rest of system software have little impact on performance as all the computationally expensive code is inside the previous linear algebra and communication libraries.

As the target of this work are large tall-and-skinny problems, we select for the evaluation problems with either 100,000 (100K) or 1,000,000 (1M) rows, and between 1,000 and 5,000 columns. All matrices have random entries following a uniform distribution in the $]-1,1[$ interval. The execution time in the experiments corresponds to the average of several executions for each problem size. In all tests a block size b of 128 was used as it is either optimal or very close to it.

3.1 Comparison with MAGMA

The first experiment in this section compares the GPU implementation of our algorithm, hereafter referred to as BMGSCQR, against the conventional approach for the QR factorization, based on (blocked) Householder reflectors, as implemented in the last version of MAGMA (v2.7.1) [1]. MAGMA follows LAPACK to implement a Householder-based factorization, with a code that is divided into two routines: DGEQRF and DORGQR. The first one computes the triangular factor R and leaves the Householder reflectors stored in a compact form. The second explicitly builds the orthogonal matrix Q. As BMGSCQR computes the orthogonal factor Q directly, for a fair comparison, the execution

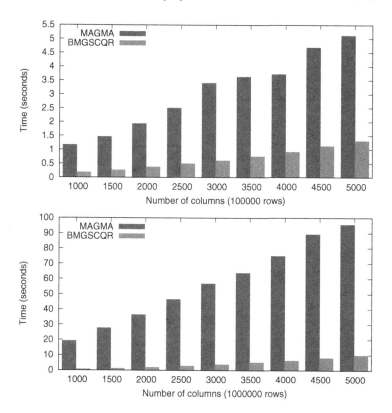

Fig. 1. Performance of BMGSCQR with matrices of 100K rows (top) and 1M rows (bottom), and varying number of columns, compared to MAGMA (DGEQRF + DORGQR) on an NVIDIA A100 GPU.

times reported in this section for MAGMA include the cost of executing both routines. In the experiments we observed that, in general, the time for DORGQR is an order of magnitude smaller than that for DGEQRF, mainly because for MAGMA, routine DORGQR is entirely executed on the GPU. MAGMA chooses the same block size that we set for BMGSCQR: 128. Therefore, the performance of the cuBLAS GEMM kernels executed from MAGMA and BMGSCQR should be similar.

Figure 1 shows the results of this first experiment. While the experimental execution times of the two algorithms should grow quadratically with n, as corresponds to a theoretical cost of $4mn^2$ flops for tall-and-skinny matrices and both algorithms, the increase looks more like linear. This is due to the large values for m, which hide the effects of varying the much smaller dimension n. In contrast, comparing the two plots in the figure, for BMGSCQR we observe a linear increase with m, while for MAGMA this increase is roughly proportional to $2m$. For example, for the matrix with 5,000 columns, the execution time for BMGSCQR grows from 1.23 to 9.75 s(econds) when m is increased from 100K to 1M. For MAGMA, the difference is 5.12 to 95.6 s for the same increase in m. Explaining this behaviour of MAGMA would require a careful inspection of the codes in this library and is beyond the scope of our work.

The direct comparison between BMGSCQR and MAGMA shows a clear balance in favor of the former for these problem sizes. The acceleration for BMGSCQR varies between 4× and 5× for the 100K matrix. For the 1M matrix the acceleration approximately ranges from 10× with 5,000 columns up to 30× with 1,000 columns. The discussion in the previous paragraph on the effect of increasing the m-dimension on the execution time also explains why the differences between both algorithms are larger for the problem with 1M rows.

3.2   Parallel Scalability

The second experiment in this section investigates the scalability of BMGSCQR as we increase the number of cluster nodes p and, correspondingly, GPUs. Since the dimensions of the target problems are (initially) fixed, being independent of the number of GPUs, this corresponds a *strong scaling* scenario. MAGMA can-

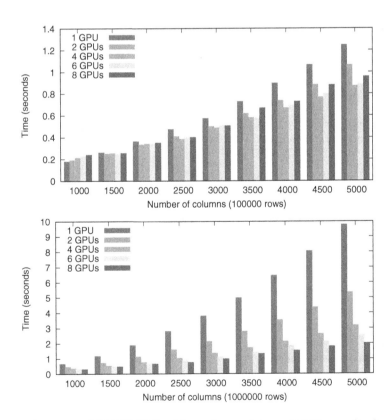

Fig. 2. Performance of BMGSCQR with random matrices of 100K rows (top) and 1M rows (bottom), and varying number of columns using several NVIDIA A100 GPUs.

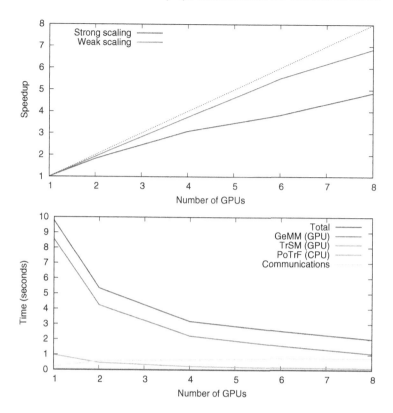

Fig. 3. Performance of BMGSCQR with a random matrix of 1M rows and 5,000 columns, for different number of nodes/NVIDIA A100 GPUs.

not operate with multiple nodes and, therefore, is not included in the following experiments.

Figure 2 displays the results of the strong scaling experiment for the two problem row-dimensions. The top plot in the figure reports the speedup for the cases with 100K rows, showing only a visible improvement for the problems with largest column-dimension and, then, only when increasing the number of GPUs up to 2. For the problems with fewer columns, there is no visible acceleration when using 2 GPUs. Independently of the number of columns, the use of more than 2 GPUs is not justified either.

The cases with 1M rows, in the bottom plot in Fig. 2, show a different scenario: For this dimension there is a clear benefit from exploiting several GPUs, with speed-ups ranging from 1.85× with 2 GPUs to 5× with 8 GPUs. This is more clearly visible in the top plot in Fig. 3, which displays the strong scaling trend for the largest problem dimension: 1M rows and 5,000 columns (line with the label "Strong scaling"). The bottom plot in that figure decomposes the execution time of that particular case into four components: GEMM, TRSM, PoTRF, and communication. The results in that plot expose that, for 8 GPUs,

316 A. S. E. Tomás and . E. S. Quintana-Ortí

the speedup is limited because the computation time decreases to the point where it is comparable to the communication costs.

To obtain a better idea of the parallelization efficiency of BMGSCQR, Fig. 3 (top) also reports the results for a *weak scaling* experiment, showing the acceleration of BMGSCQR for a problem case with 1M rows per GPU (and a fixed number of 5,000 columns). This scenario shows a speed-up near to 7× for 8 GPUs, close to the ideal rate.

4 Concluding Remarks

We have explored an alternative approach to compute the QR factorization that consists of a double-pass blocked MGS method and the CholeskyQR factorization. Compared with the conventional algorithm, based on blocked Householder reflectors, our BMGSCQR algorithm presents the same computational cost, is numerically stable for most practical problems, and offers a number of appealing properties:

- From the point of view of portability and performance, BMGSCQR is composed of a number of basic building blocks for which there exist highly tuned, parallel realizations in multi-threaded linear algebra libraries for both GPUs and multicore processors.
- BMGSCQR can be easily extended with the standardized communication primitives to obtain a message-passing version for clusters of computer nodes (with or without GPUs) as well as in multi-GPU platforms.

Our results on an NVIDIA A100 GPU show a significant acceleration over a conventional solution based on the routines in MAGMA for the same functionality. In addition, the experiments with the message-passing versions of our codes report reasonable weak and strong scalability for problems involving large tall-and-skinny matrices.

Acknowledgements. This work received funding from project PID2020-113656RB-C22 of MCIN/AEI/ 10.13039/501100011033; and the European High-Performance Computing Joint Undertaking (JU) under grant agreement No 955558 (eFlows4HPC project). The JU receives support from the European Union's Horizon 2020 research and innovation programme, and Spain, Germany, France, Italy, Poland, Switzerland, Norway.

References

1. Agullo, E., et al.: Numerical linear algebra on emerging architectures: The PLASMA and MAGMA projects, vol. 180 (2009)
2. Anderson, M., Ballard, G., Demmel, J., Keutzer, K.: Communication-avoiding QR decomposition for GPUs. In: 2011 IEEE International Parallel & Distributed Processing Symposium, pp. 48–58 (2011). https://doi.org/10.1109/IPDPS.2011.15
3. Barlow, J., Smoktunowicz, A.: Reorthogonalized block classical gram-Schmidt. Numer. Math. **123**(3), 395–423 (2013)

4. Björck, A.: Numerical Methods for Least Squares Problems. SIAM (1996)
5. Buttari, A., Langou, J., Kurzak, J., Dongarra, J.: A class of parallel tiled linear algebra algorithms for multicore architectures. Parallel Comput. **35**(1), 38–53 (2009). https://doi.org/10.1016/j.parco.2008.10.002
6. Carson, E., Lund, K., Rozložník, M., Thomas, S.: Block gram-schmidt algorithms and their stability properties. Linear Algebra Appl. **638**, 150–195 (2022). https://www.sciencedirect.com/science/article/pii/S0024379521004523
7. Demmel, J., Grigori, L., Hoemmen, M., Langou, J.: Communication-optimal parallel and sequential QR and LU factorizations. SIAM J. Sci. Comput. **34**(1), A206–A239 (2012). https://doi.org/10.1137/080731992
8. Fukaya, T., Kannan, R., Nakatsukasa, Y., Yamamoto, Y., Yanagisawa, Y.: Shifted Cholesky QR for computing the QR factorization of ill-conditioned matrices. SIAM J. Sci. Comput. **42**(1), A477–A503 (2020). https://doi.org/10.1137/18M1218212
9. Golub, G.H., Loan, C.F.V.: Matrix Computations, 3rd edn. The Johns Hopkins University Press, Baltimore (1996)
10. Gunter, B.C., van de Geijn, R.A.: Parallel out-of-core computation and updating the QR factorization. ACM Trans. Math. Soft. **31**(1), 60–78 (2005). http://doi.acm.org/10.1145/1055531.1055534
11. Leon, S.J., Björck, Å., Gander, W.: Gram-Schmidt orthogonalization: 100 years and more. Numer. Linear Algebra Appl. **20**(3), 492–532 (2013). https://onlinelibrary.wiley.com/doi/abs/10.1002/nla.1839
12. Quintana-Ortí, G., Quintana-Ortí, E.S., van de Geijn, R.A., Zee, F.G.V., Chan, E.: Programming matrix algorithms-by-blocks for thread-level parallelism. ACM Trans. Math. Softw. **36**(3), 1–26 (2009). https://doi.org/10.1145/1527286.1527288
13. Schreiber, R., Van Loan, C.: A storage-efficient WY representation for products of Householder transformations. SIAM J. Sci. Stat. Comput. **10**(1), 53–57 (1989). https://doi.org/10.1137/0910005
14. Snir, M., Otto, S.W., Huss-Lederman, S., Walker, D.W., Dongarra, J.: MPI: The Complete Reference. The MIT Press, Cambridge (1996)
15. Strazdins, P.: A comparison of lookahead and algorithmic blocking techniques for parallel matrix factorization. Technical report. TR-CS-98-07, Department of Computer Science, The Australian National University, Canberra 0200 ACT, Australia (1998)

Scheduling Fork-Joins to Heterogeneous Processors

Huijun Wang$^{(\boxtimes)}$ and Oliver Sinnen

Department of Electrical, Computer, and Software Engineering,
University of Auckland, Auckland, New Zealand
huijw@live.com

Abstract. The scheduling of task graphs with communication delays has been extensively studied. Recently, new results for the common sub-case of fork-join shaped task graphs were published, including an EPTAS and polynomial algorithms for special cases. These new results modelled the target architecture to consist of homogeneous processors. However, forms of heterogeneity become more and more common in contemporary parallel systems, such as CPU–accelerator systems, with their two types of resources. In this work, we study the scheduling of fork-join task graphs with communication delays, which is representative of highly parallel workloads, onto heterogeneous systems of related processors. We present an EPAS (efficient parameterised approximation scheme), and some polynomial time algorithms for special cases, such as with equal processing costs or unlimited resources. Lastly, we briefly look at the above described case of two resource-types and its implications. It is interesting to note, that all results here also apply to scheduling independent tasks with release times and deadlines.

1 Introduction

Task scheduling is one of the steps in parallelising a computational workload, where units of work (called tasks) are scheduled onto the available resources, to optimise for the schedule length (makespan). The structure of such a workload can be represented by a directed acyclic graph, where nodes represent tasks, edges represent data dependencies between them, and weights represent the associated costs of computation (processing) and communication (data transfer). This problem is generally intractable and difficult to approximate as well. In a typically studied model, tasks are scheduled across homogeneous processors, with communications between each other, each incurring communication delays. With varied and evolving architectures, it is becoming more appropriate to model systems of heterogeneous processors. Although results are generalised to an arbitrary number of processors, a typical example of heterogeneity consists of two types of resources, each representing a general purpose processor or one type of accelerator resource such as GPU, FPGA, or other specialised hardware, and sometimes with clusters of each kind in proximity. Many high performance parallel computing systems, in particular the largest supercomputers [16], have

D. Zeinalipour et al. (Eds.): Euro-Par 2023 Workshops, LNCS 14351, pp. 318–329, 2024.
https://doi.org/10.1007/978-3-031-50684-0_25

such an architecture. In terms of the workload structure, we use the fork-join structure in particular, which represents a significant subclass of parallel computations, as well as being a basic substructure that is common to other structures such as the series-parallel graph. It consists of a source task forking into many branch tasks, which in turn join back into a sink task. The source task prepares and divides the branch tasks, and the sink task gathers and combines results for subsequent steps. This can represent master-worker types of computations etc., and is representative of highly parallel workloads in general. More examples include MapReduce computation with frameworks like Hadoop or scatter/gather communication when using MPI parallelism [14]. Also the parallel Executor-Service in Java supports such a fork-join pattern [17]. Even if these applications may need to schedule dynamically, or have other nuances, the theoretic treatment here is important to guiding heuristic design, creating benchmarks, and adds to the completeness of theoretical results in classical scheduling.

Workloads that make use of accelerators are often highly parallel, and lend themselves to the fork-join structure. This paper investigates the optimisation problems that involve scheduling fork-join structures to heterogeneous processors, and describes some theoretical solutions to them, which have been extended from scheduling to homogeneous processors. In all cases, the algorithms also apply to the equivalent problems in scheduling independent tasks with release times and deadlines.

The rest of the paper is organised as follows. Section 2 describes the problem formally and summarises our results. Section 3 outlines related works. Section 4 describes an EPAS parameterised by the ratio of processor speeds and Sect. 5 describes some exact algorithms for special cases.

2   Problem Definition

In this section we define the problem, including models of the processing systems as well as our workload. We begin with the task graph and the fork-join structure.

2.1   Task Graph

A task graph is a directed acyclic graph with nodes representing tasks and edges representing precedence constraints (which are communications).

The shape of a fork-join task graph is shown Fig. 1. It has a set of tasks J, including the source task j_{src} and sink task j_{sink}. Each task $j \in J$ has an associated processing cost $p_j \in P$, and each branch task $j \in J \setminus \{j_{src}, j_{sink}\}$ has an incoming communication from the source, with cost $\gamma_j^{in} \in \Gamma$, and outgoing communication to the sink, with cost $\gamma_j^{out} \in \Gamma$. It is to be scheduled on the following system.

2.2   System Model

In systems of *uniformly related* heterogeneous processors, each processor $m \in M$ has a speed $s_m \in S$, and executes a task j in time p_j/s_m.

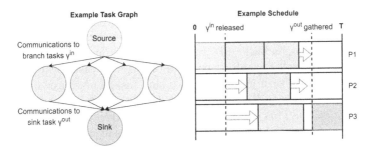

Fig. 1. Example of a parallel fork-join structure and its schedule.

Communication times are simply equal to the communication costs (there is no heterogeneity involved with the processing of communications), and no communication costs are incurred between tasks scheduled to the same processor (this is a common assumption in other works, e.g. [3,7]). Systems are modelled this way due to slower communications between processing resources not sharing memory.

Tasks scheduled to the same processor as the source or sink are said to be *local*, and tasks scheduled to other processors are said to be *remote*.

2.3 Schedule

A schedule consists of processor allocations $m_j \in M$ and start time allocations $\sigma_j \in \mathbb{N}_0$ for all tasks $j \in J$. The start time allocations are equivalent to a total order ($\leq_\sigma$) of execution over each set of tasks scheduled to the same processor, because optimally, tasks start as early as possible given their order. Therefore, for $i, j \in J$ scheduled consecutively on the same processor (meaning $i \leq_\sigma j$ and $\nexists k \in J: i \leq_\sigma k \leq_\sigma j$), the start time of j is

$$\sigma_j = \begin{cases} \max(\sigma_i + p_i/s_{m_i}, \, p_{src}/s_{m_{src}} + \gamma_j^{in}), & \text{if } m_j \neq m_{src} \\ \sigma_i + p_i/s_{m_i}, & \text{if } m_j = m_{src} \end{cases}$$

For $j = \min \leq_\sigma$, the first branch task on a processor,

$$\sigma_j = \begin{cases} p_{src}/s_{m_{src}} + \gamma_j^{in}, & \text{if } m_j \neq m_{src} \\ p_{src}/s_{m_{src}}, & \text{if } m_j = m_{src} \end{cases}$$

The objective is to find a schedule with optimal schedule length.

While with homogeneous processors we could have ignored the processing times of the source and sink tasks without loss of generality, this simplification does not hold when processor systems are heterogeneous. With the execution times of the source and sink tasks taken into account, the schedule length to be minimised is:

$$\max_{j \in J} \left(\sigma_j + p_j/s_{m_j} + \begin{cases} \gamma_j^{out}, & \text{if } m_j \neq m_{sink} \\ 0, & \text{if } m_j = m_{sink} \end{cases} \right) + p_{sink}/s_{m_{sink}}$$

2.4   Scheduling with Release Times and Deadlines

Scheduling fork-joins is related to scheduling independent tasks with release times and deadlines, where each task j has an associated release time r_j and a deadline d_j. When treated as a feasibility problem of scheduling under time T, a release time r_j would be equivalent to the incoming communication delay added to the execution time of the source $p_{src}/s_{m_{src}} + \gamma_j^{in}$, and a deadline d_j would be equivalent to $T - p_{sink}/s_{m_{sink}} - \gamma_j^{out}$. However, fork-join scheduling has to additionally consider the source and sink tasks and zeroed communication costs when tasks are scheduled to the same processor as the source or sink. Nevertheless, the results of this work for fork-joins, in particular the scheduling of the tasks allocated on remote processors, will also apply to scheduling with release times and deadlines. When extended to a minimisation problem, a minimisation objective when working with deadlines is L_{max}, the maximum lateness. [15] offers more discussion on this.

2.5   Source and Sink Allocation for Fork-Join Task Graphs

With the processing times of the source and sink tasks being different on each processor, they cannot be simplified away as with identical homogeneous processors, where the only choice that matters is whether the source and sink are on the same processor. Here, every different choice of processor type for the source and sink will affect the schedule. However, in the worst case, in a fully heterogeneous system and without any further analytical insight, an algorithm can be repeated once for each choice of source and sink processors ($|S|^2$ times in all), which would not change the class of complexity, or algorithm (for a theoretical purpose).

Proposition 1. *If a fork-join scheduling problem A can be solved in $sched(A)$ time with source and sink allocations given, then A can be solved in $|S|^2 sched(A)$ time at worst.*

The following table summarises our results using the $\alpha|\beta|\gamma$ notation from [4].

Table 1. Summary of Results.

Problem	Results	Explained in Section
$Qm\|fork\text{-}join, c_{ij}\|C_{max}$		
$Qm\|r_j\|L_{max}$	sNP-hard, EPAS	4
$Q\|fork\text{-}join, c_{ij}, p_j = p\|C_{max}$	Open,	
$Q\|r_j, p_j = p\|L_{max}$	$(OPT+p_{max})$-approx	5.1
$Q2\|fork\text{-}join, c_{ij}, p_j = p\|C_{max}$		
$Q2\|r_j, p_j = p\|L_{max}$	P	5.2
$Q\infty\|fork\text{-}join, c_{ij}, p_j = p\|C_{max}$		
$Q\infty\|r_j, p_j = p\|L_{max}$	P	5.3

3 Related Work

Heterogeneous systems have been studied as early as [8]. Recently, other theoretical results have been presented for scheduling to heterogeneous systems regarding its complexity [12], as well as an EPTAS for scheduling independent tasks to uniformly related processors [10]. There has existed a 2-approximation for scheduling to unrelated processors [9], and a PTAS for minimising the weighted finish times on related processors [5]. There is a lack of approximation schemes for precedence constrained tasks such as in this work.

Recent attention has also been on the kind of system with just two resource types (modelling the CPU–accelerator set-up), with both theoretical [2] and practical results [1], and here is a review on such studies [3].

Regarding the scheduling of fork-join structures, recent work has been presented on an EPTAS [11] and other algorithms [15] for scheduling to homogeneous systems.

4 Efficient Parameterised Approximation Scheme

We describe an Efficient Parameterised Approximation Scheme (EPAS) for heterogeneous systems of uniformly related processors, as extended from an EPTAS for the homogeneous model [11]. The EPAS is parameterised by the ratio between the fastest and slowest processor speeds $\frac{s_{max}}{s_{min}}$ and returns a solution within $1 + \mathcal{O}(\epsilon)$ of the optimal in $\mathcal{O}(f(\frac{1}{\epsilon}, \frac{s_{max}}{s_{min}}) \times poly(|J|))$ time, where $|J|$ is the number of tasks.

The basic procedure is outlined as follows. Given a feasibility problem of scheduling under makespan T, we simplify the instance and set up an ILP to decide if a schedule exists for the simplified instance - the simplifications maintain a guarantee that an optimum for the simplified instance is within a range of that to the original.

The simplifications serve to bound the number of task sizes etc., such that there is a limited number of possible schedules (configurations) on each processor. The accuracy parameter ϵ decides the resolution of the simplified instance and is inversely related to the runtime of the approximation scheme. In summary, processing and communication times are truncated, processing times too small to truncate are represented by placeholders, and sizes of gaps limited. A better summary is in [18], the supplementary version of the paper.

After the simplifications, there are $|\Gamma| = 1/\epsilon$ different communication times and $|P| = 1/\epsilon \log 1/\epsilon$ different processing times, i.e. a constant number in terms of the problem input size.

The ILP itself is what can be called a configuration ILP. We can describe a configuration as a (maximal) set of tasks that can be feasibly scheduled onto a single processor. More accurately, it is defined as a multiset of task sizes, representing the numbers of slots of each size (as created in the simplifications) that can be provided by a processor adopting such a configuration. The ILP selects a configuration for each processor, out of all possible configurations (which are bounded in number by the simplifications), such that all the configurations together provide enough slots to accommodate the given numbers of tasks of each size.

Let the set of all configurations be denoted by C. Variables x_C $\forall C \in C$ select the number of each configuration used, and each configuration C provides a $C_{p,\gamma^{in},\gamma^{out}}$ number of slots for tasks with processing time p and communication times γ^{in} and γ^{out}.

4.1 EPAS for Related Processors $Qm|fork\text{-}join, c_{ij}|C_{max}$

We now describe the formulation of the EPAS for scheduling the fork-join graph to a heterogeneous system of uniformly related processors, parameterised by the ratio in speed between the fastest and slowest processors, $\frac{s_{max}}{s_{min}}$. Remember, with related heterogeneous processors, each processor $m \in M$ completes a task j in p_j/s_m time, where $s_m \in S$ is the speed of the processor. The input to the problem is then a set of tasks with given processing costs and communication times (where communication times are as given and do not depend on processing speed), and a set of processors with given speeds.

With this, we first redefine a *small task* to be any task that takes less than $t_{\text{SMALL}} = \epsilon^2 T$ to execute on the *slowest* processor (and therefore has cost no greater than $s_{min}\epsilon^2 T$), and the rest are treated as *big tasks*. This way, a small task will never become a "big task" (in the original sense that it takes more than $\epsilon^2 T$ time to execute) moving from one processor to another, while a big task may become a "small task" (taking less than $\epsilon^2 T$ to execute) depending on the processor. The latter has no impact on the formulation of the following ILP and does not impact the complexity. Small tasks will be replaced by one or more placeholders of size $p_{\text{SMALL}} = s_{min}\epsilon^3 T$, bounding the number of processing costs. Something to note is that instead of other representations of small tasks in PTAS for scheduling, placeholders are used here to manage communication costs, and although they are fine-grained in order to reduce rounding error, they are bundled together on processor configurations so as not to increase complexity.

With the maximum processing cost being $s_{max}T$, and $(1+\epsilon)^n s_{min}\epsilon^2 T \le s_{max}T$, there are $n \le \mathcal{O}(\frac{1}{\epsilon}(\log \frac{s_{max}}{s_{min}} + \log \frac{1}{\epsilon}))$ cost sizes. On the other hand, the configurations only use $\mathcal{O}(\frac{1}{\epsilon} \log \frac{1}{\epsilon})$ different rounded processing times (as with before). Let these processing times be denoted $t \in P'$.

The input to the new ILP will again consist of the numbers of tasks of each size (cost) category $(p, \gamma^{in}, \gamma^{out})$, where p here is the processing cost (instead of the actual processing times). This includes the numbers of placeholder tasks that will replace the combined volume of small tasks for each category of $\gamma^{in}, \gamma^{out} \in \Gamma^2$. Therefore we have the following values in the right hand side of the ILP, where $N_{\text{SMALL},\gamma^{in},\gamma^{out}}$ is the number of placeholder tasks to replace the small tasks.

$$N_{p,\gamma^{in},\gamma^{out}} \quad \forall(p, \gamma^{in}, \gamma^{out}) \in P \times \Gamma^2$$
$$N_{\text{SMALL},\gamma^{in},\gamma^{out}} \quad \forall(\gamma^{in}, \gamma^{out}) \in P \times \Gamma^2$$

We round each of the processing speeds $s_m \in S$ down to the nearest $s_{min}(1 + \epsilon)^n$, $n \in \mathbb{N}_0$, where s_{max} is the highest, giving $\frac{\log(s_{max}/s_{min})}{\log(1+\epsilon)}$ types of processors.

Now, we introduce variables which select the numbers of tasks of each size (cost) to allocate to each type of processor. This includes large sizes and the placeholders for small tasks.

$$n^s_{p,\gamma^{in},\gamma^{out}} \; \forall s \in S$$

$$n^s_{\text{SMALL},\gamma^{in},\gamma^{out}} \; \forall s \in S$$

The following constraints make sure that the total number of each task size allocated on all processors is at least as large as the given number of tasks from the input.

$$\sum_{s \in S} n^s_{p,\gamma^{in},\gamma^{out}} \geq N_{p,\gamma^{in},\gamma^{out}} \tag{1}$$

$$\sum_{s \in S} n^s_{\text{SMALL},\gamma^{in},\gamma^{out}} \geq N_{p,\gamma^{in},\gamma^{out}} \tag{2}$$

$$\forall (p, \gamma^{in}, \gamma^{out}) \in P \times \Gamma^2$$

Let $(t, \gamma^{in}, \gamma^{out})$ describe the size category of a task in terms of its actual execution time $t_{p_j,s}$ on an assigned processor with speed s. For a target makespan T, the processing times of each task on each processor is put in terms of T, and from this it is known which size category $(t, \gamma^{in}, \gamma^{out})$ the task belongs to on each processor. In the end, each processor will adopt some configuration which is chosen from the same set of configurations as in the original formulation for the homogeneous-processors case, with each configuration being some set of tasks that could feasibly be scheduled together on this processor, encoded in the ILP as a vector of multiplicities of the task sizes.

Let the variables $x^s_C \; \forall s \in S, \forall C \in \boldsymbol{C}$ decide the number of processors of speed s to use configuration C, and let $C_{t,\gamma^{in},\gamma^{out}}$ denote the number of tasks of size $(t, \gamma^{in}, \gamma^{out})$ that can go into the configuration C. Then, for each processor speed s and task size $(t_{p,s}, \gamma^{in}, \gamma^{out})$, the total number of tasks of this size which can be accommodated by the selected configurations must be enough for the total number of tasks which will execute with this size on this type of processor.

$$\sum_{C \in \boldsymbol{C}} x^s_C C_{t,\gamma^{in},\gamma^{out}} - \sum_{p \in P} n^s_{p,\gamma^{in},\gamma^{out}} \cdot a_{p/s=t} \geq 0 \tag{3}$$

$$\forall s \in S, \; \forall t \in P', \; \forall (\gamma^{in}, \gamma^{out}) \in \Gamma^2$$

where $a_{p/s=t}$ is defined by

$$a_{p/s=t} = \begin{cases} 1, & \text{if with speed } s, \text{ task with cost } p \text{ executes in time category } t \\ 0, & \text{otherwise} \end{cases}$$

$$\forall s \in S, \; \forall p \in P, \; \forall t \in P'$$

The placeholders for small tasks are treated slightly differently. The different lengths of time it takes to execute a placeholder task on each type of processor is encoded into $a_{\text{SMALL}/s}$ $\forall s \in S$, where it is simply $a_{\text{SMALL}/s} = p_{\text{SMALL}}/s$. Next, for each size category (which remain differentiated by communication times) $\gamma^{in}, \gamma^{out}$, let $C_{\text{SMALL},\gamma^{in},\gamma^{out}}$ $\forall C \in \mathbf{C}$ represent the available time provided by C for placeholders of this category. Then, for each type of processor, the total time given to placeholders of each category $(\gamma^{in}, \gamma^{out})$ by the selected configurations must accommodate the total amount of time it will take to execute the placeholders assigned to it. In addition, some big tasks will take less than t_{SMALL} to execute on faster processors, where they can then be treated as small tasks and added to the total volume of small task execution time assigned to these processors. For such tasks, the factors $a_{p/s}$ $\forall s \forall p$ will give the amount of time they will each add to the total volume of small tasks on processors of speed s.

$$a_{p/s} = \begin{cases} p/s, & \text{if } p/s \leq t_{\text{SMALL}} \\ 0, & \text{otherwise} \end{cases}$$

$$\sum_{C \in \mathbf{C}} x_C^s C_{\text{SMALL},\gamma^{in},\gamma^{out}} - \sum_{p \in P} n_{p,\gamma^{in},\gamma^{out}}^s \cdot a_{p/s} - n_{\text{SMALL},\gamma^{in},\gamma^{out}}^s \cdot a_{\text{SMALL}/s} \geq 0 \quad (4)$$

$$\forall s \in S, \ \forall t \in P', \ \forall(\gamma^{in}, \gamma^{out}) \in \Gamma^2$$

Finally, for each type of processor, a number of configurations is selected that is no more than the available processors of that type.

$$\sum_{C \in \mathbf{C}} x_C^s \leq |M^s|, \ \forall s \in S \quad (5)$$

In summary, the ILP is defined by constraints 1-5, and has variables x_C^s $\forall s \forall C$, n_p^s $\forall s \forall p$, and n_{SMALL}^s $\forall s$. Proof for the following Theorem 1 is in [18].

Theorem 1. *There is an EPAS for scheduling fork-join structures to uniformly related heterogeneous systems that gives a schedule in*

$$2^{\mathcal{O}(1/\epsilon^4 \log^2 1/\epsilon \log \frac{s_{max}}{s_{min}})} \mathcal{O}(\log^2 N) + \mathcal{O}(N \log N)$$

time that is no worse than $\frac{(1+6\epsilon)}{(1-2\epsilon-\epsilon^2)} OPT.$

5   Equal Processing Costs

While the general problem $Q|fork\text{-}join, c_{ij}|C_{max}$ is sNP-hard, working with fixed computation costs can make intractable scheduling problems tractable [6] or otherwise give them faster solutions, although that is not always the case [13].

For the following we look at scheduling on related processors with a workload of **equal** processing times. Although this problem's complexity is still open, it is at least as hard as the version with homogeneous systems which is in turn harder than the open problem $P|r_j, p_j = p|\sum U$ in scheduling with release times and deadlines [15].

5.1   Approximation Algorithm for $Q|fork-join,c_{ij},p_j=p|C_{max}$

We start with a guaranteed approximation algorithms that uses a simplification together with formulating the problem as finding a bipartite graph matching. Unlike with homogeneous processors [15], this approach cannot solve the problem exactly, as not all schedules can be represented by a bipartite graph. A bipartite *hypergraph* could fully represent this scheduling problem, but its matching problem is intractable, with other approximate solutions, hence not helpful here.

Beginning with the simplification, we limit the resolution of start times to p/s_m on each processor $m \in M$, and then we have the following simple Lemma 1, where OPT is the optimal schedule length to the original instance and T^* is the optimal schedule length to the simplified instance.

Lemma 1. $T^* - (p/s_{min}) \le OPT \le T^*$

Proof. Consider an optimal schedule to the original instance. This can be transformed to a valid schedule for the simplified instance by rounding up all task start times to multiples of p/s_m on each processor $m \in M$. As we round up, the schedule length of this schedule cannot be less than OPT, but needs to be less than the optimal schedule for the simplified instance, hence $OPT \le T^*$

As no task can start later in this schedule by more than p/s_{min}, it follows $T^* - (p/s_{min}) \le OPT$.   □

In our proposed Algorithm 1, a bipartite graph $G = (U, V, E)$ is created for the simplified instance, where nodes U represent tasks, nodes V represent time slots on all processors (in p/s_m resolution), and edges E connect each task to its viable time slots.

If a maximal matching for this graph includes less than $|U| = n$ edges, the original problem $P|fork\text{-}join, p_j = 1, c_{ij}|C_{max}$ with bound T is not feasible. In a maximal matching with $|U|$ edges, each edge represents an assignment of a task to a processor and start time, while no time slot is assigned to more than once, so the schedule is valid.

Proposition 2. *An $(OPT + \frac{p}{s_{min}})$-schedule can be found for $P|fork\text{-}join, c_{ij}, p_j = p|C_{max}$ in $\mathcal{O}(|M|^2|J|^3 \log |J|)$ time.*

Due to space constraints, the proof of Proposition 2 is given in the companion report [18]. The complexity is mostly derived of the maximum matching Ford-Fulkerson algorithm. We would like to point out that this has been better formulated than the version laid out here for homogeneous systems [15], requiring only incoming communications to be simplified, which improves the bound. The amortised complexity has also been better evaluated.

5.2   Two Processors $Q2|fork\text{-}join, c_{ij}, p_j = p|C_{max}$

Scheduling to two heterogeneous processors with equal processing costs is tractable just as it is for homogeneous processors (the problem $P2|fork\text{-}join, c_{ij}, p_j = p|C_{max}$ [15]).

Algorithm 1: Formulation as bipartite graph matching problem

---

1 Binary search over T:
2   Create graph $G(U, V, E)$;
3   **for** $\forall j \in J$ **do**
4       $U \leftarrow U \cup \{u_j\}$
5   **for** $\forall m \in M$ **do**
6   **for** $\forall \sigma \in \{i\frac{p}{s_m} \mid i \in \{1, 2, ..., \lfloor \frac{T}{p/s_m} \rfloor\}\}$ **do**
7           $V \leftarrow V \cup \{v_{m,\sigma}\}$
    /* add edges   */
8   **for** $\forall u_j \in U$ **do**
9   **for** $\forall v_{m,\sigma} \in V$ **do**
10          $E \leftarrow E \cup \{e_{j,m,\sigma}\}$ /* edge from u_j to $v_{m,\sigma}$ */

11 Find if there exists a feasible matching for the bipartite graph $G(U, V, E)$
    using Ford-Fulkerson algorithm
12 **if** *feasible matching exists* **then** try lower T
13 **else** try higher T
    /* create schedule from bipartite matching   */
14 **for** $\forall v_{j,m,\sigma} \in E$ **do**
15   schedule task j to processor m at time σ

Consider the two cases separately where (case 1) the source and sink tasks are on the same processor and (case 2) where they are on separate processors. We want to reuse the same algorithms for each case (P2-SCHED1 and P2-SCHED2 [15]) as in the homogeneous case, but need to prove that they are still valid and obtain optimal length.

P2-SCHED1 casts the problem as a single processor throughput problem $1|r_j, p_j = p|\Sigma U_j$ on p_2. The tasks that are rejected then need to be executed on p_1 and a binary search finds the optimal solution. P2-SCHED1 uses an algorithm for the release time and deadline throughput problem

P2-SCHED2 is a greedy algorithm that schedules the tasks on the sink processor p_2 as they become available, ordered by non-increasing γ_i^{out}. All tasks not fitting on p_2 are put on source processor p_1 in non-increasing γ_i^{out}. Both algorithms are used with a binary search to find the optimal.

Proposition 3. P2-SCHED1 & P2-SCHED2 *obtain optimal solutions for two uniformly related heterogeneous processors* $Q2|fork\text{-}join, c_{ij}, p_j = p|C_{max}$.

Proof. P2-SCHED1 is optimal for case 1, as all tasks have the same processing time on each processor, hence the throughput argument where rejected tasks need to be scheduled on p_1 remains valid as in the homogeneous case, irrespective of a difference in processing speed between p_1 and p_2.

P2-SCHED2 is optimal for case 2 as the greedy approach fills p_2 maximally. Only swapping tasks between p_1 and p_2 could improve the schedule. However, by the greedy approach, that cannot shorten the finish time of p_2, nor can it improve the outgoing communication arrival for tasks on p_1. Due to the related heterogeneity, all tasks have the same execution time on the respective processor.

5.3 Unlimited Processors $Q\infty|fork\text{-}join, c_{ij}, p_j = p|C_{max}$

This problem is also tractable, similarly as for $P\infty|fork\text{-}join, c_{ij}, p_j = p|C_{max}$ [15]. Divide the tasks between those scheduled remotely, J_{remote}, and those scheduled locally, J_{local}, and search for a partitioning that gives the lowest schedule length. To find the schedule length given a partitioning, put each task in J_{remote} on a separate processor of the faster type, and schedule J_{local} using P2-SCHED1/2, potentially trying all combinations of processor types for the 2 local processors (the application of proposition 1), repeating P2-SCHED1/2 case by case, which adds $|S|^2$ to the complexity. Only the fastest $|J|$ processors need to be considered.

5.4 Partially Equal Communications $Q|fork\text{-}join, p_j = p, c_{in} = c, c_{out}|C_{max}$

This is also polynomially solvable. To briefly describe the algorithm, schedule the tasks in decreasing order of their communication times, filling the local processor first, and then after that, appending them to a processor that results in the earliest finish time at each stage. Again, proposition 1 can be applied here, and proof of optimality for the algorithm can be found in the companion report [18].

5.5 Grouped Processors

When we assume that communications are not incurred between processors of the same type due to close proximity or closely shared memory, this problem has similarities to scheduling with two processors, $Q2$. For the case where source and sink are on different processors types, the problem is similar enough that the same algorithm used for $Q2$ can work here. However, when source and sink are on the same processor type, with processors of the other type containing remote tasks, it again comes down to the open problem $P|p = 1, r_j|\Sigma U$. A bounded approximate solution still exists by the same technique in Sect. 5.1.

6   Conclusion

In this paper we investigated the scheduling of fork-join structures, which are typical of highly parallel workloads, to heterogeneous processor systems. We presented an EPAS for scheduling to related heterogeneous processors, and some polynomial time algorithms. We see that scheduling with two types of processors (which has special relevance as CPU–accelerator systems) has largely the same results as the general case. All of these results also apply to the equivalent problems in scheduling with release times and deadlines.

References

1. Aba, A., et al.: Efficient algorithm for scheduling parallel applications on hybrid multicore machines with communications delays and energy constraint. In: Concurrency and Computation: Practice and Experience, vol. 32(15) (2020)
2. Ait Aba, M., Munier Kordon, A., Pallez (Aupy), G.: scheduling on two unbounded resources with communication costs. In: Yahyapour, R. (ed.) Euro-Par 2019. LNCS, vol. 11725, pp. 117–128. Springer, Cham (2019). https://doi.org/10.1007/978-3-030-29400-7_9
3. Beaumont, O., et al.: Scheduling on two types of resources: a survey. ACM Comput. Surv. (CSUR) **53**(3), 1–36 (2020)
4. Graham, R.L., et al.: Optimization and approximation in deterministic sequencing and scheduling: a survey. In: Discrete Optimization II, vol. 5. Annals of Discrete Mathematics, pp. 287–326. Elsevier, Amsterdam (1979)
5. Chekuri, C., Khanna, S.: A PTAS for minimizing weighted completion time on uniformly related machines. In: Orejas, F., Spirakis, P.G., van Leeuwen, J. (eds.) ICALP 2001. LNCS, vol. 2076, pp. 848–861. Springer, Heidelberg (2001). https://doi.org/10.1007/3-540-48224-5_69
6. Davida, G.I., Linton, D.J.: A new algorithm for the scheduling of tree structured tasks. In: Proceedings of the Conference on Information Sciences and Systems, pp. 543–548. IEEE, Baltimore, MD (1976)
7. Drozdowski, M.: Scheduling for Parallel Processing. Springer (2009). https://doi.org/10.1007/978-1-84882-310-5
8. Garey, M.R., Johnson, D.S.: Strong NP-completeness results: motivation, examples, and implications. J. ACM **25**(3) (1978)
9. Shmoys, D., Lenstra, J.K., Tardos, E.: Approximation algorithms for scheduling unrelated parallel machines. Math. Progr. **46** (1990)
10. Jansen, K.: An EPTAS for scheduling jobs on uniform processors: using an MILP relaxation with a constant number of integral variables. Auto. Lang. Program (2009)
11. Jansen, K., Sinnen, O., Wang, H.: An EPTAS for scheduling fork-join graphs with communication delay. Theoret. Comput. Sci. **861**, 66–79 (2021)
12. Knop, D., Koutecky, M.: Scheduling meets n-fold integer programming. In: Proceedings of the 13th Workshop on Models and Algorithms for Planning and Scheduling Problems (MAPSP) (2017)
13. Lenstra, J.K., Rinnooy Kan, A.H.G.: Complexity of scheduling under precedence constraints. Operat. Res. **26**(1), 22–35 (1978)
14. The Open MPI project. Open MPI documentation (2004). https://www.openmpi.org/doc. Accessed: 2022-04-20. The Open MPI project
15. Sinnen, O., Wang, H.: Scheduling fork-join task graphs with communication delays and equal processing times. In: International Conference on Parallel Processing. ACM (2022)
16. The 500 most powerful computer systems. http://www.top500.org/
17. The fork/join framework. https://docs.oracle.com/javase/tutorial/essential/concurrency/forkjoin.html
18. Wang, H., Sinnen, O.: Scheduling Fork-Join Task Graphs to Heterogeneous Processors. arXiv:2305.17556 (2023)

JPACKFAAS: Profiling Java Serverless Functions Deployment Package Size in Federated FaaS

Thomas Larcher[iD] and Sashko Ristov[✉][iD]

University of Innsbruck, Innsbruck 6020, Austria
t.larcher@student.uibk.ac.at, sashko.ristov@uibk.ac.at

Abstract. Serverless computing, and in particular Function-as-a-Service (FaaS), is becoming a de-facto standard for coding the modern cloud applications. Users may code their serverless functions to use various cloud managed services that are supported by different cloud providers. However, such managed cloud services usually increase the code size of the function, which also affects the size of its deployment package due to various package dependencies, especially for Java serverless functions. In this paper, we analyze several chained cloud services and how their inclusion affects function's deployment package size. Based on the analysis, we introduce the JPACKFAAS model, which estimates deployment package size based on the managed cloud service that the function includes. We evaluated the JPACKFAAS model with fifteen serverelss functions that use three managed cloud services (storage, speech2text, and text2speech) of two cloud providers AWS and GCP. Results show that the JPACKFAAS model can accurately estimate the deployment package size with minimum measurements, even when a function uses a mixture of managed cloud services from different cloud providers. The JPACKFAAS model achieved 98.2% accuracy on average, with linear, instead of exponential number of measurements.

Keywords: Backend-as-a-Service · Deployment · FaaSification · Java · modeling · serverless

1 Introduction

Context. Serverless computing, especially with its widely used Function-as-a-Service (FaaS) representative, allow developers to simply code their functions, without bothering about underlying infrastructure and platform. Moreover, federated FaaS offers many benefits to users in terms of various pricing schemes [6], overhead [13], startup latency [7], underlying infrastructure [8,14], resources [4], scalability [16,19], cold start [1,10], resilience [15] etc. FaaS is also used for various types of applications [5].

State-of-the-Art Limitations. While research for FaaS has entered into a mature phase [9], most of the work is mainly focused on performance of the functions

D. Zeinalipour et al. (Eds.): Euro-Par 2023 Workshops, LNCS 14351, pp. 330–341, 2024.
https://doi.org/10.1007/978-3-031-50684-0_26

during runtime and rarely on the function before runtime, that is, development, packaging, and deployment [11]. The process of packaging is automatized with various FaaSifiers [2,3,17], and together with deployment tools, such as Terraform, serverless framework, or GoDeploy [12], it becomes transparent to the devops engineers. However, the packaging and deployment package size is mainly analyzed as a black box for researching mainly the cold start and invocation latency [20–22].

Research Problem. To bridge this gap in the research, in this paper we dived into details of the *deployment package* size for Java serverless functions. We have set the following research question:

To what extent we can define an accurate model that will estimate the size of the deployment package of a Java function if we know which managed cloud services it uses and which parameters are important?

Approach. To answer this research question, we conducted preliminary investigation, based on which we developed the JPACKFAAS model. Our main novelty is the splitting of deployment package overheads per *no-op* java function, *provider service overhead*, and individual *service overhead*, which are all independent and can be summed up to achieve the overall deployment package size. We evaluated the JPACKFAAS model with a total of 15 Java serverless functions that used three cloud managed services: storage, speech2text, and text2speech of two cloud providers Amazon (AWS) and Google (GCP). The evaluation showed a very high accuracy of 98.2%, which is achieved with a linear, instead of exponential complexity.

Paper Outline. The remaining of the paper is organized in several sections. Section 2 presents our initial observations, based on which we developed our JPACKFAAS model, which is elaborated in Sect. 3. We evaluate our JPACKFAAS model in Sect. 4 and discuss the related work and the limitations of the JPACK-FAAS model in Sect. 5. Finally, Sect. 6 concludes the paper and outlines the future work.

2 Preliminary Investigation and Motivation

In line with research question, we conducted a set of benchmarks that investigate the effect of adding a managed cloud service in a serverless function on the size of its deployment package. Surprisingly, our preliminary investigation revealed that introducing a new managed cloud service into a function code may cause different increase of the deployment package size, depending on the managed cloud services that the function already has. This observation led us to three observations that motivated us to model how the deployment package is affected by included managed cloud services.

2.1 Initial Scenario

Initially, we implemented two simple AWS Lambda functions and deployed them on AWS and GCP cloud regions in North Virginia, US. Each AWS Lambda function accesses different cloud object storage:

1. A copyAWS Java function that copies a file from object storage on AWS S3 and uploads it on another object storage on AWS S3, and
2. A copyGCP Java function that copies a file from object storage on GCP and uploads it on another object storage on GCP.

Although both functions perform negligible computing, they still need to load the respective dependencies to be able to access to the storage. The deployment package size of the developed AWS Lambda functions copyAWS and copyGCP was 11.6 MB and 10.7 MB, respectively.

2.2 Scenario 1: Additional AWS Service

Afterwards, we decided to add an additional package for the AWS service Polly in the functions, which synthesizes speech. We refer to these newly created serverless functions as copyAWSSyntAWS and copyGCPSyntAWS, respectively. In reality, this step is needed to be able to specify the target storage where to store the resulting synthesized speech.

Observation 1: The size of the deployment package of a serverless function may increase differently for a given AWS service. Surprisingly, although we added exactly the same package for the AWS service Polly, the deployment package size the function grew differently. Namely, the deployment package size of the function copyAWSSyntAWS increased by 1.2 MB compared to the function copyAWS, while the deployment package size of the function copyGCPSyntAWS by 9.3 MB, compared to the original function copyGCP.

2.3 Scenario 2: Additional GCP Service

Observation 1 motivated us to add the same service for speech synthesis offered by GCP (Text-To-Speech) to both functions copyAWS and copyGCP and investigate the increase of the package size. We refer to these newly created functions as copyAWSSyntGCP and copyGCPSyntGCP, respectively.

Observation 2: Package size of a function may increase differently for a given GCP service We were even more surprised when we added the GCP service for speech synthesis to both functions copyAWS and copyGCP. Although we added the same dependencies required by the GCP's Text-To-Speech service to both initial functions copyAWS and copyGCP, now the package size of the function copyAWSSyntGCP increased more than the package size of the function copyGCPSyntGCP. Namely, the former increased by 42 MB, while the latter by 33 MB.

2.4   Conclusion

As a conclusion, we can derive the following Observation 3.

Observation 3: Adding the same service of two cloud providers creates various increase of the deployment package size of functions. We conclude that the problem to determine the deployment package size of a function based on the used cloud services grows exponentially with the number of services that the function uses. Including the dependencies of the same service of different cloud providers increases the function's package size differently, not only caused by the specifics of the cloud provider, but also whether the function has already used some other services of that cloud provider.

3   JPackFaaS Model

In this section, we present our JPackFaaS model, which determines the deployment package size for a given set of managed cloud services that the Java function uses.

3.1   Cloud Provider Service Model

Cloud Provider Model. Let the set $\mathbb{P} = \bigcup_{i=1}^{p} P_i$ denotes all p cloud providers in the federated FaaS. Examples are Amazon (AWS), Google (GCP), Microsoft Azure, IBM Cloud, etc. Each cloud provider offers a set of s services $\mathbb{S}_i = \bigcup_{j=1}^{s} S_{ij}$, such that S_{ij} and S_{kj}, $i \neq k$ represent the same service that is offered by the cloud providers P_i and P_k. For instance, AWS and GCP both offer object storage services and various other managed cloud services for multimedia conversions, such as object recognition, OCR, or speech to text. We assume that each cloud provider P_i offers a Java SDK that enables serverless functions to connect to the service S_{ij}.

Service Model. We introduce the *service overhead* C_{ij}, expressed in megabytes, as the overhead to the deployment package size of a function whenever the cloud managed service S_{ij} is used in the serverless function. We model C_{ij} such that it is independent of the same service offered by the other cloud providers P_k, $k \neq i$, based on Observation 3.

Function Model. A serverless function may use any of the supported managed cloud services S_{ij}, defined with the *usage matrix* $U_{p \times s}$ with elements u_{ij}, such that $u_{ij} = 1$ if the managed cloud service S_{ij} is included in the function and $u_{ij} = 0$ otherwise.

3.2 JPACKFAAS Packaging Model

Cloud Provider Service Overhead. From the observations presented in Sect. 2, we concluded that there is a dependency between the managed cloud service S_{ij} and other services S_{im}, $m \neq j$ from the same cloud provider P_i. Therefore, we model the *cloud provider service overhead* O_i in Equation (1), measured in megabytes, which increases the deployment package size in two parts:

i) the *initial cloud provider overhead* I_i which is included only once if there is at least one managed cloud service S_{ij} of the cloud provider P_i included in the serverless function, and

ii) the sum of service overheads C_{ij} of all services of the cloud provider P_i that are included in the serverless function.

$$O_i = min(\sum_{j=1}^{j=s} u_{ij}, 1) \cdot I_i + \sum_{j=1}^{j=s} u_{ij} \cdot C_{ij} \tag{1}$$

Total Package Size PS of a Function. Finally, in Equation (2) we model the package size PS of a Java function that uses a set of services S_{ij} as a sum of all cloud provider service overheads O_i and the package size of the no-op function PS_{no-op}.

$$PS = PS_{no-op} + \sum_{i=1}^{i=p} O_i \tag{2}$$

4 Evaluation

We selected two cloud providers P_i ($P_1 = AWS$ an $P_2 = GCP$) whose managed cloud services are widely used among cloud users. We selected three managed cloud services *storage*, *speech2text*, and *text2speech*, which are supported by both cloud providers, leading to the set of six services S_{ij}, as presented in Table 1. We denote each service S_{ij} based on its position in Table 1. For instance, S_{21} denotes GCP cloud storage (GCS). We selected storage because more than 60% of functions access storage [5], as well as it is used by some managed cloud services to access the data by reference.

Table 1. The set of all managed cloud services of AWS and GCP that are used in the evaluation.

Cloud provider	storage	text2speech	speech2text
AWS	S3	Polly	Transcribe
GCP	GCS	Text-to-Speech	Speech-to-Text

4.1 Evaluated Scenarios

We evaluated three different scenarios using the given set of managed cloud services of both cloud providers AWS and GCP.

storage. This scenario copies a file from one location in cloud storage to another one. It may perform an *intra-provider* copy (e.g., copy a file from AWS S3 to AWS S3), or *inter-provider* copy (e.g., copy a file from AWS S3 to GCP Object Storage). We coded the functions for this scenario such that they receive two input parameters, which specify the source and destination URLs that point to cloud storages.

text2speech. This scenario creates natural sounding speech from a text file that is stored in cloud storage and writes the synthesized audio file back to cloud storage. Additional to cloud storages of both cloud providers, the functions of this scenario use one of the speech synthesis services of both cloud providers (AWS Polly and GCP Text-To-Speech). The result is encoded in wav format and contains the synthesized speech.

speech2text. This scenario transcribes speech contained in an audio file that is stored in cloud storage and writes the transcript back to the cloud storage. Apart from cloud storages (AWS S3 and GCP Object Storage), cloud functions for this scenario use speech recognition services (AWS Transcribe and GCP Speech-To-Text). The transcription result is encoded in json format and contains start time, end time, confidence value and the actual text of each detected word.

4.2 Developed Functions

We decided to use Java to code the functions because the difference in the package size is more significant than the scripting languages like Python or Node.js. Due to the nature of the language, Java applications contain a lot of boilerplate code, which results in larger code bases with many lines of code and larger deployment packages. Furthermore, Java is mostly used for large enterprise projects, which tend to be complex.

The three scenarios led to development of 15 serverless functions, as presented in Table 2, since each managed cloud service may be placed either on AWS or GCP, and the scenarios speech2text and text2speech needed at least one storage to read from or to store the resulting file. We also developed a "no-op"' function that simply returns immediately once it is invoked and does not use any managed cloud service. The deployment package size of the no-op function is $PS_{no-op} = 0.3$ MB.

4.3 Evaluation Metrics

We developed all 15 functions as AWS Lambda serverless functions, packaged them using the Maven build system, and measured the size of their deployment packages.

Table 2. The set of all functions used in the evaluation with different managed cloud services.

f	usage	scenario	storage		text2speech		speech2text	
			AWS	GCP	AWS	GCP	AWS	GCP
no-op	learning	–	–	–	–	–	–	–
1	learning	Storage	✓	–	–	–	–	–
2	evaluation	Storage	–	✓	–			
3	learning	Storage	✓	✓	–	–	–	–
4	learning	text2speech	✓	–	✓	–	–	–
5	evaluation	text2speech	–	✓	✓	–	–	–
6	learning	text2speech	✓	✓	✓	–	–	–
7	evaluation	text2speech	✓	–	–	✓	–	–
8	evaluation	text2speech	–	✓	–	✓	–	–
9	learning	text2speech	✓	✓	–	✓	–	–
10	learning	speech2text	✓	–	–	–	✓	–
11	evaluation	speech2text	–	✓	–	–	✓	–
12	evaluation	speech2text	✓	✓	–	–	✓	–
13	evaluation	speech2text	✓	–	–	–	–	✓
14	evaluation	speech2text	–	✓	–	–	–	✓
15	learning	speech2text	✓	✓	–	–	–	✓

The size of a deployment package includes the direct dependencies, transitive dependencies and the actual function source code itself. Large deployment packages take up more cloud storage capacity and may increase the time it takes to deploy the function. To find out how much the size of a deployment package changes when certain dependencies are added or removed, both the package sizes of individual dependencies and the deployment package sizes of function implementations with multiple dependencies were measured. Note that the size added to a deployment package of serverless function is not equivalent to the sum of sizes of the used libraries, as some transitive dependencies of the libraries might be shared, in which case they are included only once. Therefore, the deployment package size cannot be measured by adding up the sizes of individual dependencies. Instead, it was measured by including the required dependencies, running a maven build and creating a fat jar file.

4.4 JPACKFAAS Parameter Setup

We evaluated the JPACKFAAS model for all three scenarios with the 15 serverless functions, as presented in Table 2. We first determine the parameter setup of the cloud provider service model, which was presented in Sect. 3.1 and then evaluate the accuracy of the JPACKFAAS model, which was presented in Sect. 3.2.

jPackFaaS Parameter Setup. We measured the deployment package size of functions used for learning (see Table 2) and used the system of linear equations to determine the JPACKFAAS parameter setup. Table 3 presents the computed values of the initial cloud provider overhead I_i and service overheads C_{ij}, $\forall i \in \{1, 2\}$ and $\forall j \in \{1, 2, 3\}$.

Table 3. Initial cloud provider overhead I_i and service overheads C_{ij} for the three evaluated cloud services of AWS and GCP.

Cloud provider	I_i	C_{i1}	C_{i2}	C_{i3}
AWS	9.3 MB	2 MB	1.2 MB	0.5 MB
GCP	6.9 MB	3.5 MB	33 MB	31.1 MB

4.5   JPACKFAAS Accuracy

jPackFaaS Inaccuracy. We define *inaccuracy* δ_{PS} in Equation (3) as a relative deviation of simulated $\widetilde{PS}$ and measured $\overline{PS}$ deployment package size for each evaluated function, presented in percentage.

$$\delta_{PS} = \left| \frac{\widetilde{PS} - \overline{PS}}{\widetilde{PS}} \right| \cdot 100\%. \tag{3}$$

jPackFaaS Evaluation. Figure 1 presents the results of the JPACKFAAS model evaluation for all 15 functions presented in Table 2. The JPACKFAAS model correctly estimated the deployment package size of 9 functions represented with inaccuracy $\delta_{PS} = 0$ in Fig. 1. On average, the JPACKFAAS model achieved inaccuracy of only 1.8%.

5   Discussion

In this section, we compare our work with the state-of-the-art, discuss the complexity to determine the JPACKFAAS parameter setup, and present the limitations of the JPACKFAAS model. We did not determine any threat to validity to our work since the deployment package size is always constant for a function with a given code.

5.1   Related Work

Several research papers have analyzed the deployment package size. Yu *et al.* [22] evaluated how the deployment package size of Python functions affects the startup latency of a function. The authors reported that functions with larger deployment package sizes need longer startup time due to larger data transmission to the target cloud region and package import overhead. Similar conclusion derived Wen *et al.* [21], who characterized cold start latency for Python

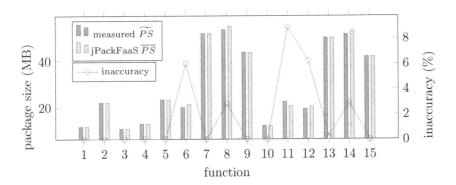

Fig. 1. Measured $\widetilde{PS}$ and simulated $\overline{PS}$ (JPACKFAAS) package size, as well as the estimation inaccuracy.

functions with different external dependencies, leading to different deployment package sizes (from 0.5 MB to 48 MB), which is comparable with the size of our functions. Unfortunately, the authors did not provide any model to estimate the function's deployment package size. Wang *et al.* [18] have also presented deployment package size, but also without providing an accurate model for it as a function of included managed cloud services. Finally, Ristov *et al.* [16] reported that the deployment time of serverless functions is positively correlated with the deployment package size and network proximity to the target cloud region.

5.2 Sensitivity Analysis

In our evaluation, we used six measurements to determine the JPACKFAAS parameter setup. In general, JPACKFAAS requires linear instead of exponential complexity, or only $O(s \cdot p)$ measurements for s services and p cloud providers in order to accurately estimate any combination of services that a function uses. Since we have already computed the initial cloud provider overhead I_i, developers need to compile the dependencies of a new managed cloud service within a no-op function and then subtract the deployment package size of the no-op function ($PS_{no-op} = 0.3$ MB) and the initial cloud provider service overhead I_i from the measured deployment package size $\widetilde{P_{ij}}$ of that function, or $C_{ij} = \widetilde{PS} - PS_{no-op} - I_i$.

5.3 JPACKFAAS Limitations

Limited Evaluation to Three Services and Two Cloud Providers. We evaluated JPACKFAAS accuracy with three managed cloud services and two cloud providers. However, a combination of other managed cloud services, such as object recognition, OCR, AI, etc., and from other cloud providers, such as Microsoft Azure, Alibaba, or IBM Cloud Functions may increase the JPACK-FAAS packaging model inaccuracy. Still, we believe that the JPACKFAAS model will retain the low inaccuracy, especially because many cloud managed services use storage, which have been already evaluated.

Limited Programming Languages. Apart from the Java programming language, serverless functions are mainly written in Python and Node.js, which may not comply with the current JPACKFAAS model. However, we believe that with the same approach, one can learn the new parameter setup and then successfully evaluate its accuracy for the other two programming languages Python and Node.js.

6 Conclusion and Future Work

We presented JPACKFAAS, a mathematical model that estimates the deployment package size of a serverless function, which uses various managed cloud services of different cloud providers. the JPACKFAAS model defines an *initial cloud provider overhead*, which is added to the deployment package size if the function uses at least one managed cloud service of that cloud provider. For each managed cloud service, the JPACKFAAS model introduces a *service overhead*, which is independent per service and is added to the deployment package size. Finally, the deployment package size of a function is increased by the deployment package size of the no-op function.

We evaluated the JPACKFAAS model with three managed cloud services storage, speech2text, and text2speech from two cloud providers AWS and GCP. The three corresponding scenarios resulted in 15 functions and only six of them (40%) were used to configure the JPACKFAAS model. The results showed that JPACKFAAS estimates the package size of all evaluated functions with accuracy of 98.2% on average.

We plan to extend our JPACKFAAS model in two directions. First, we will extend the JPACKFAAS model to support different programming languages, such as Python and Node.js. Secondly, deployment time depends on network proximity, that is, the region where the function is deployed, as well as the deployment package size for AWS Lambda functions written in Python. Therefore, we will extend JPACKFAAS to model deployment time of a serverless function based on the estimated deployment package size and the target cloud region.

Acknowledgment. This research received funding from Land Tirol, under contract F.35499.

References

1. Bermbach, D., Karakaya, A.S., Buchholz, S.: Using application knowledge to reduce cold starts in FAAS services. In: Proceedings of the 35th Annual ACM Symposium on Applied Computing (SAC 2020), pp. 134–143. Association for Computing Machinery, Brno (2020)

2. Carvalho, L., de Araújo., A.P.F.: Remote procedure call approach using the Node2FaaS framework with terraform for Function as a Service. In: International Conference on Cloud Computing and Services Science - CLOSER. SciTePress (2020)
3. Cordingly, R., et al.: The serverless application analytics framework: enabling design trade-off evaluation for serverless software. In: International Workshop on Serverless Computing (WoSC 2020), pp. 67–72 (2020). https://doi.org/10.1145/3429880.3430103
4. Eismann, S., Bui, L., Grohmann, J., Abad, C., Herbst, N., Kounev, S.: Sizeless: predicting the optimal size of serverless functions. In: Proceedings of the 22nd International Middleware Conference (Middleware 2021), pp. 248–259. Association for Computing Machinery, New York (2021). https://doi.org/10.1145/3464298.3493398
5. Eismann, S., et al.: Serverless applications: Why, when, and how? IEEE Softw. **38**(1), 32–39 (2021). https://doi.org/10.1109/MS.2020.3023302
6. Eivy, A., Weinman, J.: Be wary of the economics of "serverless" cloud computing. IEEE Cloud Comput. **4**(2), 6–12 (2017). https://doi.org/10.1109/MCC.2017.32
7. Jonas, E., Pu, Q., Venkataraman, S., Stoica, I., Recht, B.: Occupy the cloud: distributed computing for the 99%. In: Symposium on Cloud Computing, pp. 445–451 (2017)
8. Kelly, D., Glavin, F., Barrett, E.: Serverless computing: behind the scenes of major platforms. In: IEEE International Conference on Cloud Computing (CLOUD), pp. 304–312 (2020). https://doi.org/10.1109/CLOUD49709.2020.00050
9. Li, Y., Lin, Y., Wang, Y., Ye, K., Xu, C.: Serverless computing: state-of-the-art, challenges and opportunities. IEEE Trans. Serv. Comput. **16**(2), 1522–1539 (2023). https://doi.org/10.1109/TSC.2022.3166553
10. Lloyd, W., Vu, M., Zhang, B., David, O., Leavesley, G.: Improving application migration to serverless computing platforms: latency mitigation with keep-alive workloads. In: IEEE/ACM International Conference on Utility and Cloud Computing Companion (UCC Companion), pp. 195–200. IEEE (2018)
11. Pedratscher, S., Ristov, S., Fahringer, T.: M2FaaS: transparent and fault tolerant FaaSification of node.js monolith code blocks. Future Gen. Comput. Syst. **135**, 57–71 (2022). https://doi.org/10.1016/j.future.2022.04.021
12. Ristov, S., Brandacher, S., Felderer, M., Breu, R.: Godeploy: portable deployment of serverless functions in federated FAAS. In: 2022 IEEE Cloud Summit, pp. 38–43 (2022). https://doi.org/10.1109/CloudSummit54781.2022.00012
13. Ristov, S., Hautz, M., Hollaus, C., Prodan, R.: SimLess: simulate serverless workflows and their twins and siblings in federated FaaS. In: 2022 ACM Symposium on Cloud Computing (SoCC 2022), pp. 323–339. ACM, San Francisco (2022). https://doi.org/10.1145/3542929.3563478
14. Ristov, S., Hollaus, C., Hautz, M.: Colder than the warm start and warmer than the cold start! experience the spawn start in FAAS providers. In: Workshop on Advanced Tools, Programming Languages, and PLatforms for Implementing and Evaluating Algorithms for Distributed Systems (ApPLIED 2022), pp. 35–39. ACM, Salerno (2022). https://doi.org/10.1145/3524053.3542751
15. Ristov, S., Kimovski, D., Fahringer, T.: Faascinating resilience for serverless function choreographies in federated clouds. IEEE Trans. Netw. Serv. Manage. **19**(3), 2440–2452 (2022). https://doi.org/10.1109/TNSM.2022.3162036
16. Ristov, S., Pedratscher, S., Fahringer, T.: xAFCL: run scalable function choreographies across multiple FaaS systems. IEEE Trans. Serv. Comput. **16**(1), 711–723 (2023). https://doi.org/10.1109/TSC.2021.3128137

17. Ristov, S., Pedratscher, S., Wallnoefer, J., Fahringer, T.: DAF: dependency-aware faasifier for node.js monolithic applications. IEEE Softw. **38**(1), 48–53 (2021). https://doi.org/10.1109/MS.2020.3018334
18. Wang, A., et al.: Faasnet: scalable and fast provisioning of custom serverless container runtimes at Alibaba cloud function compute. In: 2021 USENIX Annual Technical Conference (USENIX ATC 21) (2021)
19. Wang, L., Li, M., Zhang, Y., Ristenpart, T., Swift, M.: Peeking behind the curtains of serverless platforms. In: USENIX Annual Technical Conference, Boston, pp. 133–145 (2018)
20. Wang, P., Zhao, C., Wei, Y., Wang, D., Zhang, Z.: An adaptive data placement architecture in multicloud environments. Sci. Program. **2020**, 1–12 (2020)
21. Wen, J., Liu, Y., Chen, Z., Chen, J., Ma, Y.: Characterizing commodity serverless computing platforms. J. Softw. Evol. Process. **35**(10), e2394 (2021)
22. Yu, T., et al.: Characterizing serverless platforms with serverlessbench. In: Proceedings of the 11th ACM Symposium on Cloud Computing (SoCC 2020), pp. 30–44. Association for Computing Machinery, Virtual Event (2020). https://doi.org/10.1145/3419111.3421280

ExaNBody: A HPC Framework for N-Body Applications

Thierry Carrard[1,2(✉)], Raphaël Prat[3], Guillaume Latu[3], Killian Babilotte[1,2], Paul Lafourcade[1,2], Lhassan Amarsid[3], and Laurent Soulard[1,2]

[1] CEA, DAM, DIF, 91297 Arpajon, France
`thierry.carrard@cea.fr`
[2] Université Paris-Saclay, LMCE, 91680 Bruyères-le-Châtel, France
[3] CEA, DES, IRESNE, DEC, Cadarache, 13108 Saint-Paul-Lez-Durance, France

Abstract. Increasing heterogeneity among HPC platforms requires applications to be frequently ported and tuned, adding burden to developers. Fast evolution of hardware mandates adaptation of algorithms and data structures to get higher performance, while application complexity constantly grows accordingly. Ensuring portability while preserving high performance at large scale along with minimal changes to an already existing application is an actual challenge. Separation of concerns to decouple performance from semantics in simulation codes are typically required. We describe a specialized programming framework for N-Body simulations that provides such separation. It allows one to develop computation kernels in the form of sequential-looking functions, while self-generating multi-level parallelism. EXANBODY possesses both an application layer with its own input data format, a way to define specific computation kernels and a separate runtime system that can address both CPUs and GPUs. The framework enables performance portability for N-Body simulations, bringing both flexibility and a set of handy tools. Performance results and speedups up to 32k cores with two distinct applications based on EXANBODY are discussed.

Keywords: N-body simulation · HPC · MPI · OpenMP · Framework

1 Introduction

Collisional N-body simulations are extensively used in several scientific domains. One challenge is the realistic modeling of atomistic systems or particle-based and granular materials containing multi-million of elements. Discrete element method (DEM), classical molecular dynamics (MD), and smoothed-particle hydrodynamics (SPH) methods fall into this category of N-body approaches. N-body modeling becomes challenging as the computational domain size and complexity rise. An always renewed challenge for tools in this field is to take advantage from the increasing power of distributed memory machines in order to mimic real systems. As supercomputers complexity tends to increase, this requires to revisit algorithms in order to use computing units at their full potential. The EXANBODY framework is modular, customizable, and allows to build a wide variety of different problems.

D. Zeinalipour et al. (Eds.): Euro-Par 2023 Workshops, LNCS 14351, pp. 342–354, 2024.
https://doi.org/10.1007/978-3-031-50684-0_27

In this paper, we focus on the scalability of a set of numerical methods for performing N-body simulations embedded into a comprehensive framework offering genericity and portable performance.

EXANBODY provides features for numerically integrating Newton's equation of motion for each particle, resulting from short/long range interactions or contact between objects (in the case of DEM simulations). Interactions computation methods rely on neighbor search algorithms and numerical time integration schemes.

To fasten developments, we propose a HPC framework to build N-body applications. The main contributions of this paper are the following. First, we introduce the framework and its features to address N-Body problems in a flexible way. Then, the framework architecture, based on a MPI+X parallelism is explained. Finally, EXANBODY is evaluated throughout target applications on thousands of CPU cores, as well as on a set of GPUs.

2   Background: N-Body Simulations

2.1   N-Body Methods

N-body methods encompass a variety of techniques used to model the behavior and interactions of a set of particles over time. These methods consist in solving Newton's equation of motion $\mathbf{f} = m\mathbf{a}$ for each particle at each time step, where $\mathbf{f}$ corresponds to the sum of the forces applied to the particle, $\mathbf{a}$ its acceleration and m its mass. The forces are deduced from the interactions between particles according to their types, *i.e.* contact, short-range, or long-range interactions, and external forces applied to the sample (i.e. gravity). Velocities are then deduced from the accelerations and subsequently used to update the particle positions at the next time step. This process is repeated, typically with a fixed time step Δ_t, according to an integration scheme[1] until the desired duration is reached. The collection of particle configurations over time allows to study a wide range of phenomena, from granular media movements, with the Discrete Element Method (DEM), to material crystal plasticity at the atomic scale using Molecular Dynamics (MD), going up to the galaxy formation with the Smoothed-Particle Hydrodynamics (SPH).

2.2   N-Body Simulation Codes

The development of a N-body code is led by the need to figure out the neighborhood of a given particle for every timestep in order to process interactions of different kinds.

Particle Interactions can be categorized as short-range and long-range. Short-range interactions are considered negligible beyond a specified cut-off radius. To optimize calculations, neighboring particle detection algorithms are employed to eliminate unnecessary computations with distant particles. Each N-Body method

---

[1] For example, Velocity Verlet integrator can be used [13].

employs a wide variety of short-range interactions that capture different particle physics. For example, visco-elastic contacts in DEM follow Hooke's law or Hertz law to model contact elasticity between rigid particles, while pair potentials like Lennard-Jones or Morse are used for gas or liquid atom interactions in classical MD. Long-range interactions, on the other hand, can sometimes not be neglected and result in algorithmic complexity of $\mathcal{O}(N^2)$. Such interactions, like gravitation in astrophysics, or electrostatic forces in MD, are typically modeled using the Ewald summation method. Fortunately, calculation approaches such as the fast multipole method can achieve a complexity of $\mathcal{O}(N)$, thanks to an octree structure, and can be efficiently parallelized [1]. Although this paper primarily focuses on short-range interactions, both types of interaction can be dealt with in EXANBODY.

Neighbor Lists are built, using different strategies, to shorten the process of finding out the neighbors of a particle within the simulation domain. It helps optimizing the default algorithm having a complexity of $\mathcal{O}(N^2)$ that tests every pair of particles (if N is the number of particles). The most common strategy to deal with any kind of simulation (static or dynamic, homogeneous and heterogeneous density) is a fusion between the linked-cell [7] method and the Verlet list method [24]. The combination of these methods has a complexity of $\mathcal{O}(N)$ and a refresh rate that depends on the displacement of the fastest particle. This algorithm is easily thread-parallelized. Others less-used neighbor search strategies have been developed to address specific simulations, such as for static simulation with particles respecting a regular layout [10].

Domain Decomposition is usually employed in N-Body methods to address distributed memory parallelization [17], assigning one subdomain to each MPI process. This implies the addition of ghost areas (replicated particles) around subdomains to ensure each particle has access to its neighborhood. Over time, many algorithms have been designed to improve load-balancing such as: Recursive Coordinate Bisection (RCB), the Recursive Inertial Bisection (RIB), the Space Filling Curve (SFC), or graph method with PARMETIS. Note that the library Zoltan gathers the most popular methods. To ease neighbor list construction (i.e. employing the linked-cell method), the simulation domain is described as a cartesian grid of cells, each of which containing embedded particles. Each subdomain then consists in a grid of entire cells assigned to one MPI process. In contrast, concurrent iteration over the cells of one subdomain's grid provides the basis for thread parallelization at the NUMA node level.

Commonalities are shared across N-body simulation codes, such as numerical schemes, neighbor particle detection, or short/long-range interactions. The computation time dedicated to interaction and force calculations can be significant (over 80% of the total time) depending on the studied phenomenon complexity. Additional factors, such as neighbor lists construction computational cost, can impact overall simulation time. For dynamic simulations involving rapidly moving particles and computationally inexpensive interactions, more than 50%

of the total time may be spent on neighbor list construction. The computationally intensive sections of the code vary depending on methods and phenomena studied, requiring optimizations such as MPI parallelization, vectorization, multi-threading, or GPU usage.

A Short Review of N-Body HPC Codes shows that a significant amount of research has been devoted to adapting N-Body specific optimizations to supercomputer architectures evolutions. One of the most significant code in the scientific community is the state-of-the-art MD code LAMMPS [22]. LAMMPS has been continuously developed for nearly three decades and includes MPI+X parallelization using native languages such as OPENMP or CUDA. An interesting package of LAMMPS is the package LIGGGHTS [12] which reuses data structures of LAMMPS to perform DEM simulations. Others widely used MD codes are GROMACS and NAMD working with a hybrid MPI+X parallelization. Although more confidential, we introduce here EXASTAMP [8,18], a MD code that has demonstrated twice the performance of the LAMMPS code on micro-jetting case composed of billions of particles [19]. Several codes are devoted to DEM applications such as MERCURYDPM including a hybrid parallelization MPI+OPENMP and non open source software like EDEM and ROCKYDEM (including multi-GPU parallelization). Overall, the HPC community has put a lot of efforts in parallelizing those physics codes on thousands of cores, as for the SPH method on both CPU [16] and GPU [6], or the DEM [12].

3   Parallel Programming Models

With the emergence of heterogeneous HPC platforms and the intensive use of GPUs, the HPC community has developed portable solutions to help developers optimize their codes on a wide variety of supercomputers. These solutions can be classified into four catgories: (1) libraries proposing a set of parallel routines and equipped with several back-ends, (2) high-level directive-based instructions, (3) algorithms accessible through a programming language with parallel execution policies, and (4) Domain Specific Language (DSL).

Two commonly used parallel libraries are KOKKOS [23] and RAJA [4]. For instance, KOKKOS is one of the available parallel back-end in LAMMPS and achieves similar multi-threaded performances compared to the OPENMP back-end [11] while being portable on GPU. Note that KOKKOS does not manage MPI level parallelization. Similarly, RAJA currently proposes back-ends support for OPENMP, TBB, SIMD, CUDA, HIP, OPENMP target offloading and SYCL. KOKKOS and RAJA provide high-level abstractions for expressing the parallel constructs that are mapped onto a runtime to achieve portable performance.

Although these programming models propose a high-level portability, the performance penalty is low but not negligible. Indeed, Martineau et al. [14,15] have reported a penalty from 5 to 30% using KOKKOS and RAJA against OPENMP, CUDA or OpenCL version. Artigues et al. [2] have evaluated the performance portability for a Particle-In-Cell (PIC) code using KOKKOS and RAJA on V100

GPU. They concluded that KOKKOS and RAJA are at least twice longer than the CUDA version to carry out the calculations while the KOKKOS version was about 14% slower than the OPENMP version on CPU. A tuning step is sometimes expected to improve performance on GPUs. On the other hand, less-intrusive programming models than KOKKOS-like solutions exist such as the directive-based programming models (2) like OPENMP for thread parallelism on CPU, or OPENMP and OPENACC on GPU. Nevertheless, the use of programming directives often requires a non-trivial tuning process according to the computing platform considered.

STDPAR is the C++ standard's parallel programming model (3) targeting both CPU and GPU. STDPAR exposes parallel versions of the STL's main algorithms like *std::for_each*, expressing potential parallelism through an execution policy, such as *std::execution::par_unseq*. STDPAR has been tested on GPU and achieved similar performances compared to KOKKOS or OPENMP for some miniapps [3] and is less intrusive. THRUST and BOOST propose similar approaches.

Finally, DSL based solutions (4) for N-body problems has been less investigated by the HPC community. Beni et al. [5] propose the unique DSL (to our knowledge) to solve N-body problems with a slight average runtime overhead of 5%. Overall, DSL has the advantage to drastically reduce the number of lines while proposing a very high-level of abstraction. Nevertheless, this DSL does not include MPI parallelization which is a major limiting factor. While identifying an efficient, flexible and portable way to model N-body problems on current supercomputers is still an open issue; our contribution aims at providing HPC optimized software shared by a wide variety of N-Body problems in a framework between a DSL and an ad-hoc N-Body code using native languages and tools.

4   Contribution

EXANBODY offers a user-friendly and practical solution to harness the power of cutting-edge supercomputers. Its flexibility enables easy extension and specialization to meet specific hardware architectures and application requirements.

4.1   ExaNBody in a Nutshell

EXANBODY is a software platform developed at the french Alternative Energies and Atomic Energy Commission (CEA) for N-body problems involved in different fields of physics. Originally designed as part of EXASTAMP, a MD code for atomistic simulation, EXANBODY has achieved nearly linear speedups on thousands of cores (100,000+) for simulations involving highly heterogeneous density scenarios, such as droplet splashing [21] or micro-jetting [20], with half a trillion atoms. Customized algorithms and data structures have been developed to achieve these results, whether for storing neighbor lists or processing communications. These advancements have made the code base increasingly generic and customizable to accommodate a growing number of physical models, while also progressively supporting GPU equipped supercomputers. As a result, the authors decided to extract the N-Body core, EXANBODY, as a standalone project, making it available for other N-Body simulation codes. EXAN-BODY now evolves alongside EXASTAMP, focusing on flexibility, performance and portability, using industry standards as its software stack basis and providing application-level customizability (see Fig. 1a). EXANBODY encompasses various aspects of N-Body simulation codes construction. Firstly, it provides a high level of flexibility through a component-based programming model. These components serve as building blocks and are assembled using YAML formatted files. Secondly, it offers portable performance by providing developers with a collection of algorithms and programming interfaces specifically designed for common N-Body compute kernels. Additionally, the programming tools aforementioned are natively compatible with different CPU and GPU architectures, thanks to the Onika execution support library. Before diving into these features, let us now describe how a simulation developer starts setting up its application.

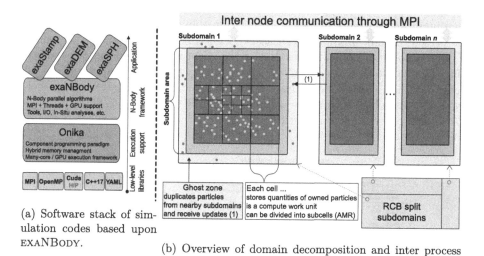

(a) Software stack of simulation codes based upon EXANBODY.

(b) Overview of domain decomposition and inter process communications in EXANBODY framework.

Fig. 1. Overview of the EXANBODY software stack (a) and coarse grain structure of a parallel application based upon it (b).

4.2 Application Level Specialization

First of all, the internal units to be used are specified as well as the physical quantities to be stored as particle attributes. These quantities (or *fields*), are defined using a symbolic name associated with a type, e.g. *velocity* as a 3D vector. A *field set* is a collection of declared fields. One of the available *field sets* is selected and used at runtime, depending on simulation specific needs. As depicted in Fig. 1b, particles are dispatched in cells of a cartesian grid spanning the simulation domain. In short, the data structure containing all particles' data will be shaped as a cartesian grid of cells, each cell containing all *fields* for all particles it (geometrically) contains. More specifically, the reason why *fields* and *field sets* are defined at compile time is that particle data storage at the cell level is handled via a specific structure guaranteeing access performance and low memory footprint, detailed in Sect. 4.4.

4.3   Flexible and User Friendly Construction of N-Body Simulations

A crucial aspect for software sustainability is to maintain performance over time while managing software complexity and evolution. Complex and rapidly evolving scientific software often encounter common pitfalls, such as code duplication, uncontrolled increase in software inter-dependencies, and obscure data/control flows. This observation has led us to develop our component-based model to avoid these pitfalls. In our model, individual software components are implemented using C++17 and are application structure oblivious, meaning they only know their input and output data flows. Application obliviousness is a crucial aspect of the present design, promoting reusability while preventing uncontrolled growth of internal software dependencies. Each component is developed as a class, inheriting from a base class *OperatorNode* and explicitly declares its input and output *slots* (data flow connection points). Once compiled, these components are hierarchically assembled at runtime using a Sequential Task Flow (STF) [1], with a YAML syntax, as shown in Fig. 2.

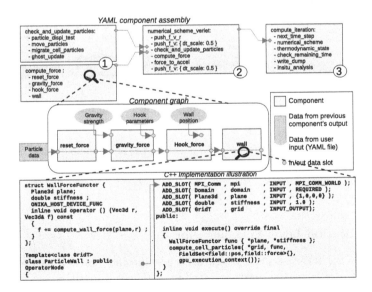

Fig. 2. Illustrative sample of components assembly using YAML description. 1) C++ developed components are assembled and connected in the manner of a STF, creating a *batch* component. 2) and 3) illustrate batch components aggregation to higher and higher level components, up to full simulation task flow.

A set of base components are already available to developers, embedded within EXANBODY, such as: common computations, checkpoint/restart, visualization and In-Situ analytics, allowing developers to focus on their application specific components. We also observed that this component based approach not only prevents some development pitfalls, but enables various simulation code structures. YAML formatted component configuration makes it simple for a user to amend or fine tune the simulation process. For instance it can be used to change the numerical scheme or even to insert In-Situ analysis components (such as proposed in [9]) at specific stages of the simulation process, leveraging In-Situ processing to limit disk I/O. Finally, this component based splitting of the code gives EXANBODY the opportunity to provide integrated profiling features that automatically give meaningful performance metrics for each part of the simulation. It allows the user to access computation time spent on CPU and GPU, as well as imbalance indicator. It can also interoperate with *nSight System* from NVIDIA and summarize memory footprint with detailed consumption.

4.4   Performance and Portability

The complex and ever-changing architectures of modern supercomputers make it difficult to maintain software performance. EXANBODY aims at providing performance portability and sustainability on those supercomputers with robust domain decomposition, automated inter-process communications algorithms, adaptable particle data layout, and a set of hybrid (CPU/GPU) parallelization templates specialized for N-Body problems.

Spatial Domain Decomposition and Inter-process Communications are critical to ensure scalability at large scales. Indeed, the coarsest parallelization level can become the main bottleneck due to network latencies and load imbalance issues. To take advantage of this first level of parallelization, the simulation domain is divided into subdomains using an RCB algorithm, as depicted in Fig. 1b, assigning one subdomain to each MPI process. This is achieved thanks to three main components: cell cost estimator, RCB domain decomposition, and particle migration. Particle migration can be used as-is by any N-Body application, thanks to the underlying generic particle data storage (see Sect. 4.4). It supports heavily multi-threaded, large scale, simulations while lowering peak memory usage. Additionally, the migration algorithm is also customizable to fit specific application needs, keeping unchanged the core implementation. For instance, MD simulations may transport per-cell data fields and DEM simulations may migrate friction information related to pair of particles. Finally, ghost particle updates are available to any N-Body application, via customizable components.

Particle Data Layout and Auxiliary Data Structures are two essential features to maximize performance at the NUMA node level. In EXANBODY, particle data are packed independently in each cell using a container specifically designed to match both CPU's SIMD and GPU's thread blocks requirements concerning data alignment and vectorization friendly padding. This generic container, available in Onika toolbox, not only adapts to specific hardware characteristics at compile time, but ensures minimal memory footprint with as low as 16 bytes overhead per cell regardless of the number of data fields, allowing for very large and sparse simulation domains. N-Body simulations also heavily depend on particles' neighbors search algorithm and storage structure. The search usually leverages the grid of cell structure to speed up the process, and neighbors lists data structure holds information during several iterations, see Sect. 2.2. However, depending on the simulation, particles may move rapidly while their distribution may be heterogeneously dense. Those two factors respectively impact neighbor list update frequency and its memory footprint. On the one hand, EXANBODY takes advantage of an Adaptive Mesh Refinement (AMR) grid [18] to accelerate (frequent) neighbor list reconstructions. On the other hand, a compressed neighbor list data structure saves up to 80% of memory (compared to uncompressed lists) while still ensuring fast access from both the CPU and the GPU.

Intra-node Parallelization API is available in EXANBODY to help developers express parallel computations within a MPI process. This API offers a set of parallelization templates associated with three types of computation kernels: local calculations on a particle, calculations coupled with reduction across all particles, and, most importantly, calculations involving each particle and its neighbors. When a developer injects a compute function into these templates, computation may be routed to CPU or GPU, as illustrated in Fig. 3. While thread parallelization on the CPU is powered by OPENMP, CUDA is employed to execute the computation kernel on the GPU, using the same provided function. The main difference between the two execution modes is that each cell is a unitary work unit for a single thread in OPENMP context but it is processed by a block of threads in CUDA. Those two parallelization levels (multi-core and GPU) are easily accessible to developers thanks to the execution support layer of Onika. Onika is the low-level software interface that powers EXANBODY building blocks. It is responsible for aforementioned data containers, memory management (unified with GPU), and it is the foundation for hybrid execution abstraction layer.

Fig. 3. Example of a particle centered computation executable on both CPU and GPU. Three ingredients: a user functor (the kernel), static execution properties (via traits specialization), a ready to use parallelization function template.

5   Numerical Experiments: MD and DEM Simulations

The present framework was evaluated with two applications: EXASTAMP, which employs MD, and EXADEM (coded with as few as 5500 lines) which relies on the DEM. Different OPENMP/MPI configurations (number of cores/threads per MPI process) have been tested to balance multi-level parallelism. Both simulations were instrumented during 1, 000 representative iterations. The performance of EXANBODY was evaluated using up to 256 cluster nodes, built on bi-socket 64-core AMD® EPYC Milan 7763 processors running at 2.45 GHz and equipped with 256 GB of RAM. We also ran CPU/GPU comparisons (512 CPU cores vs 16 NVidia A100 GPUs) to show GPU gains. Also, not included here, results show GPU gains of up to ×11 on a100 versus one node depending on the force computation kernel.

Molecular Dynamics performance is evaluated with the simulation of an impacted 640 million Tantalum atoms sample surrounded by air, leading to spallation due to shock-waves reflection on free surfaces (see Fig. 4a). This benchmark challenges MD application for two reasons: firstly, high velocity particles renders difficult to keep track of particle neighborhoods (Verlet list algorithm). Secondly, while Tantalum is a dense material, nucleation and growth of cavities creates large and increasing voided regions, leaving more and more cells empty (with no particle), making crucial subdomain partitioning for overall load balance. Moreover, the computation domain expands rapidly as the front of the bulk is propelled forward. The employed Modified Embedded Atom Model (MEAM) force model is another challenge: it involves second order neighbors, and must also be executed on ghost particles to get correct results. This intrinsically limits MPI scaling, because number of ghost particles drastically increase with smaller and smaller subdomains, and in turn prevents the 1 core per MPI process to have decent performances. Despite this flaw, we observe speedup gains when scaling from 512 to 32, 768 cores, although not ideal (*i.e.* linear). Left graph of Fig. 4b shows relative speedups for different MPI/OPENMP configurations, ranging from 1 to 128 cores per MPI process, with 32 cores per MPI process being the best combination for this case. This configuration is detailed in Fig. 4d and Fig. 4c which highlight how different parts of the simulation scale and how their relative costs evolve.

Discrete Element Method performance is evaluated with a simulation of a rotating drum containing 100 million spherical particles, see Fig. 4a. This setup is a tough benchmark as particles are rapidly moving all around the heterogeneously dense domain, due to gravity. Additionally, the employed Hooke force model has a low arithmetic intensity, and EXADEM must handle pairwise friction information, that is updated by kernel and must migrate between MPI processes when subdomains are redistributed. Those two characteristics highlight EXANBODY

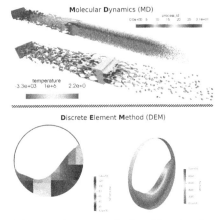

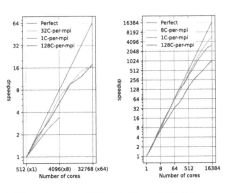

(b) Speedup for different OPENMP/MPI configurations. Left) MD simulation tested with 8, 32, and 128 threads per MPI process. Right) DEM simulation with 1, 8, and 128 threads per MPI process.

(a) Visualization of the MD simulation of metal spalling (upper) and the DEM simulation of spheres in a rotating drum.

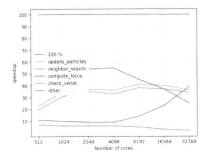

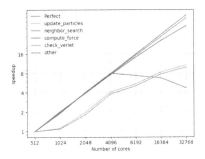

(c) Operator time ratios at different parallelization scales.

(d) Per operator speedup according to the total number of cores used.

Fig. 4. Results with two different applications: MD simulation of a 640 million atoms bulk and DEM simulation of 100 million spheres in a rotating drum.

framework overall overhead as well as its ability to fit different simulation methods. Different MPI and OPENMP configurations were also tested, showing best performance with 8 threads OPENMP per MPI process. This difference with MD demonstrates that DEM is less sensitive to subdomain decomposition and more sensitive to memory bandwidth, 8 being the number of cores sharing L3 cache. Note that compute operators (neighbors and compute), fall to respectively from 32.3% to 12.9% and from 43.5% to 13.1% for 1 and 16,384 cores whereas these operator speedups are almost perfect, respectively 14,281 and 18,943 (NUMA effect). The loss of performance is due to the expensive collective MPI functions (MPI_Allreduce), 4.74% for 128 cores, 18.8% for 2,048 cores, and 49.75% for 16,384 cores, that become predominant as the subdomains shrink. In conclusion, the application EXADEM based on EXANBODY shows good parallel performance in strong scaling from 1 to 16,384 cores for a large scale simulation on a recent HPC platform (CPU cores are used).

6   Conclusion and Future Works

Simulation codes portability on modern HPC platforms is increasingly complex and costly. As far as N-Body methods are concerned, the EXANBODY framework presented here, driven by performance and portability, provides hybrid parallelization (MPI + OPENMP + GPU) application building blocks. Our solution is halfway between a general purpose library like KOKKOS and a DSL. We have exhibited the concepts in EXANBODY architecture that address specific needs of various types of N-body methods like DEM, MD, or SPH. EXANBODY has been evaluated over largely unbalanced test cases in MD and DEM with up to $32,768$ cores on strong scaling and shows continuous performance gains.

EXANBODY should soon become open source and widely available. Before that, we want to compare current implementation of EXANBODY core, using home grown Onika execution layer, with one based on KOKKOS, RAJA or STDPAR in order to measure potential benefits of these tools regarding portability.

References

1. Agullo, E., et al.: Bridging the gap between OpenMP and task-based runtime systems for the fast multipole method. IEEE TPDS **28**(10), 2794–2807 (2017)
2. Artigues, V., et al.: Evaluation of performance portability frameworks for the implementation of a particle-in-cell code. CCPE **32**(11), e5640 (2020)
3. Asahi, Y., et al.: Performance portable Vlasov code with C++ parallel algorithm. In: IEEE/ACM International Workshop P3HPC, pp. 68–80. IEEE (2022)
4. Beckingsale, D.A., et al.: RAJA: portable performance for large-scale scientific applications. In: IEEE/ACM International Workshop P3HPC, pp. 71–81. IEEE (2019)
5. Beni, L.A., et al.: Portal: a high-performance language and compiler for parallel n-body problems. In: IPDPS, pp. 984–995. IEEE (2019)
6. Cercos-Pita, J.L.: AQUAgpusph, a new free 3D SPH solver accelerated with OpenCL. CPC **192**, 295–312 (2015)
7. Ciccotti, G., Frenkel, D.: Mc Donald. Simulation of liquids and solids, I.R. (1987)
8. Cieren, E., Colombet, L., Pitoiset, S., Namyst, R.: ExaStamp: a parallel framework for molecular dynamics on heterogeneous clusters. In: Lopes, L., et al. (eds.) Euro-Par 2014. LNCS, vol. 8806, pp. 121–132. Springer, Cham (2014). https://doi.org/10.1007/978-3-319-14313-2_11
9. Dirand, E., Colombet, L., Raffin, B.: TINS: a task-based dynamic helper core strategy for in situ analytics. In: Yokota, R., Wu, W. (eds.) Supercomputing Frontiers, pp. 159–178. Springer, Cham (2018). https://doi.org/10.1007/978-3-319-69953-0_10
10. Hu, C., et al.: Crystal MD: the massively parallel molecular dynamics software for metal with BCC structure. CPC **211**, 73–78 (2017)

11. Jeffers, J., et al.: Optimizing classical molecular dynamics in LAMMPS. In: Intel Xeon Phi Processor High Performance Programming, 2nd edn., Chap. 20, pp. 443–470 (2016)
12. Kloss, C., Goniva, C., Hager, A., Amberger, S., Pirker, S.: Models, algorithms and validation for opensource DEM and CFD-DEM. Prog. Comput. Fluid Dynam. Int. J. **12**(2–3), 140–152 (2012)
13. Leimkuhler, B.J., Reich, S., Skeel, R.D.: Integration methods for molecular dynamics. In: Mesirov, J.P., Schulten, K., Sumners, D.W. (eds.) Mathematical Approaches to Biomolecular Structure and Dynamics, pp. 161–185. Springer, New York (1996). https://doi.org/10.1007/978-1-4612-4066-2_10
14. Martineau, M., McIntosh-Smith, S., Boulton, M., Gaudin, W.: An evaluation of emerging many-core parallel programming models. In: Proceedings of the 7th International Workshop on PMAM, pp. 1–10 (2016)
15. Martineau, M., et al.: Assessing the performance portability of modern parallel programming models using TeaLeaf. CCPE **29**(15), e4117 (2017)
16. Oger, G.: Other: on distributed memory MPI-based parallelization of SPH codes in massive HPC context. CPC **200**, 1–14 (2016)
17. Plimpton, S.: Fast parallel algorithms for short-range molecular dynamics. J. Comput. Phys. **117**(1), 1–19 (1995)
18. Prat, R., et al.: Combining task-based parallelism and adaptive mesh refinement techniques in molecular dynamics simulations. In: Proceedings of the ICPP, pp. 1–10 (2018)
19. Prat, R., et al.: AMR-based molecular dynamics for non-uniform, highly dynamic particle simulations. CPC **253**, 107177 (2020)
20. Soulard, L.: Micro-jetting: a semi-analytical model to calculate the velocity and density of the jet from a triangular groove. J. Appl. Phys. **133**(8), 085901 (2023)
21. Soulard, L., Carrard, T., Durand, O.: Molecular dynamics study of the impact of a solid drop on a solid target. J. Appl. Phys. **131**(13), 135901 (2022)
22. Thompson, A.P., et al.: LAMMPS - a flexible simulation tool for particle-based materials modeling at atomic, meso, and continuum scales. CPC **271**, 108171 (2022)
23. Trott, C.R., et al.: Kokkos 3: programming model extensions for the exascale era. IEEE TPDS **33**(4), 805–817 (2022)
24. Verlet, L.: Computer experiments on classical fluids. I. Thermodynamical properties of Lennard-Jones molecules. Phys. Rev. **159**(1), 98 (1967)

Author Index

D. Zeinalipour et al. (Eds.): Euro-Par 2023 Workshops, LNCS 14351, pp. 355–357, 2024.
https://doi.org/10.1007/978-3-031-50684-0

Printed in the United States
by Baker & Taylor Publisher Services